American Literature

美国文学教程：欣赏与评析（第二版）

甘文平　编著
杨仁敬　审校

WUHAN UNIVERSITY PRESS
武汉大学出版社

图书在版编目(CIP)数据

美国文学教程:欣赏与评析:汉、英/甘文平编著;杨仁敬审校. —2版.
—武汉:武汉大学出版社,2018.12
ISBN 978-7-307-20639-7

Ⅰ.美… Ⅱ.①甘… ②杨… Ⅲ.①英语—阅读教学—高等学校—教材 ②文学欣赏—美国 ③文学评论—美国 Ⅳ.H319.4:I

中国版本图书馆CIP数据核字(2018)第258895号

责任编辑:罗晓华　　责任校对:李孟潇　　版式设计:马　佳

出版发行:**武汉大学出版社**　(430072　武昌　珞珈山)
(电子邮件:cbs22@whu.edu.cn 网址:www.wdp.whu.edu.cn)
印刷:荆州市鸿盛印务有限公司
开本:787×1092　1/16　印张:19.5　字数:456千字　插页:1
版次:2012年6月第1版　　2018年12月第2版
2018年12月第2版第1次印刷
ISBN 978-7-307-20639-7　　定价:47.00元

第二版前言

《美国文学教程：欣赏与评析》自出版以来，因为它的体例新颖、内容连贯、讲解详细、启发性强而受到广大读者的好评。英语专业本科生把它作为本科期间学习主干课程“美国文学”的辅助教材，英语专业的本科毕业生把它作为报考文学方向研究生的参考资料，年轻教师则将它视为从事美国文学教学以及研究美国文学的助手。

因此，应广大读者的要求，武汉大学出版社决定出版该教程的第二版。与 2012 年的版本相比，此次的第二版有以下三点变化：

第一，增加新内容。具体地说，“第一部分：题目”增加了一章，由姜艳老师撰写；“第三部分：人物”增加了一章，由张文老师撰写；“第五部分：修辞”也增加了一章，由周丹老师完成。三位老师都是笔者的同事。增加的内容均由笔者审校。增加部分的体例与书中的其他章节相同。

第二，调整内容编排顺序。增加内容之后，第二版的所有章节都按照作品出版的时间先后顺序排列，这样更加有利于学生的学习，更方便青年教师了解和讲授美国文学。

第三，进一步规范该教程的形式和内容。该教程的责任编辑——武汉大学出版社的罗晓华女士在书稿撰稿人校对的基础上审阅了全文，在形式的编排和内容的表述两个方面做了大量而细致的修订工作，更加有效地提高了该教程的质量。

甘文平

2018 年 10 月

序

近年来，我国出版了许多不同版本的美国文学教材，促进了美国文学在高校学生和普通读者中的普及。这些教材名称不一，有的称为“选读”，有的叫“欣赏”，也有的概括为“作品与评论”。教材的内容大多按时间顺序，选择名家名作的全文或片段加以评介，给读者有益的启迪。

甘文平教授编著的《美国文学教程：欣赏与评析》与读者见面了。它是我国高校英美文学教材园地里的一棵新苗。从体例和选材到评论和表述，它有许多创新之处。可以说，它是当前形势下一本独具特色的好教材，对丰富青年读者的美国文学知识，提高欣赏和评析能力大有帮助，也可为高校学子从事美国文学研究奠定初步基础。

《美国文学教程：欣赏与评析》有哪些特色呢？我认为主要体现在以下几个方面：

1. 体例新颖，选材恰当，内容丰富。本书改变了文学教材按时间顺序编排的习惯，以内容分类为中心，包括题目、环境、人物、主题和修辞五个部分。每个部分分别选择了相关美国名家的名作，古今兼有，小说与诗歌并列，也有剧作，以小说为主，有短篇小说名作，也有长篇小说选段。每章由五个条目组成：“作者简介”“文本选读”“题目(环境、人物、主题、修辞)解析”“难点注释”和“延伸阅读与批评”。注重作家的创作个性和独特风格，主题思想和艺术手法的评析相结合，紧扣文本，直观展示，令人耳目一新。

2. 文本分析细致、具体、生动，富有新意。文学作品的文本细读是欣赏和评论的基础。读懂读透文本就能感受作品展示的艺术魅力，理解作者的创作个性，从一般阅读层面提升到新的高度。本书特别重视文学作品文本的分析，从解题、主题赏析到延伸阅读与批评，都紧紧结合文本进行详尽而中肯的解读，为读者提供了文本细读的范例。它从作品的题目入手，深入章节，联系人物的言行，到细节描写和遣词造句的微妙之处，无不加以细致入微的评析。它使读者对不同作家、不同作品的特点和难点更容易把握和接受。这是一般美国文学选读不容易做到的。

3. 文本、理论和语境巧妙结合，评述深入浅出，朴实自然，好懂易记。本书没有孤立地停留在文本分析上，而是将文本细读与历史语境以及相关的文学批评理论结合起来，强调文学与现实的关系，密切联系名家名作产生的历史和文化语境，以加深读者对所选作品的认识和理解。它把一些深奥的术语如超验主义、“迷惘的一代”、“美国梦”和生态文学批评、现实主义、浪漫主义、现代主义、后现代主义、女权主义和新历史主义等融入生动具体的叙述中，让读者结合文本分析来了解这些文学批评理论和专门术语，比较容易理解和接受。如书中提到海明威和菲茨杰拉德同属“迷惘的一代”，但两人风格完全不同。海明威强调人的尊严，塑造了硬汉子形象，形成了独特的“冰山原则”；而菲茨杰拉德同时成了“爵士乐时代”的代言人，他的小说描绘了追求“美国梦”的破灭，大量运用象征和意象。这样生动简易的比较与选文文本的评析密切结合起来，显得有血有肉、深入浅出，令人容易明白和记住。作为一本好教材，这一点显得尤为重要。编著者要设身处地为读者着想，才能使教材发挥理想的效果。

4. 频频的“设问”和阅读的延伸促进了读者的思考和参与。与许多教材不同，本书各章里对美国名家名作的评述不是平铺直叙、人云亦云，而是叙述中不断“设问”，与读者相互沟通、共同探讨，引导读者独立思考、积极参与。比如读到福克纳的名篇《献给艾米莉的玫瑰》时，作者在“题目解析”时问道：“小说并未提到‘玫瑰’，但它的标题为何提到‘玫瑰’?”作者一开始就把小说的主题提到读者面前，非常引人注目。到了该章末了，作者又问：“是谁献给艾米莉的玫瑰?”然后答道：“是小说中的‘我们’——镇上的人，是作者福克纳，也是阅读小说的读者。”这一问一答给读者留下深刻的印象。

有时，作者提出了问题，但最后不给答案，只提供些暗示，让读者自己找答案。如评述麦尔维尔《白鲸》的主人公亚伯时，作者问道：“他是一个人、超人的神？还是一个魔鬼？或者，他是一个人与神、人与动物、人与魔鬼的‘混合物’?”但他没有回答，留待读者自己去思考，去回答。这样就可以促进读者独立思考，举一反三，取得更好的阅读效果。今天，我国读者，尤其是高校的同学们对美国文学已有了一定的了解，具备参与讨论的条件。所以，这种叙述策略有助于给读者“锦上添花”。它成了本书的一大特色。

此外，本书文字简洁、通俗、生动，作者采取一种与读者调侃聊天的方式，与读者侃侃而谈，娓娓动听，平起平坐，没有距离，与读者分享他的读书心得和体会，令读者倍感亲切，阅读兴趣油然而生。这种态度也许是美国文学教材编写的新尝试。我相信，它会受到广大读者欢迎的。

古人云：“工欲善其事，必先利其器。”要学好美国文学，必须有一本好教材。《美国文学教程：欣赏与评析》也许可以满足这种需要。当前，随着我国对外交往的发展，学习一点美国文学已成为一种社会需要，也成为新一代人的文化诉求。本书的出版无疑具有一定的现实意义。

《论语》指出：“博学而笃志，切问而近思。”学习与思考是不可偏废的。这是本书作者对读者的希望，也是读者学习本书有没有成效的关键。我衷心地希望各位读者认真学习，反复思考，将对美国文学的兴趣化成一股与时俱进的动力，学出新成效，学出新突破！

一本好教材要经得起时间的检验。关键在于不断总结，不断完善，不断创新。我热诚地建议甘文平同志在此教材试用一段时间后认真加以总结，虚心听取有关高校师生试用本教材后的意见，进一步开拓创新，精益求精，使教材更加完善，让这棵新苗茁壮成长，为高校的美国文学教材建设再作贡献！是为序。

杨仁敬

2012年3月9日

于厦大西村　书斋

目 录

Part One

Topic

“题目”是作者贴在文学作品上的“标签”，界定作品的“身份”。它的形态多样：一个短句、一个名词、一个动词、一个形容词、一个词组、一个人名或地名，乃至一个介词或数字，等等，不一而足。它是映入读者眼帘的第一个信息，是读者接触作品的第一步。它犹如一只眼睛，与读者的眼神进行第一次交流，并刻意地抓住读者的注意力，促使读者对之进行重点而持续的关注。

文学作品的题目往往是作者精心构造并有意为之，是作者重点突出的信息，甚至是作品主要意思的浓缩。透过题目，读者可以窥见作品的中心及其隐含的主题思想。因此，对于准备走进文学作品的读者来说，首先要关注题目，将题目与阅读以及思考过程结合起来。

本部分包括五个单元：三篇小说和两首诗歌，它们分别从“谁”“什么”“为什么”三个方面解读作品题目的含义。这三个问题基本上回答了题目的主要内容，而且涵盖了作品的许多信息，对更深入地解读作品大有裨益。

Chapter 1　The Law of Life

by Jack London

一、作者简介

杰克·伦敦(1876—1916)，美国19世纪末和20世纪初著名的小说家，虽英年早逝但学术影响长久。他的长篇小说有《野性的呼唤》(1903)、《海狼》(1904)、《白牙》(1906)、《铁蹄》(1908)、《马丁·伊顿》(1909)，代表性的短篇故事集有《狼之子》(1900)、《霜的孩子》(1902)、《南海故事集》(1911)等。伦敦出身贫穷，没有完成大学教育，各种工作经历让他很早就体会到世事的艰辛，同时也磨炼了他坚强不屈的性格。一方面他几乎遍尝人间百味，另一方面他勤奋好学，并立志献身文学事业。他勤于笔耕，著述颇丰，除了小说，他还涉猎诗歌、散文、文学批评、新闻报道、科幻故事，等等。因此，他是一位具有传奇色彩的作家。

杰克·伦敦的创作思想深受达尔文的进化论、马克思的社会主义、斯宾塞的社会达尔文主义、尼采的“超人”哲学、弗洛伊德和卡尔·荣格的心理学的影响，因此他的作品思想内容丰富而复杂，为读者解读他的作品带来一定的难度，同时也为读者选择分析的切入点提供了巨大的自由空间。伦敦把自己的真实经历写进小说，同时用艺术的手段描写这些经历，使之既具有真情实感，又具有艺术魅力。特别是，他的若干篇长篇和短篇小说将他自己在北美阿拉斯加的克朗代克淘金的经历作为故事情节和背景，更加令人印象深刻，极具感染力。

生命、死亡、自然的本质、自然与人的关系、与外界和自我的抗争、生命的尊严等是伦敦作品经常反映的思想主题。其作品语言朴实通俗，以写实为主，同时兼有心理描写，这些特点让他的作品染上浓厚的现实主义和自然主义色彩，同时拥有丰富的象征意蕴。

二、文本选读

The Law of Life

Old Koskoosh listened greedy. Though his sight had long since faded, his hearing was still acute, and the slightest sound penetrated to the glimmering intelligence which yet abode behind the withered forehead, but which no longer gazed forth upon the things of the world. Ah! That was Sit-cum-to-ha, shrilly anathematizing the dogs as she cuffed and beat them into the harnesses. Sit-cum-to-ha was his daughter's daughter, but she was too busy to waste a thought upon her broken grandfather, sitting alone there in the snow, forlorn and helpless. Camp must be broken[1]. The long trail waited while the short day refused to linger. Life called her, and the duties of life, not death. And he was very close to death now.

The thought made the old man panicky for the moment, and he stretched forth a palsied hand which wandered tremblingly over the small heap of dry wood beside him. Reassured that it was indeed there, his hand returned to the shelter of his mangy furs, and he again fell to listening. The sulky crackling of half-frozen hides told him that the chief's moose-skin lodge had been struck, and even then was being rammed and jammed into portable compass. The chief was his son, stalwart and strong, headman of the tribesmen, and a mighty hunter. As the women toiled with the camp luggage, his voice rose, chiding them for their slowness. Old Koskoosh strained his ears. It was the last time he would hear that voice. There went Geehow's lodge! And Tusken's! Seven, eight, nine, only the shaman's could be still standing. There! They were at work upon it now. He could hear the shaman grunt as he piled it on the sledge. A child whimpered, and a woman soothed it with soft, crooning gutturals. Little Koo-tee, the old man thought, a fretful child, and not over strong. It would die soon, perhaps, and they would burn a hole through the frozen tundra and pile rocks above to keep the wolverines away. Well, did it matter? A few years at best, and as many an empty belly as full one. And in the end, Death waited, ever-hungry and hungriest of them all.

What was that? Oh, the men lashing the sleds and drawing tight the thongs. He listened, who would listen no more. The whiplashes snarled and bit among the dongs. Hear them whine! How they hated the work and the trail! They were off! Sled after sled churned slowly away into the silence. They were gone. They had passed out of his life, and he faced the last bitter hour alone. No. The snow crunched beneath a moccasin; a man stood beside him; upon his head a hand rested gently. His son was good to do this thing. He remembered other old men whose sons had not waited after the tribe. But his son had. He wandered away into the past, till the young man's voice brought him back.

"Is it well with you?" he asked.

And the old man answered, "It is well."

"There be wood beside you," the younger man continued, "and the fire burns bright. The morning is gray, and the cold has broken. It will snow presently. Even now it is snowing."

"Aye, even now is it snowing."

"The tribesmen hurry. Their bales are heavy and their bellies flat with lack of feasting. The trail is long and they travel fast. I go now. It is well?"

"It is well. I am as a last year's leaf, clinging lightly to the stem. The first breath that blows, and I fall. My voice is become like an old woman's. My eyes no longer show me the way of my feet, and my feet are heavy, and I am tired. It is well."

He bowed his head in content till the last noise of the complaining snow had died away, and he knew his son was so beyond recall. Then his hand crept out in haste to the wood. It alone stood between him and the eternity that yawned in upon him. At last the measure of his life was a handful of faggots. One by one they would go to feed the fire, and just so, step by step, death would creep upon him. When the last stick had surrendered up its heat, the frost would begin to gather strength. First his feet would yield, then his hands; and the numbness would travel, slowly, from the extremities to the body. His head would fall forward upon his knees, and he would rest. It way easy. All men must die.

He did not complain. It was the way of life, and it was just. He had been born close to the earth, close to the earth had he lived, and the law thereof was not new to him. It was the law of all flesh. Nature[2] was not kindly to the flesh. She had no concern for that concrete thing called the individual. Her interest lay in the species, the race. This was the deepest abstraction old Koskoosh's barbaric mind was capable of, but he grasped it firmly. He saw it exemplified in all life. The rise of the sap, the bursting greenness of the willow bud, the fall of the yellow leaf—in this alone was told the whole history. But one task did Nature set the individual. Did he not perform it, he died. Did he perform it, it was all the same, he died. Nature did not care; there were plenty who were obedient, and it was only the obedience in this matter, not the obedient, which lived and lived always. The tribe of Koskoosh was very old. The old men he had known when a boy had known old men before them. Therefore it was true that the tribe lived, that it stood for the obedience of all its members, way down into the forgotten past, whose very resting places were unremembered. They did not count; they were episodes. They had passed away like clouds from a summer sky. He also was an episode and would pass away. Nature did not care. To life she set one task, gave one law. To perpetuate[3] was the task of life, its law was death. A maiden was a good creature to look upon, full-breasted and strong, with spring to her step and light in her eyes. But her task was yet before her. The light in her eyes brightened, her step quickened, she was now bold with the young men, now timid, and she gave them of her own unrest[4]. And ever she grew fairer and yet fairer to look upon, till some hunter, able no longer to withhold himself, took her to his lodge to cook and toil for him and to become the mother of his children. And with the coming of her offspring her looks left her. Her limbs dragged and shuffled, her eyes dimmed and bleared, and only the little children found joy against the withered cheek of the old squaw by the fire. Her task was done. But a little while, on the first pinch of famine or the first long trail, and she would be left, even as he had been left, in the snow, with a little pile of wood. Such was the law.

He placed a stick carefully upon the fire and resumed his meditations. It was the same everywhere, with all things. The mosquitoes vanished with the first frost. The little tree squirrel crawled away to die. When age settled upon the rabbit it became slow and heavy and could no longer outfoot its enemies. Even the big bald-face grew clumsy and blind and quarrelsome, in the end to be dragged down by a handful of yelping huskies. He remembered how he had abandoned his own father on an upper reach of the Klondike on winter, the winter before the missionary came with his talk books and his box of medicines. Many a time had Koskoosh smacked his lips over the recollection of that box, though now his mouth refused to moisten. The "painkiller" had been especially good. But the missionary was a bother after all, for he brought no meat into the camp, and he ate heartily, and the hunters grumbled. But he chilled his lungs on the divide by the

Mayo, and the dogs afterward nosed the stones away and fought over his bones.

Koskoosh placed another stick on the fire and harked back deeper into the past. There was the time of the Great Famine, when the old men crouched empty-bellied to the fire, and let fall from their lips dim traditions of the ancient day when the Yukon ran wide open for three winter, and then lay frozen for three summers. He had lost his mother in that famine. In the summer the salmon run had failed, and the tribe looked forward to the winter and the coming of the caribou. Then the winter came, but with it there were no caribou. Never had the like been known, not even in the lives of the old men. But the caribou did not come, and it was the seventh year, and the rabbits had not replenished, and the dogs were naught[5] but bundles of bones. And through the long darkness the children wailed and died, and the women, and the old men; and not one in ten of the tribe lived to meet the sun when it came back in the spring. That was a famine!

But he had seen times of plenty, too when the meat spoiled on their hands, and the dogs were fat and worthless with overeating—times when they let the game go unkilled, and the women were fertile and the lodges were cluttered with sprawling men-children and women-children. Then it was the men became high-stomached, and revived ancient quarrels, and crossed the divides to the south to kill the Pellys, and to the west that they might sit by the dead fires of the Tananas. He remembered, when a boy, during a time of plenty, when he saw a moose pulled down by the wolves. Zing-ha lay with him in the snow and watched—Zing-ha, who later became the craftiest of hunters, and who, in the end, fell through an air hole on the Yukon. They found him, a month afterward, just as he had crawled halfway out and frozen stiff to the ice.

But the moose. Zing-ha and he had gone out that day to play at hunting after the manner of their fathers. On the bed of the creek they struck the fresh track of a moose, and with it the tracks of many wolves. "An old one," Zing-ha, who was quicker at reading the sing, said, "an old one who cannot keep up with the herd. The wolves have cut him out from his brothers, and they will never leave him." And it was so. It was their way. By day and by night, never resting, snarling on his heels, snapping at his nose, they would stay by him to the end. How Zing-ha and he felt the blood lust quicken! The finish would be a sight to see!

Eager-footed, they took the trail, and even he, Koskoosh, slow of sight and an unversed tracker, could have followed it blind, it was so wide. Hot were they on the heels of the chase, reading the grim tragedy, fresh-written, at every stop. Now they came to where the moose had made a stand. Thrice the length of a grown man's body, in every direction, had the snow been stamped about and uptossed. In the midst were the deep impressions of the splay-hoofed game, and all about, everywhere, were the lighter foot marks of the wolves, some, while their brothers harried the kill, had lain to one side and rested. The full-stretched impress of their bodies in the snow was as perfect as though made the moment before. One wolf had been caught in a wild lunge of the maddened victim and trampled to death. A few bones, well picked, bore witness.

Again, they ceased the uplift of their snowshoes at a second stand. Here the great animal had fought desperately. Twice had he been dragged down, as the snow attested, and twice had he shaken his assailants clear and gained footing once more. He had done his task long since, but none the less was life dear to him. Zing-ha said it was a strange thing, a moose once down to get free again; but this one certainly had. The shaman would see sings and wonders in this when they told him.

And yet again, they came to where the moose had made to mount the bank and gain the timber. But his foes had laid on from behind, till he reared and fell back upon them, crushing two deep into the snow. It was plain the kill was at hand, for their brothers had left them untouched. Two more stands were hurried past, brief in time length and very close together. The trail was red now, and the clean stride of the great beast had grown short and slovenly. Then they heard the first sounds of the battle—not the full-throated chorus of the chase, but the short, snappy bark which spoke of close quarters and teeth to flesh. Crawling up the wind, Zing-ha bellied it through the snow, and with him crept he, Koskoosh, who was to be chief of the tribesmen in the years to come. Together they shoved aside the underbrushes of a young spruce and peered forth. It was the end they saw.

The picture, like all of youth's impressions, was still strong with him, and his dim eyes watched the end played out as vividly as in that far-off time. Koskoosh marveled at this, for in the days which followed, when he was a leader of men and a head of councilors, he had done great deeds and made his name a curse in the mouths of the Pellys, to say naught of the strange white man he had killed, knife to knife, in open fight.

For long he pondered on the days of his youth, till the fire died down and the frost bit deeper. He replenished it with two sticks this time, and gauged his grip on life by what remained. If Sit-cumto-ha dad only remembered her grandfather, and gathered a larger armful, his hours would have been longer. It would have been easy. But she was even a careless child, and honored not her ancestors from the time the Beaver, son of the son of Zing-ha, first cast eyes upon her. Well, what mattered it? Had he not done likewise in his own quick youth? For a while he listened to the silence. Perhaps the heart of his son might soften, and he would come back with the dogs to take his old father on with the tribe to where the caribou ran thick and the fat hung heavy upon them.

He strained his ears, his restless brain for the moment stilled. Not a stir, nothing. He alone took breath in the midst of the great silence. It was very lonely. Hark! What was that? A chill passed over his body. The familiar, long-drawn howl broke the void, and it was close at hand. Then on his darkened eyes was projected the vision of the moose—the old bull moose—the torn flanks and bloody sides, the riddled mane, and the great branching horns, down low and tossing to the last. He saw the flashing forms of gray, the gleaming eyes, the lolling tongues, the slavered fangs. And he saw the inexorable circle close in till it became a dark point in the midst of the stamped snow.

A cold muzzle thrust against his cheek, and at its touch his soul leaped back to the present. His hand shot into the fire and dragged out a burning faggot. Overcome for the nonce by his hereditary fear of man, the brute retreated, raising a prolonged call to his brothers; and greedily they answered, till a ring of crouching, jaw-slobbering gray was stretched round about. The old man listened to the drawing in of this circle. He waved his hand wildly, and sniffs turned to snarls; but the panting brutes refused to scatter. Now one wormed his chest forward, dragging his haunches after, now a second, now a third; but never a one drew back. Why should he cling to life? He asked, and dropped the blazing stick into the snow. It sizzled and went out. The circle grunted uneasily but held its own. Again he saw the last stand of the old bull moose, and Koskoosh dropped his head wearily upon his knees. What did it matter after all? Was it not the law of life?

三、题目解析

《生命的法则》发表于1901年，是伦敦的短篇小说代表作。如题目所示，它向读者提出了两个问题：什么是“生命”？或者说“生命”的表现形式是什么？生命的“法则”是什么？

小说主要讲述了一个古老部落首领被狼群吃掉的故事。按照时间顺序，小说先后叙述了四个小故事。第一个故事：部落首领年迈体弱，不能带领部落继续前行。他长大成人的儿子取代了他，成为部落的新首领。为了保证部落成员的安全，他们不得不留下老人，寻找新的栖息地。老人独处严寒的荒原，心生许多感慨。他明白这就是生命的轨迹：一切皆会老去，直至死亡。第二个故事是关于女性的描写：女性年轻时貌美而耐看，眼睛充满光泽，步态迅捷。继而，她进入恋爱年龄，显得更加美丽动人。然后她扮演了妻子、母亲、祖母的角色。韶华已逝，红颜不再，形容枯槁，行将就木，直到老死。第三个故事一直烙在老人的脑海：一只驼鹿遭到狼群的包围，被狼群扑倒和蚕食。第四个故事发生在老人自己身上：一群狼朝他走来，把他围住。起初，他挥棒竭力反抗，吓退狼群。但是很快，狼群不退反进。老人深知自己势单力薄，反抗毫无效果。于是，他放弃抗争，淡然迎接死亡的命运。正如小说结尾所说：“反抗又怎么样呢？这不就是生命的法则吗？”

通过以上简述，读者发现该小说如同一篇议论文。它通过若干个事实(故事片段)或曰“生命”的几个表现形式，阐明“生命”的内涵。这些生命的形式包括男人和女人、驼鹿和狼、男人和狼。不论人类(男人、女人)还是动物(驼鹿)，最终都将走向死亡。这就是“生命的法则”。同时，在弱肉强食的自然面前，弱者必将被强者毁灭：这是“生命的法则”的另一层含义。用图示表示如下：

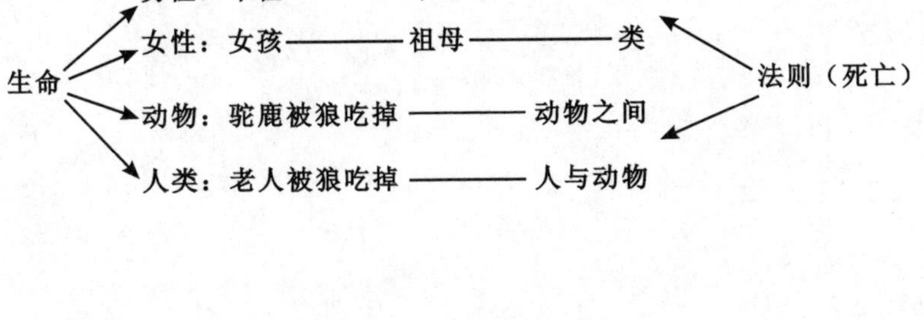

四、难点注释

1. Camp must be broken：词组，break camp，收拾行李，离开该营地。
2. Nature：大自然，造物主。
3. perpetuate：使……继续下去。
4. unrest：(情感等)不安宁，骚动。
5. naught：无；不存在。

五、延伸阅读与批评

中篇小说《野性的呼唤》被公认为杰克·伦敦的代表作之一，与长篇小说《马丁·伊登》齐名。它用自然主义的手法描写人与动物之间的曲折关系，其中既有冷漠和凶残，又有温情和真情。无论是描写人还是描写动物，都形象生动、细致入微、令人难忘。在小说的标题中，“野性”代表什么？是动物的野性，还是人类的野性？由此衍生相应的两个词语：动物的野性的“呼唤”、人类的野性的呼唤。还有人将小说译为《荒原/荒野的呼唤》，那么“呼唤”又有第三个主体：自然界，即自然界的呼唤。自然界在“呼唤”什么？小说的题目蕴涵了上述对小说理解起到重要作用的三个问题，值得读者去思考和解答。

Chapter 2 The Road Not Taken

by Robert Frost

一、作者简介

罗伯特·弗罗斯特(1874—1963)，美国20世纪著名而多产的诗人，在英国也享有盛誉。他的创作生命长达半个世纪，出版多部诗集。他的诗集有《少年的心愿》(1913)、《山间洼地》(1916)、《新罕布什尔》(1923)、《西流溪》(1928)、《又一重山脉》(1936)、《见证树》(1942)、《理智假面具》(1945)、《林中空地》(1962)，等等。《一条未走过的路》《补墙》《雪夜林边驻留》《火与冰》《摘苹果之后》等都是诗人脍炙人口的名作。

弗罗斯特当过农民和工人，乡村生活阅历丰富，思想积淀深厚。他的诗作风格纯朴，他被称为“非官方的桂冠诗人”、美国“民族诗人”、“美国最受欢迎的诗人”。他笔耕不辍，诗风贴近民众，因此也受到美国政府的关注。1961年，约翰·肯尼迪总统举行就职典礼时特邀他朗诵诗作《全心全意的奉献》。

弗罗斯特的诗歌具有浓厚的乡村田园气息，它们大多以新英格兰地区(美国东北部的六个小州：缅因、佛蒙特、新罕布什尔、马萨诸塞、罗德岛、康涅狄格)人们习以为常的事物为题材，风雪、动物、小道、水果、森林等皆入其诗。其诗常常包含一个小故事，兼有叙事诗的特征。但是，诗人不为叙述而叙述，而是平凡之中见真谛——通过描写平常事引出比较深刻的道理，甚至是人生的哲理。这恐怕是其诗受人喜爱的主要原因之一。弗罗斯特的诗歌语言朴实无华，但也讲究韵律，如双行韵、十四行诗体以及音部的抑扬格，等等，这些令其诗歌具有19世纪传统诗歌的特征。同时，他的诗歌使用意象和象征，因而超越现实而上升到哲学层面。这又使其诗歌具有现代主义思想，使诗人成为意象主义和象征主义诗人的结合体。总之，弗罗斯特的诗歌兼备古典韵味和现代气息的双重特质，在英美现代诗歌中独树一帜。

二、文本选读

The Road Not Taken

Two roads diverged in a yellow wood,
And sorry I could not travel both
And be one traveler, long I stood
And looked down one as far as I could
To where it bent in the undergrowth;

Then took the other, as just as fair[1],
And having perhaps the better claim[2],
Because it was grassy and wanted wear;
Though as for that the passing there
Had worn them really about the same,

And both that morning equally lay
In leaves no step had trodden black.
Oh, I kept the first for another day!
Yet knowing how way leads on to way[3],
I doubted if I should ever come back.

I shall be telling this with a sigh
Somewhere ages and ages hence:
Two roads diverged in a wood, and I—
I took the one less traveled by,
And that has made all the difference.

三、题目解析

《一条未走过的路》发表于1915年，是弗罗斯特的名篇。诗作由四个诗节组成。第一诗节："我"站在两条路的分岔处，思考着抉择，并眺望其中一条路的尽头；第二诗节："我"有更好的理由选择一条同样平坦但人迹罕至的路；第三诗节：两条路同样鲜有足迹，然而"我"怀疑：一旦启程前行，自己还能否重回旧地；第四诗节：多年后，"我"带着叹息诉说往事：我选择了一条有更少足迹的路，从此人生迥然不同。

诗作中的"我"是个旅行者，途中面临两条不同的路。经过思考，最终选择人迹更稀之路。他起初不确定是否能够重返原点，后来明白：回归已不可能，人生结局大不相同。

诗作描述的是现实生活中的两条可见之路。不管选择哪条，最终都有可能抵达目的地。然而，作者还是心存遗憾：如果选择了另一条，也许会更加通畅，更易完成旅程。同时，回到起点重新来过的想法已无法实现。此所谓有得必有失；过去不能假设，唯有在抉择面前更加慎重；人生不免留下这样那样的遗憾。这是人生的无奈，也是人生的现实，更是人生的意义所在。现实生活存在两条路，我们的人生、事业乃至爱情和婚姻等又何尝不是如此？也许，我们会面临更多的选择。面对选择，我们应该谨慎抉择；一旦选择，就该努力前行，不弃不止，克难奋进。唯有如此，方可减少遗憾。另外，遗憾并非坏事。有遗憾，就会更加努力，力争下次做到更好；有遗憾，说明心中有憧憬。再者，既然是自我选择，就该对结局负责。最后，如同诗人弗罗斯特本人，也许他愿意选择一条寂寞与孤独之路，以便沉寂自己，专一完成自己的创作理想。这也是一种追求、一种活法。

路，既是我们脚下可见的现实之路，也是我们的人生之路。每个人在不同的人生阶段都会面临两条"路"，每一条"路"上又会出现若干条分岔的"路"。每一次选择都有缘由，但也有遗憾。这些都是题目中“路”的含义。

四、难点注释

1. fair：没有障碍的。
2. claim：声明；理由。
3. way leads on to way：道路一条接着一条，暗指返回原点的困难。

五、延伸阅读与批评

《补墙》与《一条未走过的路》一样经常被收入美国文学选读的课本。它同样通过讲故事的方式，娓娓道来，最后提出令人深思的问题。诗歌中的“墙”存在于现实生活中，可以看见；也存在于我们的思想中，看不见，但可以感知。“墙”代表了安全、保护，还是阻碍(种族歧视)、拒绝、自闭？是谁在补墙？为何要补墙？如何理解作品中“高墙出睦邻”的观点？我们读者的生活和思想中是否也存在类似的“墙”？如果有，我们如何对待它——是补还是拆？这些问题存在于个人之间以及个人与社会之间，包含在诗歌的题目之中，值得深思。

Chapter 3 The Negro Speaks of Rivers

by Langston Hughes

一、作者简介

兰斯顿·休斯(1902—1967)，美国20世纪著名的诗人。他是20世纪20年代美国哈莱姆文艺复兴(又称新黑人运动或黑人文艺复兴运动)的领军人物，被称为美国"黑人民族的桂冠诗人"。休斯的家庭背景比较复杂，曾祖父是白人，祖母是黑人。诗人著述颇丰，主要有诗集《疲惫的布鲁斯》(1926)、《抵押给犹太人的好衣裳》(1927)以及去世后出版的诗文集《早安，革命》(1973)。此外，诗人还创作了小说《并非没有笑声》(1930)，短篇小说集《白人的行径》(1934)，剧本《混血儿》(1935)，自传作品《大海》(1940)和《我徘徊，我彷徨》(1956)，讽刺小品集三部曲《新普尔倾吐衷情》(1950)、《辛普尔的高明》(1961)、《辛普尔的汤姆叔叔》(1965)。由此可见休斯是一个多才多艺的作家。

休斯的诗作题材广泛，但大多指向历史、社会、文化，指向政治、权力、身份。黑人民族的历史和现状，黑人在白人社会的政治、经济、社会和文化地位是他诗歌关注的主要内容。塑造新黑人形象，赞美黑人的文明和智慧，歌颂黑人民族的自豪感，揭露黑人遭遇的种种不公平现象，鼓励黑人永远前进，走向美好明天是诗人始终不渝的创作追求。这些思想内涵对美国现当代黑人文学的繁荣和发展产生了极其深远的影响。在创作手法上，休斯的诗歌善于吸收传统的黑人圣歌、黑人奴隶歌曲、布鲁斯乐和爵士乐等流行音乐，并辅之朴实无华和戏剧化的语言，这些手法令他的诗作易读易颂易唱，深受不同肤色读者的欢迎。

更为可贵的是，休斯不仅心怀对黑人民族的关怀，而且放眼其他兄弟民族的未来。他十分关注中国人民的斗争与解放。1937年，休斯创作《怒吼吧，中国》，谴责帝国主义列强入侵中国，并号召中国人民团结起来，勇敢抗敌，争取解放。中华人民共和国诞生后，休斯又著文讴歌一个崭新而独立的中华民族。

二、文本选读

The Negro Speaks of Rivers

I've known rivers:
I've known rivers ancient as the world and older than the flow of human blood in human veins.
My soul has grown deep[1] like the rivers.
I bathed in the Euphrates[2] when dawns were young.
I built my hut near the Congo[3] and it lulled me to sleep.

I looked upon the Nile[4] and raised the pyramids above it.
I heard the singing of the Mississippi[5] when Abe Lincoln went down to New Orleans[6], and I've seen its muddy bosom turn all golden in the sunset.
I've known rivers:
Ancient, dusky rivers.

My soul has grown deep like the rivers.

三、题目解析

《黑人谈河流》这个题目十分醒目。“黑人”指谁？“河流”的名字是什么？它们有何特殊含义？黑人为什么要谈河流？

该诗写于1920年，当时诗人年仅18岁。从内容上看，诗作共分五个意义单元。第一，“我”了解先于人类存在的古老的河流；第二，“我”的灵魂变得像河流一样深邃；第三，“我”在幼发拉底河沐浴，与刚果河为伴，凝望尼罗河，它旁边耸立着金字塔，听见林肯访问新奥尔良时密西西比河的歌声；第四，“我”了解古老而黝黑的河流；第五，“我”的灵魂变得像河流一样深邃。其中，第三行和最后一行的内容完全相同。

诗中提到几条河流，它们都承载着丰富的历史和现实文化意义。幼发拉底河和底格里斯河并称为“两河流域”，是古代文明的发源地。尼罗河流经埃及，古埃及人民建造了象征另一个古代文明的金字塔。幼发拉底河和尼罗河孕育了人类生命，生长在那里的人民创造了灿烂的古代文明。刚果河流经非洲的腹地，同样为非洲提供人类生命之源。密西西比河是美国的最大河流，流经美国中西部的广袤大地，为美国民众提供生命的养料。综而述之，没有上述河流，就没有亚洲、非洲、美洲的人类，就没有三个大陆悠久的历史和文明(文化)。过去如此，现在也是如此。所以，河流是生命的象征、文明的象征，是人类历史的象征，也是现在乃至未来的象征。它们集自然与文明于一身，融过去、现在和未来为一体。

黑人谈河流，“我”对上述河流如此了解。因此，黑人与河流之间必有某些关联：黑人的故土在非洲，黑人民族的历史如同河流一样悠长。黑人生活在美国，他们的历史也有几个世纪。这是身处不同大陆的黑人之间的相似之处。诗作中“河流”是“黝黑的”，与黑人肤色相同，而且诗中的“我”与河流相伴。这是黑人与河流的相似点。再者，刚果河、尼罗河、密西西比河分别养育了非洲人民和美国人民，因此也是非洲文明和美国文明的创造者；非洲黑人创造了非洲文明，美国文明中也融入了非洲黑人的生命和智慧。黑人为不同大陆的文明作出了同样的贡献。于是，黝黑的河流与黑人合二为一，他们共同为人类文明作出贡献。所以，黑人需要“谈”河流，“谈”是寻求一种自我身份，一种文化认同感、民族自豪感。然而，黑人的现实如何？非洲仍然贫穷，仍然不同程度地活在被殖民的历史阴影中。美国的黑人仍然受到种族歧视，他们的历史充满黑暗、苦难和辛酸。他们的现实生活虽然大有改观，但在政治、经济、文化等方面仍然被边缘化，仍需为更加光明的未来努力拼搏。因此，黑人“谈”河流是对自我智慧和历史的歌颂，对彻底废除奴隶制的欢呼，对美国总统林肯的支持与拥戴，对欧洲新旧殖民者和美国白人的声讨，对黑人不公平历史和现实的呐喊，对种族平等的呼唤。

诗中的“黑人”，既是指个体的黑人，更是指整个黑人民族。

四、难点注释

1. deep：深邃；深沉。
2. the Euphrates：位于西南亚的幼发拉底河。
3. the Congo：非洲的刚果河。
4. the Nile：非洲的尼罗河。
5. the Mississippi：美国的密西西比河。
6. Abe Lincoln went down to New Orleans：林肯南下新奥尔良。1831年，年仅22岁的林肯到新奥尔良，看到到处都是买卖黑奴的场景后愤怒地说：“总有一天，我要砸碎这可恶的奴隶制度。”后来他当上美国总统，于1861年发表了著名的《解放奴隶宣言》，宣告美国奴隶制度的结束。

五、延伸阅读与批评

《母亲对儿子说》是休斯的另一首经常被读者吟唱的诗歌。母亲告诉儿子：生活就像爬楼梯，途中充满“杂物”，没有灯光，经常遇到曲折。但是，母亲没有放弃，坚持向前。同时母亲也鼓励儿子不要回头，更不要倒下。题目中的两个词抓住了读者的注意力：“母亲”和“儿子”。母子指谁？“说”的内容就是诗歌的内容，但它是否有特殊含义？不言而喻，诗中的“母亲”和“儿子”皆为黑人，但他们能否代表黑人民族，抑或代表整个人类？

Chapter 4 A Rose for Emily

by William Faulkner

一、作者简介

威廉·福克纳(1897—1962)，美国20世纪最杰出的小说家之一，诺贝尔文学奖获得者(1950)，美国“南方文学”的最杰出代表。他的学术生命持久，且作品很多，长篇小说有《喧哗与骚动》(1929)、《在我弥留之际》(1930)、《圣殿》(1931)、《八月之光》(1932)、《押沙龙，押沙龙!》(1936)、《村子》(1940)。此外，他还出版了几部短篇小说集，如《去吧，摩西》(1942)和《福克纳故事集》(1950)，代表性的短篇小说有《干燥的九月》等。

福克纳笔下的故事大多发生在作者虚构的一个县——约克纳帕塔法，它位于美国南方。有时，一个人物贯穿几部小说，或几部小说都在描写一个家族的兴衰变迁，这使得他的小说既各自独立，又相互勾连，形成反映美国内战前后直至作者所处时代的美国南方历史兴衰的庞大“约克纳帕塔法小说体系”。

福克纳家族和美国内战有着密切的关系，特殊的家庭背景对他的创作产生了深远的影响。美国的南方和北方在历史、政治、经济、文化方面的复杂关系，特别是美国南北战争后美国社会发生的深刻变化——南方人的怀旧情绪、南方与北方的对立、南方人对北方人的认识、南方种植园经济的走向、南方文明的重读与反思、白人与黑人的矛盾和冲突、新旧体制的更迭、生活在新旧体制夹缝中的南方人对新旧体制的思考和抉择、人与土地和自然的关系、基督教信仰危机、物质世界里人类精神的衰落等都是福克纳作品中的常见题材和主题。由于这些题材和主题既有地域性又有普遍性，读者可以从哲学或人类精神层面理解他的作品。

福克纳既是一位思想大师，也是一位语言大师。他的创作手法丰富多样。他用词考究，使用复杂句式，小说结构奇特，特别是将意识流和多角度叙述相结合等艺术手法使他的作品成为典型的欧美现代主义文学作品，也为20世纪60年代以来美国后现代主义作家提供了重要借鉴。

二、文本选读

A Rose for Emily

I

When Miss Emily Grierson died, our whole town went to her funeral: the men through a sort of respectful affection for a fallen monument[1], the women mostly out of curiosity to see the inside of her house, which no one save an old man-servant—a combined gardener and cook—had seen in at least ten years.

It was a big, squarish frame house that had once been white, decorated with cupolas and spires and scrolled balconies in the heavily lightsome style of the seventies, set on what had once been our most select street. But garages and cotton gins had encroached and obliterated even the august names of that neighborhood; only Miss Emily's house was left, lifting its stubborn and coquettish decay above the cotton wagons and the gasoline pumps-an eyesore among eyesores. And now Miss Emily had gone to join the representatives of those august[2] names where they lay in the cedar-bemused cemetery among the ranked and anonymous graves of Union and Confederate soldiers[3] who fell at the battle of Jefferson[4].

Alive, Miss Emily had been a tradition, a duty, and a care; a sort of hereditary obligation upon the town, dating from that day in 1894 when Colonel Sartoris, the mayor—he who fathered the edict that no Negro woman should appear on the streets without an apron-remitted her taxes, the dispensation dating from the death of her father on into perpetuity. Not that Miss Emily would have accepted charity. Colonel Sartoris invented an involved[5] tale to the effect that Miss Emily's father had loaned money to the town, which the town, as a matter of business, preferred this way of repaying. Only a man of Colonel Sartoris' generation and thought could have invented it, and only a woman could have believed it.

When the next generation, with its more modern ideas, became mayors and aldermen, this arrangement created some little dissatisfaction. On the first of the year they mailed her a tax notice. February came, and there was no reply. They wrote her a formal letter, asking her to call at the sheriff's office at her convenience. A week later the mayor wrote her himself, offering to call or to send his car for her, and received in reply a note on paper of an archaic shape, in a thin, flowing calligraphy in faded ink, to the effect that she no longer went out at all. The tax notice was also enclosed, without comment.

They called a special meeting of the Board of Aldermen. A deputation waited upon her, knocked at the door through which no visitor had passed since she ceased giving china-painting lessons eight or ten years earlier. They were admitted by the old Negro into a dim hall from which a stairway mounted into still more shadow. It smelled of dust and disuse—a close, dank smell. The Negro led them into the parlor. It was furnished in heavy, leather-covered furniture. When the Negro opened the blinds of one window, they could see that the leather was cracked; and when they sat down, a faint dust rose sluggishly about their thighs, spinning with slow motes in the single sun-ray. On a tarnished gilt easel before the fireplace stood a crayon portrait of Miss Emily's father.

They rose when she entered—a small, fat woman in black, with a thin gold chain descending to her waist and vanishing into her belt, leaning on an ebony cane with a tarnished gold head. Her skeleton was small and spare; perhaps that was why what would have been merely plumpness in another was obesity in her. She looked bloated, like a body long submerged in motionless water, and of that pallid hue. Her eyes, lost in the fatty ridges of her face, looked like two small pieces of coal pressed into a lump of dough as they moved from one face to another while the visitors stated their errand.

She did not ask them to sit. She just stood in the door and listened quietly until the spokesman came to a stumbling halt. Then they could hear the invisible watch ticking at the end of the gold chain.

Her voice was dry and cold. "I have no taxes in Jefferson. Colonel Sartoris explained it to me. Perhaps one of you can gain access to the city records and satisfy yourselves."

"But we have. We are the city authorities, Miss Emily. Didn't you get a notice from the sheriff, signed by him?"

"I received a paper, yes," Miss Emily said. "Perhaps he considers himself the sheriff ... I have no taxes in Jefferson."

"But there is nothing on the books to show that, you see We must go by the—"

"See Colonel Sartoris. I have no taxes in Jefferson."

"But, Miss Emily—"

"See Colonel Sartoris." (Colonel Sartoris had been dead almost ten years.) "I have no taxes in Jefferson. Tobe!" The Negro appeared. "Show these gentlemen out.

II

So she vanquished them, horse and foot, just as she had vanquished their fathers thirty years before about the smell. That was two years after her father's death and a short time after her sweetheart—the one we believed would marry her—had deserted her. After her father's death she went out very little; after her sweetheart went away, people hardly saw her at all. A few of the ladies had the temerity to call, but were not received, and the only sign of life about the place was the Negro man—a young man then—going in and out with a market basket.

"Just as if a man—any man—could keep a kitchen properly," the ladies said; so they were not surprised when the smell developed. It was another link between the gross, teeming world and the high and mighty Griersons.

A neighbor, a woman, complained to the mayor, Judge Stevens, eighty years old.

"But what will you have me do about it, madam?" he said.

"Why, send her word to stop it," the woman said. "Isn't there a law?"

"I'm sure that won't be necessary," Judge Stevens said. "It's probably just a snake or a rat that nigger of hers killed in the yard. I'll speak to him about it."

The next day he received two more complaints, one from a man who came in diffident deprecation. "We really must do something about it, Judge. I'd be the last[6] one in the world to bother Miss Emily, but we've got to do something." That night the Board of Aldermen met—three graybeards and one younger man, a member of the rising generation.

"It's simple enough," he said. "Send her word to have her place cleaned up. Give her a certain time to do it in, and if she don't..."

"Dammit, sir," Judge Stevens said, "will you accuse a lady to her face of smelling bad?"

So the next night, after midnight, four men crossed Miss Emily's lawn and slunk about the house like burglars, sniffing along the base of the brickwork and at the cellar openings while one of them performed a regular sowing motion with his hand out of a sack slung from his shoulder. They broke open the cellar door and sprinkled lime there, and in all the outbuildings. As they recrossed the lawn, a window that had been dark was lighted and Miss Emily sat in it, the light behind her, and her upright torso motionless as that of an idol. They crept quietly across the lawn and into the shadow of the locusts that lined the street. After a week or two the smell went away.

That was when people had begun to feel really sorry for her. People in our town, remembering how old lady Wyatt, her great-aunt, had gone completely crazy at last, believed that the Griersons held themselves a little too high for what they really were. None of the young men were quite good enough for Miss Emily and such. We had long thought of them as a tableau, Miss Emily a slender figure in white in the background, her father a spraddled silhouette in the foreground, his back to her and clutching a horsewhip, the two of them framed by the back-flung front door. So when she got to be thirty and was still single, we were not pleased exactly, but vindicated; even with insanity in the family she wouldn't have turned down all of her chances if they had really materialized[7].

When her father died, it got about that the house was all that was left to her; and in a way, people were glad. At last they could pity Miss Emily. Being left alone, and a pauper, she had become humanized. Now she too would know the old thrill and the old despair of a penny more or less.

The day after his death all the ladies prepared to call at the house and offer condolence and aid, as is our custom Miss Emily met them at the door, dressed as usual and with no trace of grief on her face. She told them that her father was not dead. She did that for three days, with the ministers calling on her, and the doctors, trying to persuade her to let them dispose of the body. Just as they were about to resort to law and force, she broke down, and they buried her father quickly.

We did not say she was crazy then. We believed she had to do that. We remembered all the young men her father had driven away, and we knew that with nothing left, she would have to cling to that which had robbed her, as people will.

III

She was sick for a long time. When we saw her again, her hair was cut short, making her look like a girl, with a vague resemblance to those angels in colored church windows—sort of tragic and serene.

The town had just let the contracts for paving the sidewalks, and in the summer after her father's death they began the work. The construction company came with riggers and mules and machinery, and a foreman named Homer Barron, a Yankee[8]—a big, dark, ready man, with a big voice and eyes lighter than his face. The little boys would follow in groups to hear him cuss the riggers, and the riggers singing in time to the rise and fall of picks. Pretty soon he knew everybody in town. Whenever you heard a lot of laughing anywhere about the square, Homer Barron would be in the center of the group. Presently we began to see him and Miss Emily on Sunday afternoons driving in the yellow-wheeled buggy and the matched team of bays from the livery stable.

At first we were glad that Miss Emily would have an interest, because the ladies all said, "Of course a Grierson would not think seriously of a Northerner, a day laborer." But there were still others, older people, who said that even grief could not cause a real lady to forget noblesse oblige—without calling it noblesse oblige. They just said, "Poor Emily. Her kinsfolk should come to her." She had some kin in Alabama; but years ago her father had fallen out with them over the estate of old lady Wyatt, the crazy woman, and there was no communication between the two families. They had not even been represented at the funeral.

And as soon as the old people said, "Poor Emily," the whispering began. "Do you suppose it's really so?" they said to one another. "Of course it is. What else could ..." This behind their hands; rustling of craned silk and satin behind jalousies closed upon the sun of Sunday afternoon as the thin, swift clop-clop-clop of the matched team passed: "Poor Emily."

She carried her head high enough—even when we believed that she was fallen. It was as if she demanded more than ever the recognition of her dignity as the last Grierson; as if it had wanted that touch of earthiness to reaffirm her imperviousness. Like when she bought the rat poison, the arsenic. That was over a year after they had begun to say "Poor Emily," and while the two female cousins were visiting her.

"I want some poison," she said to the druggist. She was over thirty then, still a slight woman, though thinner than usual, with cold, haughty black eyes in a face the flesh of which was strained across the temples and about the eyesockets as you imagine a lighthouse-keeper's face ought to look. "I want some poison," she said.

"Yes, Miss Emily. What kind? For rats and such? I'd recom—"

"I want the best you have. I don't care what kind."

The druggist named several. "They'll kill anything up to an elephant. But what you want is—"

"Arsenic," Miss Emily said. "Is that a good one?"

"Is ... arsenic? Yes, ma'am. But what you want—"

"I want arsenic."

The druggist looked down at her. She looked back at him, erect, her face like a strained flag. "Why, of course," the druggist said. "If that's what you want. But the law requires you to tell what you are going to use it for."

Miss Emily just stared at him, her head tilted back in order to look him eye for eye, until he looked away and went and got the arsenic and wrapped it up. The Negro delivery boy brought her the package; the druggist didn't come back. When she opened the package at home there was written on the box, under the skull and bones: "For rats."

Ⅳ

So the next day we all said, "She will kill herself"; and we said it would be the best thing. When she had first begun to be seen with Homer Barron, we had said, "She will marry him." Then we said, "She will persuade him yet," because Homer himself had remarked—he liked men, and it was known that he drank with the younger men in the Elks' Club—that he was not a marrying man. Later we said, "Poor Emily" behind the jalousies as they passed on Sunday afternoon in the glittering buggy, Miss Emily with her head high and Homer Barron with his hat cocked and a cigar in his teeth, reins and whip in a yellow glove.

Then some of the ladies began to say that it was a disgrace to the town and a bad example to the young people. The men did not want to interfere, but at last the ladies forced the Baptist minister—Miss Emily's people were Episcopal—to call upon her. He would never divulge what happened during that interview, but he refused to go back again. The next Sunday they again drove about the streets, and the following day the minister's wife wrote to Miss Emily's relations in Alabama.

So she had blood-kin under her roof again and we sat back to watch developments. At first nothing happened. Then we were sure that they were to be married. We learned that Miss Emily had been to the jeweler's and ordered a man's toilet set in silver, with the letters H. B. on each piece. Two days later we learned that she had bought a complete outfit of men's clothing, including a nightshirt, and we said, "They are married." We were really glad. We were glad because the two female cousins were even more Grierson than Miss Emily had ever been.

So we were not surprised when Homer Barron—the streets had been finished some time since—was gone. We were a little disappointed that there was not a public blowing-off, but we believed that he had gone on to prepare for Miss Emily's coming, or to give her a chance to get rid of the cousins. (By that time it was a cabal, and we were all Miss Emily's allies to help circumvent the cousins.) Sure enough, after another week they departed. And, as we had expected all along, within three days Homer Barron was back in town. A neighbor saw the Negro man admit him at the kitchen door at dusk one evening.

And that was the last we saw of Homer Barron. And of Miss Emily for some time. The Negro man went in and out with the market basket, but the front door remained closed. Now and then we would see her at a window for a moment, as the men did that night when they sprinkled the lime, but for almost six months she did not appear on the streets. Then we knew that this was to be expected too; as if that quality of her father which had thwarted her woman's life so many times had been too virulent and too furious to die.

When we next saw Miss Emily, she had grown fat and her hair was turning gray. During the next few years it grew grayer and grayer until it attained an even pepper-and-salt iron-gray, when it ceased turning. Up to the day of her death at seventy-four it was still that vigorous iron-gray, like the hair of an active man.

From that time on her front door remained closed, save for a period of six or seven years, when she was about forty, during which she gave lessons in china-painting. She fitted up a studio in one of the downstairs rooms, where the daughters and granddaughters of Colonel Sartoris' contemporaries were sent to her with the same regularity and in the same spirit that they were sent to church on Sundays with a twenty-five-cent piece for the collection plate. Meanwhile her taxes had been remitted.

Then the newer generation became the backbone and the spirit of the town, and the painting pupils grew up and fell away and did not send their children to her with boxes of color and tedious brushes and pictures cut from the ladies' magazines. The front door closed upon the last one and remained closed for good. When the town got free postal delivery, Miss Emily alone refused to let them fasten the metal numbers above her door and attach a mailbox to it. She would not listen to them.

Daily, monthly, yearly we watched the Negro grow grayer and more stooped, going in and out with the market basket. Each December we sent her a tax notice, which would be returned by the post office a week later, unclaimed. Now and then we would see her in one of the downstairs windows—she had evidently shut up the top floor of the house—like the carven torso of an idol in a niche, looking or not looking at us, we could never tell which. Thus she passed from generation to generation—dear, inescapable, impervious, tranquil, and perverse.

And so she died. Fell ill in the house filled with dust and shadows, with only a doddering Negro man to wait on her. We did not even know she was sick; we had long since given up trying to get any information from the Negro. He talked to no one, probably not even to her, for his voice had grown harsh and rusty, as if from disuse.

She died in one of the downstairs rooms, in a heavy walnut bed with a curtain, her gray head propped on a pillow yellow and moldy with age and lack of sunlight.

V

The Negro met the first of the ladies at the front door and let them in, with their hushed, sibilant voices and their quick, curious glances, and then he disappeared. He walked right through the house and out the back and was not seen again.

The two female cousins came at once. They held the funeral on the second day, with the town coming to look at Miss Emily beneath a mass of bought flowers, with the crayon face of her father musing profoundly above the bier and the ladies sibilant and macabre; and the very old men—some in their brushed Confederate uniforms—on the porch and the lawn, talking of Miss Emily as if she had been a contemporary of theirs, believing that they had danced with her and courted her perhaps, confusing time with its mathematical progression, as the old do, to whom all the past is not a diminishing road but, instead, a huge meadow which no winter ever quite touches, divided from them now by the narrow bottle-neck of the most recent decade of years.

Already we knew that there was one room in that region above stairs which no one had seen in forty years, and which would have to be forced. They waited until Miss Emily was decently in the ground before they opened it.

The violence of breaking down the door seemed to fill this room with pervading dust. A thin, acrid pall as of the tomb seemed to lie everywhere upon this room decked and furnished as for a bridal: upon the valance curtains of faded rose color, upon the rose-shaded lights, upon the dressing table, upon the delicate array of crystal and the man's toilet things backed with tarnished silver, silver so tarnished that the monogram was obscured. Among them lay a collar and tie, as if they had just been removed, which, lifted, left upon the surface a pale crescent in the dust. Upon a chair hung the suit, carefully folded; beneath it the two mute shoes and the discarded socks.

The man himself lay in the bed.

For a long while we just stood there, looking down at the profound and fleshless grin. The body had apparently once lain in the attitude[9] of an embrace, but now the long sleep that outlasts love, that conquers even the grimace of love, had cuckolded him. What was left of him, rotted beneath what was left of the nightshirt, had become inextricable from the bed in which he lay; and upon him and upon the pillow beside him lay that even coating of the patient and biding dust.

Then we noticed that in the second pillow was the indentation of a head. One of us lifted something from it, and leaning forward, that faint and invisible dust dry and acrid in the nostrils, we saw a long strand of iron-gray hair.

三、题目解析

《献给艾米莉的玫瑰》出版于1930年，是福克纳中短篇小说里的一朵奇葩。小说并未提到"玫瑰"，但它的标题为何要提到"玫瑰"？它代表什么？是谁要献给艾米莉玫瑰？

小说共分五个部分。第一部分：艾米莉死了，镇上的男女怀着尊敬和好奇的心情前往探访她的住处——该镇昔日辉煌而显赫建筑中的最后一座房屋。她的墓园里躺着她的祖先，还有在美国南北战争时期战死的南方和北方士兵。艾米莉在世时被认为是该镇传统的象征。时代更迭，新人掌权，但她拒不交税。第二部分：她年届三十，仍孑然一身。房子是父亲留给她的唯一家产。第三部分讲述艾米莉的爱情故事。父亲死后的那个夏天，由北方汉子带领的建筑公司来到艾米莉的家乡。不久镇民就看到她与北方汉子经常在一起。但是他们认为她根本看不上"北方佬"。后来人们看到她到药店买了耗子药。第四部分续写第三部分。人们对艾米莉的买药行为表示不解，同时也为她有伤风俗的交友举动感到羞愧。"北方佬"进到艾米莉的屋子后他俩再也没有露面，直到艾米莉七十四岁去世。第五部分呼应第一部分。全镇的人为艾米莉举行葬礼。打开尘封四十年的一间房，床上躺着早已腐烂的一具男尸，它就是那个"北方佬"。

小说向读者交代了几个关键事件：南北战争给故事发生地——小镇带来观念上的变化、艾米莉的家世、艾米莉的处境、艾米莉与北方工头的交往、北方工头之死。这些片断向读者描绘了艾米莉所处的时代环境和她本人的生活轨迹。所以，我们可以从社会历史和个人两个层面解读艾米莉。

从社会历史层面：首先，艾米莉是美国内战之前美国南方历史的一个符号——南方贵族的后裔，象征着成功、高贵、显赫、辉煌；她得到全镇的尊敬和认同，是南方历史的“传统”和“纪念碑”，是南方文明的守候者和继承者。因此，她与“北方佬”的交往被认为是“羞耻”。其次，她是美国内战之后美国南方历史从辉煌走向没落的受害者，是身处南方新旧历史更迭路口的“过客”：镇上的老民离她渐行渐远；镇上的新民对她敬而远之。严厉的家教使之孑然一身；她虽有家产房屋，但它们恰似囚牢，禁锢着她的身体和思想。她被高悬在空中，脱离社会，与孤独和寂寞为伴。

从个人层面：艾米莉反权威，反世俗，反等级制度，抛弃古老的历史戒律，追求自由而纯洁的爱情。纵使心理变态、手段残忍，但那也许是她拥有爱情的唯一方式。她对人性和爱情的追求令人感动和敬佩。

“玫瑰”在西方文化中意义丰赡：爱之女神维纳斯的象征、处女玛丽的象征。白色玫瑰代表天真之爱；粉红玫瑰表示初爱；红色玫瑰象征真爱。福克纳没有说明献给艾米莉的“玫瑰”是何种颜色，但它或许包含上述所有含义，因为我们从艾米莉身上读出了高贵、敬意、坚强、初爱、真爱、悲情之爱。

是谁献给艾米莉玫瑰？是小说中的“我们”——镇上的人，是作者福克纳，也是阅读小说的读者。

四、难点注释

1. fallen monument：坍塌的纪念碑。
2. august：令人敬畏的。
3. Union and Confederate soldiers：美国内战时期的北部联军士兵和南部联军士兵。
4. Jefferson：杰斐逊，小说作者福克纳虚构的一个美国南方小镇，是作者笔下许多故事的发生地。
5. involved：十分复杂的。
6. last：最不愿意干的。
7. materialized：成为现实；出现。
8. Yankee：(美国)北方诸州的人，北方佬。
9. attitude：姿势，姿态。

五、延伸阅读与批评

长篇小说《喧嚣与骚动》是福克纳的代表作。它叙述了美国南方没落贵族康普生一家的遭遇，展现了南方贵族庄园制解体的图景，并深刻地揭示了第一次世界大战后在西方精神危机浪潮的冲击下南方“现代人”的异化感和失落感。“喧嚣与骚动”来自莎士比亚的剧本《麦克白》第五幕第五场中麦克白的独白：“人生不过是一个行走的影子，一个在舞台上指手画脚的拙劣的演员，登场片刻，就在无声无息中悄然退下；它是一个白痴所讲的故事，充满着喧嚣与骚动，却找不到一点意义。”小说中没有明示“喧嚣与骚动”，但它与小说的三个叙述者、老康普生的三个儿子有什么关系？建议读者在解读该小说时先了解《麦克白》的大意之后再把握《喧嚣与骚动》的三个叙事者的性格特征。

Chapter 5 The Grapes of Wrath

by John Steinbeck

(*Excerpts*)

一、作者简介

约翰·斯坦贝克(1902—1968)，20世纪美国著名小说家，1962年获得诺贝尔文学奖，美国"左翼文学"的杰出代表。他一生共创作16部小说、6部非小说类文学作品和2部短篇小说集。代表作品有中篇小说《人鼠之间》(1937)、长篇小说《愤怒的葡萄》(1939)、中篇小说《月亮下去了》(1942)、长篇小说《伊甸之东》(1952)、长篇小说《烦恼的冬天》(1961)等。

斯坦贝克是一位地域作家，作品中带有强烈的地域色彩。斯坦贝克大部分作品中的故事都发生在加利福尼亚州中部，特别是在萨利纳斯河谷和加利福尼亚海岸区域。斯坦贝克自幼在加利福尼亚的萨利纳斯河谷长大，那里有着丰富的迁徙和移民历史，是一个多元文化聚集地。这种生长环境给斯坦贝克的写作增添了地方风味，使他的许多作品有了鲜明的区域感。

斯坦贝克是一位左翼作家，他的作品经常探索命运和不公正的主题，特别是一些受压迫的主人公或普通民众。斯坦贝克与左翼作家、记者和工会人士的交往对他的写作产生了一定的影响。1935年，他加入了一个共产主义组织，即美国作家联盟。因此，斯坦贝克的许多作品都以美国的土地和人民为题材，反映社会现实和劳动人民的斗争。

斯坦贝克是一位艺术大师，创作手法新颖独特。他用一种诗性化的小说语言来表现作品宏大和崇高的主题。他在小说情节发展过程中插入充满激情的抒情描写，以一种伤感的抒情和自然的文笔来表达他对普通贫民的同情。他将插入章节与叙述章节有机地融合在一起，两种章节互相交替，章节衔接艺术体现了小说结构的巧妙和创新。

正如诺贝尔文学奖颁奖词中所说，"斯坦贝克的创作既关注现实又富有想象，以蕴涵同情的幽默和对社会的敏锐洞察力而著称"。斯坦贝克作品大多以贫困、奋斗、劳动人民之间的友谊为主题思想。斯坦贝克具有纯熟而多样的写作技巧和艺术风格，其整体创作风格是以现实主义手法为主，兼用浪漫主义、幽默、象征等写作方式。他的作品致力于反映社会现实和劳动人民的斗争，代表了左翼文学一个重要的方面。其代表作——长篇小说《愤怒的葡萄》有史诗般的气势，是美国左翼文学的一个巅峰。斯坦贝克在美国被认为是仅次于马克·吐温的最受欢迎的作家，其作品对后来的美国文学，尤其是西部文学的发展起到了重大的影响。

二、文本选读

The Grapes of Wrath

10

WHEN THE TRUCK had gone, loaded with implements, with heavy tools, with beds and springs, with every movable thing that might be sold, Tom hung around the place. He mooned into the barn shed, into the empty stalls, and he walked into the implement leanto and kicked the refuse that was left, turned a broken mower tooth with his foot. He visited places he remembered—the red bank where the swallows nested, the willow tree over the pig pen. Two shoats grunted and squirmed at him through the fence, black pigs, sunning and comfortable. And then his pilgrimage was over, and he went to sit on the doorstep where the shade was lately fallen. Behind him Ma moved about in the kitchen, washing children's clothes in a bucket; and her strong freckled arms dripped soapsuds from the elbows. She stopped her rubbing when he sat down. She looked at him a long time, and at the back of his head when he turned and stared out at the hot sunlight. And then she went back to her rubbing.

She said, "Tom, I hope things is all right in California."

He turned and looked at her. "What makes you think they ain't?" he asked.

"Well—nothing. Seems too nice, kinda. I seen the han'bills fellas pass out, an' how much work they is, an' high wages an' all; an' I seen in the paper how they want folks to come an' pick grapes an' oranges an' peaches. That'd be nice work, Tom, pickin' peaches. Even if they wouldn't let you eat none, you could maybe snitch a little ratty one sometimes. An' it'd be nice under the trees, workin' in the shade. I'm scared of stuff so nice. I ain't got faith. I'm scared somepin ain't so nice about it."

Tom said, "Don't roust your faith bird-high an' you won't do no crawlin' with the worms."

"I know that's right. That's Scripture, ain't it?"

"I guess so," said Tom. "I never could keep Scripture straight sence I read a book name *The Winning of Barbara Worth*[1]."

Ma chuckled lightly and scrounged the clothes in and out of the bucket. And she wrung out overalls and shirts, and the muscles of her forearms corded out. "Your Pa's pa, he quoted Scripture all the time. He got it all roiled up, too. It was the *Dr. Miles' Almanac* he got mixed up. Used to read ever' word in that almanac out loud—letters from folks that couldn't sleep or had lame backs. An' later he'd give them people for a lesson, an' he'd say, 'That's a par'ble from Scripture.' Your Pa an' Uncle John troubled 'im some about it when they'd laugh." She piled wrung clothes like cord wood on the table. "They say it's two thousan' miles where we're goin'. How far ya think that is, Tom? I seen it on a map, big mountains like on a post card, an' we're goin' right through 'em. How long ya s'pose it'll take to go that far, Tommy?

"I dunno," he said. "Two weeks, maybe ten days if we got luck. Look, Ma, stop your worryin'. I'm a-gonna tell you somepin about bein' in the pen. You can't go thinkin' when you're gonna be out. You'd go nuts. You got to think about that day, an' then the nex' day, about the ball game Sat'dy. That's what you got to do. Ol' timers does that. A new young fella gets buttin' his head on the cell door. He's thinkin' how long it's gonna be. Whyn't you do that? Jus' take ever' day."

"That's a good way," she said, and she filled up her bucket with hot water from the stove, and she put in dirty clothes and began punching them down into the soapy water. "Yes, that's a good way. But I like to think how nice it's gonna be, maybe, in California. Never cold. An' fruit ever'place, an' people just bein' in the nicest places, little white houses in among the orange trees. I wonder—that is, if we all get jobs an' all work—maybe we can get one of them little white houses. An' the little fellas go out an' pick oranges right off the tree. They ain't gonna be able to stand it, they'll get to yellin' so."

Tom watched her working, and his eyes smiled. "It done you good jus' thinkin' about it. I knowed a fella from California. He didn't talk like us. You'd of knowed he come from some far-off place jus' the way he talked. But he says they's too many folks lookin' for work right there now. An' he says the folks that pick the fruit live in dirty ol' camps an' don't hardly get enough to eat. He says wages is low an' hard to get any."

A shadow crossed her face. "Oh, that ain't so," she said. "Your father got a han'bill on yella paper, tellin' how they need folks to work. They wouldn't go to that trouble if they wasn't plenty work. Costs 'em good money to get them han'bills out. What'd they want ta lie for, an' costin' 'em money to lie?"

Tom shook his head. "I don't know, Ma. It's kinda hard to think why they done it. Maybe—" He looked out at the hot sun, shining on the red earth.

"Maybe what?"

"Maybe it's nice, like you says. Where'd Grampa go? Where'd the preacher go?"

Ma was going out of the house, her arms loaded high with the clothes. Tom moved aside to let her pass. "Preacher says he's gonna walk aroun'. Grampa's asleep here in the house. He comes in here in the day an' lays down sometimes." She walked to the line and began to drape pale blue jeans and blue shirts and long gray underwear over the wire.

Behind him Tom heard a shuffling step, and he turned to look in. Grampa was emerging from the bedroom, and as in the morning, he fumbled with the buttons of his fly. "I heerd talkin'," he said. "Sons-a-bitches won't let a ol' fella sleep. When you bastards get dry behin' the ears, you'll maybe learn to let a ol' fella sleep." His furious fingers managed to flip open the only two buttons on his fly that had been buttoned. And his hand forgot what it had been trying to do. His hand reached in and contentedly scratched under the testicles. Ma came in with wet hands, and her palms puckered and bloated from hot water and soap.

"Thought you was sleepin'. Here, let me button you up." And though he struggled, she held him and buttoned his underwear and his shirt and his fly. "You go aroun' a sight," she said, and let him go.

And he spluttered angrily, "Fella's come to a nice—to a nice—when somebody buttons 'em. I want ta be let be to button my own pants."

Ma said playfully, "They don't let people run aroun' with their clothes unbutton' in California."

"They don't, hey! Well, I'll show 'em. They think they're gonna show me how to act out there? Why, I'll go aroun' a-hangin' out if I wanta!"

Ma said, "Seems like his language gets worse ever' year. Showin' off, I guess."

The old man thrust out his bristly chin, and he regarded Ma with his shrewd, mean, merry eyes. "Well, sir," he said, "we'll be a-startin' 'fore long now. An', by God, they's grapes out there, just a-hangin' over inta the road. Know what I'm a-gonna do? I'm gonna pick me a wash tub full a grapes, an' I'm gonna set in 'em, an' scrooge aroun', an' let the juice run down my pants."

Tom laughed. "By God, if he lives to be two hundred you never will get Grampa house broke," he said. "You're all set on goin', ain't you, Grampa?"

The old man pulled out a box and sat down heavily on it. "Yes, sir," he said. "An' goddamn near time, too. My brother went on out there forty years ago. Never did hear nothin' about him. Sneaky son-of-a-bitch, he was. Nobody loved him. Run off with a single-action Colt of mine. If I ever run across him or his kids, if he got any out in California, I'll ask 'em for that Colt. But if I know 'im, an' he got any kids, he cuckoo'd 'em, an' somebody else is a-raisin' 'em. I sure will be glad to get out there. Got a feelin' it'll make a new fella outa me. Go right to work in the fruit."

Ma nodded. "He means it, too," she said. "Worked right up to three months ago, when he throwed his hip out the last time."

"Damn right," said Grampa.

Tom looked outward from his seat on the doorstep. "Here comes that preacher, walkin' aroun' from the back side a the barn."

Ma said, "Curiousest grace I ever heerd, that he give this mornin'. Wasn't hardly no grace at all. Jus' talkin', but the sound of it was like a grace."

"He's a funny fella," said Tom. "Talks funny all the time. Seems like he's talkin' to hisself, though. He ain't tryin' to put nothin' over."

"Watch the look in his eye," said Ma. "He looks baptized. Got that look they call lookin' through. He sure looks baptized. An' a-walkin' with his head down, a-starin' at nothin' on the groun'. There is a man that's baptized." And she was silent, for Casy had drawn near the door.

"You gonna get sun-shook, walkin' around like that," said Tom.

Casy said, "Well, yeah—maybe." He appealed to them all suddenly, to Ma and Grampa and Tom. "I got to get goin' west. I got to go. I wonder if I kin go along with you folks." And then he stood, embarrassed by his own speech.

Ma looked to Tom to speak, because he was a man, but Tom did not speak. She let him have the chance that was his right, and then she said, "Why, we'd be proud to have you. 'Course I can't say right now; Pa says all the men'll talk tonight and figger when we gonna start. I guess maybe we better not say till all the men come. John an' Pa an' Noah an' Tom an' Grampa an' Al an' Connie, they're gonna figger soon's they get back. But if they's room I'm pretty sure we'll be proud to have ya."

The preacher sighed. "I'll go anyways," he said. "Somepin's happening. I went up an' I looked, an' the houses is all empty, an' the lan' is empty, an' this whole country is empty. I can't stay here no more. I got to go where the folks is goin'. I'll work in the fiel's, an' maybe I'll be happy."

"An' you ain't gonna preach?" Tom asked.

"I ain't gonna preach."

"An' you ain't gonna baptize?" Ma asked.

"I ain't gonna baptize. I'm gonna work in the fiel's, in the green fiel's, an' I'm gonna be near to folks. I ain't gonna try to teach 'em nothin'. I'm gonna try to learn. Gonna learn why the folks walks in the grass, gonna hear 'em talk, gonna hear 'em sing. Gonna listen to kids eatin' mush. Gonna hear husban' an' wife a-poundin' the mattress in the night. Gonna eat with 'em an' learn." His eyes were wet and shining. "Gonna lay in the grass, open an' honest with anybody that'll have me. Gonna cuss an' swear an' hear the poetry of folks talkin'. All that's holy, all that's what I didn't understan'. All them things is the good things."

The preacher sat humbly down on the chopping block beside the door. "I wonder what they is for a fella so lonely."

Tom coughed delicately. "For a fella that don't preach no more—" he began.

"Oh, I'm a talker!" said Casy. "No gettin' away from that. But I ain't preachin'. Preachin' is tellin' folks stuff. I'm askin' 'em. That ain't preachin', is it?"

"I don' know," said Tom. "Preachin's a kinda tone a voice, an' preachin's a way a lookin' at things. Preachin's bein' good to folks when they wanna kill ya for it. Las' Christmus in McAlester, Salvation Army come an' done us good. Three solid hours a cornet music, an' we set there. They was bein' nice to us. But if one of us tried to walk out, we'd a-drawed solitary. That's preachin. Doin' good to a fella that's down an' can't smack ya in the puss for it. No, you ain't no preacher. But don't you blow no cornets aroun' here."

Ma threw some sticks into the stove. "I'll get you a bite now, but it ain't much."

Grampa brought his box outside and sat on it and leaned against the wall, and Tom and Casy leaned back against the house wall. And the shadow of the afternoon moved out from the house.

In the late afternoon the truck came back, bumping and rattling through the dust, and there was a layer of dust in the bed, and the hood was covered with dust, and the headlights were obscured with a red flour. The sun was setting when the truck came back, and the earth was bloody in its setting light. Al sat bent over the wheel, proud and serious and efficient, and Pa and

Uncle John, as befitted the heads of the clan, had the honor seats beside the driver. Standing in the truck bed, holding onto the bars of the sides, rode the others, twelve-year-old Ruthie and ten-year-old Winfield, grime-faced and wild, their eyes tired but excited, their fingers and the edges of their mouths black and sticky from licorice whips, whined out of their father in town. Ruthie, dressed in a real dress of pink muslin that came below her knees, was a little serious in her youngladiness. But Winfield was still a trifle of a snot-nose, a little of a brooder back of the barn, and an inveterate collector and smoker of snipes. And whereas Ruthie felt the might, the responsibility, and the dignity of her developing breasts, Winfield was kidwild and calfish. Beside them, clinging lightly to the bars, stood Rose of Sharon, and she balanced, swaying on the balls of her feet, and took up the road shock in her knees and hams. For Rose of Sharon was pregnant and careful. Her hair, braided and wrapped around her head, made an ash-blond crown. Her round soft face, which had been voluptuous and inviting a few months ago, had already put on the barrier of pregnancy, the self-sufficient smile, the knowing perfection-look; and her plump body—full soft breasts and stomach, hard hips and buttocks that had swung so freely and provocatively as to invite slapping and stroking—her whole body had become demure and serious. Her whole thought and action were directed inward on the baby. She balanced on her toes now, for the baby's sake. And the world was pregnant to her; she thought only in terms of reproduction and of motherhood. Connie, her nineteenyear-old husband, who had married a plump, passionate hoyden, was still frightened and bewildered at the change in her; for there were no more cat fights in bed, biting and scratching with muffled giggles and final tears. There was a balanced, careful, wise creature who smiled shyly but very firmly at him. Connie was proud and fearful of Rose of Sharon. Whenever he could, he put a hand on her or stood close, so that his body touched her at hip and shoulder, and he felt that this kept a relation that might be departing. He was a sharp-faced, lean young man of a Texas strain, and his pale blue eyes were sometimes dangerous and sometimes kindly, and sometimes frightened. He was a good hard worker and would make a good husband. He drank enough, but not too much; fought when it was required of him; and never boasted. He sat quietly in a gathering and yet managed to be there and to be recognized.

Had he not been fifty years old, and so one of the natural rulers of the family, Uncle John would have preferred not to sit in the honor place beside the driver. He would have liked Rose of Sharon to sit there. This was impossible, because she was young and a woman. But Uncle John sat uneasily, his lonely haunted eyes were not at ease, and his thin strong body was not relaxed. Nearly all the time the barrier of loneliness cut Uncle John off from people and from appetites. He ate little, drank nothing, and was celibate. But underneath, his appetites swelled into pressures until they broke through. Then he would eat of some craved food until he was sick; or he would drink jake or whisky until he was a shaken paralytic with red wet eyes; or he would raven with lust for some whore in Sallisaw. It was told of him that once he went clear to Shawnee and hired three whores in one bed, and snorted and rutted on their unresponsive bodies for an hour. But when one of his appetites was sated, he was sad and ashamed and lonely again. He hid from people, and by gifts tried to make up to all people for himself. Then he crept into houses and left gum under pillows for children; then he cut wood and took no pay. Then he gave away any possession he might have: a saddle, a horse, a new pair of shoes. One could not talk to him then, for he ran away, or if confronted hid within himself and peeked out of frightened eyes. The death of his wife, followed by months of being alone, had marked him with guilt and shame and had left an unbreaking loneliness on him. But there were things he could not escape. Being one of the heads of the family, he had to govern; and now he had to sit on the honor seat beside the driver.

The three men on the seat were glum as they drove toward home over the dusty road. Al, bending over the wheel, kept shifting eyes from the road to the instrument panel, watching the ammeter needle, which jerked suspiciously, watching the oil gauge and the heat indicator. And his mind was cataloguing weak points and suspicious things about the car. He listened to the whine, which might be the rear end, dry; and he listened to tappets lifting and falling. He kept his hand on the gear lever, feeling the turning gears through it. And he had let the clutch out against the brake to test for slipping clutch plates. He might be a musking goat sometimes, but this was his responsibility, this truck, its running, and its maintenance. If something went wrong it would be his fault, and while no one would say it, everyone, and Al most of all, would know it was his fault. And so he felt it, watched it, and listened to it. And his face was serious and responsible. And everyone respected him and his responsibility. Even Pa, who was the leader, would hold a wrench and take orders from Al.

They were all tired on the truck. Ruthie and Winfield were tired from seeing too much movement, too many faces, from fighting to get licorice whips; tired from the excitement of having Uncle John secretly slip gum into their pockets.

And the men in the seat were tired and angry and sad, for they had got eighteen dollars for every movable thing from the farm: the horses, the wagon, the implements, and all the furniture from the house. Eighteen dollars. They had assailed the buyer, argued; but they were routed when his interest seemed to flag and he had told them he didn't want the stuff at any price. Then they were beaten, believed him, and took two dollars less than he had first offered. And now they were weary and frightened because they had gone against a system they did not understand and it had beaten them. They knew the team and the wagon were worth much more. They knew the buyer man would get much more, but they didn't know how to do it. Merchandising was a secret to them.

Al, his eyes darting from road to panel board, said, "That fella, he ain't a local fella. Didn' talk like a local fella. Clothes was different, too."

And Pa explained, "When I was in the hardware store I talked to some men I know. They say there's fellas comin' in jus' to buy up the stuff us fellas got to sell when we get out. They say these new fellas is cleaning up. But there ain't nothin' we can do about it. Maybe Tommy should of went. Maybe he could of did better."

John said, "But the fella wasn't gonna take it at all. We couldn't haul it back."

"These men I know told about that," said Pa. "Said the buyer fellas always done that. Scairt folks that way. We jus' don't know how to go about stuff like that. Ma's gonna be disappointed. She'll be mad an' disappointed."

Al said, "When ya think we're gonna go, Pa?"

"I dunno. We'll talk her over tonight an' decide. I'm sure glad Tom's back. That makes me feel good. Tom's a good boy."

Al said, "Pa, some fellas was talkin' about Tom, an' they says he's parole'. An' they says that means he can't go outside the State, or if he goes, an' they catch him, they send 'im back for three years."

Pa looked startled. "They said that? Seem like fellas that knowed? Not jus' blowin' off?"

"I don't know," said Al. "They was just a-talkin' there, an' I didn't let on he's my brother. I jus' stood an' took it in."

Pa said, "Jesus Christ, I hope that ain't true! We need Tom. I'll ask 'im about that. We got trouble enough without they chase the hell out of us. I hope it ain't true. We got to talk that out in the open."

Uncle John said, "Tom, he'll know."

They fell silent while the truck battered along. The engine was noisy, full of little clashings, and the brake rods banged. There was a wooden creaking from the wheels, and a thin jet of steam escaped through a hole in the top of the radiator cap. The truck pulled a high whirling column of red dust behind it. They rumbled up the last little rise while the sun was still half-face above the horizon, and they bore down on the house as it disappeared. The brakes squealed when they stopped, and the sound printed in Al's head—no lining left.

Ruthie and Winfield climbed yelling over the side walls and dropped to the ground. They shouted, "Where is he? Where's Tom?" And then they saw him standing beside the door, and they stopped, embarrassed, and walked slowly toward him and looked shyly at him.

And when he said, "Hello, how you kids doin'?" they replied softly, "Hello! All right." And they stood apart and watched him secretly, the great brother who had killed a man and been in prison. They remembered how they had played prison in the chicken coop and fought for the right to be prisoner.

Connie Rivers lifted the high tail-gate out of the truck and got down and helped Rose of Sharon to the ground; and she accepted it nobly, smiling her wise, selfsatisfied smile, mouth tipped at the corners a little fatuously.

Tom said, "Why, it Rosasharn. I didn't know you was comin' with them."

"We was walkin'," she said. "The truck come by an' picked us up." And then she said, "This is Connie, my husband." And she was grand, saying it.

The two shook hands, sizing each other up, looking deeply into each other; and in a moment each was satisfied, and Tom said, "Well, I see you been busy."

She looked down. "You do not see, not yet."

"Pa tol' me. When's it gonna be?"

"Oh, not for a long time! Not till nex' winter."

Tom laughed. "Gonna get 'im bore in a orange ranch, huh? In one a them white houses with orange trees all aroun'."

Rose of Sharon felt her stomach with both her hands. "You do not see," she said, and she smiled her complacent smile and went into the house. The evening was hot, and the thrust of light still flowed up from the western horizon. And without any signal the family gathered by the truck, and the congress, the family government, went into session.

The film of evening light made the red earth lucent, so that its dimensions were deepened, so that a stone, a post, a building had greater depth and more solidity than in the daytime light; and these objects were curiously more individual—a post was more essentially a post, set off from the earth it stood in and the field of corn it stood out against. All plants were individuals, not the mass of crop; and the ragged willow tree was itself, standing free of all other willow trees. The earth contributed a light to the evening. The front of the gray, paintless house, facing the west, was luminous as the moon is. The gray dusty truck, in the yard before the door, stood out magically in this light, in the overdrawn perspective of a stereopticon.

The people too were changed in the evening, quieted. They seemed to be a part of an organization of the unconscious. They obeyed impulses which registered only faintly in their thinking minds. Their eyes were inward and quiet, and their eyes, too, were lucent in the evening, lucent in dusty faces.

The family met at the most important place, near the truck. The house was dead, and the fields were dead; but this truck was the active thing, the living principle. The ancient Hudson, with bent and scarred radiator screen, with grease in dusty globules at the worn edge of every moving part, with hub caps gone and caps of red dust in their places—this was the new hearth, the living center of the family; half passenger car and half truck, high-sided and clumsy.

Pa walked around the truck, looking at it, and then he squatted down in the dust and found a stick to draw with. One foot was flat to the ground, the other rested on the ball and slightly back, so that one knee was higher than the other. Left forearm rested on the lower, left, knee; the right elbow on the right knee, and the right fist cupped for the chin. Pa squatted there, looking at the truck, his chin in his cupped fist. And Uncle John moved toward him and squatted down beside him. Their eyes were brooding. Grampa came out of the house and saw the two squatting together, and he jerked over and sat on the running board of the truck, facing them. That was the nucleus. Tom and Connie and Noah strolled in and squatted, and the line was a half-circle with Grampa in the opening. And then Ma came out of the house, and Granma with her, and Rose of Sharon behind, walking daintily. They took their places behind the squatting men; they stood up and put their hands on their hips. And the children, Ruthie and Winfield, hopped from foot to foot beside the women; the children squidged their toes in the red dust, but they made no sound. Only the preacher was not there. He, out of delicacy, was sitting on the ground behind the house. He was a good preacher and knew his people.

The evening light grew softer, and for a while the family sat and stood silently. Then Pa, speaking to no one, but to the group, made his report. "Got skinned on the stuff we sold. The fella knowed we couldn't wait. Got eighteen dollars only."

Ma stirred restively, but she held her peace.

Noah, the oldest son, asked, "How much, all added up, we got?"

Pa drew figures in the dust and mumbled to himself for a moment. "Hundred fiftyfour," he said. "But Al here says we gonna need better tires. Says these here won't last."

This was Al's first participation in the conference. Always he had stood behind with the women before. And now he made his report solemnly. "She's old an' she's ornery," he said gravely. "I gave the whole thing a good goin'-over 'fore we bought her. Didn' listen to the fella talkin' what a hell of a bargain she was. Stuck my finger in the differential and they wasn't no sawdust. Opened the gear box an' they wasn't no sawdust. Test' her clutch an' rolled her wheels for line. Went under her an' her frame ain't splayed none. She never been rolled. Seen they was a cracked cell in her battery an' made the fella put in a good one. The tires ain't worth a damn, but they're a good size. Easy to get. She'll ride like a bull calf, but she ain't shootin' no oil. Reason I says buy her is she was a pop'lar car. Wreckin' yards is full a Hudson Super-Sixes, an' you can buy parts cheap. Could a got a bigger, fancier car for the same money, but parts too hard to get, an' too dear. That's how I figgered her anyways." The last was his submission to the family. He stopped speaking and waited for their opinions.

Grampa was still the titular head, but he no longer ruled. His position was honorary and a matter of custom. But he did have the right of first comment, no matter how silly his old mind might be. And the squatting men and the standing women waited for him. "You're all right, Al," Grampa said. "I was a squirt jus' like you, a-fartin' aroun' like a dog-wolf. But when they was a job, I done it. You've growed up good." He finished in the tone of a benediction, and Al reddened a little with pleasure.

Pa said, "Sounds right-side-up to me. If it was horses we wouldn't have to put the blame on Al. But Al's the on'y automobile fella here."

Tom said, "I know some. Worked some in McAlester. Al's right. He done good." And now Al was rosy with the compliment. Tom went on, "I'd like to say—well, that preacher—he wants to go along." He was silent. His words lay in the group, and the group was silent. "He's a nice fella," Tom added. "We've knowed him a long time. Talks a little wild sometimes, but he talks sensible." And he relinquished the proposal to the family.

The light was going gradually. Ma left the group and went into the house, and the iron clang of the stove came from the house. In a moment she walked back to the brooding council.

Grampa said, "They was two ways a thinkin'. Some folks use' ta figger that a preacher was poison luck."

Tom said, "This fella says he ain't a preacher no more."

Grampa waved his hand back and forth. "Once a fella's a preacher, he's always a preacher.

That's somepin you can't get shut of. They was some folks figgered it was a good respectable thing to have a preacher along. Ef somebody died, preacher buried 'em. Weddin' come due, or overdue, an' there's your preacher. Baby come, an' you got a christener right under the roof. Me, I always said they was preachers an' preachers. Got to pick 'em. I kinda like this fella. He ain't stiff."

Pa dug his stick into the dust and rolled it between his fingers so that it bored a little hole. "They's more to this than is he lucky, or is he a nice fella," Pa said. "We got to figger close. It's a sad thing to figger close. Le's see, now. There's Grampa an' Granma—that's two. An' me an' John an' Ma—that's five. An' Noah an' Tommy an' Al—that's eight. Rosasharn an' Connie is ten, an' Ruthie an' Winfiel' is twelve. We got to take the dogs 'cause what'll we do else? Can't shoot a good dog, an' there ain't nobody to give 'em to. An' that's fourteen."

"Not countin' what chickens is left, an' two pigs," said Noah.

Pa said, "I aim to get those pigs salted down to eat on the way. We gonna need meat. Carry the salt kegs right with us. But I'm wonderin' if we can all ride, an' the preacher too. An' kin we feed a extra mouth?" Without turning his head he asked, "Kin we, Ma?"

Ma cleared her throat. "It ain't kin we? It's will we?" she said firmly. "As far as 'kin,' we can't do nothin', not go to California or nothin'; but as far as 'will,' why, we'll do what we will. An' as far as 'will'—it's a long time our folks been here and east before, an' I never heerd tell of no Joads or no Hazletts, neither, ever refusin' food an' shelter or a lift on the road to anybody that asked. They's been mean Joads, but never that mean."

Pa broke in, "But s'pose there just ain't room?" He had twisted his neck to look up at her, and he was ashamed. Her tone had made him ashamed. "S'pose we jus' can't all get in the truck?"

"There ain't room now," she said. "There ain't room for more'n six, an' twelve is goin' sure. One more ain't gonna hurt; an' a man, strong an' healthy, ain't never no burden. An' any time when we got two pigs an' over a hundred dollars, an' we wonderin' if we kin feed a fella—" She stopped, and Pa turned back, and his spirit was raw from the whipping.

Granma said, "A preacher is a nice thing to be with us. He give a nice grace this morning."

Pa looked at the face of each one for dissent, and then he said, "Want to call 'im over, Tommy? If he's goin', he ought to be here."

Tom got up from his hams and went toward the house, calling, "Casy—oh, Casy!"

A muffled voice replied from behind the house. Tom walked to the corner and saw the preacher sitting back against the wall, looking at the flashing evening star in the light sky. "Calling me?" Casy asked.

"Yeah. We think long as you're goin' with us, you ought to be over with us, helpin' to figger things out."

Casy got to his feet. He knew the government of families, and he knew he had been taken into the family. Indeed his position was eminent, for Uncle John moved sideways, leaving space between Pa and himself for the preacher. Casy squatted down like the others, facing Grampa enthroned on the running board.

Ma went to the house again. There was a screech of a lantern hood and the yellow light flashed up in the dark kitchen. When she lifted the lid of the big pot, the smell of boiling side-meat and beet greens came out the door. They waited for her to come back across the darkening yard, for Ma was powerful in the group.

Pa said, "We got to figger when to start. Sooner the better. What we got to do 'fore we go is get them pigs slaughtered an' in salt, an' pack our stuff an' go. Quicker the better, now."

Noah agreed, "If we pitch in, we kin get ready tomorrow, an' we kin go bright the nex' day."

Uncle John objected, "Can't chill no meat in the heat a the day. Wrong time a year for slaughterin'. Meat'll be sof' if it don' chill."

"Well, le's do her tonight. She'll chill tonight some. Much as she's gonna. After we eat, le's get her done. Got salt?"

Ma said, "Yes. Got plenty salt. Got two nice kegs, too."

"Well, le's get her done, then," said Tom.

Grampa began to scrabble about, trying to get a purchase to arise. "Gettin' dark," he said. "I'm gettin' hungry. Come time we get to California I'll have a big bunch a grapes in my han' all the time, a-nibblin' off it all the time, by God!" He got up, and the men arose.

Ruthie and Winfield hopped excitedly about in the dust, like crazy things. Ruthie whispered hoarsely to Winfield, "Killin' pigs and goin' to California. Killin' pigs and goin'—all the same time."

And Winfield was reduced to madness. He stuck his finger against his throat, made a horrible face, and wobbled about, weakly shrilling, "I'm a ol' pig. Look. I'm a ol' pig. Look at the blood, Ruthie!" And he staggered and sank to the ground, and waved arms and legs weakly.

But Ruthie was older, and she knew the tremendousness of the time. "And goin' to California," she said again. And she knew this was the great time in her life so far.

The adults moved toward the lighted kitchen through the deep dusk, and Ma served them greens and side-meat in tin plates. But before Ma ate, she put the big round wash tub on the stove and started the fire to roaring. She carried buckets of water until the tub was full, and then around the tub she clustered the buckets, full of water. The kitchen became a swamp of heat, and the family ate hurriedly, and went out to sit on the doorstep until the water should get hot. They sat looking out at the dark, at the square of light the kitchen lantern threw on the ground outside the door, with a hunched shadow of Grampa in the middle of it. Noah picked his teeth thoroughly with a broom straw. Ma and Rose of Sharon washed up the dishes and piled them on the table.

And then, all of a sudden, the family began to function. Pa got up and lighted another lantern. Noah from a box in the kitchen, brought out the bow-bladed butchering knife and whetted it on a worn little carborundum stone. And he laid the scraper on the chopping block, and the knife beside it. Pa brought two sturdy sticks, each three feet long, and pointed the ends with the ax, and he tied strong ropes, double half-hitched, to the middle of the sticks.

He grumbled, "Shouldn't of sold those singletrees—all of 'em."

The water in the pots steamed and rolled.

Noah asked, "Gonna take the water down there or bring the pigs up here?"

"Pigs up here," said Pa. "You can't spill a pig and scald yourself like you can hot water. Water about ready?"

"Jus' about," said Ma.

"Aw right. Noah, you an' Tom an' Al come along. I'll carry the light. We'll slaughter down there an' bring 'em up here."

Noah took his knife, and Al the ax, and the four men moved down on the sty, their legs flickering in the lantern light. Ruthie and Winfield skittered along, hopping over the ground. At the sty Pa leaned over the fence holding the lantern. The sleepy young pigs struggled to their feet, grunting suspiciously. Uncle John and the preacher walked down to help.

"All right," said Pa. "Stick 'em, an' we'll run 'em up and bleed an' scald at the house." Noah and Tom stepped over the fence. They slaughtered quickly and efficiently. Tom struck twice with the blunt head of the ax; and Noah, leaning over the felled pigs, found the great artery with his curving knife and released the pulsing streams of blood. Then over the fence with the squealing pigs. The preacher and Uncle John dragged one by the hind legs, and Tom and Noah the other. Pa walked along with the lantern, and the black blood made two trails in the dust.

At the house, Noah slipped his knife between tendon and bone of the hind legs; the pointed sticks held the legs apart, and the carcasses were hung from the two-by-four rafters that stuck out from the house. Then the men carried the boiling water and poured it over the black bodies. Noah slit the bodies from end to end and dropped the entrails out on the ground. Pa sharpened two more sticks to hold the bodies open to the air, while Tom with the scrubber and Ma with a dull knife scraped the skins to take out the bristles. Al brought a bucket and shoveled the entrails into it, and dumped them on the ground away from the house, and two cats followed him, mewing loudly, and the dogs followed him, growling lightly at the cats.

Pa sat on the doorstep and looked at the pigs hanging in the lantern light. The scraping was done now, and only a few drops of blood continued to fall from the carcasses into the black pool on the ground. Pa got up and went to the pigs and felt them with his hand, and then he sat down again. Granma and Grampa went toward the barn to sleep, and Grampa carried a candle lantern in his hand. The rest of the family sat quietly about the doorstep, Connie and Al and Tom on the ground, leaning their backs against the house wall, Uncle John on a box. Pa in the doorway. Only Ma and Rose of Sharon continued to move about. Ruthie and Winfield were sleepy now, but fighting it off. They quarreled sleepily out in the darkness, Noah and the preacher squatted side by side, facing the house. Pa scratched himself nervously, and took off his hat and ran his fingers through his hair. "Tomorra we'll get that pork salted early in the morning, an' then we'll get the truck loaded, all but the beds, an' nex' morning off we'll go. Hardly is a day's work in all that," he said uneasily.

Tom broke in, "We'll be moonin' aroun' all day, lookin' for somepin to do." The group stirred uneasily. "We could get ready by daylight an' go," Tom suggested. Pa rubbed his knee with his hand. And the restiveness spread to all of them.

Noah said, "Prob'ly wouldn't hurt that meat to git her right down in salt. Cut her up, she'd cool quicker anyways."

It was Uncle John who broke over the edge, his pressures too great. "What we hangin' aroun' for? I want to get shut of this. Now we're goin', why don't we go?"

And the revulsion spread to the rest. "Whyn't we go? Get sleep on the way." And a sense of hurry crept into them.

Pa said, "They say it's two thousan' miles. That's a hell of a long ways. We oughta go. Noah, you an' me can get that meat cut up an' we can put all the stuff in the truck."

Ma put her head out of the door. "How about if we forgit somepin, not seein' it in the dark?"

"We could look 'round after daylight," said Noah. They sat still then, thinking about it. But in a moment Noah got up and began to sharpen the bow-bladed knife on his little worn stone. "Ma," he said, "git that table cleared." And he stepped to a pig, cut a line down one side of the backbone and began peeling the meat forward, off the ribs.

Pa stood up excitedly. "We got to get the stuff together," he said. "Come on, you fellas."

Now that they were committed to going, the hurry infected all of them. Noah carried the slabs of meat into the kitchen and cut it into small salting blocks, and Ma patted the coarse salt in, laid it piece by piece in the kegs, careful that no two pieces touched each other. She laid the slabs like bricks, and pounded salt in the spaces. And Noah cut up the side-meat and he cut up the legs. Ma kept her fire going, and as Noah cleaned the ribs and the spines and leg bones of all the meat he could, she put them in the oven to roast for gnawing purposes.

In the yard and in the barn the circles of lantern light moved about, and the men brought together all the things to be taken, and piled them by the truck. Rose of Sharon brought out all the clothes the family possessed: the overalls, the thick-soled shoes, the rubber boots, the worn best suits, the sweaters and sheepskin coats. And she packed these tightly into a wooden box and got into the box and tramped them down. And then she brought out the print dresses and shawls, the black cotton stockings and the children's clothes—small overalls and cheap print dresses—and she put these in the box and tramped them down.

Tom went to the tool shed and brought what tools were left to go, a hand saw and a set of wrenches, a hammer and a box of assorted nails, a pair of pliers and a flat file and a set of rat-tail files.

And Rose of Sharon brought out the big piece of tarpaulin and spread it on the ground behind the truck. She struggled through the door with the mattresses, three double ones and a single. She piled them on the tarpaulin and brought arm-loads of folded ragged blankets and piled them up.

Ma and Noah worked busily at the carcasses, and the smell of roasting pork bones came from the stove. The children had fallen by the way in the late night. Winfield lay curled up in the dust outside the door; and Ruthie, sitting on a box in the kitchen where she had gone to watch the butchering, had dropped her head back against the wall. She breathed easily in her sleep, and her lips were parted over her teeth.

Tom finished with the tools and came into the kitchen with his lantern, and the preacher followed him. "God in a buckboard," Tom said, "smell that meat! An' listen to her crackle."

Ma laid the bricks of meat in a keg and poured salt around and over them and covered the layer with salt and patted it down. She looked up at Tom and smiled a little at him, but her eyes were serious and tired. "Be nice to have pork bones for breakfas'," she said.

The preacher stepped beside her. "Leave me salt down this meat," he said. "I can do it. There's other stuff for you to do."

She stopped her work then and inspected him oddly, as though he suggested a curious thing. And her hands were crusted with salt, pink with fluid from the fresh pork. "It's women's work," she said finally.

"It's all work," the preacher replied. "They's too much of it to split it up to men's or women's work. You got stuff to do. Leave me salt the meat."

Still for a moment she stared at him, and then she poured water from a bucket into the tin wash basin and she washed her hands. The preacher took up the blocks of pork and patted on the salt while she watched him. And he laid them in the kegs as she had. Only when he had finished a layer and covered it carefully and patted down the salt was she satisfied. She dried her bleached and bloated hands.

Tom said, "Ma, what stuff we gonna take from here?"

She looked quickly about the kitchen. "The bucket," she said. "All the stuff to eat with: plates an' the cups, the spoons an' knives an' forks. Put all them in that drawer, an' take the drawer. The big fry pan an' the big stew kettle, the coffee pot. When it gets cool, take the rack outa the oven. That's good over a fire. I'd like to take the wash tub, but I guess there ain't room. I'll wash clothes in the bucket. Don't do no good to take little stuff. You can cook little stuff in a big kettle, but you can't cook big stuff in a little pot. Take the bread pans, all of 'em. They fit down inside each other." She stood and looked about the kitchen. "You jus' take that stuff I tol' you, Tom. I'll fix up the rest, the big can a pepper an' the salt an' the nutmeg an' the grater. I'll take all that stuff jus' at the last." She picked up a lantern and walked heavily into the bedroom, and her bare feet made no sound on the floor.

The preacher said, "She looks tar'd."

"Women's always tar'd," said Tom. "That's just the way women is, 'cept at meetin' once an' again."

"Yeah, but tar'der'n that. Real tar'd like she's sick-tar'd."

Ma was just through the door, and she heard his words. Slowly her relaxed face tightened, and the lines disappeared from the taut muscular face. Her eyes sharpened and her shoulders straightened. She glanced about the stripped room. Nothing was left in it except trash. The mattresses which had been on the floor were gone. The bureaus were sold. On the floor lay a broken comb, an empty talcum powder can, and a few dust mice. Ma set her lantern on the floor. She reached behind one of the boxes that had served as chairs and brought out a stationery box, old and soiled and cracked at the corners. She sat down and opened the box. Inside were letters, clippings, photographs, a pair of earrings, a little gold signet ring, and a watch chain braided of hair and tipped with gold swivels. She touched the letters with her fingers, touched them lightly, and she smoothed a newspaper clipping on which there was an account of Tom's trial. For a long time she held the box, looking over it, and her fingers disturbed the letters and then lined them up again. She bit her lower lip, thinking, remembering. And at last she made up her mind. She picked out the ring, the watch charm, the earrings, dug under the pile and found one gold cuff link. She took a letter from an envelope and dropped the trinkets in the envelope. Then gently and tenderly she closed the box and smoothed the top carefully with her fingers. Her lips parted. Then she stood up, took her lantern, and went back into the kitchen. She lifted the stove lid and laid the box gently among the coals. Quickly the heat browned the paper. A flame licked up and over the box. She replaced the stove lid and instantly the fire sighed up and breathed over the box.

25

THE SPRING IS BEAUTIFUL in California. Valleys in which the fruit blossoms are fragrant pink and white waters in a shallow sea. Then the first tendrils of the grapes swelling from the old gnarled vines, cascade down to cover the trunks. The full green hills are round and soft as breasts. And on the level vegetable lands are the mile-long rows of pale green lettuce and the spindly little cauliflowers, the gray-green unearthly artichoke plants.

And then the leaves break out on the trees, and the petals drop from the fruit trees and carpet the earth with pink and white. The centers of the blossoms swell and grow and color: cherries and apples, peaches and pears, figs which close the flower in the fruit. All California quickens with produce, and the fruit grows heavy, and the limbs bend gradually under the fruit so that little crutches must be placed under them to support the weight.

Behind the fruitfulness are men of understanding and knowledge, and skill, men who experiment with seed, endlessly developing the techniques for greater crops of plants whose roots will resist the million enemies of the earth: the molds, the insects, the rusts, the blights. These men work carefully and endlessly to perfect the seed, the roots. And there are the men of chemistry who spray the trees against pests, who sulphur[2] the grapes, who cut out disease and rots, mildews and sicknesses. Doctors of preventive medicine, men at the borders who look for fruit flies, for Japanese beetle, men who quarantine the sick trees and root them out and burn them, men of knowledge. The men who graft the young trees, the little vines, are the cleverest of all, for theirs is a surgeon's job, as tender and delicate; and these men must have surgeons' hands and surgeons' hearts to slit the bark, to place the grafts, to bind the wounds and cover them from the air. These are great men.

Along the rows, the cultivators move, tearing the spring grass and turning it under to make a fertile earth, breaking the ground to hold the water up near the surface, ridging the ground in little pools for the irrigation, destroying the weed roots that may drink the water away from the trees.

And all the time the fruit swells and the flowers break out in long clusters on the vines. And in the growing year the warmth grows and the leaves turn dark green. The prunes lengthen like little green bird's eggs, and the limbs sag down against the crutches under the weight. And the hard little pears take shape, and the beginning of the fuzz comes out on the peaches. Grape blossoms shed their tiny petals and the hard little beads become green buttons, and the buttons grow heavy. The men who work in the fields, the owners of the little orchards, watch and calculate. The year is heavy with produce. And the men are proud, for of their knowledge they can make the year heavy. They have transformed the world with their knowledge. The short, lean wheat has been made big and productive. Little sour apples have grown large and sweet, and that old grape that grew among the trees and fed the birds its tiny fruit has mothered a thousand varieties, red and black, green and pale pink, purple and yellow; and each variety with its own flavor. The men who work in the experimental farms have made new fruits: nectarines and forty kinds of plums, walnuts with paper shells. And always they work, selecting, grafting, changing, driving themselves, driving the earth to produce.

And first the cherries ripen. Cent and a half a pound. Hell, we can't pick 'em for that. Black cherries and red cherries, full and sweet, and the birds eat half of each cherry and the yellowjackets buzz into the holes the birds made. And on the ground the seeds drop and dry with black shreds hanging from them.

The purple prunes soften and sweeten. My God, we can't pick them and dry and sulphur them. We can't pay wages, no matter what wages. And the purple prunes carpet the ground. And first the skins wrinkle a little and swarms of flies come to feast, and the valley is filled with the odor of sweet decay. The meat turns dark and the crop shrivels on the ground.

And the pears grow yellow and soft. Five dollars a ton. Five dollars for forty fifty-pound boxes; trees pruned and sprayed, orchards cultivated—pick the fruit, put it in boxes, load the trucks, deliver the fruit to the cannery—forty boxes for five dollars. We can't do it. And the yellow fruit falls heavily to the ground and splashes on the ground. The yellowjackets dig into the soft meat, and there is a smell of ferment and rot.

Then the grapes—we can't make good wine. People can't buy good wine. Rip the grapes from the vines, good grapes, rotten grapes, wasp-stung grapes. Press stems, press dirt and rot.

But there's mildew and formic acid in the vats.

Add sulphur and tannic acid.

The smell from the ferment is not the rich odor of wine, but the smell of decay and chemicals.

Oh, well. It has alcohol in it, anyway. They can get drunk.

The little farmers watched debt creep up on them like the tide. They sprayed the trees and sold no crop, they pruned and grafted and could not pick the crop. And the men of knowledge have worked, have considered, and the fruit is rotting on the ground, and the decaying mash in the wine vat is poisoning the air. And taste the wine—no grape flavor at all, just sulphur and tannic acid and alcohol.

This little orchard will be a part of a great holding next year, for the debt will have choked the owner.

This vineyard will belong to the bank. Only the great owners can survive, for they own the canneries, too. And four pears peeled and cut in half, cooked and canned, still cost fifteen cents. And the canned pears do not spoil. They will last for years.

The decay spreads over the State, and the sweet smell is a great sorrow on the land. Men who can graft the trees and make the seed fertile and big can find no way to let the hungry people eat their produce. Men who have created new fruits in the world cannot create a system whereby their fruits may be eaten. And the failure hangs over the State like a great sorrow.

The works of the roots of the vines, of the trees, must be destroyed to keep up the price, and this is the saddest, bitterest thing of all. Carloads of oranges dumped on the ground. The people came for miles to take the fruit, but this could not be. How would they buy oranges at twenty cents a dozen if they could drive out and pick them up? And men with hoses squirt kerosene on the oranges, and they are angry at the crime, angry at the people who have come to take the fruit. A million people hungry, needing the fruit—and kerosene sprayed over the golden mountains.

And the smell of rot fills the country.

Burn coffee for fuel in the ships. Burn corn to keep warm, it makes a hot fire. Dump potatoes in the rivers and place guards along the banks to keep the hungry people from fishing them out. Slaughter the pigs and bury them, and let the putrescence drip down into the earth.

There is a crime here that goes beyond denunciation. There is a sorrow here that weeping cannot symbolize. There is a failure here that topples all our success. The fertile earth, the straight tree rows, the sturdy trunks, and the ripe fruit. And children dying of pellagra must die because a profit cannot be taken from an orange. And coroners must fill in the certificate—died of malnutrition—because the food must rot, must be forced to rot.

The people come with nets to fish for potatoes in the river, and the guards hold them back; they come in rattling cars to get the dumped oranges, but the kerosene is sprayed. And they stand still and watch the potatoes float by, listen to the screaming pigs being killed in a ditch and covered with quick-lime, watch the mountains of oranges slop down to a putrefying ooze; and in the eyes of the people there is the failure; and in the eyes of the hungry there is a growing wrath. In the souls of the people the grapes of wrath are filling and growing heavy, growing heavy for the vintage.

29

OVER THE HIGH COAST mountains and over the valleys the gray clouds marched in from the ocean. The wind blew fiercely and silently, high in the air, and it swished in the brush, and it roared in the forests. The clouds came in brokenly, in puffs, in folds, in gray crags; and they piled in together and settled low over the west. And then the wind stopped and left the clouds deep and solid. The rain began with gusty showers, pauses and downpours; and then gradually it settled to a single tempo, small drops and a steady beat, rain that was gray to see through, rain that cut midday light to evening. And at first the dry earth sucked the moisture down and blackened. For two days the earth drank the rain, until the earth was full. Then puddles formed, and in the low places little lakes formed in the fields. The muddy lakes rose higher, and the steady rain whipped the shining water. At last the mountains were full, and the hillsides spilled into the streams, built them to freshets, and sent them roaring down the canyons into the valleys. The rain beat on steadily. And the streams and the little rivers edged up to the bank sides and worked at willows and tree roots, bent the willows deep in the current, cut out the roots of cottonwoods and brought down the trees. The muddy water whirled along the bank sides and crept up the banks until at last it spilled over, into the fields, into the orchards, into the cotton patches where the black stems stood. Level fields became lakes, broad and gray, and the rain whipped up the surfaces. Then the water poured over the highways, and cars moved slowly, cutting the water ahead, and leaving a boiling muddy wake behind. The earth whispered under the beat of the rain, and the streams thundered under the churning freshets.

When the first rain started, the migrant people huddled[3] in their tents, saying, It'll soon be over, and asking, How long's it likely to go on?

And when the puddles formed, the men went out in the rain with shovels and built little dikes around the tents. The beating rain worked at the canvas until it penetrated and sent streams down. And then the little dikes washed out and the water came inside, and the streams wet the beds and the blankets. The people sat in wet clothes. They set up boxes and put planks on the boxes. Then, day and night, they sat on the planks.

Beside the tents the old cars stood, and water fouled the ignition wires and water fouled the carburetors. The little gray tents stood in lakes. And at last the people had to move. Then the cars wouldn't start because the wires were shorted; and if the engines would run, deep mud engulfed the wheels. And the people waded away, carrying their wet blankets in their arms. They splashed along, carrying the children, carrying the very old, in their arms. And if a barn stood on high ground, it was filled with people, shivering and hopeless.

Then some went to the relief offices, and they came sadly back to their own people.

They's rules—you got to be here a year before you can git relief. They say the gov'ment is gonna help. They don' know when.

And gradually the greatest terror of all came along.

They ain't gonna be no kinda work for three months.

In the barns, the people sat huddled together; and the terror came over them, and their faces were gray with terror. The children cried with hunger, and there was no food.

Then the sickness came, pneumonia, and measles that went to the eyes and to the mastoids.

And the rain fell steadily, and the water flowed over the highways, for the culverts could not carry the water.

Then from the tents, from the crowded barns, groups of sodden men went out, their clothes slopping rags, their shoes muddy pulp. They splashed out through the water, to the towns, to the country stores, to the relief offices, to beg for food, to cringe and beg for food, to beg for relief, to try to steal, to lie. And under the begging, and under the cringing, a hopeless anger began to smolder. And in the little towns pity for the sodden men changed to anger, and anger at the hungry people changed to fear of them. Then sheriffs[4] swore in deputies in droves, and orders were rushed for rifles, for tear gas, for ammunition. Then the hungry men crowded the alleys behind the stores to beg for bread, to beg for rotting vegetables, to steal when they could.

Frantic men pounded on the doors of the doctors; and the doctors were busy. And sad men left word at country stores for the coroner to send a car. The coroners were not too busy. The coroners' wagons backed up through the mud and took out the dead.

And the rain pattered relentlessly down, and the streams broke their banks and spread out over the country.

Huddled under sheds, lying in wet hay, the hunger and the fear bred anger. Then boys went out, not to beg, but to steal; and men went out weakly, to try to steal.

The sheriffs swore in new deputies and ordered new rifles; and the comfortable people in tight houses felt pity at first and then distaste, and finally hatred for the migrant people.

In the wet hay of leaking barns babies were born to women who panted with pneumonia. And old people curled up in corners and died that way, so that the coroners could not straighten them. At night, the frantic men walked boldly to hen roosts and carried off the squawking chickens. If they were shot at, they did not run, but splashed sullenly away; and if they were hit, they sank tiredly in the mud.

The rain stopped. On the fields the water stood, reflecting the gray sky, and the land whispered with moving water. And the men came out of the barns, out of the sheds. They squatted on their hams and looked out over the flooded land. And they were silent. And sometimes they talked very quietly.

No work till spring. No work.

And if no work—no money, no food.

Fella had a team of horses, had to use 'em to plow an' cultivate an' mow, wouldn' think a turnin' 'em out to starve when they wasn't workin'.

Them's horses—we're men.

The women watched the men, watched to see whether the break had come at last. The women stood silently and watched. And where a number of men gathered together, the fear went from their faces, and anger took its place. And the women sighed with relief, for they knew it was all right—the break had not come; and the break would never come as long as fear could turn to wrath.

Tiny points of grass came through the earth, and in a few days the hills were pale green with the beginning year.

30

IN THE BOXCAR CAMP the water stood in puddles, and the rain splashed in the mud. Gradually the little stream crept up the bank toward the low flat where the boxcars stood.

On the second day of the rain Al took the tarpaulin down from the middle of the car. He carried it out and spread it on the nose of the truck, and he came back into the car and sat down on his mattress. Now, without the separation, the two families in the car were one. The men sat together, and their spirits were damp. Ma kept a little fire going in the stove, kept a few twigs burning, and she conserved her wood. The rain poured down on the nearly flat roof of the boxcar.

On the third day the Wainwrights grew restless. "Maybe we better go 'long," Mrs. Wainwright said.

And Ma tried to keep them. "Where'd you go an' be sure of a tight roof?"

"I dunno, but I got a feelin' we oughta go along." They argued together, and Ma watched Al.

Ruthie and Winfield tried to play for a while, and then they too relapsed into sullen inactivity, and the rain drummed down on the roof.

On the third day the sound of the stream could be heard above the drumming rain. Pa and Uncle John stood in the open door and looked out on the rising stream. At both ends of the camp the water ran near to the highway, but at the camp it looped away so that the highway embankment surrounded the camp at the back and the stream closed it in on the front. And Pa said, "How's it look to you, John? Seems to me if that crick comes up, she'll flood us."

Uncle John opened his mouth and rubbed his bristling chin. "Yeah," he said. "Might at that."

Rose of Sharon was down with a heavy cold, her face flushed and her eyes shining with fever. Ma sat beside her with a cup of hot milk. "Here," she said. "Take this here. Got bacon grease in it for strength. Here, drink it!"

Rose of Sharon shook her head weakly. "I ain't hungry."

Pa drew a curved line in the air with his finger. "If we was all to get our shovels an' throw up a bank, I bet we could keep her out. On'y have to go from up there down to there."

"Yeah," Uncle John agreed. "Might. Dunno if them other fellas'd wanta. They maybe ruther move somewheres else."

"But these here cars is dry," Pa insisted. "Couldn' find no dry place as good as this. You wait." From the pile of brush in the car he picked a twig. He ran down the catwalk, splashed through the mud to the stream and he set his twig upright on the edge of the swirling water. In a moment he was back in the car. "Jesus, ya get wet through," he said.

Both men kept their eyes on the little twig on the water's edge. They saw the water move slowly up around it and creep up the bank. Pa squatted down in the doorway. "Comin' up fast," he said. "I think we oughta go talk to the other fellas. See if they'll help ditch up. Got to git outa here if they won't." Pa looked down the long car to the Wainwright end. Al was with them, sitting beside Aggie. Pa walked into their precinct. "Water's risin'," he said. "How about if we throwed up a bank? We could do her if ever'body helped."

Wainwright said, "We was jes' talkin'. Seems like we oughta be gettin' outa here."

Pa said, "You been aroun'. You know what chancet we got a gettin' a dry place to stay." "I know. But jes' the same—"

Al said, "Pa, if they go, I'm a-goin' too."

Pa looked startled. "You can't, Al. The truck—We ain't fit to drive that truck."

"I don' care. Me an' Aggie got to stick together."

"Now you wait," Pa said. "Come on over here." Wainwright and Al got to their feet and approached the door. "See?" Pa said, pointing. "Jus' a bank from there an' down to there." He looked at his stick. The water swirled about it now, and crept up the bank.

"Be a lot a work, an' then she might come over anyways," Wainwright protested.

"Well, we ain't doin' nothin', might's well be workin'. We ain't gonna find us no nice place to live like this. Come on, now. Le's go talk to the other fellas. We can do her if ever'body helps."

Al said, "If Aggie goes, I'm a-goin' too."

Pa said, "Look, Al, if them fellas won't dig, then we'll all hafta go. Come on, le's go talk to 'em." They hunched their shoulders and ran down the cat-walk to the next car and up the walk into its open door.

Ma was at the stove, feeding a few sticks to the feeble flame. Ruthie crowded close beside her. "I'm hungry," Ruthie whined.

"No, you ain't," Ma said. "You had good mush."

"Wisht I had a box a Cracker Jack[5]. There ain't nothin' to do. Ain't no fun."

"They'll be fun," Ma said. "You jus' wait. Be fun purty soon. Git a house an' a place, purty soon."

"Wisht we had a dog," Ruthie said.

"We'll have a dog; have a cat, too."

"Yella cat?" "Don't bother me," Ma begged.

"Don't go plaguin' me now, Ruthie. Rosasharn's sick. Jus' you be a good girl a little while. They'll be fun." Ruthie wandered, complaining, away.

From the mattress where Rose of Sharon lay covered up there came a quick sharp cry, cut off in the middle. Ma whirled and went to her. Rose of Sharon was holding her breath and her eyes were filled with terror.

"What is it?" Ma cried. The girl expelled her breath and caught it again. Suddenly Ma put her hand under the covers. Then she stood up. "Mis' Wainwright," she called. "Oh, Mis' Wainwright!"

The fat little woman came down the car. "Want me?"

"Look!" Ma pointed at Rose of Sharon's face. Her teeth were clamped on her lower lip and her forehead was wet with perspiration, and the shining terror was in her eyes.

"I think it's come," Ma said. "It's early."

The girl heaved a great sigh and relaxed. She released her lip and closed her eyes. Mrs. Wainwright bent over her.

"Did it kinda grab you all over—quick? Open up an' answer me." Rose of Sharon nodded weakly. Mrs. Wainwright turned to Ma. "Yep," she said. "It's come. Early, ya say?"

"Maybe the fever brang it."

"Well, she oughta be up on her feet. Oughta be walkin' aroun'."

"She can't," Ma said. "She ain't got the strength."

"Well, she oughta." Mrs. Wainwright grew quiet and stern with efficiency. "I he'ped with lots," she said. "Come on, le's close that door, nearly. Keep out the draf'." The two women pushed on the heavy sliding door, boosted it along until only a foot was open. "I'll git our lamp, too," Mrs. Wainwright said. Her face was purple with excitement. "Aggie," she called. "You take care of these here little fellas."

Ma nodded, "Tha's right. Ruthie! You an' Winfiel' go down with Aggie. Go on now."

"Why?" they demanded.

"Cause you got to. Rosasharn gonna have her baby."

"I wanta watch, Ma. Please let me."

"Ruthie! You git now. You git quick." There was no argument against such a tone. Ruthie and Winfield went reluctantly down the car. Ma lighted the lantern. Mrs. Wainwright brought her Rochester lamp down and set it on the floor, and its big circular flame lighted the boxcar brightly.

Ruthie and Winfield stood behind the brush pile and peered over. "Gonna have a baby, an' we're a-gonna see," Ruthie said softly. "Don't you make no noise now. Ma won't let us watch. If she looks this-a-way, you scrunch down behin' the brush. Then we'll see."

"There ain't many kids seen it," Winfield said.

"There ain't no kids seen it," Ruthie insisted proudly. "On'y us."

Down by the mattress, in the bright light of the lamp, Ma and Mrs. Wainwright held conference. Their voices were raised a little over the hollow beating of the rain. Mrs. Wainwright took a paring knife from her apron pocket and slipped it under the mattress. "Maybe it don't do no good," she said apologetically. "Our folks always done it. Don't do no harm, anyways."

Ma nodded. "We used a plow point. I guess anything sharp'll work, long as it can cut birth pains. I hope it ain't gonna be a long one."

"You feelin' awright now?"

Rose of Sharon nodded nervously. "Is it a-comin'?"

"Sure," Ma said. "Gonna have a nice baby. You jus' got to help us. Feel like you could get up an' walk?"

"I can try."

"That's a good girl," Mrs. Wainwright said. "That is a good girl. We'll he'p you, honey. We'll walk with ya." They helped her to her feet and pinned a blanket over her shoulders. Then Ma held her arm from one side, and Mrs. Wainwright from the other. They walked her to the brush pile and turned slowly and walked her back, over and over; and the rain drummed deeply on the roof.

Ruthie and Winfield watched anxiously. "When's she goin' to have it?" he demanded.

"Sh! Don't draw 'em. We won't be let to look."

Aggie joined them behind the brush pile. Aggie's lean face and yellow hair showed in the lamplight, and her nose was long and sharp in the shadow of her head on the wall.

Ruthie whispered, "You ever saw a baby bore?"

"Sure," said Aggie.

"Well, when's she gonna have it?"

"Oh, not for a long, long time."

"Well, how long?"

"Maybe not 'fore tomorrow mornin'."

"Shucks!" said Ruthie. "Ain't no good watchin' now, then. Oh! Look!"

The walking women had stopped. Rose of Sharon had stiffened, and she whined with pain. They laid her down on the mattress and wiped her forehead while she grunted and clenched her fists. And Ma talked softly to her. "Easy," Ma said. "Gonna be all right—all right. Jus' grip ya hans'. Now then, take your lip inta your teeth. Tha's good—tha's good." The pain passed on. They let her rest awhile, and then helped her up again, and the three walked back and forth, back and forth between the pains.

Pa stuck his head in through the narrow opening. His hat dripped with water. "What ya shut the door for?" he asked. And then he saw the walking women.

Ma said, "Her time's come."

"Then—then we couldn' go 'f we wanted to."

"No."

"Then we got to buil' that bank."

"You got to."

Pa sloshed through the mud to the stream. His marking stick was four inches down. Twenty men stood in the rain. Pa cried, "We got to build her. My girl got her pains." The men gathered about him.

"Baby?"

"Yeah. We can't go now."

A tall man said, "It ain't our baby. We kin go."

"Sure," Pa said. "You can go. Go on. Nobody's stoppin' you. They's only eight shovels." He hurried to the lower part of the bank and drove his shovel into the mud. The shovelful lifted with a sucking sound. He drove it again, and threw the mud into the low place on the stream bank. And beside him the other men ranged themselves. They heaped the mud up in a long embankment, and those who had no shovels cut live willow whips and wove them in a mat and kicked them into the bank. Over the men came a fury of work, a fury of battle. When one man dropped the shovel, another took it up. They had shed their coats and hats. Their shirts and trousers clung tightly to their bodies, their shoes were shapeless blobs of mud. A shrill scream came from the Joad car. The men stopped, listened uneasily, and then plunged to work again. And the little levee of earth extended until it connected with the highway embankment on either end. They were tired now, and the shovels moved more slowly. And the stream rose slowly. It edged above the place where the first dirt had been thrown.

Pa laughed in triumph. "She'd come over if we hadn' a built up!" he cried.

The stream rose slowly up the side of the new wall, and tore at the willow mat. "Higher!" Pa cried. "We got to git her higher!"

The evening came, and the work went on. And now the men were beyond weariness. Their faces were set and dead. They worked jerkily, like machines. When it was dark the women set lanterns in the car doors, and kept pots of coffee handy. And the women ran one by one to the Joad car and wedged themselves inside.

The pains were coming close now, twenty minutes apart. And Rose of Sharon had lost her restraint. She screamed fiercely under the fierce pains. And the neighbor women looked at her and patted her gently and went back to their own cars.

Ma had a good fire going now, and all her utensils, filled with water, sat on the stove to heat. Every little while Pa looked in the car door. "All right?" he asked.

"Yeah! I think so," Ma assured him.

As it grew dark, someone brought out a flashlight to work by. Uncle John plunged on, throwing mud on top of the wall.

"You take it easy," Pa said. "You'll kill yaself."

"I can't he'p it. I can't stan' that yellin'. It's like—it's like when—"

"I know," Pa said. "But jus' take it easy."

Uncle John blubbered, "I'll run away. By God, I got to work or I'll run away."

Pa turned from him. "How's she stan' on the last marker?"

The man with the flashlight threw the beam on the stick. The rain cut whitely through the light. "Comin' up."

"She'll come up slower now," Pa said. "Got to flood purty far on the other side."

"She's comin' up, though."

The women filled the coffee pots and set them out again. And as the night went on, the men moved slower and slower, and they lifted their heavy feet like draft horses. More mud on the levee, more willows interlaced. The rain fell steadily. When the flashlight turned on faces, the eyes showed staring, and the muscles on the cheeks were welted out.

For a long time the screams continued from the car, and at last they were still.

Pa said, "Ma'd call me if it was bore." He went on shoveling the mud sullenly.

The stream eddied and boiled against the bank. Then, from up the stream there came a ripping crash. The beam of the flashlight showed a great cottonwood toppling. The men stopped to watch. The branches of the tree sank into the water and edged around with the current while the stream dug out the little roots. Slowly the tree was freed, and slowly it edged down the stream. The weary men watched, their mouths hanging open. The tree moved slowly down. Then a branch caught on a stump, snagged and held. And very slowly the roots swung around and hooked themselves on the new embankment. The water piled up behind. The tree moved and tore the bank. A little stream slipped through. Pa threw himself forward and jammed mud in the break. The water piled against the tree. And then the bank washed quickly down, washed around ankles, around knees. The men broke and ran, and the current worked smoothly into the flat, under the cars, under the automobiles.

Uncle John saw the water break through. In the murk he could see it. Uncontrollably his weight pulled him down. He went to his knees, and the tugging water swirled about his chest.

Pa saw him go. "Hey! What's the matter?" He lifted him to his feet. "You sick? Come on, the cars is high."

Uncle John gathered his strength. "I dunno," he said apologetically. "Legs give out. Jus' give out." Pa helped him along toward the cars.

When the dike swept over, Al turned and ran. His feet moved heavily. The water was about his calves when he reached the truck. He flung the tarpaulin off the nose and jumped into the car. He stepped on the starter, The engine turned over and over, and there was no bark of the motor. He choked the engine deeply. The battery turned the sodden motor more and more slowly, and there was no cough. Over and over, slower and slower. Al set the spark high. He felt under the seat for the crank and jumped out. The water was higher than the running board. He ran to the front end. Crank case was under water now. Frantically he fitted the crank and twisted around and around, and his clenched hand on the crank splashed in the slowly flowing water at each turn. At last his frenzy gave out. The motor was full of water, the battery fouled by now. On slightly higher ground two cars were started and their lights on. They floundered in the mud and dug their wheels down until finally the drivers cut off the motors and sat still, looking into the headlight beams. And the rain whipped white streaks through the lights. Al went slowly around the truck, reached in, and turned off the ignition.

When Pa reached the cat-walk, he found the lower end floating. He stepped it down into the mud, under water. "Think ya can make it awright, John?" he asked.

"I'll be awright. Jus' go on."

Pa cautiously climbed the cat-walk and squeezed himself in the narrow opening. The two lamps were turned low. Ma sat on the mattress beside Rose of Sharon, and Ma fanned her still face with a piece of cardboard. Mrs. Wainwright poked dry brush into the stove, and a dank smoke edged out around the lids and filled the car with a smell of burning tissue. Ma looked up at Pa when he entered, and then quickly down.

"How—is she?" Pa asked.

Ma did not look up at him again. "Awright, I think. Sleepin'."

The air was fetid and close with the smell of the birth. Uncle John clambered in and held himself upright against the side of the car. Mrs. Wainwright left her work and came to Pa. She pulled him by the elbow toward the corner of the car. She picked up a lantern and held it over an apple box in the corner. On a newspaper lay a blue shriveled little mummy.

"Never breathed," said Mrs. Wainwright softly. "Never was alive."

Uncle John turned and shuffled tiredly down the car to the dark end. The rain whished softly on the roof now, so softly that they could hear Uncle John's tired sniffling from the dark.

Pa looked up at Mrs. Wainwright. He took the lantern from her hand and put it on the floor. Ruthie and Winfield were asleep on their own mattress, their arms over their eyes to cut out the light.

Pa walked slowly to Rose of Sharon's mattress. He tried to squat down, but his legs were too tired. He knelt instead. Ma fanned her square of cardboard back and forth. She looked at Pa for a moment, and her eyes were wide and staring, like a sleepwalker's eyes.

Pa said, "We—done—what we could."

"I know."

"We worked all night. An' a tree cut out the bank."

"I know."

"You can hear it under the car."

"I know. I heard it."

"Think she's gonna be all right?"

"I dunno."

"Well—couldn' we—of did nothin'?"

Ma's lips were stiff and white. "No. They was on'y one thing to do—ever—an' we done it."

"We worked till we dropped, an' a tree—Rain's lettin' up some."

Ma looked at the ceiling, and then down again. Pa went on, compelled to talk. "I dunno how high she'll rise. Might flood the car."

"I know."

"You know ever'thing."

She was silent, and the cardboard moved slowly back and forth.

"Did we slip up?" he pleaded. "Is they anything we could of did?"

Ma looked at him strangely. Her white lips smiled in a dreaming compassion. "Don't take no blame. Hush! It'll be awright. They's changes—all over."

"Maybe the water—maybe we'll have to go."

"When it's time to go—we'll go. We'll do what we got to do. Now hush. You might wake her."

Mrs. Wainwright broke twigs and poked them in the sodden, smoking fire.

From outside came the sound of an angry voice. "I'm goin' in an' see the son-of-abitch myself."

And then, just outside the door, Al's voice, "Where you think you're goin'?"

"Goin' in to see that bastard Joad."

"No, you ain't. What's the matter'th you?"

"If he didn't have that fool idear about the bank, we'd a got out. Now our car is dead."

"You think ours is burnin' up the road?"

"I'm a-goin' in."

Al's voice was cold. "You're gonna fight your way in."

Pa got slowly to his feet and went to the door. "Awright, Al, I'm comin' out. It's awright, Al." Pa slid down the cat-walk. Ma heard him say, "We got sickness. Come on down here."

The rain scattered lightly on the roof now, and a new-risen breeze blew it along in sweeps. Mrs. Wainwright came from the stove and looked down at Rose of Sharon. "Dawn's a-comin' soon, ma'am. Whyn't you git some sleep? I'll set with her."

"No," Ma said. "I ain't tar'd."

"In a pig's eye," said Mrs. Wainwright. "Come on, you lay down awhile."

Ma fanned the air slowly with her cardboard. "You been frien'ly," she said. "We thank you."

The stout woman smiled. "No need to thank. Ever'body's in the same wagon. S'pose we was down. You'd a give us a han'."

"Yes," Ma said, "we would."

"Or anybody."

"Or anybody. Use' ta be the fambly was fust. It ain't so now. It's anybody. Worse off we get, the more we got to do."

"We couldn' a saved it."

"I know," said Ma.

Ruthie sighed deeply and took her arm from over her eyes. She looked blindly at the lamp for a moment, and then turned her head and looked at Ma. "Is it bore?" she demanded. "Is the baby out?"

Mrs. Wainwright picked up a sack and spread it over the apple box in the corner.

"Where's the baby?" Ruthie demanded.

Ma wet her lips. "There ain't no baby. They never was no baby. We was wrong."

"Shucks!" Ruthie yawned. "I wisht it had a been a baby."

Mrs. Wainwright sat down beside Ma and took the cardboard from her and fanned the air. Ma folded her hands in her lap, and her tired eyes never left the face of Rose of Sharon, sleeping in exhaustion. "Come on," Mrs. Wainwright said. "Jus' lay down. You'll be right beside her. Why, you'd wake up if she took a deep breath, even."

"Awright, I will." Ma stretched out on the mattress beside the sleeping girl. And Mrs. Wainwright sat on the floor and kept watch.

Pa and Al and Uncle John sat in the car doorway and watched the steely dawn come. The rain had stopped, but the sky was deep and solid with cloud. As the light came, it was reflected on the water. The men could see the current of the stream, slipping swiftly down, bearing black branches of trees, boxes, boards. The water swirled into the flat where the boxcars stood. There was no sign of the embankment left. On the flat the current stopped. The edges of the flood were lined with yellow foam. Pa leaned out the door and placed a twig on the cat-walk, just above the water line. The men watched the water slowly climb to it, lift it gently and float it away. Pa placed another twig an inch above the water and settled back to watch.

"Think it'll come inside the car?" Al asked.

"Can't tell. They's a hell of a lot of water got to come down from the hills yet. Can't tell. Might start up to rain again."

Al said, "I been a-thinkin'. If she come in, ever'thing'll get soaked."

"Yeah."

"Well, she won't come up more'n three-four feet in the car 'cause she'll go over the highway an' spread out first."

"How you know?" Pa asked.

"I took a sight on her, off the end of the car." He held his hand. "'Bout this far up she'll come."

"Awright," Pa said. "What about it? We won't be here."

"We got to be here. Truck's here. Take a week to get the water out of her when the flood goes down."

"Well—what's your idear?"

"We can tear out the side-boards of the truck an' build a kinda platform in here to pile our stuff an' to set up on."

"Yeah? How'll we cook—how'll we eat?"

"Well, it'll keep our stuff dry."

The light grew stronger outside, a gray metallic light. The second little stick floated away from the cat-walk. Pa placed another one higher up. "Sure climbin'," he said. "I guess we better do that."

Ma turned restlessly in her sleep. Her eyes started wide open. She cried sharply in warning, "Tom! Oh, Tom! Tom!"

Mrs. Wainwright spoke soothingly. The eyes flicked closed again and Ma squirmed under her dream. Mrs. Wainwright got up and walked to the doorway. "Hey!" she said softly. "We ain't gonna git out soon." She pointed to the corner of the car where the apple box was. "That ain't doin' no good. Jus' cause trouble and sorra. Couldn' you fellas kinda—take it out an' bury it?"

The men were silent. Pa said at last, "Guess you're right. Jus' cause sorra. 'Gainst the law to bury it."

"They's lots a things 'gainst the law that we can't he'p doin'."

"Yeah." Al said, "We oughta git them truck sides tore off 'fore the water comes up much more."

Pa turned to Uncle John. "Will you take an' bury it while Al an' me git that lumber in?"

Uncle John said sullenly, "Why do I got to do it? Why don' you fellas? I don' like it." And then, "Sure. I'll do it. Sure, I will. Come on, give it to me." His voice began to rise. "Come on! Give it to me."

"Don' wake 'em up," Mrs. Wainwright said. She brought the apple box to the doorway and straightened the sack decently over it.

"Shovel's standin' right behin' you," Pa said.

Uncle John took the shovel in one hand. He slipped out the doorway into the slowly moving water, and it rose nearly to his waist before he struck bottom. He turned and settled the apple box under his other arm.

Pa said, "Come on, Al. Le's git that lumber in."

In the gray dawn light Uncle John waded around the end of the car, past the Joad truck; and he climbed the slippery bank to the highway. He walked down the highway, past the boxcar flat, until he came to a place where the boiling stream ran close to the road, where the willows grew along the road side. He put his shovel down, and holding the box in front of him, he edged through the brush until he came to the edge of the swift stream. For a time he stood watching it swirl by, leaving its yellow foam among the willow stems. He held the apple box against his chest. And then he leaned over and set the box in the stream and steadied it with his hand. He said fiercely, "Go down an' tell 'em. Go down in the street an' rot an' tell 'em that way. That's the way you can talk. Don' even know if you was a boy or a girl. Ain't gonna find out. Go on down now, an' lay in the street. Maybe they'll know then." He guided the box gently out into the current and let it go. It settled low in the water, edged sideways, whirled around, and turned slowly over. The sack floated away, and the box, caught in the swift water, floated quickly away, out of sight, behind the brush. Uncle John grabbed the shovel and went rapidly back to the boxcars. He sloshed down into the water and waded to the truck, where Pa and Al were working, taking down the one-by-six planks.

Pa looked over at him. "Get it done?"

"Yeah."

"Well, look," Pa said. "If you'll he'p Al, I'll go down the store an' get some stuff to eat."

"Get some bacon," Al said. "I need some meat."

"I will," Pa said. He jumped down from the truck and Uncle John took his place.

When they pushed the planks into the car door, Ma awakened and sat up. "What you doin'?"

"Gonna build up a place to keep outa the wet."

"Why?" Ma asked. "It's dry in here."

"Ain't gonna be. Water's comin' up."

Ma struggled up to her feet and went to the door. "We got to git outa here."

"Can't," Al said. "All our stuff's here. Truck's here. Ever'thing we got."

"Where's Pa?"

"Gone to get stuff for breakfas'."

Ma looked down at the water. It was only six inches down from the floor by now. She went back to the mattress and looked at Rose of Sharon. The girl stared back at her.

"How you feel?" Ma asked.

"Tar'd. Jus' tar'd out."

"Gonna get some breakfas' into you."

"I ain't hungry."

Mrs. Wainwright moved beside Ma. "She looks all right. Come through it fine."

Rose of Sharon's eyes questioned Ma, and Ma tried to avoid the question. Mrs. Wainwright walked to the stove.

"Ma?"

"Yeah? What you want?"

"Is—it—all right?"

Ma gave up the attempt. She kneeled down on the mattress. "You can have more," she said. "We done ever'thing we knowed."

Rose of Sharon struggled and pushed herself up. "Ma!"

"You couldn' he'p it."

The girl lay back again, and covered her eyes with her arms. Ruthie crept close and looked down in awe. She whispered harshly, "She sick, Ma? She gonna die?"

"Course not. She's gonna be awright. Awright."

Pa came in with his armload of packages. "How is she?"

"Awright," Ma said. "She's gonna be awright."

Ruthie reported to Winfield. "She ain't gonna die. Ma says so."

And Winfield, picking his teeth with a splinter in a very adult manner, said, "I knowed it all the time."

"How'd you know?"

"I won't tell," said Winfield, and he spat out a piece of the splinter.

Ma built the fire up with the last twigs and cooked the bacon and made gravy. Pa had brought store bread. Ma scowled when she saw it. "We got any money lef'?"

"Nope," said Pa. "But we was so hungry."

"An' you got store bread," Ma said accusingly.

"Well, we was awful hungry. Worked all night long."

Ma sighed. "Now what we gonna do?"

As they ate, the water crept up and up. Al gulped his food and he and Pa built the platform. Five feet wide, six feet long, four feet above the floor. And the water crept to the edge of the doorway, seemed to hesitate a long time, and then moved slowly inward over the floor. And outside the rain began again, as it had before, big heavy drops splashing on the water, pounding hollowly on the roof.

Al said, "Come on now, let's get the mattresses up. Let's put the blankets up, so they don't git wet." They piled their possessions up on the platform, and the water crept over the floor. Pa and Ma, Al and Uncle John, each at a corner, lifted Rose of Sharon's mattress, with the girl on it, and put it on top of the pile.

And the girl protested, "I can walk. I'm awright." And the water crept over the floor, a thin film of it. Rose of Sharon whispered to Ma, and Ma put her hand under the blanket and felt her breast and nodded.

In the other end of the boxcar, the Wainwrights were pounding, building a platform for themselves. The rain thickened, and then passed away.

Ma looked down at her feet. The water was half an inch deep on the car floor by now. "You, Ruthie—Winfiel'!" she called distractedly. "Come get on top of the pile. You'll get cold." She saw them safely up, sitting awkwardly beside Rose of Sharon. Ma said suddenly, "We got to git out."

"We can't," Pa said. "Like Al says, all our stuff's here. We'll pull off the boxcar door an' make more room to set on."

THE FAMILY huddled on the platforms, silent and fretful. The water was six inches deep in the car before the flood spread evenly over the embankment and moved into the cotton field on the other side. During that day and night the men slept soddenly, side by side on the boxcar door. And Ma lay close to Rose of Sharon. Sometimes Ma whispered to her and sometimes sat up quietly, her face brooding. Under the blanket she hoarded the remains of the store bread.

The rain had become intermittent now—little wet squalls and quiet times. On the morning of the second day Pa splashed through the camp and came back with ten potatoes in his pockets. Ma watched him sullenly while he chopped out part of the inner wall of the car, built a fire, and scooped water into a pan. The family ate the steaming boiled potatoes with their fingers. And when this last food was gone, they stared at the gray water; and in the night they did not lie down for a long time.

When the morning came they awakened nervously. Rose of Sharon whispered to Ma.

Ma nodded her head. "Yes," she said. "It's time for it." And then she turned to the car door, where the men lay. "We're a-gettin' outa here," she said savagely, "gettin' to higher groun'. An' you're comin' or you ain't comin', but I'm takin' Rosasharn an' the little fellas outa here."

"We can't!" Pa said weakly.

"Awright, then. Maybe you'll pack Rosasharn to the highway, anyways, an' then come back. It ain't rainin' now, an' we're a'goin'."

"Awright, we'll go," Pa said.

Al said, "Ma, I ain't goin'."

"Why not?"

"Well—Aggie—why, her an' me—"

Ma smiled. "'Course," she said. "You stay here, Al. Take care of the stuff. When the water goes down—why, we'll come back. Come quick, 'fore it rains again," she told Pa. "Come on, Rosasharn. We're goin' to a dry place."

"I can walk."

"Maybe a little, on the road. Git your back bent, Pa."

Pa slipped into the water and stood waiting. Ma helped Rose of Sharon down from the platform and steadied her across the car. Pa took her in his arms, held her as high as he could, and pushed his way carefully through the deep water, around the car, and to the highway. He set her down on her feet and held onto her. Uncle John carried Ruthie and followed. Ma slid down into the water, and for a moment her skirts billowed out around her.

"Winfiel', set on my shoulder. Al—we'll come back soon's the water's down. Al—" She paused. "If—if Tom comes—tell him we'll be back. Tell him be careful. Winfiel'! Climb on my shoulder—there! Now, keep your feet still." She staggered off through the breast-high water. At the highway embankment they helped her up and lifted Winfield from her shoulder.

They stood on the highway and looked back over the sheet of water, the dark red blocks of the cars, the trucks and automobiles deep in the slowly moving water. And as they stood, a little misting rain began to fall.

"We got to git along," Ma said. "Rosasharn, you feel like you could walk?"

"Kinda dizzy," the girl said. "Feel like I been beat."

Pa complained, "Now we're a-goin', where we goin'?"

"I dunno. Come on, give your han' to Rosasharn." Ma took the girl's right arm to steady her, and Pa her left. "Goin' someplace where it's dry. Got to. You fellas ain't had dry clothes on for two days." They moved slowly along the highway. They could hear the rushing of the water in the stream beside the road. Ruthie and Winfield marched together, splashing their feet against the road. They went slowly along the road. The sky grew darker and the rain thickened. No traffic moved along the highway.

"We got to hurry," Ma said. "If this here girl gits good an' wet—I don't know what'll happen to her."

"You ain't said where-at we're a-hurryin' to," Pa reminded her sarcastically. The road curved along beside the stream. Ma searched the land and the flooded fields. Far off the road, on the left, on a slight rolling hill a rain-blackened barn stood. "Look!" Ma said. "Look there! I bet it's dry in that barn. Let's go there till the rain stops."

Pa sighed. "Prob'ly get run out by the fella owns it."

Ahead, beside the road, Ruthie saw a spot of red. She raced to it. A scraggly geranium gone wild, and there was one rain-beaten blossom on it. She picked the flower. She took a petal carefully off and stuck it on her nose. Winfield ran up to see.

"Lemme have one?" he said.

"No, sir! It's all mine. I foun' it." She stuck another red petal on her forehead, a little bright-red heart.

"Come on, Ruthie! Lemme have one. Come on, now." He grabbed at the flower in her hand and missed it, and Ruthie banged him in the face with her open hand. He stood for a moment, surprised, and then his lips shook and his eyes welled.

The others caught up. "Now what you done?" Ma asked. "Now what you done?"

"He tried to grab my fl'ar."

Winfield sobbed, "I—on'y wanted one—to—stick on my nose."

"Give him one, Ruthie."

"Leave him find his own. This here's mine."

"Ruthie! You give him one."

Ruthie heard the threat in Ma's tone, and changed her tactics. "Here," she said with elaborate kindness. "I'll stick on one for you." The older people walked on. Winfield held his nose near to her. She wet a petal with her tongue and jabbed it cruelly on his nose. "You little son-of-a-bitch," she said softly. Winfield felt for the petal with his fingers, and pressed it down on his nose. They walked quickly after the others. Ruthie felt how the fun was gone. "Here," she said. "Here's some more. Stick some on your forehead."

From the right of the road there came a sharp swishing. Ma cried, "Hurry up. They's a big rain. Le's go through the fence here. It's shorter. Come on, now! Bear on, Rosasharn." They half dragged the girl across the ditch, helped her through the fence. And then the storm struck them. Sheets of rain fell on them. They plowed through the mud and up the little incline. The black barn was nearly obscured by the rain. It hissed and splashed, and the growing wind drove it along. Rose of Sharon's feet slipped and she dragged between her supporters.

"Pa! Can you carry her?"

Pa leaned over and picked her up. "We're wet through anyways," he said. "Hurry up. Winfiel'—Ruthie! Run on ahead."

They came panting up to the rain-soaked barn and staggered into the open end. There was no door in this end. A few rusty farm tools lay about, a disk plow and a broken cultivator, an iron wheel. The rain hammered on the room and curtained the entrance. Pa gently set Rose of Sharon down on an oily box. "God Awmighty!" he said.

Ma said, "Maybe they's hay inside. Look, there's a door." She swung the door on its rusty hinges. "They is hay," she cried. "Come on in, you."

It was dark inside. A little light came in through the cracks between the boards.

"Lay down, Rosasharn," Ma said. "Lay down an' res'. I'll try to figger some way to dry you off."

Winfield said, "Ma!" and the rain roaring on the roof drowned his voice. "Ma!"

"What is it? What you want?"

"Look! In the corner."

Ma looked. There were two figures in the gloom; a man who lay on his back, and a boy sitting beside him, his eyes wide, staring at the newcomers. As she looked, the boy got slowly up to his feet and came toward her. His voice croaked. "You own this here?"

"No," Ma said. "Jus' come in outa the wet. We got a sick girl. You got a dry blanket we could use an' get her wet clothes off?"

The boy went back to the corner and brought a dirty comfort and held it out to Ma.

"Thank ya," she said. "What's the matter'th that fella?"

The boy spoke in a croaking monotone. "Fust he was sick—but now he's starvin'."

"What?"

"Starvin'. Got sick in the cotton. He ain't et for six days."

Ma walked to the corner and looked down at the man. He was about fifty, his whiskery face gaunt, and his open eyes were vague and staring. The boy stood beside her. "Your pa?" Ma asked.

"Yeah! Says he wasn' hungry, or he jus' et. Give me the food. Now he's too weak. Can't hardly move."

The pounding of the rain decreased to a soothing swish on the roof. The gaunt man moved his lips. Ma knelt beside him and put her ear close. His lips moved again.

"Sure," Ma said. "You jus' be easy. He'll be awright. You jus' wait'll I get them wet clo'es off'n my girl."

Ma went back to the girl. "Now slip 'em off," she said. She held the comfort up to screen her from view. And when she was naked, Ma folded the comfort about her.

The boy was at her side again explaining, "I didn' know. He said he et, or he wasn' hungry. Las' night I went an' bust a winda an' stoled some bread. Made 'im chew 'er down. But he puked it all up, an' then he was weaker. Got to have soup or milk. You folks got money to git milk?"

Ma said, "Hush. Don' worry. We'll figger somepin out."

Suddenly the boy cried, "He's dyin', I tell you! He's starvin' to death, I tell you."

"Hush," said Ma. She looked at Pa and Uncle John standing helplessly gazing at the sick man. She looked at Rose of Sharon huddled in the comfort. Ma's eyes passed Rose of Sharon's eyes, and then came back to them. And the two women looked deep into each other. The girl's breath came short and gasping.

She said "Yes."

Ma smiled. "I knowed you would. I knowed!" She looked down at her hands, tightlocked in her lap.

Rose of Sharon whispered, "Will—will you all—go out?" The rain whisked lightly on the roof.

Ma leaned forward and with her palm she brushed the tousled hair back from her daughter's forehead, and she kissed her on the forehead. Ma got up quickly. "Come on, you fellas," she called. "You come out in the tool shed."

Ruthie opened her mouth to speak. "Hush," Ma said. "Hush and git." She herded them through the door, drew the boy with her; and she closed the squeaking door.

For a minute Rose of Sharon sat still in the whispering barn. Then she hoisted her tired body up and drew the comfort about her. She moved slowly to the corner and stood looking down at the wasted face, into the wide, frightened eyes. Then slowly she lay down beside him. He shook his head slowly from side to side. Rose of Sharon loosened one side of the blanket and bared her breast. "You got to," she said. She squirmed closer and pulled his head close. "There!" she said. "There." Her hand moved behind his head and supported it. Her fingers moved gently in his hair. She looked up and across the barn, and her lips came together and smiled mysteriously.

三、题目解析

《愤怒的葡萄》发表于1939年，是斯坦贝克的长篇小说代表作，也是左翼文学一部重要的作品，荣获美国国家图书奖和普利策文学奖。小说题目的隐喻性向读者提出以下两类问题：一是有关"葡萄"的问题，例如葡萄代表什么？有何象征意义？为何是葡萄而不是其他？二是有关"愤怒"的问题，例如葡萄为何愤怒？是什么让葡萄如此愤怒？愤怒的表现形式是什么？因愤怒有何行为？

小说共有30章，主要讲述了美国20世纪30年代经济大萧条时期以乔德为代表的破产佃农丧失家园，被迫离开俄克拉荷马州的故土，前往加利福尼亚西行路上逃荒的艰难经历以及到达加利福尼亚以后的不幸遭遇。失业、饥饿和迫害激起佃农们的满腔怨愤，他们团结起来，为获得工作和土地，为自己的尊严和将来而奋起抗争。这些题材和主题是美国左翼文学的主要特征。

小说的题目来自1861年美国诗人、废奴主义者朱莉亚·沃德·豪的《共和国之战歌》："我看到了上帝降临的荣耀/他在踩踏满园愤怒的葡萄。"斯坦贝克采用此题目，原因在于"我喜欢这首歌，因为它是一种进行曲，这本书也是一种进行曲"，以此表达劳动人民集体的力量和共同抗争的决心。

小说题目中的"葡萄"是什么？为什么是"葡萄"？起初，"葡萄"象征着富饶和希望。第10章中乔德的祖父说道："我们要到那边去。上帝啊！那边到处都是葡萄，一直垂到路上来。知道我想干嘛吗？我要摘一澡盆的葡萄，在盆里打滚，用葡萄汁来洗裤子。"在无家可归的破产佃农眼中，加利福尼亚土地肥沃、物产富饶，尤其盛产葡萄，是一个可以安居乐业的希望之乡和理想乐园。“葡萄”代表了破产佃农未来美好生活的愿景，指引着他们的逃荒之旅，给予他们在长途跋涉中战胜苦难的勇气。然而，事与愿违。“葡萄”象征着丰收，却与俄克拉荷马的饥饿形成了鲜明的对比和反差。当破产佃农们找寻幸福生活的希望成为泡影时，他们无比愤怒。这时“葡萄”象征着失望和痛苦。第25章结尾处写道：“他们静静地站着，眼看着土豆顺水漂流，听着别人将惨叫的猪杀死在干水沟里，然后掩埋在生石灰底下，眼看着堆积成山的橙子坍下去，变成一片腐烂的泥浆；人们看到了失败；饥饿的人们眼中闪现着一股越来越强烈的怒火。愤怒的葡萄充塞着人们的心灵，沉甸甸的，等待收获期来临。”这里出现了小说的标题，希望的“葡萄”变成了愤怒的“葡萄”。除了表征“勇气”“力量”“智慧”“营养”。“葡萄”在这里也象征着耶稣的子民，他们是“葡萄树”的“枝子”，意指成千上万受尽压迫的劳苦大众。

小说题目中“愤怒”的起因是什么？“愤怒”的对象是什么？“愤怒”的行为是什么？“愤怒”的结果是什么？第25章结尾处已提及愤怒的原因，第29章再一次对此进行了强化：“大家在棚舍里挤着，在干草堆上躺着，饥饿和恐惧便酿成了愤怒。”“男人们聚在一起，他们的恐惧已变成了愤怒。”饥饿和恐惧是佃农们如此愤怒的直接原因，肉体的伤害和精神的折磨把他们逼到了死亡线上。归根结底，“愤怒”的对象是当时的美国资本主义。佃农们被压低工资，屡遭当地势力的敲诈勒索和迫害。他们身处绝境，苦苦挣扎，“于是男孩们走出去，不是去讨饭，而是去盗窃；男人们也软弱无力地走出去，准备行窃”。他们进行有力的对抗，在行为上宣泄着愤怒的情绪。此外，佃农们互助友爱，这一自救方式是另一种有力的抗争。第30章中，乔德一家人在一个谷仓里躲避洪水。罗莎香忍受着孩子夭折的极大痛苦，用自己的乳汁去救另一位饿得奄奄一息的陌生人。这种温馨而甜蜜的场面与感觉，仿佛与“葡萄”的蜜甜如出一辙。关于小说题目中“愤怒”的理解，读者还可以从农民与土地的关系等方面来思考“愤怒”的深层次原因；除了自救，读者还可以以暴力斗争为切入点来解读“愤怒”这一行为；“愤怒”之后将产生什么样的结果，小说最后一句中罗莎香脸上“神秘的微笑”发人深思，这一结尾说明了人类在面临生存威胁时，除了进行暴力反抗，还可以团结互助进行自救，最终的希望在于每个人的仁爱之心。

四、难点注释

1. *The Winning of Barbara Worth*：《芭芭拉·沃斯的胜利》，美国作家哈罗德·贝尔·赖特（Harold Bell Wright，1872—1944）于1911年出版的长篇小说。
2. sulphur：用硫磺处理。
3. huddled：（因寒冷或害怕）蜷缩。这里是huddle的过去式。
4. sheriffs：英国、美国的郡县治安官，有时也译作“警长”。这里是sheriff的复数。
5. Cracker Jack：焦糖裹层玉米花和花生混合成的一种零食，目前为百事食品公司旗下的商标。它最著名的特色是包装内附有一个玩具。

五、延伸阅读与批评

中篇小说《人鼠之间》(1937)是斯坦贝克的代表作之一。它叙述了20世纪30年代美国经济大萧条时期，两个一贫如洗却又相依为命的美国流动农业工人莱尼和乔治因失去赖以生存的土地，像四处逃窜的田鼠一样到处漂泊，最终，乔治万般无奈之中打死莱尼，他们“安居乐业”的梦想随之破灭的悲惨故事。小说的题目把人和鼠联系在一起，蕴涵了对小说理解起到关键作用的一系列问题。其一，“人”除了指主人公莱尼和乔治，是否还有其他含义，例如指代所有流动工人？其二，“鼠”代表什么？为什么是鼠而非其他动物？除了英文题目中/m/押头韵，是否还有其他理解，例如人鼠之间有何相似之处？其三，人鼠之间到底发生了什么？人和鼠的结局如何？所有这些问题有待读者进一步去思考和解答。

（姜艳撰写，甘文平审校）

Part Two

Environment

"环境"是文学作品中故事发生的场景，或者故事人物周围的人和物。它包括可见或可感、静态或动态的自然环境和社会环境，如各种人或物的动作和声音等，也涵盖人物的心理和思想环境(状态)。故事人物不可能存在于真空(也是一种环境)里，一定处于某种特殊的境况中。"环境"往往是作者为作品刻意营造的一种氛围，为故事"定调"，为作品"调色"，对故事人物产生影响，并最终影响情节的发展、人物关系的走向、主题思想的形成。所以，把握"环境"的特征和内涵意义，理清环境描写与故事人物和事件之间的关系是读者阅读文学作品的一个重要切入点，或者说是一把重要的钥匙。

一般说来，文学作品中的人物和环境是认同或疏离的关系。前者是人物把自己认同于环境(的某个元素)，并对之产生亲近感。后者是人物对环境产生疏离感，环境的敌对和冷漠"面孔"让人物产生恐惧感。它如同一张网，让人欲逃不能，只能在不安和焦虑中挣扎。

本部分选取四篇小说，分别分析自然环境和社会(战争)环境对作品解读、人物心理和行为造成的影响。有时候环境本身是文本的内容乃至主题思想的一部分。

Chapter 1　A Cask of Amontillado

by Adgar Allan Poe

一、作者简介

埃德加·爱伦·坡(1809—1849)，美国19世纪著名的诗人、小说家、文学批评家。坡的诗集有《埃德加·爱伦·坡诗集》(1831)，其中《乌鸦》《致海伦》《安娜贝尔·李》等是他的诗作名篇。1840年他出版了短篇小说集《天方夜谭》。代表性的短篇小说有《厄舍屋的倒塌》《丽吉娅》《黑猫》《失窃的信》《莫格街谋杀案》《金甲虫》《红死病假面具》《一桶蒙特亚白葡萄酒》等。论文《诗歌原理》和《创作哲学》等集中反映了他的诗歌和小说创作理论。

坡年幼便失去双亲，被人收养，但又与养父不和。他生活阅历丰富、生活艰辛、命运多舛。特殊的人生履历造就了他坚韧而反叛的性格。文学创作、酗酒、追求女人成为他的三大生活内容。

爱伦·坡只活了40岁，但他的作品在美国文坛乃至世界文坛占有特殊的地位。他是现代美国短篇小说之父，开美国侦探小说之先河，引领了整个西方现代文学的潮流。他特别强调文学的整体效果，注重作品留给读者的感受和读者对作品的反应。因此，他的诗歌和小说都向读者传递特殊的艺术效果。

学界一般将坡的小说分为“侦探小说”或“恐怖小说”和“心理小说”。前者讲求推理，描写可怕的环境和经历，侦探的过程往往是展示恐怖的过程；后者侧重人物的心理活动。美、死亡、复仇是坡作品中常见的主题。其小说大多采用第一人称叙事，善于运用推理和制造恐怖氛围，达到他所强调的美学效果。同时，坡注重挖掘人物的内心活动和深层心理世界。有学者如此概述他的小说特色：“理智与激情，清醒与迷狂，现实与想象”的对立及其界限的消弭是其小说作品在主题思想和艺术手法两方面的突出特色。同时坡是“唯美主义”诗派的代表，讲究意象美、音乐美、形式美、对称美。他的诗和诗论受到法国浪漫主义作家波特莱尔等人的推崇。

20世纪以来，坡一直受到学者的关注。人们先后从社会—历史、弗洛伊德精神分析、结构主义、后现代主义、大众文化等视角分析他的小说。

二、文本选读

The Cask of Amontillado[1]

The thousand injuries of Fortunato I had borne as I best could, but when he ventured upon insult I vowed revenge. You, who so well know the nature of my soul, will not suppose, however, that I gave utterance to[2] a threat. At length I would be avenged; this was a point definitively settled—but the very definitiveness with which it was resolved precluded the idea of risk. I must not only punish but punish with impunity. A wrong is unredressed when retribution overtakes its redresser[3]. It is equally unredressed when the avenger fails to make himself felt as such to him who has done the wrong. It must be understood that neither by word nor deed had I given Fortunato cause to doubt my good will. I continued as was my wont[4], to smile in his face, and he did not perceive that my smile now was at the thought of his immolation.

He had a weak point—this Fortunato—although in other regards he was a man to be respected and even feared. He prided himself on his connoisseurship[5] in wine. Few Italians have the true virtuoso spirit. For the most part their enthusiasm is adopted to suit the time and opportunity, to practice imposture upon the British and Austrian millionaires. In painting and gemmary, Fortunato, like his countrymen, was a quack, but in the matter of old wines he was sincere. In this respect I did not differ from him materially;—I was skilful in the Italian vintages myself, and bought largely whenever I could.

It was about dusk, one evening during the supreme madness of the carnival season, that I encountered my friend. He accosted me with excessive warmth, for he had been drinking much. The man wore motley. He had on a tight-fitting parti-striped dress, and his head was surmounted by the conical cap and bells. I was so pleased to see him that I thought I should never have done wringing his hand.

I said to him—"My dear Fortunato, you are luckily met. How remarkably well you are looking today! But I have received a pipe of what passes for[6] Amontillado, and I have my doubts."

"How?" said he, "Amontillado? A pipe? Impossible? And in the middle of the carnival!"

"I have my doubts," I replied; "and I was silly enough to pay the full Amontillado price without consulting you in the matter. You were not to be found, and I was fearful of losing a bargain."

"Amontillado!"

"I have my doubts."

"Amontillado!"

"And I must satisfy them."

"Amontillado!"

"As you are engaged, I am on my way to Luchresi. If any one has a critical turn it is he. He will tell me—"

"Luchresi cannot tell Amontillado from Sherry[7]."

"And yet some fools will have it that his taste is a match for your own."

"Come, let us go."

"Whither?"

"To your vaults."

"My friend, no; I will not impose upon your good nature. I perceive you have an engagement Luchresi—"

"I have no engagement; —come."

"My friend, no. It is not the engagement, but the severe cold with which I perceive you are afflicted. The vaults are insufferably damp. They are encrusted with nitre."

"Let us go, nevertheless. The cold is merely nothing. Amontillado! You have been imposed upon. And as for Luchresi, he cannot distinguish Sherry from Amontillado."

Thus speaking, Fortunato possessed himself of my arm; and putting on a mask of black silk and drawing a roquelaire closely about my person, I suffered him to hurry me to my palazzo. There were no attendants at home; they had absconded to make merry in honour of the time. I had told them that I should not return until the morning and had given them explicit orders not to stir from the house. These orders were sufficient, I well knew, to insure their immediate disappearance, one and all, as soon as my back was turned.

I took from their sconces two flambeaux, and giving one to Fortunato, bowed him through several suites of rooms to the archway that led into the vaults. I passed down a long and winding staircase, requesting him to be cautious as he followed. We came at length to the foot of the descent, and stood together on the damp ground of the catacombs of the Montresors. The gait of my friend was unsteady, and the bells upon his cap jingled as he strode.

"The pipe," said he.

"It is farther on," said I; "but observe the white web-work which gleams from these cavern walls."

He turned towards me and looked into my eyes with two filmy orbs that distilled the rheum of intoxication.

"Nitre?" he asked, at length.

"Nitre," I replied. "How long have you had that cough?"

"Ugh! ugh! ugh! —ugh! ugh! ugh! —ugh! ugh! ugh! —ugh! ugh! ugh! —ugh! ugh! ugh!

My poor friend found it impossible to reply for many minutes.

"It is nothing," he said, at last.

"Come," I said, with decision, "we will go back; your health is precious. You are rich, respected, admired, beloved; you are happy, as once I was. You are a man to be missed. For me it is no matter. We will go back; you will be ill, and I cannot be responsible. Besides, there is Luchresi—"

"Enough," he said; "the cough is a mere nothing; it will not kill me. I shall not die of a cough."

"True—true," I replied; "and, indeed, I had no intention of alarming you unnecessarily—but you should use all proper caution. A draught of this Medoc[8] will defend us from the damps." Here I knocked off the neck of a bottle which I drew from a long row of its fellows that lay upon the mould.

"Drink," I said, presenting him the wine.

He raised it to his lips with a leer. He paused and nodded to me familiarly, while his bells jingled.

"I drink," he said, "to the buried that repose around us."

"And I to your long life."

He again took my arm and we proceeded.

"These vaults," he said, "are extensive."

"The Montresors," I replied, "were a great numerous family."

"I forget your arms."

"A huge human foot d'or, in a field azure; the foot crushes a serpent rampant whose fangs are imbedded in the heel."

"And the motto?"

"Nemo me impune lacessit[9]."

"Good!" he said.

The wine sparkled in his eyes and the bells jingled. My own fancy grew warm with the Medoc. We had passed through long walls of piled skeletons, with casks and puncheons intermingling, into the inmost recesses of the catacombs. I paused again, and this time I made bold to seize Fortunato by an arm above the elbow.

"The nitre!" I said; "see, it increases. It hangs like moss upon the vaults. We are below the river's bed. The drops of moisture trickle among the bones. Come, we will go back ere it is too late. Your cough—"

"It is nothing," he said; "let us go on. But first, another draught of the Medoc."

I broke and reached him a flaçon of De Grâve. He emptied it at a breath. His eyes flashed with a fierce light. He laughed and threw the bottle upwards with a gesticulation I did not understand. I looked at him in surprise. He repeated the movement—a grotesque one.

"You do not comprehend?" he said.

"Not I," I replied.

"Then you are not of the brotherhood."

"How?"

"You are not of the masons[10]."

"Yes, yes," I said "yes, yes."

"You? Impossible! A mason?"

"A mason," I replied.

"A sign," he said, "a sign."

"It is this," I answered, producing from beneath the folds of my roquelaire a trowel.

"You jest," he exclaimed, recoiling a few paces. "But let us proceed to the Amontillado."

"Be it so," I said, replacing the tool beneath the cloak and again offering him my arm. He leaned upon it heavily. We continued our rout in search of the Amontillado. We passed through a range of low arches, descended, passed on, and descending again, arrived at a deep crypt, in which the foulness of the air caused our flambeaux rather to glow than flame.

At the most remote end of the crypt there appeared another less spacious. Its walls had been lined with human remains piled to the vault overhead, in the fashion of the great catacombs of Paris. Three sides of this interior crypt were still ornamented in this manner. From the fourth side the bones had been thrown down, and lay promiscuously upon the earth, forming at one point a mound of some size. Within the wall thus exposed by the displacing of the bones, we perceived a still interior cryptic of recess, in depth about four feet, in width three, in height six or seven. It seemed to have been constructed for no especial use within itself, but formed merely the interval between two of the colossal supports of the roof of the catacombs, and was backed by one of their circumscribing walls of solid granite.

It was in vain that Fortunato, uplifting his dull torch, endeavoured to pry into the depths of the recess. Its termination the feeble light did not enable us to see.

"Proceed," I said; "herein is the Amontillado. As for Luchresi—"

"He is an ignoramus," interrupted my friend, as he stepped unsteadily forward, while I followed immediately at his heels. In an instant he had reached the extremity of the niche, and finding his progress arrested by the rock, stood stupidly bewildered. A moment more and I had fettered him to the granite. In its surface were two iron staples, distant from each other about two feet, horizontally. From one of these depended a short chain. from the other a padlock. Throwing the links about his waist, it was but the work of a few seconds to secure it. He was too much astounded to resist. Withdrawing the key I stepped back from the recess. "Pass your hand," I said, "over the wall; you cannot help feeling the nitre. Indeed it is very damp. Once more let me implore you to return. No? Then I must positively leave you. But I must first render you all the little attentions in my power."

"The Amontillado!" ejaculated my friend, not yet recovered from his astonishment.

"True," I replied; "the Amontillado."

As I said these words I busied myself among the pile of bones of which I have before spoken. Throwing them aside, I soon uncovered a quantity of building stone and mortar. With these materials and with the aid of my trowel, I began vigorously to wall up the entrance of the niche.

I had scarcely laid the first tier of my masonry when I discovered that the intoxication of Fortunato had in a great measure worn off. The earliest indication I had of this was a low moaning cry from the depth of the recess. It was not the cry of a drunken man. There was then a long and obstinate silence. I laid the second tier, and the third, and the fourth; and then I heard the furious vibration of the chain. The noise lasted for several minutes, during which, that I might hearken to it with the more satisfaction, I ceased my labours and sat down upon the bones. When at last the clanking subsided, I resumed the trowel, and finished without interruption the fifth, the sixth, and the seventh tier. The wall was now nearly upon a level with my breast. I again paused, and holding the flambeaux over the mason-work, threw a few feeble rays upon the figure within.

A succession of loud and shrill screams, bursting suddenly from the throat of the chained form, seemed to thrust me violently back. For a brief moment I hesitated, I trembled. Unsheathing my rapier, I began to grope with it about the recess; but the thought of an instant reassured me. I placed my hand upon the solid fabric of the catacombs and felt satisfied. I reapproached the wall. I replied to the yells of him who clamoured. I re-echoed, I aided, I surpassed them in volume and in strength. I did this, and the clamourer grew still.

It was now midnight, and my task was drawing to a close. I had completed the eighth, the ninth, and the tenth tier. I had finished a portion of the last and the eleventh; there remained but a single stone to be fitted and plastered in. I struggled with its weight; I placed it partially in its destined position. But now there came from out the niche a low laugh that erected the hairs upon my head. It was succeeded by a sad voice, which I had difficulty in recognising as that of the noble Fortunato. The voice said—

"Ha! ha! ha! —he! he! he! —a very good joke, indeed—an excellent jest. We will have many a rich laugh about it at the palazzo—he! he! he! —over our wine—he! he! he!"

"The Amontillado!" I said.

"He! he! he! —he! he! he! —yes, the Amontillado. But is it not getting late? Will not they be awaiting us at the palazzo, the Lady Fortunato and the rest? Let us be gone."

"Yes," I said "let us be gone."

"For the love of God, Montresor!"

"Yes," I said, "for the love of God!"

But to these words I hearkened in vain for a reply. I grew impatient. I called aloud—"Fortunato!"

No answer. I called again—

"Fortunato!"

No answer still. I thrust a torch through the remaining aperture and let it fall within. There came forth in return only a jingling of the bells. My heart grew sick; it was the dampness of the catacombs that made it so. I hastened to make an end of my labour. I forced the last stone into its position; I plastered it up. Against the new masonry I re-erected the old rampart of bones. For the half of a century no mortal[11] has disturbed them. In pace requiescat[12]!

三、环境解析

《一桶蒙特亚白葡萄酒》发表于1846年，是关于"复仇"主题的恐怖小说名篇。小说的叙述者"我"为了报复福尔图纳托而设计出一条妙计。

福尔图纳托对"我"伤害无数，为此"我"决心寻机报仇雪恨。"我"买了一桶蒙特亚白葡萄酒，但不知真伪，故希望得到确认。狂欢节的晚上，趁福尔图纳托醉酒之际，"我"邀请他去辨认。福尔图纳托不以为然，提出要亲自鉴赏。"我们"二人手擎火把，来到藏酒地点——"我"家的地窖。途中，"我"几次暗示对方：地窖潮湿、阴冷、恐怖，建议返回地上，但福尔图纳托执意前行，无视尸骨遍地的骇人环境，直至地窖的最深处——凹洞的尽头。他全然不顾危险的降临。见时机已到，“我”用锁链将福尔图纳托锁在花岗石墙上，并快速砌墙抹灰，封住洞口。等到福尔图纳托明白过来后便竭力嘶叫，但“我”置之不理，直到完全封死洞口。“我”为报复成功自鸣得意。半个世纪以来无人光顾那些尸骨。

小说为读者营造了两种环境：有形(静态)环境和无形(动态)环境。它们制造出阴森、恐怖、死亡的氛围。它们是小说主题的“外衣”，也是主题的一部分。有形环境指的是地窖——黑暗而阴冷，湿气逼人；到处是尸骨，还伴以滴水的声音。它们衬托死一般的寂静。此环境是“我”和福尔图纳托的活动场所，是后者的葬身之地。不久，福尔图纳托成为环境的牺牲品，是环境的“新成员”，融入环境之中，成为环境的一部分。他的尸骨与其他尸骨一起，构成一个让读者读后望而却步、不寒而栗、充满死亡意义的环境。

受到眼前静态环境和“我”的所作所为的影响，清醒后的福尔图纳托“创造”了一个无形的动态环境——回荡在地窖的尖叫声。那是一种充满理性和激情、现实和想象、绝望和死亡的呐喊。它的寓意在于：也许是他应得的报应和作恶者的忏悔，抑或是对“我”的哀求和警示——不要杀人，否则也会遭此报应。这一点在爱伦·坡的另一篇小说《泄密的心》中得到印证。读完小说对该部分的描述，读者将对它的声音环境产生深刻的印象。

由此可见，环境与故事人物的关系是多方面的：既有海明威《在异乡》中“物”与“我”的对应关系，也有包含与被包含的关系，它们都对作品的主题思想起到暗示作用。而且，故事人物如同小说的作者，可以在一种环境影响下创造另一种环境。环境既是小说的形式，也是小说的内容。

四、难点注释

1. Amontillado：西班牙产的蒙特亚白葡萄酒。
2. give utterance to：表达，吐露。
3. A wrong is unredressed when retribution overtakes its redresser：如果报应降临到报复者的头上，那么其报复行为不算成功，所蒙之冤未被洗雪。
4. wont：习惯做法。
5. connoisseurship：鉴赏家(行家)身份。
6. pass for：被当成。
7. Sherry：雪利酒，西班牙产的另一种白葡萄酒。
8. Medoc：法国产的梅多克葡萄酒。
9. Nemo me impune lacessit：凡伤我者必受惩罚。
10. mason：西方民间秘密团体“共济会”的会员，共济会员互称兄弟，通过暗语秘密活动；又指泥瓦工。
11. mortal：人。
12. In pace requiescat：拉丁语，即英语的 may he rest in peace(愿灵魂安息)。

五、延伸阅读与批评

《黑猫》也属于爱伦·坡的恐怖小说。小说对黑猫及其所处地点的描写令读者铭记于心。

“黑猫”名叫普路托，是故事的叙述者“我”的宠物和朋友。但它与其他事物一起构成故事中四个十分特殊的场景：“我”把一只被“我”挖掉眼睛的黑猫吊死在一根树枝上；遭受火灾的一堵墙上印着一只与吊死在树上完全相同的猫；酒馆的大酒桶上坐着一只有白斑的猫，那白斑是与普路托相比的唯一不同之处；被“我”杀死的妻子被“我”嵌进地窖的墙里，妻子的尸体已腐朽，但她的头上坐着那只独眼黑猫。这四种场景呈现递进关系，一步步地引导“我”走向理智的对立面，直到自我灭亡。

“猫环境”代表何种意义？物质层面的“猫环境”对情节推动有何作用？是否左右着故事人物命运的走向？精神层面的“猫环境”是否指涉故事人物的非理性状况？或者，“猫”与叙述者“我”是否存在某种对应？这些问题的本身也许就是问题的答案。

Chapter 2 The Red Badge of Courage

by Stephen Crane

(*Excerpts*)

一、作者简介

斯蒂芬·克莱恩(1871—1900)，美国文学史上的一位早慧者和早逝者：小说家、诗人、记者。他一生发表了5部长篇小说，2部诗集，300多篇短篇故事、报道和特写。代表作有长篇小说《街头女郎梅季》(1893)和《红色英勇勋章》(1895)等，短篇小说集《海上扁舟及其他冒险故事》(1898)和《魔鬼和其他故事》(1899)，《海上扁舟》和《蓝色旅馆》是其中的短篇小说名篇。诗集有《黑衣骑者及其他》(1895)和《战争是仁慈的》(1899)。其诗作《战争是仁慈的》经常被人称道。

克莱恩9岁便失去父亲，母子俩的居住地在当时被视为性的天堂和酗酒赌博的场所。他一度成为那里的常客。后来他去南非、古巴、欧洲报道当地的战争。特殊的人生经历、对美国内战历史的兴趣、独特的文学想象力为克莱恩的创作提供了丰富的素材。

《街头女郎梅季》是美国第一部自然主义小说，它第一次向读者揭示了大城市里底层人们的生活、贫民窟、妓女、酗酒等题材。《红色英勇勋章》是美国第一部战争小说，它对士兵在战争之前、战争期间、战后的感受，战争的性质，战争与英雄主义和道德体系之间的关系等方面的描写，深深地影响了美国第一次世界大战、第二次世界大战和越南战争文学。他在诗歌领域同样颇有造诣，有评论家认为克莱恩和女诗人艾米莉·迪金森同为美国现代诗歌的先驱。

人与自然的关系——环境的压力、宇宙的冷漠、人对环境的无助抗争是克莱恩作品普遍关注的命题。自然主义的冷峻、现实主义的客观、印象主义的细致、象征主义的意蕴、讽刺式幽默等是克莱恩作品的主要创作特色。同时，克莱恩的作品语言简练有力，且常用口语化的语言。因此，也有学者认为克莱恩是美国现代文学的“父亲”，因为《街头女郎梅季》“是现代美国写作的开始”。

二、文本选读

The Red Badge of Courage

CHAPTER 3

When another night came, the columns[1] changed to purple streaks, filed across two pontoon bridges. A glaring fire wine-tinted the waters of the river. Its rays, shining upon the moving masses of troops, brought forth here and there sudden gleams of silver or gold. Upon the other shore a dark and mysterious range of hills was curved against the sky. The insect voices of the night sang solemnly.

After this crossing the youth assured himself that at any moment they might be suddenly and fearfully assaulted from the caves of the lowering woods. He kept his eyes watchfully upon the darkness.

But his regiment went unmolested to a camping place, and its soldiers slept the brave sleep of wearied men. In the morning they were routed out with early energy, and hustled along a narrow road that led deep into the forest.

It was during this rapid march that the regiment lost many of the marks of a new command.

The men had begun to count the miles upon their fingers, and they grew tired. "Sore feet an' damned short rations, that's all," said the loud soldier[2]. There was perspiration and grumblings. After a time they began to shed their knapsacks. Some tossed them unconcernedly down; others hid them carefully, asserting their plans to return for them at some convenient time. Men extricated themselves from thick shirts. Presently few carried anything but their necessary clothing, blankets, haversacks, canteens, and arms and ammunition. "You can now eat and shoot," said the tall soldier to the youth. "That's all you want to do."

There was sudden change from the ponderous infantry of theory to the light and speedy infantry of practice. The regiment, relieved of a burden, received a new impetus. But there was much loss of valuable knapsacks, and, on the whole, very good shirts.

But the regiment was not yet veteranlike in appearance. Veteran regiments in the army were likely to be very small aggregations of men. Once, when the command had first come to the field, some perambulating veterans, noting the length of their column, had accosted them thus: "Hey, fellers, what brigade is that?" And when the men had replied that they formed a regiment and not a brigade, the older soldiers had laughed, and said, "O Gawd!"

Also, there was too great a similarity in the hats. The hats of a regiment should properly represent the history of headgear for a period of years. And, moreover, there were no letters of faded gold speaking from the colors. They were new and beautiful, and the color bearer habitually oiled the pole.

Presently the army again sat down to think. The odor of the peaceful pines was in the men's nostrils. The sound of monotonous axe blows rang through the forest, and the insects, nodding upon their perches, crooned like old women. The youth returned to his theory of a blue demonstration.

One gray dawn, however, he was kicked in the leg by the tall soldier, and then, before he was entirely awake, he found himself running down a wood road in the midst of men who were panting from the first effects of speed. His canteen banged rythmically upon his thigh, and his haversack bobbed softly. His musket bounced a trifle from his shoulder at each stride and made his cap feel uncertain upon his head.

He could hear the men whisper jerky sentences: "Say—what's all this—about?" "What th' thunder—we—skedaddlin' this way for?" "Billie—keep off m' feet. Yeh run—like a cow." And the loud soldier's shrill voice could be heard: "What th' devil they in such a hurry for?"

The youth thought the damp fog of early morning moved from the rush of a great body of troops. From the distance came a sudden spatter of firing.

He was bewildered. As he ran with his comrades he strenuously tried to think, but all he knew was that if he fell down those coming behind would tread upon him. All his faculties seemed to be needed to guide him over and past obstructions. He felt carried along by a mob.

The sun spread disclosing rays, and, one by one, regiments burst into view like armed men just born of the earth. The youth perceived that the time had come. He was about to be measured[3]. For a moment he felt in the face of his great trial like a babe, and the flesh over his heart seemed very thin. He seized time to look about him calculatingly.

But he instantly saw that it would be impossible for him to escape from the regiment. It inclosed him. And there were iron laws of tradition and law on four sides. He was in a moving box.

As he perceived this fact it occurred to him that he had never wished to come to the war. He had not enlisted of his free will. He had been dragged by the merciless government. And now they were taking him out to be slaughtered.

The regiment slid down a bank and wallowed across a little stream. The mournful current moved slowly on, and from the water, shaded black, some white bubble eyes looked at the men.

As they climbed the hill on the farther side artillery began to boom. Here the youth forgot many things as he felt a sudden impulse of curiosity. He scrambled up the bank with a speed that could not be exceeded by a bloodthirsty man.

He expected a battle scene.

There were some little fields girted and squeezed by a forest. Spread over the grass and in among the tree trunks, he could see knots and waving lines of skirmishers who were running hither and thither and firing at the landscape. A dark battle line lay upon a sunstruck clearing that gleamed orange color. A flag fluttered.

Other regiments floundered up the bank. The brigade was formed in line of battle, and after a pause started slowly through the woods in the rear of the receding skirmishers, who were continually melting into the scene to appear again farther on. They were always busy as bees, deeply absorbed in their little combats.

The youth tried to observe everything. He did not use care to avoid trees and branches, and his forgotten feet were constantly knocking against stones or getting entangled in briers. He was aware that these battalions with their commotions were woven red and startling into the gentle fabric of softened greens and browns. It looked to be a wrong place for a battle field.

The skirmishers in advance fascinated him. Their shots into thickets and at distant and prominent trees spoke to him of tragedies—hidden, mysterious, solemn.

Once the line encountered the body of a dead soldier. He lay upon his back staring at the sky. He was dressed in an awkward suit of yellowish brown. The youth could see that the soles of his shoes had been worn to the thinness of writing paper, and from a great rent in one the dead foot projected piteously. And it was as if fate had betrayed the soldier. In death it exposed to his enemies that poverty which in life he had perhaps concealed from his friends.

The ranks opened covertly to avoid the corpse. The invulnerable dead man forced a way for himself. The youth looked keenly at the ashen face. The wind raised the tawny beard. It moved as if a hand were stroking it. He vaguely desired to walk around and around the body and stare; the impulse of the living to try to read in dead eyes the answer to the Question.

During the march the ardor which the youth had acquired when out of view of the field rapidly faded to nothing. His curiosity was quite easily satisfied. If an intense scene had caught him with its wild swing as he came to the top of the bank, he might have gone gone roaring on. This advance upon Nature was too calm. He had opportunity to reflect. He had time in which to wonder about himself and to attempt to probe his sensations.

Absurd ideas took hold upon him. He thought that he did not relish the landscape. It threatened him. A coldness swept over his back, and it is true that his trousers felt to him that they were no fit for his legs at all.

A house standing placidly in distant fields had to him an ominous look. The shadows of the woods were formidable. He was certain that in this vista there lurked fierce-eyed hosts. The swift thought came to him that the generals did not know what they were about. It was all a trap. Suddenly those close forests would bristle with rifle barrels. Ironlike brigades would appear in the rear. They were all going to be sacrificed. The generals were stupids. The enemy would presently swallow the whole command. He glared about him, expecting to see the stealthy approach of his death.

He thought that he must break from the ranks and harangue his comrades. They must not all be killed like pigs; and he was sure it would come to pass unless they were informed of these dangers. The generals were idiots to send them marching into a regular pen. There was but one pair of eyes in the corps. He would step forth and make a speech. Shrill and passionate words came to his lips.

The line, broken into moving fragments by the ground, went calmly on through fields and woods. The youth looked at the men nearest him, and saw, for the most part, expressions of deep interest, as if they were investigating something that had fascinated them. One or two stepped with overvaliant airs as if they were already plunged into war. Others walked as upon thin ice. The greater part of the untested men appeared quiet and absorbed. They were going to look at war, the red animal—war, the blood-swollen god. And they were deeply engrossed in this march.

As he looked the youth gripped his outcry at his throat. He saw that even if the men were tottering with fear they would laugh at his warning. They would jeer him, and, if practicable, pelt him with missiles. Admitting that he might be wrong, a frenzied declamation of the kind would turn him into a worm.

He assumed, then, the demeanor of one who knows that he is doomed alone to unwritten responsibilities. He lagged, with tragic glances at the sky.

He was surprised presently by the young lieutenant of his company, who began heartily to beat him with a sword, calling out in a loud and insolent voice: "Come, young man, get up into ranks there. No skulking 'll do here." He mended his pace with suitable haste. And he hated the lieutenant, who had no appreciation of fine minds. He was a mere brute.

After a time the brigade was halted in the cathedral light of a forest. The busy skirmishers were still popping. Through the aisles of the wood could be seen the floating smoke from their rifles. Sometimes it went up in little balls, white and compact.

During this halt many men in the regiment began erecting tiny hills in front of them. They used stones sticks, earth, and anything they thought might turn a bullet. Some built comparatively large ones, while others seems content with little ones.

This procedure caused a discussion among the men. Some wished to fight like duelists, believing it to be correct to stand erect and be, from their feet to their foreheads, a mark. They said they scorned the devices of the cautious. But the others scoffed in reply, and pointed to the veterans on the flanks who were digging at the ground like terriers. In a short time there was quite a barricade along the regimental fronts. Directly, however, they were ordered to withdraw from that place.

This astounded the youth. He forgot his stewing over the advance movement. "Well, then, what did they march us out here for?" he demanded of the tall soldier. The latter with calm faith began a heavy explanation, although he had been compelled to leave a little protection of stones and dirt to which he had devoted much care and skill.

When the regiment was aligned in another position each man's regard for his safety caused another line of small intrenchments. They ate their noon meal behind a third one. They were moved from this one also. They were marched from place to place with apparent aimlessness.

The youth had been taught that a man became another thing in a battle. He saw his salvation in such a change. Hence this waiting was an ordeal to him. He was in a fever of impatience. He considered that there was denoted a lack of purpose on the part of the generals. He began to complain to the tall soldier. "I can't stand this much longer," he cried. "I don't see what good it does to make us wear out our legs for nothin'." He wished to return to camp, knowing that this affair was a blue demonstration; or else to go into a battle and discover that he had been a fool in his doubts, and was, in truth, a man of traditional courage. The strain of present circumstances he felt to be intolerable.

The philosophical tall soldier measured a sandwich of cracker and pork and swallowed it in a nonchalant manner. "Oh, I suppose we must go reconnoitering around the country jest to keep 'em from getting too close, or to develop 'em, or something."

"Huh!" said the loud soldier.

"Well," cried the youth, still fidgeting, "I'd rather do anything 'most than go tramping' round the country all day doing no good to nobody and jest tiring ourselves out."

"So would I," said the loud soldier. "It ain't right. I tell you if anybody with any sense was a-runnin' this army it—"

"Oh, shut up!" roared the tall private. "You little fool. You little damn' cuss. You ain't had that there coat and them pants on for six months, and yet you talk as if—"

"Well, I wanta do some fighting anyway," interrupted the other. "I didn't come here to walk. I could 'ave walked to home— 'round an' 'round the barn, if I jest wanted to walk."

The tall one, red-faced, swallowed another sandwich as if taking poison in despair.

But gradually, as he chewed, his face became again quiet and contented. He could not rage in fierce argument in the presence of such sandwiches. During his meals he always wore an air of blissful contemplation of the food he had swallowed. His spirit seemed then to be communing with the viands.

He accepted new environment and circumstance with great coolness, eating from his haversack at every opportunity. On the march he went along with the stride of a hunter, objecting to neither gait nor distance[4]. And he had not raised his voice when he had been ordered away from three little protective piles of earth and stone, each of which had been an engineering feat worthy of being made sacred to the name of his grandmother.

In the afternoon, the regiment went out over the same ground it had taken in the morning. The landscape then ceased to threaten the youth. He had been close to it and become familiar with it.

When, however, they began to pass into a new region, his old fears of stupidity and incompetence reassailed him, but this time he doggedly let them babble. He was occupied with his problem, and in his desperation he concluded that the stupidity did not greatly matter.

Once he thought he had concluded that it would be better to get killed directly and end his troubles. Regarding death thus out of the corner of his eye, he conceived it to be nothing but rest, and he was filled with a momentary astonishment that he should have made an extraordinary commotion over the mere matter of getting killed. He would die; he would go to some place where he would be understood. It was useless to expect appreciation of his profound and fine sense from such men as the lieutenant. He must look to the grave for comprehension.

The skirmish fire increased to a long clattering sound. With it was mingled far-away cheering. A battery spoke.

Directly the youth could see the skirmishers running. They were pursued by the sound of musketry fire. After a time the hot, dangerous flashes of the rifles were visible. Smoke clouds went slowly and insolently across the fields like observant phantoms. The din became crescendo, like the roar of an oncoming train.

A brigade ahead of them and on the right went into action with a rending roar. It was as if it had exploded. And thereafter it lay stretched in the distance behind a long gray wall, that one was obliged to look twice at to make sure that it was smoke.

The youth, forgetting his neat plan of getting killed, gazed spell bound. His eyes grew wide and busy with the action of the scene. His mouth was a little ways open.

Of a sudden he felt a heavy and sad hand laid upon his shoulder. Awakening from his trance of observation he turned and beheld the loud soldier.

"It's my first and last battle, old boy," said the latter, with intense gloom. He was quite pale and his girlish lip was trembling.

"Eh?" murmured the youth in great astonishment.

"It's my first and last battle, old boy," continued the loud soldier. "Something tells me—"

"What?"

"I'm a gone coon this first time and—and I w-want you to take these here things—to—my—folks." He ended in a quavering sob of pity for himself. He handed the youth a little packet done up in a yellow envelope.

"Why, what the devil—" began the youth again.

But the other gave him a glance as from the depths of a tomb, and raised his limp hand in a prophetic manner and turned away.

CHAPTER 5

There were moments of waiting. The youth thought of the village street at home before the arrival of the circus parade on a day in the spring. He remembered how he had stood, a small, thrillful boy, prepared to follow the dingy lady upon the white horse, or the band in its faded chariot. He saw the yellow road, the lines of expectant people, and the sober houses. He particularly remembered an old fellow who used to sit upon a cracker box in front of the store and feign to despise such exhibitions. A thousand details of color and form surged in his mind. The old fellow upon the cracker box appeared in middle prominence.

Some one cried, "Here they come!"

There was rustling and muttering among the men. They displayed a feverish desire to have every possible cartridge ready to their hands. The boxes were pulled around into various positions, and adjusted with great care. It was as if seven hundred new bonnets were being tried on.

The tall soldier, having prepared his rifle, produced a red handkerchief of some kind. He was engaged in knitting it about his throat with exquisite attention to its position, when the cry was repeated up and down the line in a muffled roar of sound.

"Here they come! Here they come!" Gun locks clicked.

Across the smoke-infested fields came a brown swarm of running men who were giving shrill yells. They came on, stooping and swinging their rifles at all angles. A flag, tilted forward, sped near the front.

As he caught sight of them the youth was momentarily startled by a thought that perhaps his gun was not loaded. He stood trying to rally his faltering intellect so that he might recollect the moment when he had loaded, but he could not.

A hatless general pulled his dripping horse to a stand near the colonel of the 304th. He shook his fist in the other's face. "You've got to hold 'em back!" he shouted, savagely; "you've got to hold 'em back!"

In his agitation the colonel began to stammer. "A-all r-right, General, all right, by Gawd! We-we'll do our—we-we'll d-d-do-do our best, General." The general made a passionate gesture and galloped away. The colonel, perchance to relieve his feelings, began to scold like a wet parrot. The youth, turning swiftly to make sure that the rear was unmolested, saw the commander regarding his men in a highly resentful manner, as if he regretted above everything his association with them.

The man at the youth's elbow was mumbling, as if to himself: "Oh, we're in for it[5] now! oh, we're in for it now!"

The captain of the company had been pacing excitedly to and fro in the rear. He coaxed in schoolmistress fashion, as to a congregation of boys with primers. His talk was an endless repetition. "Reserve your fire, boys—don't shoot till I tell you—save your fire—wait till they get close up—don't be damned fools—"

Perspiration streamed down the youth's face, which was soiled like that of a weeping urchin. He frequently, with a nervous movement, wiped his eyes with his coat sleeve. His mouth was still a little ways ope.

He got the one glance at the foe-swarming field in front of him, and instantly ceased to debate the question of his piece being loaded. Before he was ready to begin—before he had announced to himself that he was about to fight—he threw the obedient well-balanced rifle into position and fired a first wild shot. Directly he was working at his weapon like an automatic affair.

He suddenly lost concern for himself, and forgot to look at a menacing fate. He became not a man but a member. He felt that something of which he was a part—a regiment, an army, a cause, or a country—was in crisis. He was welded into a common personality which was dominated by a single desire. For some moments he could not flee no more than a little finger can commit a revolution from a hand.

If he had thought the regiment was about to be annihilated perhaps he could have amputated himself from it. But its noise gave him assurance. The regiment was like a firework that, once ignited, proceeds superior to circumstances until its blazing vitality fades. It wheezed and banged with a mighty power. He pictured the ground before it as strewn with the discomfited.

There was a consciousness always of the presence of his comrades about him. He felt the subtle battle brotherhood more potent even than the cause for which they were fighting. It was a mysterious fraternity born of the smoke and danger of death.

He was at a task. He was like a carpenter who has made many boxes, making still another box, only there was furious haste in his movements. He, in his thoughts, was careering[6] off in other places, even as the carpenter who as he works whistles and thinks of his friend or his enemy, his home or a saloon. And these jolted dreams were never perfect to him afterward, but remained a mass of blurred shapes.

Presently he began to feel the effects of the war atmosphere—a blistering sweat, a sensation that his eyeballs were about to crack like hot stones. A burning roar filled his ears.

Following this came a red rage. He developed the acute exasperation of a pestered animal, a well-meaning cow worried by dogs. He had a mad feeling against his rifle, which could only be used against one life at a time. He wished to rush forward and strangle with his fingers. He craved a power that would enable him to make a world-sweeping gesture and brush all back. His impotency appeared to him, and made his rage into that of a driven beast.

Buried in the smoke of many rifles his anger was directed not so much against the men whom he knew were rushing toward him as against the swirling battle phantoms which were choking him, stuffing their smoke robes down his parched throat. He fought frantically for respite for his senses, for air, as a babe being smothered attacks the deadly blankets.

There was a blare of heated rage mingled with a certain expression of intentness on all faces. Many of the men were making low-toned noises with their mouths, and these subdued cheers, snarls, imprecations, prayers, made a wild, barbaric song that went as an undercurrent of sound, strange and chantlike with the resounding chords of the war march. The man at the youth's elbow was babbling. In it there was something soft and tender like the monologue of a babe. The tall soldier was swearing in a loud voice. From his lips came a black procession of curious oaths. Of a sudden another broke out in a querulous way like a man who has mislaid his hat. "Well, why don't they support us? Why don't they send supports? Do they think—"

The youth in his battle sleep heard this as one who dozes hears.

There was a singular absence of heroic poses. The men bending and surging in their haste and rage were in every impossible attitude. The steel ramrods clanked and clanged with incessant din as the men pounded them furiously into the hot rifle barrels. The flaps of the cartridge boxes were all unfastened, and bobbed idiotically with each movement. The rifles, once loaded, were jerked to the shoulder and fired without apparent aim into the smoke or at one of the blurred and shifting forms which upon the field before the regiment had been growing larger and larger like puppets under a magician's hand.

The officers, at their intervals, rearward, neglected to stand in picturesque attitudes. They were bobbing to and fro roaring directions and encouragements. The dimensions of their howls were extraordinary. They expended their lungs with prodigal wills. And often they nearly stood upon their heads in their anxiety to observe the enemy on the other side of the tumbling smoke.

The lieutenant of the youth's company had encountered a soldier who had fled screaming at the first volley of his comrades. Behind the lines these two were acting a little isolated scene. The man was blubbering and staring with sheeplike eyes at the lieutenant, who had seized him by the collar and was pommeling him. He drove him back into the ranks with many blows. The soldier went mechanically, dully, with his animal-like eyes upon the officer. Perhaps there was to him a divinity expressed in the voice of the other—stern, hard, with no reflection of fear in it. He tried to reload his gun, but his shaking hands prevented. The lieutenant was obliged to assist him.

The men dropped here and there like bundles. The captain of the youth's company had been killed in an early part of the action. His body lay stretched out in the position of a tired man resting, but upon his face there was an astonished and sorrowful look, as if he thought some friend had done him an ill turn. The babbling man was grazed by a shot that made the blood stream widely down his face. He clapped both hands to his head. "Oh!" he said, and ran. Another grunted suddenly as if he had been struck by a club in the stomach. He sat down and gazed ruefully. In his eyes there was mute, indefinite reproach. Farther up the line a man, standing behind a tree, had had his knee joint splintered by a ball. Immediately he had dropped his rifle and gripped the tree with both arms. And there he remained, clinging desperately and crying for assistance that he might withdraw his hold upon the tree.

At last an exultant yell went along the quivering line. The firing dwindled from an uproar to a last vindictive popping. As the smoke slowly eddied away, the youth saw that the charge had been repulsed. The enemy were scattered into reluctant groups. He saw a man climb to the top of the fence, straddle the rail, and fire a parting shot. The waves[7] had receded, leaving bits of dark "debris" upon the ground.

Some in the regiment began to whoop frenziedly. Many were silent. Apparently they were trying to contemplate themselves.

After the fever had left his veins, the youth thought that at last he was going to suffocate. He became aware of the foul atmosphere in which he had been struggling. He was grimy and dripping like a laborer in a foundry. He grasped his canteen and took a long swallow of the warmed water.

A sentence with variations went up and down the line. "Well, we've helt 'em back. We've helt 'em back; derned if we haven't." The men said it blissfully, leering at each other with dirty smiles.

The youth turned to look behind him and off to the right and off to the left. He experienced the joy of a man who at last finds leisure in which to look about him.

Under foot there were a few ghastly forms motionless. They lay twisted in fantastic contortions. Arms were bent and heads were turned in incredible ways. It seemed that the dead men must have fallen from some great height to get into such positions. They looked to be dumped out upon the ground from the sky.

From a position in the rear of the grove a battery was throwing shells over it. The flash of the guns startled the youth at first. He thought they were aimed directly at him. Through the trees he watched the black figures of the gunners as they worked swiftly and intently. Their labor seemed a complicated thing. He wondered how they could remember its formula in the midst of confusion.

The guns squatted in a row like savage chiefs. They argued with abrupt violence. It was a grim pow-wow. Their busy servants ran hither and thither.

A small procession of wounded men were going drearily toward the rear. It was a flow of blood from the torn body of the brigade.

To the right and to the left were the dark lines of other troops. Far in front he thought he could see lighter masses protruding in points from the forest. They were suggestive of unnumbered thousands.

Once he saw a tiny battery go dashing along the line of the horizon. The tiny riders were beating the tiny horses.

From a sloping hill came the sound of cheerings and clashes. Smoke welled slowly through the leaves.

Batteries were speaking with thunderous oratorical effort. Here and there were flags, the red in the stripes dominating. They splashed bits of warm color upon the dark lines of troops.

The youth felt the old thrill at the sight of the emblems. They were like beautiful birds strangely undaunted in a storm.

As he listened to the din from the hillside, to a deep pulsating thunder that came from afar to the left, and to the lesser clamors which came from many directions, it occurred to him that they were fighting, too, over there, and over there, and over there. Heretofore he had supposed that all the battle was directly under his nose.

As he gazed around him the youth felt a flash of astonishment at the blue, pure sky and the sun gleamings on the trees and fields. It was surprising that Nature had gone tranquilly on with her golden process in the midst of so much devilment.

CHAPTER 6

The youth awakened slowly. He came gradually back to a position from which he could regard himself. For moments he had been scrutinizing his person in a dazed way as if he had never before seen himself. Then he picked up his cap from the ground. He wriggled in his jacket to make a more comfortable fit, and kneeling relaced his shoe. He thoughtfully mopped his reeking features.

So it was all over at last! The supreme trial had been passed. The red, formidable difficulties of war had been vanquished.

He went into an ecstasy of self-satisfaction. He had the most delightful sensations of his life. Standing as if apart from himself, he viewed that last scene. He perceived that the man who had fought thus was magnificent.

He felt that he was a fine fellow. He saw himself even with those ideals which he had considered as far beyond him. He smiled in deep gratification.

Upon his fellows he beamed tenderness and good will. "Gee! ain't it hot, hey?" he said affably to a man who was polishing his streaming face with his coat sleeves.

"You bet!" said the other, grinning sociably. "I never seen sech dumb hotness." He sprawled out luxuriously on the ground. "Gee, yes! An' I hope we don't have no more fightin' till a week from Monday."

There were some handshakings and deep speeches with men whose features were familiar, but with whom the youth now felt the bonds of tied hearts. He helped a cursing comrade to bind up a wound of the shin.

But, of a sudden, cries of amazement broke out along the ranks of the new regiment. "Here they come ag'in! Here they come ag'in!" The man who had sprawled upon the ground started up and said, "Gosh!"

The youth turned quick eyes upon the field. He discerned forms begin to swell in masses out of a distant wood. He again saw the tilted flag speeding forward.

The shells, which had ceased to trouble the regiment for a time, came swirling again, and exploded in the grass or among the leaves of the trees. They looked to be strange war flowers bursting into fierce bloom.

The men groaned. The luster faded from their eyes. Their smudged countenances now expressed a profound dejection. They moved their stiffened bodies slowly, and watched in sullen mood the frantic approach of the enemy. The slaves toiling in the temple of this god began to feel rebellion at his harsh tasks.

They fretted and complained each to each. "Oh, say, this is too much of a good thing! Why can't somebody send us supports?"

"We ain't never goin' to stand this second banging. I didn't come here to fight the hull damn' rebel army."

There was one who raised a doleful cry. "I wish Bill Smithers had trod on my hand, insteader me treddin' on his'n." The sore joints of the regiment creaked as it painfully floundered into position to repulse.

The youth stared. Surely, he thought, this impossible thing was not about to happen. He waited as if he expected the enemy to suddenly stop, apologize, and retire bowing. It was all a mistake.

But the firing began somewhere on the regimental line and ripped along in both directions. The level sheets of flame developed great clouds of smoke that tumbled and tossed in the mild wind near the ground for a moment, and then rolled through the ranks as through a gate. The clouds were tinged an earthlike yellow in the sunrays and in the shadow were a sorry blue. The flag was sometimes eaten and lost in this mass of vapor, but more often it projected, sun-touched, resplendent.

Into the youth's eyes there came a look that one can see in the orbs of a jaded horse. His neck was quivering with nervous weakness and the muscles of his arms felt numb and bloodless. His hands, too, seemed large and awkward as if he was wearing invisible mittens. And there was a great uncertainty about his knee joints.

The words that comrades had uttered previous to the firing began to recur to him. "Oh, say, this is too much of a good thing! What do they take us for—why don't they send supports? I didn't come here to fight the hull damned rebel army."

He began to exaggerate the endurance, the skill, and the valor of those who were coming. Himself reeling from exhaustion, he was astonished beyond measure at such persistency. They must be machines of steel. It was very gloomy struggling against such affairs, wound up perhaps to fight until sundown.

He slowly lifted his rifle and catching a glimpse of the thickspread field he blazed at a cantering cluster. He stopped then and began to peer as best as he could through the smoke. He caught changing views of the ground covered with men who were all running like pursued imps, and yelling.

To the youth it was an onslaught of redoubtable dragons. He became like the man who lost his legs at the approach of the red and green monster. He waited in a sort of a horrified, listening attitude. He seemed to shut his eyes and wait to be gobbled.

A man near him who up to this time had been working feverishly at his rifle suddenly stopped and ran with howls. A lad whose face had borne an expression of exalted courage, the majesty of he who dares give his life, was, at an instant, smitten abject. He blanched like one who has come to the edge of a cliff at midnight and is suddenly made aware. There was a revelation. He, too, threw down his gun and fled. There was no shame in his face. He ran like a rabbit.

Others began to scamper away through the smoke. The youth turned his head, shaken from his trance by this movement as if the regiment was leaving him behind. He saw the few fleeting forms.

He yelled then with fright and swung about. For a moment, in the great clamor, he was like a proverbial chicken. He lost the direction of safety. Destruction threatened him from all points.

Directly he began to speed toward the rear in great leaps. His rifle and cap were gone. His unbuttoned coat bulged in the wind. The flap of his cartridge box bobbed wildly, and his canteen, by its slender cord, swung out behind. On his face was all the horror of those things which he imagined.

The lieutenant sprang forward bawling. The youth saw his features wrathfully red, and saw him make a dab with his sword. His one thought of the incident was that the lieutenant was a peculiar creature to feel interested in such matters upon this occasion.

He ran like a blind man. Two or three times he fell down. Once he knocked his shoulder so heavily against a tree that he went headlong.

Since he had turned his back upon the fight his fears had been wondrously magnified. Death about to thrust him between the shoulder blades was far more dreadful than death about to smite him between the eyes. When he thought of it later, he conceived the impression that it is better to view the appalling than to be merely within hearing. The noises of the battle were like stones; he believed himself liable to be crushed.

As he ran on he mingled with others. He dimly saw men on his right and on his left, and he heard footsteps behind him. He thought that all the regiment was fleeing, pursued by those ominous crashes.

In his flight the sound of these following footsteps gave him his one meager relief. He felt vaguely that death must make a first choice of the men who were nearest; the initial morsels for the dragons would be then those who were following him. So he displayed the zeal of an insane sprinter in his purpose to keep them in the rear. There was a race.

As he, leading, went across a little field, he found himself in a region of shells. They hurtled over his head with long wild screams. As he listened he imagined them to have rows of cruel teeth that grinned at him. Once one lit before him and the livid lightning of the explosion effectually barred the way in his chosen direction. He groveled on the ground and then springing up went careering off through some bushes.

He experienced a thrill of amazement when he came within view of a battery in action. The men there seemed to be in conventional moods, altogether unaware of the impending annihilation. The battery was disputing with a distant antagonist and the gunners were wrapped in admiration of their shooting. They were continually bending in coaxing postures over the guns. They seemed to be patting them on the back and encouraging them with words. The guns, stolid and undaunted, spoke with dogged valor.

The precise gunners were coolly enthusiastic. They lifted their eyes every chance to the smoke-wreathed hillock from whence the hostile battery addressed them. The youth pitied them as he ran. Methodical idiots! Machine-like fools! The refined joy of planting shells in the midst of the other battery's formation would appear a little thing when the infantry came swooping out of the woods.

The face of a youthful rider, who was jerking his frantic horse with an abandon of temper he might display in a placid barnyard, was impressed deeply upon his mind. He knew that he looked upon a man who would presently be dead.

Too, he felt a pity for the guns, standing, six good comrades, in a bold row.

He saw a brigade going to the relief of its pestered fellows. He scrambled upon a wee hill and watched it sweeping finely, keeping formation in difficult places. The blue of the line was crusted with steel color, and the brilliant flags projected. Officers were shouting.

This sight also filled him with wonder. The brigade was hurrying briskly to be gulped into the infernal mouths of the war god. What manner of men were they, anyhow? Ah, it was some wondrous breed! Or else they didn't comprehend—the fools.

A furious order caused commotion in the artillery. An officer on a bounding horse made maniacal motions with his arms. The teams went swinging up from the rear, the guns were whirled about, and the battery scampered away. The cannon with their noses poked slantingly at the ground grunted and grumbled like stout men, brave but with objections to hurry.

The youth went on, moderating his pace since he had left the place of noises.

Later he came upon a general of division seated upon a horse that pricked its ears in an interested way at the battle. There was a great gleaming of yellow and patent leather about the saddle and bridle. The quiet man astride looked mouse-colored upon such a splendid charger.

A jingling staff was galloping hither and thither. Sometimes the general was surrounded by horsemen and at other times he was quite alone. He looked to be much harassed. He had the appearance of a business man whose market is swinging up and down.

The youth went slinking around this spot. He went as near as he dared trying to overhear words. Perhaps the general, unable to comprehend chaos, might call upon him for information. And he could tell him. He knew all concerning it. Of a surety the force was in a fix, and any fool could see that if they did not retreat while they had opportunity—why—

He felt that he would like to thrash the general, or at least approach and tell him in plain words exactly what he thought him to be. It was criminal to stay calmly in one spot and make no effort to stay destruction. He loitered in a fever of eagerness for the division commander to apply to him.

As he warily moved about, he heard the general call out irritably: "Tompkins, go over an' see Taylor, an' tell him not t' be in such an all-fired hurry; tell him t' halt his brigade in th' edge of th' woods; tell him t' detach a reg'ment—say I think th' center'll break if we don't help it out some; tell him t' hurry up."

A slim youth on a fine chestnut horse caught these swift words from the mouth of his superior. He made his horse bound into a gallop almost from a walk in his haste to go upon his mission. There was a cloud of dust.

A moment later the youth saw the general bounce excitedly in his saddle.

"Yes, by heavens, they have!" The officer leaned forward. His face was aflame with excitement. "Yes, by heavens, they've held 'im! They've held 'im!"

He began to blithely roar at his staff: "We'll wallop'im now. We'll wallop 'im now. We've got 'em sure." He turned suddenly upon an aid: "Here—you—Jones—quick—ride after Tompkins—see Taylor—tell him t' go in—everlastingly—like blazes—anything."

As another officer sped his horse after the first messenger, the general beamed upon the earth like a sun. In his eyes was a desire to chant a paean. He kept repeating, "They've held 'em, by heavens!"

His excitement made his horse plunge, and he merrily kicked and swore at it. He held a little carnival of joy on horseback.

CHAPTER 7

The youth cringed as if discovered in a crime. By heavens, they had won after all! The imbecile line had remained and become victors. He could hear cheering.

He lifted himself upon his toes and looked in the direction of the fight. A yellow fog lay wallowing on the treetops. From beneath it came the clatter of musketry. Hoarse cries told of an advance.

He turned away amazed and angry. He felt that he had been wronged.

He had fled, he told himself, because annihilation approached. He had done a good part in saving himself, who was a little piece of the army. He had considered the time, he said, to be one in which it was the duty of every little piece to rescue itself if possible. Later the officers could fit the little pieces together again, and make a battle front. If none of the little pieces were wise enough to save themselves from the flurry of death at such a time, why, then, where would be the army? It was all plain that he had proceeded according to very correct and commendable rules. His actions had been sagacious things. They had been full of strategy. They were the work of a master's legs.

Thoughts of his comrades came to him. The brittle blue line had withstood the blows and won. He grew bitter over it. It seemed that the blind ignorance and stupidity of those little pieces had betrayed him. He had been overturned and crushed by their lack of sense in holding the position, when intelligent deliberation would have convinced them that it was impossible. He, the enlightened man who looks afar in the dark, had fled because of his superior perceptions and knowledge. He felt a great anger against his comrades. He knew it could be proved that they had been fools.

He wondered what they would remark when later he appeared in camp. His mind heard howls of derision. Their density would not enable them to understand his sharper point of view.

He began to pity himself acutely. He was ill used. He was trodden beneath the feet of an iron injustice. He had proceeded with wisdom and from the most righteous motives under heaven's blue only to be frustrated by hateful circumstances.

A dull, animal-like rebellion against his fellows, war in the abstract, and fate grew within him. He shambled along with bowed head, his brain in a tumult of agony and despair. When he looked loweringly up, quivering at each sound, his eyes had the expression of those of a criminal who thinks his guilt little and his punishment great, and knows that he can find no words.

He went from the fields into a thick woods, as if resolved to bury himself. He wished to get out of hearing of the crackling shots which were to him like voices.

The ground was cluttered with vines and bushes, and the trees grew close and spread out like bouquets. He was obliged to force his way with much noise. The creepers, catching against his legs, cried out harshly as their sprays were torn from the barks of trees. The swishing saplings tried to make known his presence to the world. He could not conciliate the forest. As he made his way, it was always calling out protestations. When he separated embraces of trees and vines the disturbed foliages waved their arms and turned their face leaves toward him. He dreaded lest these noisy motions and cries should bring men to look at him. So he went far, seeking dark and intricate places.

After a time the sound of musketry grew faint and the cannon boomed in the distance. The sun, suddenly apparent, blazed among the trees. The insects were making rhythmical noises. They seemed to be grinding their teeth in unison. A woodpecker stuck his impudent head around the side of a tree. A bird flew on lighthearted wing.

Off was the rumble of death. It seemed now that Nature had no ears.

This landscape gave him assurance. A fair field holding life. It was the religion of peace. It would die if its timid eyes were compelled to see blood. He conceived Nature to be a woman with a deep aversion to tragedy.

He threw a pine cone at a jovial squirrel, and he ran with chattering fear. High in a treetop he stopped, and, poking his head cautiously from behind a branch, looked down with an air of trepidation.

The youth felt triumphant at this exhibition. There was the law, he said. Nature had given him a sign. The squirrel, immediately upon recognizing danger, had taken to his legs without ado. He did not stand stolidly baring his furry belly to the missile, and die with an upward glance at the sympathetic heavens. On the contrary, he had fled as fast as his legs could carry him; and he was but an ordinary squirrel, too—doubtless no philosopher of his race. The youth wended, feeling that Nature was of his mind. She re-enforced his argument with proofs that lived where the sun shone.

Once he found himself almost into a swamp. He was obliged to walk upon bog tufts and watch his feet to keep from the oily mire. Pausing at one time to look about him he saw, out at some black water, a small animal pounce in and emerge directly with a gleaming fish.

The youth went again into the deep thickets. The brushed branches made a noise that drowned the sounds of cannon. He walked on, going from obscurity into promises of a greater obscurity[8].

At length he reached a place where the high, arching boughs made a chapel. He softly pushed the green doors aside and entered. Pine needles were a gentle brown carpet. There was a religious half light.

Near the threshold he stopped, horror-stricken at the sight of a thing.

He was being looked at by a dead man who was seated with his back against a columnlike tree. The corpse was dressed in a uniform that once had been blue, but was now faded to a melancholy shade of green. The eyes, staring at the youth, had changed to the dull hue to be seen on the side of a dead fish. The mouth was open. Its red had changed to an appalling yellow. Over the gray skin of the face ran little ants. One was trundling some sort of bundle along the upper lip.

The youth gave a shriek as he confronted the thing. He was for moments turned to stone before it. He remained staring into the liquid-looking eyes. The dead man and the living man exchanged a long look. Then the youth cautiously put one hand behind him and brought it against a tree. Leaning upon this he retreated, step by step, with his face still toward the thing. He feared that if he turned his back the body might spring up and stealthily pursue him.

The branches, pushing against him, threatened to throw him over upon it. His unguided feet, too, caught aggravatingly in brambles; and with it all he received a subtle suggestion to touch the corpse. As he thought of his hand upon it he shuddered profoundly.

At last he burst the bonds which had fastened him to the spot and fled, unheeding the underbrush. He was pursued by the sight of black ants swarming greedily upon the gray face and venturing horribly near to the eyes.

After a time he paused, and, breathless and panting, listened. He imagined some strange voice would come from the dead throat and squawk after him in horrible menaces.

The trees about the portal of the chapel moved soughingly in a soft wind. A sad silence was upon the little guarding edifice.

三、环境解析

《红色英勇勋章》的情节比较简单。美国内战时期，主人公亨利·弗莱明为实现自己的英雄梦参加了北方军。他对战争一无所知，因此战斗刚一打响他便在本能的驱动下临阵逃跑。他一方面为此惭愧不已，一方面为自己开脱。其间，他遇上"高个子士兵"，并目睹其惨死场景。后来，他在追问另一个逃兵时被对方用枪托伤了头部，留下伤疤。归队后，同伴们认为他是英勇作战受伤，视他为英雄。第二天的战斗又开始了，弗莱明紧握军旗，冲锋在前，极大地鼓舞了士气，他因此受到官兵的表扬。战斗结束了，弗莱明认为自己成长为真正的男子汉。然而，他仍然在思考自己以前的逃跑行为、一个普通士兵在战场上的表现、战争本身、战争与死亡的关系、人与自然的关系等问题。从某种意义上说，弗莱明对英雄主义神话不再抱有幻想，但另一方面他成为一名真正的英雄。只不过，他意识到他的英勇之举并非刻意为之，而是在愤怒和战斗的混乱中形成的。

环境与人的关系是该小说重点探讨的主题之一，因此《红色英勇勋章》被称为自然主义的杰作。

本文节选的四个章节比较集中地反映了环境对小说主人公弗莱明的影响以及他对自然的解读。在他看来，自然万物总是按照自己的方式行进着，对人类的一切漠不关心。

第三章：弗莱明入伍后兵团一直在行军，他们感到疲惫，希望直面一场真正的战斗。远处传来枪声，突然其他士兵逃跑起来，弗莱明惊恐之余也随之跑起来。他此时认为自己不该参战，是无情的政府将他拖到战场。随后，他们碰到一个死亡的士兵。他对死者的一切感到好奇，但找不到答案。他焦虑、不安、无助，对一切感到陌生。于是，他觉得周围的环境成为威胁之物：

> 寒冷扫过他的背部，他感到穿的裤子根本不合身，不能为他的双腿御寒……远处田野里的房子露出不祥的面孔。树木的影子狰狞恐怖，从这里望去那里面一定隐藏着眼神凶猛的敌人。将军们不知道他们的方向。前面一定是个陷阱。突然，茂密的森林布满了敌人的枪管……他们都将送死……他盯着周围的一切，希望看到自己的死亡偷偷临近。

弗莱明处在紧张与不安的心理状态中，他对环境的陌生和环境对他的冷漠使他在思考对方时产生了与自己心态类似的想法。他似乎觉得，环境是他的敌人，是他产生恐惧心理的源泉。内部的心理环境和外部的物质环境加深了他的恐惧感，进一步激发他在后来行动中生物般的本能冲动。

第五章：弗莱明疯狂地对着烟雾扫射。他惊奇地发现大自然面对枪林弹雨竟然无动于衷。

第六章：战斗又打响了。弗莱明与其他人一起，扔掉抢，像一只兔子、一个瞎子，恐惧地叫喊着，逃跑起来。他们在进行一场逃跑比赛。

第七章：弗莱明发表他的“逃跑哲学”演说。他一方面为自己的逃跑行为感到自责，另一方面又对之感到自鸣得意：兴奋、负罪感、愤怒等各种心理都有。此时，他又开始与大自然“对话”：

> 他认为死亡在远处隆隆作响，可是大自然好像没有长耳朵。
>
> 他认为大自然像一个对悲剧十分反感的女人。
>
> 他将一枚松果扔向一只松鼠，松鼠恐惧地跑到树顶，探头谨慎而惊恐地瞅着下方。他对此露出喜悦之情，认为自己明白了大自然给予他的法则。松鼠意识到危险后立刻拔腿就跑，而不会将自己的肚子暴露给子弹。相反，它会竭尽全力逃跑。它不过是一只普通的松鼠——不是它种族的哲学家。他感到大自然明白他的心理。它用放之四海而皆准的证据证明他的论断是正确的。

在此，弗莱明对环境有了完全不同的认识——环境成为他的“知音”。为什么？因为他通过驱赶松鼠而“读懂”了大自然的心声，实现了与自然的“物我统一”。他明白：逃生是宇宙中一切生物之本能。动物如此，人类亦不例外。因此，他的逃跑无可厚非。他无需为此背负负疚感。诚如他的“逃跑哲学”所言：只有保留生命才能同敌人战斗；没有生命的个体就没有生命的集体，就没有一个团，或者一个旅，就不能形成战斗力。至于它是否与伦理和道理有关，无关紧要。然而，以松鼠为代表的大自然认同弗莱明的看法吗？当然不。人类之间的自相残杀已经扰乱自然的安宁；更有甚者，人类将肮脏的双手伸向自然本身。自然当然不欢迎以弗莱明为代表的人类。

弗莱明用自己的独特方式感受和认知周围的环境。不同的心理和思想状况决定他解读环境的视角和意义，而伦理标准和道德准则不在其中。他似乎总能够在自己和自然环境之间找到“契合点”。可是自然对人类的入侵表示警觉与戒备；环境不为人类所动，它始终是它自己，按照自己的方式存在着。这些特征是不是自然主义文学的主要特征呢？

四、难点注释

1. columns：行军的队伍。
2. the loud soldier：大嗓门士兵。下文的 the tall soldier 指的是高个子士兵。作者不用具体的名字，而是用他们的各自特点指代不同的士兵。
3. He was about to be measured：他即将接受检验。
4. objecting to neither gait nor distance：既不反对行军速度的快慢，也不反对行军距离的远近。
5. we're in for it：词组 be in for it 意为“骑虎难下；没有退路”。
6. careering：急行；猛冲。
7. waves：一次次的攻击。
8. ...from obscurity into promises of a greater obscurity：obscurity 黑暗，昏暗；promises 可能；征兆。

五、延伸阅读与批评

《海上扁舟》发表于1897年，是斯蒂芬·克莱恩的短篇小说代表作。小说受到英国作家的高度赞扬，H. G. 威尔斯甚至认为它是“他[斯蒂芬·克莱恩]全部作品的顶峰”。该小说的第一句话就明白地告诉读者小说全文的主要内容：“一个目的在于反映事实的故事：‘海军准将号’沉没后，船上4人劫后余生的经历。”四个人驾驶的小船时刻都在与惊涛骇浪、黑夜、大风、鲨鱼和冰冷的海水斗争。他们随时都有被大海吞没的危险。他们一方面忙于跟死神搏斗，另一方面他们的思维十分活跃：既有对生的留恋和追求，又想到死之后的解脱；既有对过去事物的回忆，又有对自然本身以及自然与人类关系的思考。

故事人物对环境的反思多次触及小说的主题思想。例如，“人们眼中的大自然。对他来说，大自然似乎既不残酷，也不仁慈；既不是变化莫测，也不是谨慎明智。但它是冷漠的，彻底完全的冷漠”。那么，故事人物是在什么情形下对环境产生如此印象？再如，“大地对海上来人的欢迎是热烈的、慷慨的。然而一个一动也不动、水一滴一滴往下掉的形体慢慢地被抬上了海滩。对他来说，大地的欢迎只能是另外一种不祥的接待，坟墓的接待”。他们历经辛苦，最终到达梦寐以求的陆地，但为什么视大地为坟墓？

Chapter 3 Sister Carrie

by Theodore Dreiser

(Excerpts)

一、作者简介

西奥多·德莱塞(1871—1945)，美国20世纪第一位杰出的小说家。他的作品以小说为主，兼有札记、诗歌、戏剧和自传等。代表性的小说有《嘉莉妹妹》(1900)、《珍妮姑娘》(1911)、《欲望三部曲》:《金融家》(1912)、《巨人》(1914)、《斯多葛》(1947)，短篇小说集《自由及其他故事》(1918)、《美国的悲剧》(1925)，剧本《陶工之手》(1918)，自传《关于我自己的书》(1922)，政论集《悲剧的美国》等。其中，《嘉莉妹妹》是德莱塞的成名作，《美国的悲剧》是他的代表作。

德莱塞自幼家境贫寒，12岁便离开学校开始自谋生计。他先后当过报童、店员、洗碗工。18岁时受人资助上大学学习一年，接着又从事各种体力劳动。21岁之后在芝加哥和纽约等大城市当记者和编辑。虽然生活艰辛，但他从不屈服，勤奋好学，笔耕不辍，成为一位自学成才的作家。

德莱塞被称为现实主义作家或者自然主义作家，其作品同时具有超验主义、神秘主义和悲观主义色彩。他是美国资本主义的“黑幕揭发者”，具有激进的社会主义思想和反清教主义倾向。他认同美国从资本主义向帝国主义发展时期的消费文化观。他在颠覆传统社会道德的同时又不能完全摆脱它的桎梏。这些评价基本概括了德莱塞创作的思想内容。他作品的题材和主题包括资本社会里各个阶层的人间万象，如金钱、社会地位、消费、享受、女人、成功、辛酸、幻灭等各种“美国梦”的形态。德莱塞最大的创作特色是运用通俗而质朴的语言真实而细致地再现美国现实社会，给读者强烈的真实感。

德莱塞站在20世纪的门槛上，是美国现代文学的先驱，他对美国新型城市生活题材的集中处理极大地影响了他同时代的作家，如著名的短篇小说家舍伍德·安德森和美国第一位诺贝尔文学奖得主辛克莱·刘易斯。

二、文本选读

Sister Carrie

Chapter 1
THE MAGNET ATTRACTING
—*A WAIF AMID FORCES*

When Caroline Meeber boarded the afternoon train for Chicago, her total outfit consisted of a small trunk, a cheap imitation alligator-skin satchel, a small lunch in a paper box, and a yellow leather snap purse, containing her ticket, a scrap of paper with her sister's address in Van Buren Street, and four dollars in money. It was in August, 1889. She was eighteen years of age, bright, timid, and full of the illusions of ignorance and youth. Whatever touch of regret at parting characterised her thoughts, it was certainly not for advantages now being given up. A gush of tears at her mother's farewell kiss, a touch in her throat when the cars clacked by the flour mill where her father worked by the day, a pathetic sigh as the familiar green environs of the village passed in review, and the threads which bound her so lightly to girlhood and home were irretrievably broken.

To be sure there was always the next station, where one might descend and return. There was the great city, bound more closely by these very trains which came up daily. Columbia City was not so very far away, even once she was in Chicago. What, pray, is a few hours—a few hundred miles? She looked at the little slip bearing her sister's address and wondered. She gazed at the green landscape, now passing in swift review, until her swifter thoughts replaced its impression with vague conjectures of what Chicago might be.

When a girl leaves her home at eighteen, she does one of two things. Either she falls into saving hands and becomes better, or she rapidly assumes the cosmopolitan standard of virtue and becomes worse. Of an intermediate balance, under the circumstances, there is no possibility. The city has its cunning wiles, no less than the infinitely smaller and more human tempter. There are large forces which allure with all the soulfulness of expression possible in the most cultured human. The gleam of a thousand lights is often as effective as the persuasive light in a wooing and fascinating eye. Half the undoing of the unsophisticated and natural mind is accomplished by forces wholly superhuman. A blare of sound, a roar of life, a vast array of human hives, appeal to the astonished senses in equivocal terms. Without a counsellor at hand to whisper cautious interpretations, what falsehoods may not these things breathe into the unguarded ear! Unrecognised for what they are, their beauty, like music, too often relaxes, then weakens, then perverts the simpler human perceptions[1].

Caroline, or Sister Carrie, as she had been half affectionately termed by the family, was possessed of a mind rudimentary in its power of observation and analysis. Self-interest with her was high, but not strong. It was, nevertheless, her guiding characteristic. Warm with the fancies of youth, pretty with the insipid prettiness of the formative period, possessed of a figure promising eventual shapeliness and an eye alight with certain native intelligence, she was a fair example of the middle American class—two generations removed from the emigrant. Books were beyond her interest—knowledge a sealed book[2]. In the intuitive graces she was still crude. She could scarcely toss her head gracefully. Her hands were almost ineffectual. The feet, though small, were set flatly. And yet she was interested in her charms, quick to understand the keener pleasures of life, ambitious to gain in material things. A half-equipped little knight she was, venturing to reconnoitre the mysterious city and dreaming wild dreams of some vague, far-off supremacy, which should make it prey and subject—the proper penitent, groveling[3] at a woman's slipper.

"That," said a voice in her ear, "is one of the prettiest little resorts in Wisconsin."

"Is it?" she answered nervously.

The train was just pulling out of Waukesha. For some time she had been conscious of a man behind. She felt him observing her mass of hair. He had been fidgeting, and with natural intuition she felt a certain interest growing in that quarter. Her maidenly reserve, and a certain sense of what was conventional under the circumstances, called her to forestall and deny this familiarity, but the daring and magnetism of the individual, born of past experiences and triumphs, prevailed. She answered.

He leaned forward to put his elbows upon the back of her seat and proceeded to make himself volubly agreeable.

"Yes, that is a great resort for Chicago people. The hotels are swell. You are not familiar with this part of the country, are you?"

"Oh, yes, I am," answered Carrie. "That is, I live at Columbia City. I have never been through here, though."

"And so this is your first visit to Chicago," he observed.

All the time she was conscious of certain features out of the side of her eye. Flush, colourful cheeks, a light moustache, a grey fedora hat. She now turned and looked upon him in full, the instincts of self-protection and coquetry mingling confusedly in her brain.

"I didn't say that," she said.

"Oh," he answered, in a very pleasing way and with an assumed air of mistake, "I thought you did."

Here was a type of the travelling canvasser for a manufacturing house—a class which at that time was first being dubbed by the slang of the day "drummers." He came within the meaning of a still newer term, which had sprung into general use among Americans in 1880, and which concisely expressed the thought of one whose dress or manners are calculated to elicit the admiration of susceptible young women—a "masher." His suit was of a striped and crossed pattern of brown wool, new at that time, but since become familiar as a business suit. The low crotch of the vest revealed a stiff shirt bosom of white and pink stripes. From his coat sleeves protruded a pair of linen cuffs of the same pattern, fastened with large, gold plate buttons, set with the common yellow agates known as "cat's-eyes." His fingers bore several rings—one, the ever-enduring heavy seal—and from his vest dangled a neat gold watch chain, from which was suspended the secret insignia of the Order of Elks. The whole suit was rather tight-fitting, and was finished off with heavy-soled tan shoes, highly polished, and the grey fedora hat. He was, for the order of intellect represented, attractive, and whatever he had to recommend him, you may be sure was not lost upon Carrie, in this, her first glance.

Lest this order of individual should permanently pass, let me put down some of the most striking characteristics of his most successful manner and method. Good clothes, of course, were the first essential, the things without which he was nothing. A strong physical nature, actuated by a keen desire for the feminine, was the next. A mind free of any consideration of the problems or forces of the world and actuated not by greed, but an insatiable love of variable pleasure. His method was always simple. Its principal element was daring, backed, of course, by an intense desire and admiration for the sex[4]. Let him meet with a young woman once and he would approach her with an air of kindly familiarity, not unmixed with pleading, which would result in most cases in a tolerant acceptance. If she showed any tendency to coquetry he would be apt to straighten her tie, or if she "took up" with him at all, to call her by her first name. If he visited a department store it was to lounge familiarly over the counter and ask some leading questions. In more exclusive circles, on the train or in waiting stations, he went slower. If some seemingly vulnerable object appeared he was all attention—to pass the compliments of the day, to lead the way to the parlor car, carrying her grip, or, failing that, to take a seat next her with the hope of being able to court her to her destination. Pillows, books, a footstool, the shade lowered; all these figured in the things which he could do. If, when she reached her destination he did not alight and attend her baggage for her, it was because, in his own estimation, he had signally failed.

A woman should some day write the complete philosophy of clothes. No matter how young, it is one of the things she wholly comprehends. There is an indescribably faint line in the matter of man's apparel which somehow divides for her those who are worth glancing at and those who are not. Once an individual has passed this faint line on the way downward he will get no glance from her. There is another line at which the dress of a man will cause her to study her own. This line the individual at her elbow now marked for Carrie. She became conscious of an inequality. Her own plain blue dress, with its black cotton tape trimmings, now seemed to her shabby. She felt the worn state of her shoes.

"Let's see," he went on, "I know quite a number of people in your town. Morgenroth the clothier and Gibson the dry goods man."

"Oh, do you?" she interrupted, aroused by memories of longings their show windows had cost her.

At last he had a clew to her interest, and followed it deftly. In a few minutes he had come about into her seat. He talked of sales of clothing, his travels, Chicago, and the amusements of that city.

"If you are going there, you will enjoy it immensely. Have you relatives?"

"I am going to visit my sister," she explained.

"You want[5] to see Lincoln Park," he said, "and Michigan Boulevard. They are putting up great buildings there. It's a second New York—great. So much to see—theatres, crowds, fine houses—oh, you'll like that."

There was a little ache in her fancy of all he described. Her insignificance in the presence of so much magnificence faintly affected her. She realised that hers was not to be a round of pleasure, and yet there was something promising in all the material prospect he set forth. There was something satisfactory in the attention of this individual with his good clothes. She could not help smiling as he told her of some popular actress of whom she reminded him. She was not silly, and yet attention of this sort had its weight.

"You will be in Chicago some little time, won't you?" he observed at one turn of the now easy conversation.

"I don't know," said Carrie vaguely—a flash vision of the possibility of her not securing employment rising in her mind.

"Several weeks, anyhow," he said, looking steadily into her eyes.

There was much more passing now than the mere words indicated. He recognised the indescribable thing that made up for fascination and beauty in her. She realised that she was of interest to him from the one standpoint which a woman both delights in and fears. Her manner was simple, though for the very reason that she had not yet learned the many little affectations with which women conceal their true feelings. Some things she did appeared bold. A clever companion—had she ever had one—would have warned her never to look a man in the eyes so steadily.

"Why do you ask?" she said.

"Well, I'm going to be there several weeks. I'm going to study stock at our place and get new samples. I might show you 'round."

"I don't know whether you can or not. I mean I don't know whether I can. I shall be living with my sister, and—"

"Well, if she minds, we'll fix that." He took out his pencil and a little pocket note-book as if it were all settled. "What is your address there?"

She fumbled her purse which contained the address slip.

He reached down in his hip pocket and took out a fat purse. It was filled with slips of paper, some mileage books, a roll of greenbacks. It impressed her deeply. Such a purse had never been carried by any one attentive to her. Indeed, an experienced traveller, a brisk man of the world, had never come within such close range before. The purse, the shiny tan shoes, the smart new suit, and the air with which he did things, built up for her a dim world of fortune, of which he was the centre. It disposed her pleasantly toward all he might do.

He took out a neat business card, on which was engraved Bartlett, Caryoe & Company, and down in the left-hand corner, Chas. H. Drouet.

"That's me," he said, putting the card in her hand and touching his name. "It's pronounced Drew-eh. Our family was French, on my father's side."

She looked at it while he put up his purse. Then he got out a letter from a bunch in his coat pocket. "This is the house I travel for," he went on, pointing to a picture on it, "corner of State and Lake." There was pride in his voice. He felt that it was something to be connected with such a place, and he made her feel that way.

"What is your address?" he began again, fixing his pencil to write.

She looked at his hand.

"Carrie Meeber," she said slowly. "Three hundred and fifty-four West Van Buren Street, care S. C. Hanson."

He wrote it carefully down and got out the purse again. "You'll be at home if I come around Monday night?" he said.

"I think so," she answered.

How true it is that words are but the vague shadows of the volumes we mean. Little audible links, they are, chaining together great inaudible feelings and purposes. Here were these two, bandying little phrases, drawing purses, looking at cards, and both unconscious of how inarticulate all their real feelings were. Neither was wise enough to be sure of the working of the mind of the other. He could not tell how his luring succeeded. She could not realise that she was drifting, until he secured her address. Now she felt that she had yielded something—he, that he had gained a victory. Already they felt that they were somehow associated. Already he took control in directing the conversation. His words were easy. Her manner was relaxed.

They were nearing Chicago. Signs were everywhere numerous. Trains flashed by them. Across wide stretches of flat, open prairie they could see lines of telegraph poles stalking across the fields toward the great city. Far away were indications of suburban towns, some big smokestacks towering high in the air.

Frequently there were two-story frame houses standing out in the open fields, without fence or trees, lone outposts of the approaching army of homes.

To the child, the genius with imagination, or the wholly untravelled, the approach to a great city for the first time is a wonderful thing. Particularly if it be evening—that mystic period between the glare and gloom of the world when life is changing from one sphere or condition to another. Ah, the promise of the night. What does it not hold for the weary! What old illusion of hope is not here forever repeated! Says the soul of the toiler to itself, "I shall soon be free. I shall be in the ways and the hosts of the merry. The streets, the lamps, the lighted chamber set for dining, are for me. The theatre, the halls, the parties, the ways of rest and the paths of song-these are mine in the night." Though all humanity be still enclosed in the shops, the thrill runs abroad. It is in the air. The dullest feel something which they may not always express or describe. It is the lifting of the burden of toil.

Sister Carrie gazed out of the window. Her companion, affected by her wonder, so contagious are all things, felt anew some interest in the city and pointed out its marvels.

"This is Northwest Chicago," said Drouet. "This is the Chicago River," and he pointed to a little muddy creek, crowded with the huge masted wanderers from far-off waters nosing the black-posted banks. With a puff, a clang, and a clatter of rails it was gone. "Chicago is getting to be a great town," he went on. "It's a wonder. You'll find lots to see here."

She did not hear this very well. Her heart was troubled by a kind of terror. The fact that she was alone, away from home, rushing into a great sea of life and endeavour, began to tell. She could not help but feel a little choked for breath—a little sick as her heart beat so fast. She half closed her eyes and tried to think it was nothing, that Columbia City was only a little way off.

"Chicago! Chicago!" called the brakeman, slamming open the door. They were rushing into a more crowded yard, alive with the clatter and clang of life. She began to gather up her poor little grip and closed her hand firmly upon her purse. Drouet arose, kicked his legs to straighten his trousers, and seized his clean yellow grip.

"I suppose your people will be here to meet you?" he said. "Let me carry your grip."

"Oh, no," she said. "I'd rather you wouldn't. I'd rather you wouldn't be with me when I meet my sister."

"All right," he said in all kindness. "I'll be near, though, in case she isn't here, and take you out there safely."

"You're so kind," said Carrie, feeling the goodness of such attention in her strange situation.

"Chicago!" called the brakeman, drawing the word out long. They were under a great shadowy train shed, where the lamps were already beginning to shine out, with passenger cars all about and the train moving at a snail's pace. The people in the car were all up and crowding about the door.

"Well, here we are," said Drouet, leading the way to the door. "Good-bye, till I see you Monday."

"Good-bye," she answered, taking his proffered hand.

"Remember, I'll be looking till you find your sister."

She smiled into his eyes.

They filed out, and he affected to take no notice of her. A lean-faced, rather commonplace woman recognised Carrie on the platform and hurried forward.

"Why, Sister Carrie!" she began, and there was embrace of welcome.

Carrie realised the change of affectional atmosphere at once. Amid all the maze, uproar, and novelty she felt cold reality taking her by the hand. No world of light and merriment. No round of amusement. Her sister carried with her most of the grimness of shift and toil.

"Why, how are all the folks at home?" she began; "how is father, and mother?"

Carrie answered, but was looking away. Down the aisle, toward the gate leading into the waiting-room and the street, stood Drouet. He was looking back. When he saw that she saw him and was safe with her sister he turned to go, sending back the shadow of a smile. Only Carrie saw it. She felt something lost to her when he moved away. When he disappeared she felt his absence thoroughly. With her sister she was much alone, a lone figure in a tossing, thoughtless sea.

Chapter 2
WHAT POVERTY THREATENED
—*OF GRANITE AND BRASS*

Minnie's flat, as the one-floor resident apartments were then being called, was in a part of West Van Buren Street inhabited by families of labourers and clerks, men who had come, and were still coming, with the rush of population pouring in at the rate of 50,000 a year. It was on the third floor, the front windows looking down into the street, where, at night, the lights of grocery stores were shining and children were playing. To Carrie, the sound of the little bells upon the horse-cars, as they tinkled in and out of hearing, was as pleasing as it was novel. She gazed into the lighted street when Minnie brought her into the front room, and wondered at the sounds, the movement, the murmur of the vast city which stretched for miles and miles in every direction.

Mrs. Hanson, after the first greetings were over, gave Carrie the baby and proceeded to get supper. Her husband asked a few questions and sat down to read the evening paper. He was a silent man, American born, of a Swede father, and now employed as a cleaner of refrigerator cars at the stock-yards. To him the presence or absence of his wife's sister was a matter of indifference. Her personal appearance did not affect him one way or the other. His one observation to the point was concerning the chances of work in Chicago.

"It's a big place," he said. "You can get in somewhere in a few days. Everybody does."

It had been tacitly understood beforehand that she was to get work and pay her board. He was of a clean, saving disposition, and had already paid a number of monthly instalments on two lots far out on the West Side. His ambition was some day to build a house on them.

In the interval which marked the preparation of the meal Carrie found time to study the flat. She had some slight gift of observation and that sense, so rich in every woman—intuition.

She felt the drag of a lean and narrow life[6]. The walls of the rooms were discordantly papered. The floors were covered with matting and the hall laid with a thin rag carpet. One could see that the furniture was of that poor, hurriedly patched together quality sold by the instalment houses.

She sat with Minnie, in the kitchen, holding the baby until it began to cry. Then she walked and sang to it, until Hanson, disturbed in his reading, came and took it. A pleasant side to his nature came out here. He was patient. One could see that he was very much wrapped up in his offspring.

"Now, now," he said, walking. "There, there," and there was a certain Swedish accent noticeable in his voice.

"You'll want to see the city first, won't you?" said Minnie, when they were eating. "Well, we'll go out Sunday and see Lincoln Park."

Carrie noticed that Hanson had said nothing to this. He seemed to be thinking of something else.

"Well," she said, "I think I'll look around tomorrow. I've got Friday and Saturday, and it won't be any trouble. Which way is the business part?"

Minnie began to explain, but her husband took this part of the conversation to himself.

"It's that way," he said, pointing east. "That's east." Then he went off into the longest speech he had yet indulged in, concerning the lay of Chicago. "You'd better look in those big manufacturing houses along Franklin Street and just the other side of the river," he concluded. "Lots of girls work there. You could get home easy, too. It isn't very far."

Carrie nodded and asked her sister about the neighbourhood. The latter talked in a subdued tone, telling the little she knew about it, while Hanson concerned himself with the baby. Finally he jumped up and handed the child to his wife.

"I've got to get up early in the morning, so I'll go to bed," and off he went, disappearing into the dark little bedroom off the hall, for the night.

"He works way down at the stock-yards," explained Minnie, "so he's got to get up at half-past five."

"What time do you get up to get breakfast?" asked Carrie.

"At about twenty minutes of five."

Together they finished the labour of the day, Carrie washing the dishes while Minnie undressed the baby and put it to bed. Minnie's manner was one of trained industry, and Carrie could see that it was a steady round of toil with her.

She began to see that her relations with Drouet would have to be abandoned. He could not come here. She read from the manner of Hanson, in the subdued air of Minnie, and, indeed, the whole atmosphere of the flat, a settled opposition to anything save a conservative round of toil. If Hanson sat every evening in the front room and read his paper, if he went to bed at nine, and Minnie a little later, what would they expect of her? She saw that she would first need to get work and establish herself on a paying basis before she could think of having company of any sort. Her little flirtation with Drouet seemed now an extraordinary thing.

"No," she said to herself, "he can't come here."

She asked Minnie for ink and paper, which were upon the mantel in the dining-room, and when the latter had gone to bed at ten, got out Drouet's card and wrote him.

"I cannot have you call on me here. You will have to wait until you hear from me again. My sister's place is so small."

She troubled herself over what else to put in the letter. She wanted to make some reference to their relations upon the train, but was too timid. She concluded by thanking him for his kindness in a crude way, then puzzled over the formality of signing her name, and finally decided upon the severe, winding up with a "Very truly," which she subsequently changed to "Sincerely." She sealed and addressed the letter, and going in the front room, the alcove of which contained her bed, drew the one small rocking-chair up to the open window, and sat looking out upon the night and streets in silent wonder. Finally, wearied by her own reflections, she began to grow dull in her chair, and feeling the need of sleep, arranged her clothing for the night and went to bed.

When she awoke at eight the next morning, Hanson had gone. Her sister was busy in the dining-room, which was also the sitting-room, sewing. She worked, after dressing, to arrange a little breakfast for herself, and then advised with Minnie as to which way to look. The latter had changed considerably since Carrie had seen her. She was now a thin, though rugged, woman of twenty-seven, with ideas of life coloured by her husband's, and fast hardening into narrower conceptions of pleasure and duty than had ever been hers in a thoroughly circumscribed youth. She had invited Carrie, not because she longed for her presence, but because the latter was dissatisfied at home, and could probably get work and pay her board here. She was pleased to see her in a way but reflected her husband's point of view in the matter of work. Anything was good enough so long as it paid—say, five dollars a week to begin with. A shop girl was the destiny prefigured for the newcomer. She would get in one of the great shops and do well enough until—well, until something happened. Neither of them knew exactly what. They did not figure on promotion. They did not exactly count on marriage. Things would go on, though, in a dim kind of way until the better thing would eventuate, and Carrie would be rewarded for coming and toiling in the city. It was under such auspicious circumstances that she started out this morning to look for work.

Before following her in her round of seeking, let us look at the sphere in which her future was to lie. In 1889 Chicago had the peculiar qualifications of growth which made such adventuresome pilgrimages even on the part of young girls plausible. Its many and growing commercial opportunities gave it widespread fame, which made of it a giant magnet, drawing to itself, from all quarters, the hopeful and the hopeless—those who had their fortune yet to make and those whose fortunes and affairs had reached a disastrous climax elsewhere. It was a city of over 500,000, with the ambition, the daring, the activity of a metropolis of a million. Its streets and houses were already scattered over an area of seventy-five square miles. Its population was not so much thriving upon established commerce as upon the industries which prepared for the arrival of others. The sound of the hammer engaged upon the erection of new structures was everywhere heard. Great industries were moving in. The huge railroad corporations which had long before recognised the prospects of the place had seized upon vast tracts of land for transfer and shipping purposes. Street-car lines had been extended far out into the open country in anticipation of rapid growth. The city had laid miles and miles of streets and sewers through regions where, perhaps, one solitary house stood out alone—a pioneer of the populous ways to be. There were regions open to the sweeping winds and rain, which were yet lighted throughout the night with long, blinking lines of gas-lamps, fluttering in the wind. Narrow board walks extended out, passing here a house, and there a store, at far intervals, eventually ending on the open prairie.

In the central portion was the vast wholesale and shopping district, to which the uninformed seeker for work usually drifted. It was a characteristic of Chicago then, and one not generally shared by other cities, that individual firms of any pretension occupied individual buildings. The presence of ample ground made this possible. It gave an imposing appearance to most of the wholesale houses, whose offices were upon the ground floor and in plain view of the street. The large plates of window glass, now so common, were then rapidly coming into use, and gave to the ground floor offices a distinguished and prosperous look. The casual wanderer could see as he passed a polished array of office fixtures, much frosted glass, clerks hard at work, and genteel businessmen in "nobby" suits and clean linen lounging about or sitting in groups. Polished brass or nickel signs at the square stone entrances announced the firm and the nature of the business in rather neat and reserved terms. The entire metropolitan centre possessed a high and mighty air calculated to overawe and abash the common applicant, and to make the gulf between poverty and success seem both wide and deep.

Into this important commercial region the timid Carrie went. She walked east along Van Buren Street through a region of lessening importance, until it deteriorated into a mass of shanties and coal-yards, and finally verged upon the river. She walked bravely forward, led by an honest desire to find employment and delayed at every step by the interest of the unfolding scene, and a sense of helplessness amid so much evidence of power and force which she did not understand. These vast buildings, what were they? These strange energies and huge interests, for what purposes were they there? She could have understood the meaning of a little stone-cutter's yard at Columbia City, carving little pieces of marble for individual use, but when the yards of some huge stone corporation came into view, filled with spur tracks and flat cars, transpierced by docks from the river and traversed overhead by immense trundling cranes of wood and steel, it lost all significance in her little world[7].

It was so with the vast railroad yards, with the crowded array of vessels she saw at the river, and the huge factories over the way, lining the water's edge. Through the open windows she could see the figures of men and women in working aprons, moving busily about. The great streets were wall-lined mysteries to her; the vast offices, strange mazes which concerned far-off individuals of importance. She could only think of people connected with them as counting money, dressing magnificently, and riding in carriages. What they dealt in, how they laboured, to what end it all came, she had only the vaguest conception. It was all wonderful, all vast, all far removed, and she sank in spirit inwardly and fluttered feebly at the heart as she thought of entering any one of these mighty concerns and asking for something to do—something that she could do—anything.

Chapter 3
WEE QUESTION OF FORTUNE
—*FOUR-FIFTY A WEEK*

Once across the river and into the wholesale district, she glanced about her for some likely door at which to apply. As she contemplated the wide windows and imposing signs, she became conscious of being gazed upon and understood for what she was-a wage-seeker. She had never done this thing before, and lacked courage. To avoid a certain indefinable shame she felt at being caught spying about for a position, she quickened her steps and assumed an air of indifference supposedly common to one upon an errand. In this way she passed many manufacturing and wholesale houses without once glancing in. At last, after several blocks of walking, she felt that this would not do, and began to look about again, though without relaxing her pace. A little way on she saw a great door which, for some reason, attracted her attention. It was ornamented by a small brass sign, and seemed to be the entrance to a vast hive of six or seven floors. "Perhaps," she thought, "they may want some one," and crossed over to enter. When she came within a score of feet of the desired goal, she saw through the window a young man in a grey checked suit. That he had anything to do with the concern, she could not tell, but because he happened to be looking in her direction her weakening heart misgave her and she hurried by, too overcome with shame to enter. Over the way stood a great six-story structure, labelled Storm and King, which she viewed with rising hope. It was a wholesale dry goods concern and employed women. She could see them moving about now and then upon the upper floors. This place she decided to enter, no matter what. She crossed over and walked directly toward the entrance. As she did so, two men came out and paused in the door. A telegraph messenger in blue dashed past her and up the few steps that led to the entrance and disappeared. Several pedestrians out of the hurrying throng which filled the sidewalks passed about her as she paused, hesitating. She looked helplessly around, and then, seeing herself observed, retreated. It was too difficult a task. She could not go past them.

So severe a defeat told sadly upon her nerves. Her feet carried her mechanically forward, every foot of her progress being a satisfactory portion of a flight which she gladly made. Block after block passed by. Upon streetlamps at the various corners she read names such as Madison, Monroe, La Salle, Clark, Dearborn, State, and still she went, her feet beginning to tire upon the broad stone flagging. She was pleased in part that the streets were bright and clean. The morning sun, shining down with steadily increasing warmth, made the shady side of the streets pleasantly cool. She looked at the blue sky overhead with more realisation of its charm than had ever come to her before.

Her cowardice began to trouble her in a way. She turned back, resolving to hunt up Storm and King[8] and enter. On the way, she encountered a great wholesale shoe company, through the broad plate windows of which she saw an enclosed executive department, hidden by frosted glass. Without this enclosure, but just within the street entrance, sat a grey-haired gentleman at a small table, with a large open ledger before him. She walked by this institution several times hesitating, but, finding herself unobserved, faltered past the screen door and stood humble waiting.

"Well, young lady," observed the old gentleman, looking at her somewhat kindly, "what is it you wish?"

"I am, that is, do you—I mean, do you need any help?" she stammered.

"Not just at present," he answered smiling. "Not just at present. Come in some time next week. Occasionally we need some one."

She received the answer in silence and backed awkwardly out. The pleasant nature of her reception rather astonished her. She had expected that it would be more difficult, that something cold and harsh would be said—she knew not what. That she had not been put to shame and made to feel her unfortunate position, seemed remarkable.

Somewhat encouraged, she ventured into another large structure. It was a clothing company, and more people were in evidence—well-dressed men of forty and more, surrounded by brass railings.

An office boy approached her.

"Who is it you wish to see?" he asked.

"I want to see the manager," she said. He ran away and spoke to one of a group of three men who were conferring together. One of these came towards her.

"Well?" he said coldly. The greeting drove all courage from her at once.

"Do you need any help?" she stammered.

"No," he replied abruptly, and turned upon his heel.

She went foolishly out, the office boy deferentially swinging the door for her, and gladly sank into the obscuring crowd. It was a severe setback to her recently pleased mental state.

Now she walked quite aimlessly for a time, turning here and there, seeing one great company after another, but finding no courage to prosecute her single inquiry. High noon came, and with it hunger. She hunted out an unassuming restaurant and entered, but was disturbed to find that the prices were exorbitant for the size of her purse. A bowl of soup was all that she could afford, and, with this quickly eaten, she went out again. It restored her strength somewhat and made her moderately bold to pursue the search.

In walking a few blocks to fix upon some probable place, she again encountered the firm of Storm and King, and this time managed to get in. Some gentlemen were conferring close at hand, but took no notice of her. She was left standing, gazing nervously upon the floor. When the limit of her distress had been nearly reached, she was beckoned to by a man at one of the many desks within the near-by railing.

"Who is it you wish to see?" he required.

"Why, any one, if you please," she answered. "I am looking for something to do."

"Oh, you want to see Mr. McManus," he returned. "Sit down," and he pointed to a chair against the neighbouring wall. He went on leisurely writing, until after a time a short, stout gentleman came in from the street.

"Mr. McManus," called the man at the desk, "this young woman wants to see you."

The short gentleman turned about towards Carrie, and she arose and came forward.

"What can I do for you, miss?" he inquired, surveying her curiously.

"I want to know if I can get a position," she inquired.

"As what?" he asked.

"Not as anything in particular," she faltered.

"Have you ever had any experience in the wholesale dry goods business?" he questioned.

"No, sir," she replied.

"Are you a stenographer or typewriter?"

"No, sir."

"Well, we haven't anything here," he said. "We employ only experienced help."

She began to step backward toward the door, when something about her plaintive face attracted him.

"Have you ever worked at anything before?" he inquired.

"No, sir," she said.

"Well, now, it's hardly possible that you would get anything to do in a wholesale house of this kind. Have you tried the department stores?"

She acknowledged that she had not.

"Well, if I were you," he said, looking at her rather genially, "I would try the department stores. They often need young women as clerks."

"Thank you," she said, her whole nature relieved by this spark of friendly interest.

"Yes," he said, as she moved toward the door, "you try the department stores," and off he went.

At that time the department store was in its earliest form of successful operation, and there were not many. The first three in the United States, established about 1884, were in Chicago. Carrie was familiar with the names of several through the advertisements in the "Daily News," and now proceeded to seek them. The words of Mr. McManus had somehow managed to restore her courage, which had fallen low, and she dared to hope that this new line would offer her something. Some time she spent in wandering up and down, thinking to encounter the buildings by chance, so readily is the mind, bent upon prosecuting a hard but needful errand, eased by that self-deception which the semblance of search, without the reality, gives. At last she inquired of a police officer, and was directed to proceed "two blocks up," where she would find "The Fair."

The nature of these vast retail combinations, should they ever permanently disappear, will form an interesting chapter in the commercial history of our nation. Such a flowering out of a modest trade principle the world had never witnessed up to that time. They were along the line of the most effective retail organisation, with hundreds of stores coordinated into one and laid out upon the most imposing and economic basis. They were handsome, bustling, successful affairs, with a host of clerks and a swarm of patrons. Carrie passed along the busy aisles, much affected by the remarkable displays of trinkets, dress goods, stationery, and jewelry. Each separate counter was a show place of dazzling interest and attraction. She could not help feeling the claim of each trinket and valuable[9] upon her personally, and yet she did not stop. There was nothing there which she could not have used—nothing which she did not long to own. The dainty slippers and stockings, the delicately frilled skirts and petticoats, the laces, ribbons, hair-combs, purses, all touched her with individual desire, and she felt keenly the fact that not any of these things were in the range of her purchase. She was a work-seeker, an outcast without employment, one whom the average employee could tell at a glance was poor and in need of a situation[10].

It must not be thought that any one could have mistaken her for a nervous, sensitive, high-strung nature, cast unduly upon a cold, calculating, and unpoetic world. Such certainly she was not. But women are peculiarly sensitive to their adornment.

Not only did Carrie feel the drag of desire for all which was new and pleasing in apparel for women, but she noticed too, with a touch at the heart, the fine ladies who elbowed and ignored her, brushing past in utter disregard of her presence, themselves eagerly enlisted in the materials which the store contained. Carrie was not familiar with the appearance of her more fortunate sisters of the city. Neither had she before known the nature and appearance of the shop girls with whom she now compared poorly. They were pretty in the main, some even handsome, with an air of independence and indifference which added, in the case of the more favoured, a certain piquancy. Their clothes were neat, in many instances fine, and wherever she encountered the eye of one it was only to recognise in it a keen analysis of her own position—her individual shortcomings of dress and that shadow of manner which she thought must hang about her and make clear to all who and what she was. A flame of envy lighted in her heart. She realised in a dim way how much the city held—wealth, fashion, ease—every adornment for women, and she longed for dress and beauty with a whole heart.

On the second floor were the managerial offices, to which, after some inquiry, she was now directed. There she found other girls ahead of her, applicants like herself, but with more of that self-satisfied and independent air which experience of the city lends; girls who scrutinised her in a painful manner. After a wait of perhaps three-quarters of an hour, she was called in turn.

"Now," said a sharp, quick-mannered Jew, who was sitting at a roll-top desk near the window, "have you ever worked in any other store?"

"No, sir," said Carrie.

"Oh, you haven't," he said, eyeing her keenly.

"No, sir," she replied.

"Well, we prefer young women just now with some experience. I guess we can't use you."

Carrie stood waiting a moment, hardly certain whether the interview had terminated.

"Don't wait!" he exclaimed. "Remember we are very busy here."

Carrie began to move quickly to the door.

"Hold on," he said, calling her back. "Give me your name and address. We want girls occasionally."

When she had gotten safely into the street, she could scarcely restrain the tears. It was not so much the particular rebuff which she had just experienced, but the whole abashing trend of the day. She was tired and nervous. She abandoned the thought of appealing to the other department stores and now wandered on, feeling a certain safety and relief in mingling with the crowd.

In her indifferent wandering she turned into Jackson Street, not far from the river, and was keeping her way along the south side of that imposing thoroughfare, when a piece of wrapping paper, written on with marking ink and tacked up on the door, attracted her attention. It read, "Girls wanted—wrappers & stitchers." She hesitated a moment, then entered.

The firm of Speigelheim & Co., makers of boys' caps, occupied one floor of the building, fifty feet in width and some eighty feet in depth. It was a place rather dingily lighted, the darkest portions having incandescent lights, filled with machines and work benches. At the latter laboured quite a company of girls and some men. The former were drably-looking creatures, stained in face with oil and dust, clad in thin, shapeless, cotton dresses and shod with more or less worn shoes. Many of them had their sleeves rolled up, revealing bare arms, and in some cases, owing to the heat, their dresses were open at the neck. They were a fair type of nearly the lowest order of shop-girls—careless, slouchy, and more or less pale from confinement. They were not timid, however; were rich in curiosity, and strong in daring and slang.

Carrie looked about her, very much disturbed and quite sure that she did not want to work here. Aside from making her uncomfortable by sidelong glances, no one paid her the least attention. She waited until the whole department was aware of her presence. Then some word was sent around, and a foreman, in an apron and shirt sleeves, the latter rolled up to his shoulders, approached.

"Do you want to see me?" he asked.

"Do you need any help?" said Carrie, already learning directness of address.

"Do you know how to stitch caps?" he returned.

"No, sir," she replied.

"Have you ever had any experience at this kind of work?" he inquired.

She answered that she had not.

"Well," said the foreman, scratching his ear meditatively, "we do need a stitcher. We like experienced help, though. We've hardly got time to break people in." He paused and looked away out of the window. "We might, though, put you at finishing," he concluded reflectively.

"How much do you pay a week?" ventured Carrie, emboldened by a certain softness in the man's manner and his simplicity of address.

"Three and a half," he answered.

"Oh," she was about to exclaim, but checked herself and allowed her thoughts to die without expression.

"We're not exactly in need of anybody," he went on vaguely, looking her over as one would a package. "You can come on Monday morning, though," he added, "and I'll put you to work."

"Thank you," said Carrie weakly.

"If you come, bring an apron," he added.

He walked away and left her standing by the elevator, never so much as inquiring her name. While the appearance of the shop and the announcement of the price paid per week operated very much as a blow to Carrie's fancy, the fact that work of any kind was offered after so rude a round of experience was gratifying. She could not begin to believe that she would take the place, modest as her aspirations were. She had been used to better than that. Her mere experience and the free out-of-door life of the country caused her nature to revolt at such confinement. Dirt had never been her share. Her sister's flat was clean. This place was grimy and low, the girls were careless and hardened. They must be bad-minded and hearted, she imagined. Still, a place had been offered her. Surely Chicago was not so bad if she could find one place in one day. She might find another and better later.

Her subsequent experiences were not of a reassuring nature, however. From all the more pleasing or imposing places she was turned away abruptly with the most chilling formality. In others where she applied only the experienced were required. She met with painful rebuffs, the most trying of which had been in a manufacturing cloak house, where she had gone to the fourth floor to inquire.

"No, no," said the foreman, a rough, heavily built individual, who looked after a miserably lighted workshop, "we don't want any one. Don't come here."

With the wane of the afternoon went her hopes, her courage, and her strength. She had been astonishingly persistent. So earnest an effort was well deserving of a better reward. On every hand, to her fatigued senses, the great business portion grew larger, harder, more stolid in its indifference. It seemed as if it was all closed to her, that the struggle was too fierce for her to hope to do anything at all. Men and women hurried by in long, shifting lines. She felt the flow of the tide of effort and interest—felt her own helplessness without quite realising the wisp on the tide that she was. She cast about vainly for some possible place to apply, but found no door which she had the courage to enter. It would be the same thing all over. The old humiliation of her plea, rewarded by curt denial. Sick at heart and in body, she turned to the west, the direction of Minnie's flat, which she had now fixed in mind, and began that wearisome, baffled retreat which the seeker for employment at nightfall too often makes. In passing through Fifth Avenue, south towards Van Buren Street, where she intended to take a car, she passed the door of a large wholesale shoe house, through the plate-glass windows of which she could see a middle-aged gentleman sitting at a small desk. One of those forlorn impulses which often grow out of a fixed sense of defeat, the last sprouting of a baffled and uprooted growth of ideas, seized upon her. She walked deliberately through the door and up to the gentleman, who looked at her weary face with partially awakened interest.

"What is it?" he said.

"Can you give me something to do?" said Carrie.

"Now, I really don't know," he said kindly. "What kind of work is it you want—you're not a typewriter, are you?"

"Oh, no," answered Carrie.

"Well, we only employ book-keepers and typewriters here. You might go around to the side and inquire upstairs. They did want some help upstairs a few days ago. Ask for Mr. Brown."

She hastened around to the side entrance and was taken up by the elevator to the fourth floor.

"Call Mr. Brown, Willie," said the elevator man to a boy near by.

Willie went off and presently returned with the information that Mr. Brown said she should sit down and that he would be around in a little while.

It was a portion of the stock room which gave no idea of the general character of the place, and Carrie could form no opinion of the nature of the work.

"So you want something to do," said Mr. Brown, after he inquired concerning the nature of her errand. "Have you ever been employed in a shoe factory before?"

"No, sir," said Carrie.

"What is your name?" he inquired, and being informed, "Well, I don't know as I have anything for you. Would you work for four and a half a week?"

Carrie was too worn by defeat not to feel that it was considerable. She had not expected that he would offer her less than six. She acquiesced, however, and he took her name and address.

"Well," he said, finally, "you report here at eight o'clock Monday morning. I think I can find something for you to do."

He left her revived by the possibilities, sure that she had found something at last. Instantly the blood crept warmly over her body. Her nervous tension relaxed. She walked out into the busy street and discovered a new atmosphere. Behold, the throng was moving with a lightsome step. She noticed that men and women were smiling. Scraps of conversation and notes of laughter floated to her. The air was light. People were already pouring out of the buildings, their labour ended for the day. She noticed that they were pleased, and thoughts of her sister's home and the meal that would be awaiting her quickened her steps. She hurried on, tired perhaps, but no longer weary of foot. What would not Minnie say! Ah, the long winter in Chicago-the lights, the crowd, the amusement! This was a great, pleasing metropolis after all. Her new firm was a goodly institution. Its windows were of huge plate glass. She could probably do well there. Thoughts of Drouet returned—of the things he had told her. She now felt that life was better, that it was livelier, sprightlier. She boarded a car in the best of spirits, feeling her blood still flowing pleasantly. She would live in Chicago, her mind kept saying to itself. She would have a better time than she had ever had before—she would be happy.

三、环境解析

18 岁的农村女孩嘉罗琳·米伯(家人昵称她为“嘉莉妹妹”)怀揣对大都市繁华生活的憧憬来到芝加哥，投奔她的姐姐。她在火车上初识年轻的推销员杜洛埃，对方浑身散发的豪华气质深深地吸引了她。分手后，嘉莉在鞋厂找到工作。低薪和劳累让她难以忍受，她感到心灰意冷。命运安排她与杜洛埃重逢，她成为他的情妇，享受了一时的欢悦。后来，杜洛埃将嘉莉介绍给地位更高和金钱更多的酒店经理赫斯特伍德。经理为嘉莉的美貌痴迷而丧失理智。他偷钱后弃家而去，携嘉莉到纽约过着纸醉金迷的生活。然而，纽约非芝加哥，赫斯特伍德的生意每况愈下，俩人不禁为生计担忧。这时，嘉莉利用自己的美色，成为一名有名的演员。赫斯特伍德遭嘉莉抛弃，靠救济和乞讨为生，最终在收容所用煤气了此一生。成名后的嘉莉并不开心，伴随她的是孤独与寂寞。

作为美国20世纪第一部描写城市生活的小说，《嘉莉妹妹》向读者展示了19世纪末美国绚丽而诱人的城市风景。对乡下人来说，城市成为荣华和富贵、快乐和享受的代名词，因而城市环境对挣扎在穷苦深渊的人们具有令人难以抗拒的诱惑力。繁华和消费世界里高楼、霓虹灯、珠宝、名贵服饰等紧紧地拉扯着那些天真无知的穷者的双眼，攫住他们的身和心。这就是《嘉莉妹妹》前三章描写的主要内容之一。

在驶往芝加哥的火车上，嘉莉碰到了推销员杜洛埃。杜洛埃的动人谈吐、新潮西装和西装背心、镀金的扣子、沉甸甸的戒指、精致的金表链、锃亮的皮鞋和软呢帽，还有鼓鼓的钱包——深深地吸引她，让她第一次强烈地感受到大都市的魅力。他似乎成了她心中芝加哥那个花花世界的中心、整个城市风景的“浓缩品”、城市各种诱人物品的“嵌合体”。他犹如一块巨大的磁铁，将嘉莉的心吸往火车前行的方向——芝加哥。

走在芝加哥的大街上，嘉莉第一次目睹大都市的“容貌”：长长的马路和煤气街灯、气势宏伟的批发商行、宽大的玻璃窗、各种闪光的铜牌，还有悠闲的富商，等等。“整个都市中心显出一种财大气粗、高不可攀的气势，为的是让那些普通的求职者望而生畏，不敢问津。”如果说火车上的杜洛埃只是芝加哥“缩影”，这里就是它的放大镜。嘉莉为此感到既激动又怯生。她期望自己立即投入它的怀抱，拥抱它，或被它拥抱。正如小说所描述的：“一想到要走进这么气派的商号找工作，她能做的工作——不管是什么工作，她就感到怦然心跳了。”

深入都市的“腹地”，走在商场里和人群中，嘉莉观察到都市奢华的具体内涵：富丽堂皇的商场设计和布局、气派热闹的百货商场、忙碌的店员，络绎不绝的顾客。各种漂亮的首饰、衣服、文具和珠宝琳琅满目、光彩夺目，令人眼花缭乱、流连忘返，“她不由感到每件饰物和珠宝都在向她招手。”还有，那些精美的舞鞋和长筒袜，饰有漂亮绉边的裙子和衬裙，还有花边、缎带、梳子、钱包；还有一群群长相漂亮、穿着华丽，但对嘉莉视而不见的夫人和小姐们。她为此激动而兴奋，妒忌而自卑。所有这些极大地勾起了嘉莉的占有欲望。

城市环境的组成部分——火车上的商人杜洛埃、芝加哥城市的概貌、商场的奢侈品和衣着华丽的美女——在嘉莉面前一一展现出来。芝加哥的外表和男女显贵们将嘉莉的朦胧梦想明朗化，抽象的追求具体化。城市环境左右着嘉莉的思想和言行。她为之忍受自卑，付出肉体和灵魂。她一步步地走进他们、她们、它们，走到这一切的中央，甚至爬到它的顶端。

你能分析小说第10章和最后一章中的环境描写与人物身份和心理之间的关系吗？

四、难点注释

1. Unrecognised… simpler human perceptions：they 指代上面的 a blare of sound，a roar of life，a vast array of human hives。动词 relax，weaken 和 pervert 为递进关系，共同的对象是 perceptions。

2. knowledge a sealed book：完整的表达是 knowledge is a sealed book to her。词组 sealed book 不可理解的事物。该句的意思为：她不知道知识为何物。
3. grovel：奴颜婢膝。
4. sex：性。
5. want：口语表达，后接不定式，表“应该”。
6. drag of a lean and narrow life：日子艰辛，生活拮据。
7. it lost all significance in her little world：她的见识有限，不知道这些东西的意义。
8. Storm and King：公司名称。
9. valuable：贵重物品，尤指首饰。
10. situation：职位。求职广告的英文表达是 situations wanted。

五、延伸阅读与批评

长篇小说《美国的悲剧》被公认为是西奥多·德莱塞最优秀的代表作。年轻的主人公克莱德生活在一个穷牧师家庭，他的父母笃信上帝，常带着他们的孩子上街宣传上帝的旨意，高唱《赞美诗》。可围观者对他们不是投以白眼，便是讽刺挖苦。他们一家人也并没有因为崇拜耶稣而得到幸福，相反却弄得衣食无着。为了追求幸福，克莱德离家独自闯荡世界。贪慕虚荣的他虽然凭着聪明机灵在伯父的工厂里找到了稳定的工作，还遇到爱恋自己的美丽女孩，但他并不就此满足。为了追求更高的社会地位，他开始追求富家女，并狠心地把自己已经怀孕的女友害死。最终，克莱德非但没有实现自己的美梦，反倒受到法律的制裁。

德莱塞认为，在当时的美国社会里克莱德的悲剧是不可避免的，它既是一个个体现象，更是美国社会的写照——整个美国的悲剧。为什么？你能从小说的第二章找到部分答案吗？通过比照《嘉莉妹妹》我们可以发现，两部小说的前几章都在介绍主人公的基本信息。嘉莉妹妹和克莱德在对环境的敏感度方面是否存在某些共同点？

Chapter 4 In Another Country

by Ernest Hemingway

一、作者简介

欧内斯特·海明威(1899—1961)，美国20世纪最著名的小说家之一，诺贝尔文学奖获得者(1954)，美国文学中"迷惘的一代"的代言人。他的作品以长篇小说为主，也有非小说和诗歌。长篇小说主要有《太阳照样升起》(1926)、《永别了，武器》(1929)、《有钱人和没钱人》(1937)、《丧钟为谁而鸣》(1940)、《老人与海》(1952)，短篇小说集有《在我们的时代》(1925)、《没有女人的男人》(1927)、《胜者无所得》(1933)、《尼克·亚当斯故事集》(1972)，以及描述西班牙斗牛赛和阐述作者创作思想的非小说《死在午后》(1932)。

海明威是一位富有传奇色彩的人物：小时候随父亲打猎和钓鱼；长大后参加过第一次世界大战和第二次世界大战，到过意大利、西班牙、中国和东南亚；后来移居古巴的哈瓦那。他先后娶了四位妻子，最后用猎枪自杀结束了自己的生命。他的一生似乎一直生活"在路上"。

海明威的创作题材丰富多样，人与自然的关系、战争、死亡、创伤、爱情、人的尊严是他作品关注的主要对象。特别是他笔下的"硬汉子"形象和"重压下的体面""一个人可以被毁灭，但不能给打败"的精神最令人感动。在写作手法上，"冰山原则"是海明威留给读者的最大财富：用简洁而普通、少用形容词的对话表达深刻而丰富的思想内涵。海明威的成名之路上有几个作家值得一提：美国文学史上第一位描写战争的斯蒂芬·克莱恩，要求他阅读马克·吐温和惠特曼作品的舍伍德·安德森，为他指点创作迷津的格特鲁德·斯泰因，亲自帮他改稿的菲茨杰拉德，当然还包括他的妻子。就为美国文学作出贡献方面而言，海明威作品的主题思想挖掘和艺术手法运用同等重要。

总的说来，海明威的短篇小说与其长篇小说齐名。国内曾有学者认为他的短篇小说有时晦涩难懂，造成意义的不确定性，原因之一可能是这些作品"省略"的信息过多。但这也许是它们艺术魅力的一部分。

二、文本选读

In Another Country

In the fall the war was always there, but we did not go to it any more. It was cold in the fall in Milan and the dark came very early. Then the electric lights came on, and it was pleasant along the streets looking in the windows. There was much game[1] hanging outside the shops, and the snow powdered in the fur of the foxes and the wind blew their tails. The deer hung stiff and heavy and empty, and small birds blew in the wind and the wind turned their feathers. It was a cold fall and the wind came down from the mountains.

We were all at the hospital every afternoon, and there were different ways of walking across the town through the dusk to the hospital. Two of the ways were alongside canals, but they were long. Always, though, you crossed a bridge across a canal to enter the hospital. There was a choice of three bridges. On one of them a woman sold roasted chestnuts. It was warm, standing in front of her charcoal fire, and the chestnuts were warm afterward in your pocket. The hospital was very old and very beautiful, and you entered a gate and walked across a court-yard and out a gate on the other side. There were usually funerals starting from the courtyard. Beyond the old hospital were the new brick pavilions, and there we met every afternoon and were all very polite and interested in what was the matter, and sat in the machines[2] that were to make so much difference.

The doctor came up to the machine where I was sitting and said: "What did you like best to do before the war? Did you practice a sport?"

I said: "Yes, football."

"Good," he said. "You will be able to play football again better than ever."

My knee did not bend and the leg dropped straight from the knee to the ankle without a calf, and the machine was to bend the knee and make it move as in riding a tricycle. But it did not bend yet, and instead the machine lurched when it came to the bending part. The doctor said: "That will all pass. You are a fortunate young man. You will play football again like a champion."

In the next machine was a major who had a little hand like a baby's. He winked at me when the doctor examined his hand, which was between two leather straps that bounced up and down and flapped the stiff fingers, and said: "And will I too play football, captain-doctor?" He had been a very great fencer, and before the war the greatest fencer in Italy.

The doctor went to his office in a back room and brought a photograph which showed a hand that had been withered almost as small as the major's, before it had taken a machine course, and after was a little larger. The major held the photograph with his good hand and looked at it very carefully. "A wound?" he asked.

"An industrial accident," the doctor said.

"Very interesting, very interesting," the major said, and handed it back to the doctor.

"You have confidence?"

"No," said the major.

There were three boys who came each day who were about the same age I was. They were all three from Milan, and one of them was to be a lawyer, and one was to be a painter, and one had intended to be a soldier, and after we were finished with the machines, sometimes we walked back together to the Café Cova, which was next door to the Scala. We walked the short way through the communist quarter because we were four together. The people hated us because we were officers, and from a wine-shop someone called out, "A basso gli ufficiali[3]!" as we passed. Another boy who walked with us sometimes and made us five wore a black silk handkerchief across his face because he had no nose then and his face was to be rebuilt. He had gone out to the front from the military academy and been wounded within an hour after he had gone into the front line for the first time. They rebuilt his face, but he came from a very old family and they could never get the nose exactly right. He went to South America and worked in a bank. But this was a long time ago, and then we did not any of us know how it was going to be afterward. We only knew then that there was always the war, but that we were not going to it any more.

We all had the same medals, except the boy with the black silk bandage across his face, and he had not been at the front long enough to get any medals. The tall boy with a very pale face who was to be a lawyer had been lieutenant of Arditi and had three medals of the sort we each had only one of. He had lived a very long time with death and was a little detached. We were all a little detached, and there was nothing that held us together except that we met every afternoon at the hospital. Although, as we walked to the Cova through the tough part of town, walking in the dark, with light and singing coming out of the wine-shops, and sometimes having to walk into the street when the men and women would crowd together on the sidewalk so that we would have had to jostle them to get by, we felt held together by there being something that had happened that they, the people who disliked us, did not understand.

We ourselves all understood the Cova, where it was rich and warm and not too brightly lighted, and noisy and smoky at certain hours, and there were always girls at the tables and the illustrated papers on a rack on the wall. The girls at the Cova were very patriotic, and I found that the most patriotic people in Italy were the café girls—and I believe they are still patriotic.

The boys at first were very polite about my medals and asked me what I had done to get them. I showed them the papers, which were written in a very beautiful language and full of fratellanza and abnegazione[4], but which really said, with the adjectives removed, that I had been given the medals because I was an American. After that their manner changed a little toward me, although I was their friend against outsiders. I was a friend, but I was never really one of them after they had read the citations, because it had been different with them and they had done very different things to get their medals. I had been wounded, it was true; but we all knew that being wounded, after all, was really an accident. I was never ashamed of the ribbons, though, and sometimes, after the cocktail hour, I would imagine myself having done all the things they had done to get their medals; but walking home at night through the empty streets with the cold wind and all the shops closed, trying to keep near the street lights, I knew that I would never have done such things, and I was very much afraid to die, and often lay in bed at night by myself, afraid to die and wondering how I would be when I went back to the front again.

The three with the medals were like hunting-hawks; and I was not a hawk, although I might seem a hawk to those who had never hunted; they, the three, knew better and so we drifted apart. But I stayed good friends with the boy who had been wounded his first day at the front, because he would never know now how he would have turned out; so he could never be accepted either, and I liked him because I thought perhaps he would not have turned out to be a hawk either.

The major, who had been a great fencer, did not believe in bravery, and spent much time while we sat in the machines correcting my grammar. He had complimented me on how I spoke Italian, and we talked together very easily. One day I had said that Italian seemed such an easy language to me that I could not take a great interest in it; everything was so easy to say. "Ah, yes," the major said. "Why, then, do you not take up the use of grammar?" So we took up the use of grammar, and soon Italian was such a difficult language that I was afraid to talk to him until I had the grammar straight in my mind.

The major came very regularly to the hospital. I do not think he ever missed a day, although I am sure he did not believe in the machines. There was a time when none of us believed in the machines, and one day the major said it was all nonsense. The machines were new then and it was we who were to prove them. It was an idiotic idea, he said, "A theory[5], like another." I had not learned my grammar, and he said I was a stupid impossible disgrace, and he was a fool to have bothered with me. He was a small man and he sat straight up in his chair with his right hand thrust into the machine and looked straight ahead at the wall while the straps thumbed up and down with his fingers in them.

"What will you do when the was is over if it is over?" he asked me. "Speak grammatically!"

"I will go to the States."

"Are you married?"

"No, but I hope to be."

"The more of a fool you are," he said. He seemed very angry. "A man must not marry."

"Why, Signor Maggiore?"

"Don't call me 'Signor Maggiore'."

"Why must not a man marry?"

"He cannot marry. He cannot marry," he said angrily. "If he is to lose everything, he should not place himself in a position to lose that. He should not place himself in a position to lose. He should find things he cannot lose."

He spoke very angrily and bitterly, and looked straight ahead while he talked.

"But why should he necessarily lose it?"

"He'll lose it," the major said. He was looking at the wall. Then he looked down at the machine and jerked his little hand out from between the straps and slapped it hard against his thigh. "He'll lose it," he almost shouted. "Don't argue with me!" Then he called to the attendant who ran the machines. "Come and turn this damned thing off."

He went back into the other room for the light treatment and the massage. Then I heard him ask the doctor if he might use his telephone and he shut the door. When he came back into the room, I was sitting in another machine. He was wearing his cape and had his cap on, and he came directly toward my machine and put his arm on my shoulder.

"I am so sorry," he said, and patted me on the shoulder with his good hand. "I would not be rude. My wife has just died. You must forgive me."

"Oh—" I said, feeling sick for him. "I am so sorry."

He stood there biting his lower lip. "It is very difficult," he said. "I cannot resign myself."

He looked straight past me and out through the window. Then he began to cry. "I am utterly unable to resign myself," he said and choked. And then crying, his head up looking at nothing, carrying himself straight and soldierly, with tears on both his cheeks and biting his lips, he walked past the machines and out the door.

The doctor told me that the major's wife, who was very young and whom he had not married until he was definitely invalided out of the war, had died of pneumonia. She had been sick only a few days. No one expected her to die. The major did not come to the hospital for three days. Then he came at the usual hour, wearing a black band on the sleeve of his uniform. When he came back, there were large framed photographs around the wall, of all sorts of wounds before and after they had been cured by the machines. In front of the machine the major used were three photographs of hands like his that were completely restored. I do not know where the doctor got them. I always understood we were the first to use the machines. The photographs did not make much difference to the major because he only looked out of the window.

三、环境解析

《在异乡》发表于1938年，是与《白象似的群山》《杀人者》《一个干净明亮的地方》《雨中的猫》等齐名的短篇小说名篇。它是海明威重视自然环境描写的代表作品。

战争一直在进行着。一个很冷的秋天夜晚。冷风吹，雪花飘。店外挂着野味：狐狸身上裹着雪，尾巴在风中摇曳；内脏被掏的鹿僵硬而沉甸；小鸟的羽毛随风舞动。"我"——受伤的青年美国士兵，每天到意大利米兰的一家医院做康复理疗。"我"从膝盖到踝关节之间的小腿僵直，需要坐在特制的轮椅上治疗。同来理疗的还有几位意大利年轻士兵。意大利少校的手受伤，萎缩成娃娃的手，一位士兵的鼻子被毁。他们在一起讨论各自的理想和勋章；他们不认同"我"因为偶然负伤而接受勋章；少校心情极坏，因为他的新婚妻子去世了；医生安慰我们：一切都会好起来，我们都会梦想成真。然而大家明白：康复希望渺茫，故而对医生反应冷淡。

小说的第一段为读者描写了一个背景和一个场景：战争下的欧洲和意大利米兰的一个秋天的晚上，但重点描述离开战争的一个秋天场景。秋天的冷、黑、风、雪、死成为小说故事发生的自然环境，故事人物在如此环境下展开他们的言、行、思。第一，小说的开篇就向读者呈现这个特殊的自然环境，很显然，它为小说设定了特殊的色调：冷漠而寂寞，充满悲剧和死亡气息。它必将对故事人物产生不同程度的影响。第二，特殊环境传递的信息与人物的现实情绪相互认同：故事发生在医院，故事人物是受伤的士兵——他们缺乏温情，只有创伤，心情如同冰一样寒冷，充满悲情。第三，环境内容与人物当时的境遇类同：环境中的"人物"皆为死亡的动物，没有生命、希望、意义；故事中的士兵伤势严重，有的无法治愈。少校的妻子离世，他的前途未卜。目睹店外的"物"，追思身边的"人"，二者不无相似之处。第四，环境内容的结局对人物心理活动产生某种"预设"作用。小说结尾处，尽管医生为少校展示治愈后正常人的手，但少校对此很淡漠。他"只是向着窗外，凝望着”。妻子死了，少校对治疗和治愈漠不关心，他的心接近窗外的死亡境况。最后，以第一次世界大战为大背景的真实性与人物心理感受的真实性形成共时上的对应：士兵们对未来的一切不能确定，只有伤和痛切切实实地包围着他们，如同前方不断进行的战争。

总之，小说首段的自然环境描写对人物心理和小说主题思想的形成起到感染、照应、预示和催化的作用。为什么？值得三思。

四、难点注释

1. game：(总称)猎物。
2. machines：医疗器材。
3. A basso gli ufficiali：(意大利语)打倒军官。
4. fratellanza and abnegazione：(意大利语)友爱和克己。
5. theory：推测。

五、延伸阅读与批评

海明威另一部有名的短篇小说《白象似的群山》同样注重对自然环境的描写，而且环境勾描与故事情节推进交替出现。故事的发生地是某车站。其开篇即自然景观的描写：河谷的一边是绵延起伏的山，没有树木。随后有四个地方呼应开篇的自然环境：阳光下的山是白色的，乡野则是灰褐色、干巴巴的；透过树木看到的山是白色的；铁路对面的河流两岸是农田和树木，还有粮田和大河；对面是干涸的河谷和群山。自然中的白色和绿色及其各自的含义形成反差，故事男女主人公的心理活动也呈相反的走势。环境传递的内涵与故事人物的谈话和思考的内容是否构成对应关系？作者对男主人公的动作描写有什么明显的特色？值得三思。

Part Three

Character

“人物”或“形象”(image)是指文学作品中行为或活动的主体，通常是一个或一个以上的人(也可以是动物)。根据作者着墨的多少和赋予内涵的多寡，“人物”通常分为主要人物和次要人物、“丰满人物”和“扁平人物”、正面人物和反面人物。无论属于哪一类，“人物”身上都具有某种品质，是作者想要借以表达自己观点或立场的“媒介”，是作品主题思想的一部分。一般说来，分析“人物”就是分析作品的主题思想，因此把握作品中的“人物”特征十分必要。

分析“人物”的特征主要有两个途径：一是关注“人物”本身，包括外貌特征、语言、行为、思想(心理)活动；二是关注“人物”周围的人(群)对该“人物”的看法，以及他们之间的互动关系。“人物”的外部特征往往给读者某种暗示或联想，是该“人物”内心世界某个侧面的“投射”；行动是内心世界的反映；言为心声，即所说是所想。心理活动是言行的“孵化器”和“调节器”，所以它们皆有意义。上述两个途径相互补充，形成对“人物”比较完整的认识。

该部分包括五篇小说，分别从“人物”的外表、言行、心理活动和人物关系来解析某个特定“人物”对故事发展和主题思想形成所起的作用。

Chapter 1 The Scarlet Letter

by Nathaniel Hawthorne

(*Excerpts*)

一、作者简介

纳撒尼尔·霍桑(1804—1864)，美国19世纪著名的浪漫主义小说家。他以长篇小说和短篇小说闻名。长篇小说有《红字》(1850)、《七个尖角阁的房子》(1851)、《福谷传奇》(1852)、《大理石雕像》(1860)，短篇小说集有《故事重述》(1837)、《古屋青苔》(1846)、《雪的意象及其他重述的故事》(1852)、《历史与传记故事演义》(1851)。短篇小说代表作有《年轻的古德曼·布朗》《教长的黑面纱》《拉普齐尼博士的女儿》《海德格尔博士的书房》等。此外，霍桑参加了朋友富兰克林·皮尔斯的总统竞选活动，并为他写了竞选传记《富兰克林·皮尔斯传》(1852)，1862年发表了关于美国内战的文章《关于战争时局》。

霍桑出生在新英格兰的塞勒姆镇——英国殖民者在美国最早的据点之一。他的祖父曾担任殖民长官和清教法官，参与迫害宗教异端分子的活动。特殊的家庭背景使得霍桑对美国早期殖民地时期的社会历史和宗教产生浓厚的兴趣，并对它们进行不断的思考和书写。

霍桑深受清教主义中"内在堕落"和"原罪说"的影响，因此反映社会和人性中的"恶"以及人们对待犯罪的态度和行为方式成为他作品思想内容的主旋律。同时，他擅长挖掘人物的内心世界，探析人物在善与恶之间做出选择时的心理活动。他因此被称为美国心理小说的开创者，对亨利·詹姆斯和威廉·福克纳等人产生了重大的影响。霍桑在思想上充满矛盾，对清教主义的主张持模棱两可的态度。一方面，他抨击清教思想的严厉和非人性特征；另一方面，他视清教思想的某些信条为人们的言行准则。尽管霍桑的作品大多取材美国早期的社会和历史，但它们借古喻今，从侧面反映了美国19世纪社会和人们的思想和行为现实。

霍桑是一位语言风格大师。他的想象力十分丰富；用词正规，词汇量大，句子较长；作品构思巧妙，结构严谨；善用意象、明喻、暗喻、象征、寓言，因此其作品具有较强的现代主义文学色彩。这些创作手法为他的作品增添了浪漫气息和思想深度，丰富了读者的阅读视角。

二、文本选读

The Scarlet Letter

CHAPTER II THE MARKET-PLACE

The grass-plot before the jail, in Prison Lane, on a certain summer morning, not less than two centuries ago, was occupied by a pretty large number of the inhabitants of Boston, all with their eyes intently fastened on the iron-clamped oaken door. Amongst any other population, or at a later period in the history of New England, the grim rigidity that petrified the bearded physiognomies of these good people would have augured some awful business in hand. It could have betokened nothing short of the anticipated execution of some noted culprit, on whom the sentence of a legal tribunal had but confirmed the verdict of public sentiment. But, in that early severity of the Puritan character, an inference of this kind could not so indubitably be drawn. It might be that a sluggish bond-servant, or an undutiful child, whom his parents had given over to the civil authority, was to be corrected at the whipping-post. It might be that an Antinomian, a Quaker[1], or other heterodox religionist, was to be scourged out of the town, or an idle or vagrant Indian, whom the white man's firewater had made riotous about the streets, was to be driven with stripes into the shadow of the forest. It might be, too, that a witch, like old Mistress Hibbins, the bitter-tempered widow of the magistrate, was to die upon the gallows. In either case, there was very much the same solemnity of demeanour on the part of the spectators, as befitted a people among whom religion and law were almost identical, and in whose character both were so thoroughly interfused, that the mildest and severest acts of public discipline were alike made venerable and awful. Meagre, indeed, and cold, was the sympathy that a transgressor might look for, from such bystanders, at the scaffold. On the other hand, a penalty which, in our days, would infer a degree of mocking infamy and ridicule, might then be invested with almost as stern a dignity as the punishment of death itself.

It was a circumstance to he noted on the summer morning when our story begins its course, that the women, of whom there were several in the crowd, appeared to take a peculiar interest in whatever penal infliction might be expected to ensue. The age had not so much refinement, that any sense of impropriety restrained the wearers of petticoat and farthingale from stepping forth into the public ways, and wedging their not unsubstantial persons, if occasion were, into the throng nearest to the scaffold at an execution. Morally, as well as materially, there was a coarser fibre in those wives and maidens of old English birth and breeding than in their fair descendants, separated from them by a series of six or seven generations; for, throughout that chain of ancestry, every successive mother had transmitted to her child a fainter bloom, a more delicate and briefer beauty, and a slighter physical frame, if not character of less force and solidity than her own. The women who were now standing about the prison-door stood within less than half a century of the period when the man-like Elizabeth[2] had been the not altogether unsuitable representative of the sex. They were her countrywomen: and the beef and ale of their native land, with a moral diet not a whit more refined, entered largely into their composition. The bright morning sun, therefore, shone on broad shoulders and well-developed busts, and on round and ruddy cheeks, that had ripened in the far-off island, and had hardly yet grown paler or thinner in the atmosphere of New England. There was, moreover, a boldness and rotundity of speech among these matrons, as most of them seemed to be, that would startle us at the present day, whether in respect to its purport or its volume of tone.

"Goodwives," said a hard-featured dame of fifty, "I'll tell ye a piece of my mind. It would be greatly for the public behoof if we women, being of mature age and church-members in good repute, should have the handling of such malefactresses as this Hester Prynne. What think ye, gossips[3]? If the hussy stood up for judgment before us five, that are now here in a knot together, would she come off with such a sentence as the worshipful magistrates have awarded? Marry, I trow not."

"People say," said another, "that the Reverend Master Dimmesdale, her godly pastor, takes it very grievously to heart that such a scandal should have come upon his congregation."

"The magistrates are God-fearing gentlemen, but merciful overmuch—that is a truth," added a third autumnal matron. "At the very least, they should have put the brand of a hot iron on Hester Prynne's forehead. Madame Hester would have winced at that, I warrant me. But she—the naughty baggage—little will she care what they put upon the bodice of her gown! Why, look you, she may cover it with a brooch, or such like heathenish adornment, and so walk the streets as brave as ever!"

"Ah, but," interposed, more softly, a young wife, holding a child by the hand, "let her cover the mark as she will, the pang of it will be always in her heart."

"What do we talk of marks and brands, whether on the bodice of her gown or the flesh of her forehead?" cried another female, the ugliest as well as the most pitiless of these self-constituted judges. "This woman has brought shame upon us all, and ought to die. Is there not law for it? Truly there is, both in the Scripture and the statute-book. Then let the magistrates, who have made it of no effect, thank themselves if their own wives and daughters go astray!"

"Mercy on us, goodwife." exclaimed a man in the crowd, "is there no virtue in woman, save what springs from a wholesome fear of the gallows? That is the hardest word yet! Hush now, gossips! For the lock is turning in the prison-door, and here comes Mistress Prynne herself."

The door of the jail being flung open from within there appeared, in the first place, like a black shadow emerging into sunshine, the grim and gristly presence of the town-beadle, with a sword by his side, and his staff of office in his hand. This personage prefigured and represented in his aspect the whole dismal severity of the Puritanic code of law, which it was his business to administer in its final and closest application to the offender. Stretching forth the official staff in his left hand, he laid his right upon the shoulder of a young woman, whom he thus drew forward, until, on the threshold of the prison-door, she repelled him, by an action marked with natural dignity and force of character, and stepped into the open air as if by her own free will. She bore in her arms a child, a baby of some three months old, who winked and turned aside its little face from the too vivid light of day; because its existence, heretofore, had brought it acquaintance only with the grey twilight of a dungeon, or other darksome apartment of the prison.

When the young woman—the mother of this child—stood fully revealed before the crowd, it seemed to be her first impulse to clasp the infant closely to her bosom; not so much by an impulse of motherly affection, as[4] that she might thereby conceal a certain token, which was wrought or fastened into her dress. In a moment, however, wisely judging that one token of her shame would but poorly serve to hide another, she took the baby on her arm, and with a burning blush, and yet a haughty smile, and a glance that would not be abashed, looked around at her townspeople and neighbours. On the breast of her gown, in fine red cloth, surrounded with an elaborate embroidery and fantastic flourishes of gold thread, appeared the letter A. It was so artistically done, and with so much fertility and gorgeous luxuriance of fancy, that it had all the effect of a last and fitting decoration to the apparel which she wore, and which was of a splendour in accordance with the taste of the age, but greatly beyond what was allowed by the sumptuary regulations of the colony.

The young woman was tall, with a figure of perfect elegance on a large scale. She had dark and abundant hair, so glossy that it threw off the sunshine with a gleam; and a face which, besides being beautiful from regularity of feature and richness of complexion, had the impressiveness belonging to a marked brow and deep black eyes. She was ladylike, too, after the manner of the feminine gentility of those days; characterised by a certain state and dignity, rather than by the delicate, evanescent, and indescribable grace which is now recognised as its indication. And never had Hester Prynne appeared more ladylike, in the antique interpretation of the term, than as she issued from the prison. Those who had before known her, and had expected to behold her dimmed and obscured by a disastrous cloud, were astonished, and even startled, to perceive how her beauty shone out, and made a halo of the misfortune and ignominy in which she was enveloped. It may be true that, to a sensitive observer, there was some thing exquisitely painful in it. Her attire, which indeed, she had wrought for the occasion in prison, and had modelled much after her own fancy, seemed to express the attitude of her spirit, the desperate recklessness of her mood, by its wild and picturesque peculiarity. But the point which drew all eyes, and, as it were, transfigured the wearer—so that both men and women who had been familiarly acquainted with Hester Prynne were now impressed as if they beheld her for the first time—was that SCARLET LETTER, so fantastically embroidered and illuminated upon her bosom. It had the effect of a spell, taking her out of the ordinary relations with humanity, and enclosing her in a sphere by herself.

"She hath good skill at her needle, that's certain," remarked one of her female spectators; "but did ever a woman, before this brazen hussy, contrive such a way of showing it? Why, gossips, what is it but to laugh in the faces of our godly magistrates, and make a pride out of what they, worthy gentlemen, meant for a punishment?"

"It were well," muttered the most iron-visaged of the old dames, "if we stripped Madame Hester's rich gown off her dainty shoulders; and as for the red letter which she hath stitched so curiously, I'll bestow a rag of mine own rheumatic flannel to make a fitter one!"

"Oh, peace, neighbours—peace!" whispered their youngest companion; "do not let her hear you! Not a stitch in that embroidered letter but she has felt it in her heart."

The grim beadle now made a gesture with his staff.

"Make way, good people—make way, in the King's name!" cried he. "Open a passage; and I promise ye, Mistress Prynne shall be set where man, woman, and child may have a fair sight of her brave apparel from this time till an hour past meridian. A blessing on the righteous colony of the Massachusetts, where iniquity is dragged out into the sunshine! Come along, Madame Hester, and show your scarlet letter in the market-place!"

A lane was forthwith opened through the crowd of spectators. Preceded by the beadle, and attended by an irregular procession of stern-browed men and unkindly visaged women, Hester Prynne set forth towards the place appointed for her punishment. A crowd of eager and curious schoolboys, understanding little of the matter in hand, except that it gave them a half-holiday, ran before her progress, turning their heads continually to stare into her face and at the winking baby in her arms, and at the ignominious letter on her breast. It was no great distance, in those days, from the prison door to the market-place. Measured by the prisoner's experience, however, it might be reckoned a journey of some length; for haughty as her demeanour was, she perchance underwent an agony from every footstep of those that thronged to see her, as if her heart had been flung into the street for them all to spurn and trample upon. In our nature, however, there is a provision, alike marvellous and merciful, that the sufferer should never know the intensity of what he endures by its present torture, but chiefly by the pang that rankles after it. With almost a serene deportment, therefore, Hester Prynne passed through this portion of her ordeal, and came to a sort of scaffold, at the western extremity of the market-place. It stood nearly beneath the eaves of Boston's earliest church, and appeared to be a fixture there.

In fact, this scaffold constituted a portion of a penal machine, which now, for two or three generations past, has been merely historical and traditionary among us, but was held, in the old time, to be as effectual an agent, in the promotion of good citizenship, as ever was the guillotine among the terrorists of France. It was, in short, the platform of the pillory; and above it rose the framework of that instrument of discipline, so fashioned as to confine the human head in its tight grasp, and thus hold it up to the public gaze. The very ideal of ignominy was embodied and made manifest in this contrivance of wood and iron. There can be no outrage, methinks, against our common nature—whatever be the delinquencies of the individual—no outrage more flagrant than to forbid the culprit to hide his face for shame; as it was the essence of this punishment to do. In Hester Prynne's instance, however, as not unfrequently in other cases, her sentence bore that she should stand a certain time upon the platform, but without undergoing that gripe about the neck and confinement of the head, the proneness to which was the most devilish characteristic of this ugly engine. Knowing well her part, she ascended a flight of wooden steps, and was thus displayed to the surrounding multitude, at about the height of a man's shoulders above the street.

Had there been a Papist among the crowd of Puritans, he might have seen in this beautiful woman, so picturesque in her attire and mien, and with the infant at her bosom, an object to remind him of the image of Divine Maternity, which so many illustrious painters have vied with one another to represent; something which should remind him, indeed, but only by contrast, of that sacred image of sinless motherhood, whose infant was to redeem the world. Here, there was the taint of deepest sin in the most sacred quality of human life, working such effect, that the world was only the darker for this woman's beauty, and the more lost for the infant that she had borne[5].

The scene was not without a mixture of awe, such as must always invest the spectacle of guilt and shame in a fellow-creature, before society shall have grown corrupt enough to smile, instead of shuddering at it. The witnesses of Hester Prynne's disgrace had not yet passed beyond their simplicity. They were stern enough to look upon her death, had that been the sentence, without a murmur at its severity, but had none of the heartlessness of another social state, which would find only a theme for jest in an exhibition like the present. Even had there been a disposition to turn the matter into ridicule, it must have been repressed and overpowered by the solemn presence of men no less dignified than the governor, and several of his counsellors, a judge, a general, and the ministers of the town, all of whom sat or stood in a balcony of the meeting-house, looking down upon the platform. When such personages could constitute a part of the spectacle, without risking the majesty, or reverence of rank and office, it was safely to be inferred that the infliction of a legal sentence would have an earnest and effectual meaning. Accordingly, the crowd was sombre and grave. The unhappy culprit sustained herself as best a woman might, under the heavy weight of a thousand unrelenting eyes, all fastened upon her, and concentrated at her bosom. It was almost intolerable to be borne. Of an impulsive and passionate nature, she had fortified herself to encounter the stings and venomous stabs of public contumely, wreaking itself in every variety of insult; but there was a quality so much more terrible in the solemn mood of the popular mind, that she longed rather to behold all those rigid countenances contorted with scornful merriment, and herself the object. Had a roar of laughter burst from the multitude—each man, each woman, each little shrill-voiced child, contributing their individual parts—Hester Prynne might have repaid them all with a bitter and disdainful smile. But, under the leaden infliction which it was her doom to endure, she felt, at moments, as if she must needs shriek out with the full power of her lungs, and cast herself from the scaffold down upon the ground, or else go mad at once.

Yet there were intervals when the whole scene, in which she was the most conspicuous object, seemed to vanish from her eyes, or, at least, glimmered indistinctly before them, like a mass of imperfectly shaped and spectral images. Her mind, and especially her memory, was preternaturally active, and kept bringing up other scenes than this roughly hewn street of a little town, on the edge of the western wilderness: other faces than were lowering upon her from beneath the brims of those steeple-crowned hats. Reminiscences, the most trifling and immaterial, passages of infancy and school-days, sports, childish quarrels, and the little domestic traits of her maiden years, came swarming back upon her, intermingled with recollections of whatever was gravest in her subsequent life; one picture precisely as vivid as another; as if all were of similar importance, or all alike a play. Possibly, it was an instinctive device of her spirit to relieve itself by the exhibition of these phantasmagoric forms, from the cruel weight and hardness of the reality.

Be that as it might, the scaffold of the pillory was a point of view that revealed to Hester Prynne the entire track along which she had been treading, since her happy infancy. Standing on that miserable eminence, she saw again her native village, in Old England, and her paternal home: a decayed house of grey stone, with a poverty-stricken aspect, but retaining a half obliterated shield of arms over the portal, in token of antique gentility. She saw her father's face, with its bold brow, and reverend white beard that flowed over the old-fashioned Elizabethan ruff; her mother's, too, with the look of heedful and anxious love which it always wore in her remembrance, and which, even since her death, had so often laid the impediment of a gentle remonstrance in her daughter's pathway. She saw her own face, glowing with girlish beauty, and illuminating all the interior of the dusky mirror in which she had been wont to gaze at it. There she beheld another countenance, of a man well stricken in years, a pale, thin, scholar-like visage, with eyes dim and bleared by the lamp-light that had served them to pore over many ponderous books. Yet those same bleared optics had a strange, penetrating power, when it was their owner's purpose to read the human soul. This figure of tile study and the cloister, as Hester Prynne's womanly fancy failed not to recall, was slightly deformed, with the left shoulder a trifle higher than the right. Next rose before her in memory's picture-gallery, the intricate and narrow thoroughfares, the tall, gray houses, the huge cathedrals, and the public edifices, ancient in date and quaint in architecture, of a Continental city; where new life had awaited her, still in connection with the misshapen scholar: a new life, but feeding itself on time-worn materials, like a tuft of green moss on a crumbling wall. Lastly, in lieu of these shifting scenes, came back the rude market-place of the Puritan settlement, with all the townspeople assembled, and levelling their stern regards at Hester Prynne—yes, at herself—who stood on the scaffold of the pillory, an infant on her arm, and the letter A, in scarlet, fantastically embroidered with gold thread, upon her bosom!

Could it be true? She clutched the child so fiercely to her breast that it sent forth a cry; she turned her eyes downward at the scarlet letter, and even touched it with her finger, to assure herself that the infant and the shame were real. Yes! —these were her realities—all else had vanished!

CHAPTER III THE RECOGNITION

From this intense consciousness of being the object of severe and universal observation, the wearer of the scarlet letter was at length relieved, by discerning, on the outskirts of the crowd, a figure which irresistibly took possession of her thoughts. An Indian in his native garb was standing there; but the red men were not so infrequent visitors of the English settlements that one of them would have attracted any notice from Hester Prynne at such a time; much less would he have excluded all other objects and ideas from her mind. By the Indian's side, and evidently sustaining a companionship with him, stood a white man, clad in a strange disarray of civilized and savage costume.

He was small in stature, with a furrowed visage, which as yet could hardly be termed aged. There was a remarkable intelligence in his features, as of a person who had so cultivated his mental part that it could not fail to mould the physical to itself and become manifest by unmistakable tokens. Although, by a seemingly careless arrangement of his heterogeneous garb, he had endeavoured to conceal or abate the peculiarity, it was sufficiently evident to Hester Prynne that one of this man's shoulders rose higher than the other. Again, at the first instant of perceiving that thin visage, and the slight deformity of the figure, she pressed her infant to her bosom with so convulsive a force that the poor babe uttered another cry of pain. But the mother did not seem to hear it.

At his arrival in the market-place, and some time before she saw him, the stranger had bent his eyes on Hester Prynne. It was carelessly at first, like a man chiefly accustomed to look inward, and to whom external matters are of little value and import, unless they bear relation to something within his mind. Very soon, however, his look became keen and penetrative. A writhing horror twisted itself across his features, like a snake gliding swiftly over them, and making one little pause, with all its wreathed intervolutions in open sight. His face darkened with some powerful emotion, which, nevertheless, he so instantaneously controlled by an effort of his will, that, save at a single moment, its expression might have passed for calmness. After a brief space, the convulsion grew almost imperceptible, and finally subsided into the depths of his nature. When he found the eyes of Hester Prynne fastened on his own, and saw that she appeared to recognize him, he slowly and calmly raised his finger, made a gesture with it in the air, and laid it on his lips.

Then touching the shoulder of a townsman who stood near to him, he addressed him, in a formal and courteous manner.

"I pray you, good Sir," said he, "who is this woman? —and wherefore is she here set up to public shame?"

"You must needs be a stranger in this region, friend," answered the townsman, looking curiously at the questioner and his savage companion, "else you would surely have heard of Mistress Hester Prynne and her evil doings. She hath raised a great scandal, I promise you, in godly Master Dimmesdale's church."

"You say truly," replied the other; "I am a stranger, and have been a wanderer, sorely against my will. I have met with grievous mishaps by sea and land, and have been long held in bonds among the heathen-folk to the southward; and am now brought hither by this Indian to be redeemed out of my captivity. Will it please you, therefore, to tell me of Hester Prynne's—have I her name rightly? —of this woman's offences, and what has brought her to yonder scaffold?"

"Truly, friend; and methinks it must gladden your heart, after your troubles and sojourn in the wilderness," said the townsman, "to find yourself at length in a land where iniquity is searched out and punished in the sight of rulers and people, as here in our godly New England.

Yonder woman, Sir, you must know, was the wife of a certain learned man, English by birth, but who had long dwelt in Amsterdam, whence some good time agone he was minded to cross over and cast in his lot with us of the Massachusetts. To this purpose he sent his wife before him, remaining himself to look after some necessary affairs. Marry, good Sir, in some two years, or less, that the woman has been a dweller here in Boston, no tidings have come of this learned gentleman, Master Prynne; and his young wife, look you, being left to her own misguidance—"

"Ah! —aha! —I conceive you," said the stranger with a bitter smile. "So learned a man as you speak of should have learned this too in his books. And who, by your favour, Sir, may be the father of yonder babe—it is some three or four months old, I should judge—which Mistress Prynne is holding in her arms?"

"Of a truth, friend, that matter remaineth a riddle; and the Daniel[6] who shall expound it is yet a-wanting," answered the townsman. "Madame Hester absolutely refuseth to speak, and the magistrates have laid their heads together in vain. Peradventure the guilty one stands looking on at this sad spectacle, unknown of man, and forgetting that God sees him."

"The learned man," observed the stranger with another smile, "should come himself to look into the mystery."

"It behooves him well if he be still in life," responded the townsman. "Now, good Sir, our Massachusetts magistracy, bethinking themselves that this woman is youthful and fair, and doubtless was strongly tempted to her fall, and that, moreover, as is most likely, her husband may be at the bottom of the sea, they have not been bold to put in force the extremity of our righteous law against her. The penalty thereof is death. But in their great mercy and tenderness of heart they have doomed Mistress Prynne to stand only a space of three hours on the platform of the pillory, and then and thereafter, for the remainder of her natural life to wear a mark of shame upon her bosom."

"A wise sentence," remarked the stranger, gravely, bowing his head. "Thus she will be a living sermon against sin, until the ignominious letter be engraved upon her tombstone. It irks me, nevertheless, that the partner of her iniquity should not, at least, stand on the scaffold by her side. But he will be known—he will be known! —he will be known!"

He bowed courteously to the communicative townsman, and whispering a few words to his Indian attendant, they both made their way through the crowd.

While this passed, Hester Prynne had been standing on her pedestal, still with a fixed gaze towards the stranger—so fixed a gaze that, at moments of intense absorption, all other objects in the visible world seemed to vanish, leaving only him and her. Such an interview, perhaps, would have been more terrible than even to meet him as she now did, with the hot mid-day sun burning down upon her face, and lighting up its shame; with the scarlet token of infamy on her breast; with the sin-born infant in her arms; with a whole people, drawn forth as to a festival, staring at the features that should have been seen only in the quiet gleam of the fireside, in the happy shadow of a home, or beneath a matronly veil at church. Dreadful as it was, she was conscious of a shelter in the presence of these thousand witnesses. It was better to stand thus, with so many betwixt him and her, than to greet him face to face—they two alone. She fled for refuge, as it were, to the public exposure, and dreaded the moment when its protection should be withdrawn from her. Involved in these thoughts, she scarcely heard a voice behind her until it had repeated her name more than once, in a loud and solemn tone, audible to the whole multitude.

"Hearken unto me, Hester Prynne!" said the voice.

It has already been noticed that directly over the platform on which Hester Prynne stood was a kind of balcony, or open gallery, appended to the meeting-house. It was the place whence proclamations were wont to be made, amidst an assemblage of the magistracy, with all the ceremonial that attended such public observances in those days. Here, to witness the scene which we are describing, sat Governor Bellingham[7] himself with four sergeants about his chair, bearing halberds, as a guard of honour. He wore a dark feather in his hat, a border of embroidery on his cloak, and a black velvet tunic beneath—a gentleman advanced in years, with a hard experience written in his wrinkles. He was not ill-fitted to be the head and representative of a community which owed its origin and progress, and its present state of development, not to the impulses of youth, but to the stern and tempered energies of manhood and the sombre sagacity of age; accomplishing so much, precisely because it imagined and hoped so little[8]. The other eminent characters by whom the chief ruler was surrounded were distinguished by a dignity of mien, belonging to a period when the forms of authority were felt to possess the sacredness of Divine institutions. They were, doubtless, good men, just and sage. But, out of the whole human family, it would not have been easy to select the same number of wise and virtuous persons, who should he less capable of sitting in judgment on an erring woman's heart, and disentangling its mesh of good and evil, than the sages of rigid aspect towards whom Hester Prynne now turned her face. She seemed conscious, indeed, that whatever sympathy she might expect lay in the larger and warmer heart of the multitude; for, as she lifted her eyes towards the balcony, the unhappy woman grew pale, and trembled. The voice which had called her attention was that of the reverend and famous John Wilson, the eldest clergyman of Boston, a great scholar, like most of his contemporaries in the profession, and withal a man of kind and genial spirit. This last attribute, however, had been less carefully developed than his intellectual gifts, and was, in truth, rather a matter of shame than self-congratulation with him. There he stood, with a border of grizzled locks beneath his skull-cap, while his grey eyes, accustomed to the shaded light of his study, were winking, like those of Hester's infant, in the unadulterated sunshine. He looked like the darkly engraved portraits which we see prefixed to old volumes of sermons, and had no more right than one of those portraits would have to step forth, as he now did, and meddle with a question of human guilt, passion, and anguish.

"Hester Prynne," said the clergyman, "I have striven with my young brother here, under whose preaching of the Word you have been privileged to sit"—here Mr. Wilson laid his hand on the shoulder of a pale young man beside him—"I have sought, I say, to persuade this godly youth, that he should deal with you, here in the face of Heaven, and before these wise and upright rulers, and in hearing of all the people, as touching the vileness and blackness of your sin. Knowing your natural temper better than I, he could the better judge what arguments to use, whether of tenderness or terror, such as might prevail over your hardness and obstinacy, insomuch that you should no longer hide the name of him who tempted you to this grievous fall. But he opposes to me—with a young man's over-softness, albeit wise beyond his years—that it were wronging the very nature of woman to force her to lay open her heart's secrets in such broad daylight, and in presence of so great a multitude. Truly, as I sought to convince him, the shame lay in the commission of the sin, and not in the showing of it forth. What say you to it, once again, brother Dimmesdale? Must it be thou, or I, that shall deal with this poor sinner's soul?"

There was a murmur among the dignified and reverend occupants of the balcony; and Governor Bellingham gave expression to its purport, speaking in an authoritative voice, although tempered with respect towards the youthful clergyman whom he addressed:

"Good Master Dimmesdale," said he, "the responsibility of this woman's soul lies greatly with you. It behoves you; therefore, to exhort her to repentance and to confession, as a proof and consequence thereof."

The directness of this appeal drew the eyes of the whole crowd upon the Reverend Mr. Dimmesdale—young clergyman, who had come from one of the great English universities, bringing all the learning of the age into our wild forest land. His eloquence and religious fervour had already given the earnest of high eminence in his profession. He was a person of very striking aspect, with a white, lofty, and impending brow; large, brown, melancholy eyes, and a mouth which, unless when he forcibly compressed it, was apt to be tremulous, expressing both nervous sensibility and a vast power of self restraint. Notwithstanding his high native gifts and scholar-like attainments, there was an air about this young minister—an apprehensive, a startled, a half-frightened look—as of a being who felt himself quite astray, and at a loss in the pathway of human existence, and could only be at ease in some seclusion of his own. Therefore, so far as his duties would permit, he trod in the shadowy by-paths, and thus kept himself simple and childlike, coming forth, when occasion was, with a freshness, and fragrance, and dewy purity of thought, which, as many people said, affected them like tile speech of an angel.

Such was the young man whom the Reverend Mr. Wilson and the Governor had introduced so openly to the public notice, bidding him speak, in the hearing of all men, to that mystery of a woman's soul, so sacred even in its pollution. The trying nature of his position drove the blood from his cheek, and made his lips tremulous.

"Speak to the woman, my brother," said Mr. Wilson. "It is of moment to her soul, and, therefore, as the worshipful Governor says, momentous to thine own, ill whose charge hers is. Exhort her to confess the truth!"

The Reverend Mr. Dimmesdale bent his head, silent prayer, as it seemed, and then came forward.

"Hester Prynne," said he, leaning over the balcony and looking down steadfastly into her eyes, "thou hearest what this good man says, and seest the accountability under which I labour. If thou feelest it to be for thy soul's peace, and that thy earthly punishment will thereby be made more effectual to salvation, I charge thee to speak out the name of thy fellow-sinner and fellow-sufferer! Be not silent from any mistaken pity and tenderness for him; for, believe me, Hester, though he were to step down from a high place, and stand there beside thee, on thy pedestal of shame, yet better were it so than to hide a guilty heart through life. What can thy silence do for him, except it tempt him—yea, compel him, as it were—to add hypocrisy to sin? Heaven hath granted thee an open ignominy, that thereby thou mayest work out an open triumph over the evil within thee and the sorrow without. Take heed how thou deniest to him—who, perchance, hath not the courage to grasp it for himself—the bitter, but wholesome, cup that is now presented to thy lips!"

The young pastor's voice was tremulously sweet, rich, deep, and broken. The feeling that it so evidently manifested, rather than the direct purport of the words, caused it to vibrate within all hearts, and brought the listeners into one accord of sympathy. Even the poor baby at Hester's bosom was affected by the same influence, for it directed its hitherto vacant gaze towards Mr. Dimmesdale, and held up its little arms with a half-pleased, half-plaintive murmur. So powerful seemed the minister's appeal that the people could not believe but that Hester Prynne would speak out the guilty name, or else that the guilty one himself in whatever high or lowly place he stood, would be drawn forth by an inward and inevitable necessity, and compelled to ascend the scaffold. Hester shook her head.

"Woman, transgress not beyond the limits of Heaven's mercy!" cried the Reverend Mr. Wilson, more harshly than before. "That little babe hath been gifted with a voice, to second[9] and confirm the counsel which thou hast heard. Speak out the name! That, and thy repentance, may avail to take the scarlet letter off thy breast."

"Never," replied Hester Prynne, looking, not at Mr. Wilson, but into the deep and troubled eyes of the younger clergyman. "It is too deeply branded. Ye cannot take it off. And would that I might endure his agony as well as mine!"

"Speak, woman!" said another voice, coldly and sternly, proceeding from the crowd about the scaffold, "Speak; and give your child a father!"

"I will not speak!" answered Hester, turning pale as death, but responding to this voice, which she too surely recognised. "And my child must seek a heavenly father; she shall never know an earthly one!"

"She will not speak!" murmured Mr. Dimmesdale, who, leaning over the balcony, with his hand upon his heart, had awaited the result of his appeal. He now drew back with a long respiration. "Wondrous strength arid generosity of a woman's heart! She will not speak!"

Discerning the impracticable state of the poor culprit's mind, the elder clergyman, who had carefully prepared himself for the occasion, addressed to the multitude a discourse on sin, in all its branches, but with continual reference to the ignominious letter. So forcibly did he dwell upon this symbol, for the hour or more during which is periods were rolling over the people's heads, that it assumed new terrors in their imagination, and seemed to derive its scarlet hue from the flames of the infernal pit. Hester Prynne, meanwhile, kept her place upon the pedestal of shame, with glazed eyes, and an air of weary indifference. She had borne that morning all that nature could endure; and as her temperament was not of the order that escapes from too intense suffering by a swoon, her spirit could only shelter itself beneath a stony crust of insensibility, while the faculties of animal life remained entire. In this state, the voice of the preacher thundered remorselessly, but unavailingly, upon her ears. The infant, during the latter portion of her ordeal, pierced the air with its wailings and screams; she strove to hush it mechanically, but seemed scarcely to sympathise with its trouble. With the same hard demeanour, she was led back to prison, and vanished from the public gaze within its iron-clamped portal. It was whispered by those who peered after her that the scarlet letter threw a lurid gleam along the dark passage-way of the interior.

CHAPTER XII THE MINISTER's VIGIL

Walking in the shadow of a dream, as it were, and perhaps actually under the influence of a species of somnambulism, Mr. Dimmesdale reached the spot where, now so long since, Hester Prynne had lived through her first hours of public ignominy. The same platform or scaffold, black and weather-stained with the storm or sunshine of seven long years, and foot-worn, too, with the tread of many culprits who had since ascended it, remained standing beneath the balcony of the meeting-house. The minister went up the steps.

It was an obscure night in early May. An unwearied pall of cloud muffled the whole expanse of sky from zenith to horizon. If the same multitude which had stood as eye-witnesses while Hester Prynne sustained her punishment could now have been summoned forth, they would have discerned no face above the platform nor hardly the outline of a human shape, in the dark grey of the midnight. But the town was all asleep. There was no peril of discovery. The minister might stand there, if it so pleased him, until morning should redden in the east, without other risk than that the dank and chill night air would creep into his frame, and stiffen his joints with rheumatism, and clog his throat with catarrh and cough; thereby defrauding the expectant audience of to-morrow's prayer and sermon. No eye could see him, save that ever-wakeful one which had seen him in his closet, wielding the bloody scourge. Why, then, had he come hither? Was it but the mockery of penitence? A mockery, indeed, but in which his soul trifled with itself! A mockery at which angels blushed and wept, while fiends rejoiced with jeering laughter! He had been driven hither by the impulse of that Remorse which dogged him everywhere, and whose own sister and closely linked companion was that Cowardice which invariably drew him back, with her tremulous gripe, just when the other impulse had hurried him to the verge of a disclosure. Poor, miserable man! what right had infirmity like his to burden itself with crime? Crime is for the iron-nerved, who have their choice either to endure it, or, if it press too hard, to exert their fierce and savage strength for a good purpose, and fling it off at once! This feeble and most sensitive of spirits could do neither, yet continually did one thing or another, which intertwined, in the same inextricable knot, the agony of heaven-defying guilt and vain repentance.

And thus, while standing on the scaffold, in this vain show of expiation, Mr. Dimmesdale was overcome with a great horror of mind, as if the universe were gazing at a scarlet token on his naked breast, right over his heart. On that spot, in very truth, there was, and there had long been, the gnawing and poisonous tooth of bodily pain. Without any effort of his will, or power to restrain himself, he shrieked aloud: an outcry that went pealing through the night, and was beaten back from one house to another, and reverberated from the hills in the background; as if a company of devils, detecting so much misery and terror in it, had made a plaything of the sound, and were bandying it to and fro.

"It is done!" muttered the minister, covering his face with his hands. "The whole town will awake and hurry forth, and find me here!"

But it was not so. The shriek had perhaps sounded with a far greater power, to his own startled ears, than it actually possessed. The town did not awake; or, if it did, the drowsy slumberers mistook the cry either for something frightful in a dream, or for the noise of witches, whose voices, at that period, were often heard to pass over the settlements or lonely cottages, as they rode with Satan through the air. The clergyman, therefore, hearing no symptoms of disturbance, uncovered his eyes and looked about him. At one of the chamber-windows of Governor Bellingham's mansion, which stood at some distance, on the line of another street, he beheld the appearance of the old magistrate himself with a lamp in his hand a white night-cap on his head, and a long white gown enveloping his figure. He looked like a ghost evoked unseasonably from the grave. The cry had evidently startled him. At another window of the same house, moreover appeared old Mistress Hibbins, the Governor's sister, also with a lamp, which even thus far off revealed the expression of her sour and discontented face. She thrust forth her head from the lattice, and looked anxiously upward Beyond the shadow of a doubt, this venerable witch-lady had heard Mr. Dimmesdale's outcry, and interpreted it, with its multitudinous echoes and reverberations, as the clamour of the fiends and night-hags, with whom she was well known to make excursions in the forest.

Detecting the gleam of Governor Bellingham's lamp, the old lady quickly extinguished her own, and vanished. Possibly, she went up among the clouds. The minister saw nothing further of her motions. The magistrate, after a wary observation of the darkness—into which, nevertheless, he could see but little further than he might into a mill-stone—retired from the window.

The minister grew comparatively calm. His eyes, however, were soon greeted by a little glimmering light, which, at first a long way off was approaching up the street. It threw a gleam of recognition, on here a post, and there a garden fence, and here a latticed window-pane, and there a pump, with its full trough of water, and here again an arched door of oak, with an iron knocker, and a rough log for the door-step. The Reverend Mr. Dimmesdale noted all these minute particulars, even while firmly convinced that the doom of his existence was stealing onward, in the footsteps which he now heard; and that the gleam of the lantern would fall upon him in a few moments more, and reveal his long-hidden secret. As the light drew nearer, be beheld, within its illuminated circle, his brother clergyman—or, to speak more accurately, his professional father, as well as highly valued friend—the Reverend Mr. Wilson, who, as Mr. Dimmesdale now conjectured, had been praying at the bedside of some dying man. And so he had. The good old minister came freshly from the death-chamber of Governor Winthrop[10], who had passed from earth to heaven within that very hour. And now surrounded, like the saint-like personage of olden times, with a radiant halo, that glorified him amid this gloomy night of sin—as if the departed Governor had left him an inheritance of his glory, or as if he had caught upon himself the distant shine of the celestial city, while looking thitherward to see the triumphant pilgrim pass within its gates—now, in short, good Father Wilson was moving homeward, aiding his footsteps with a lighted lantern! The glimmer of this luminary suggested the above conceits to Mr. Dimmesdale, who smiled—nay, almost laughed at them—and then wondered if he was going mad.

As the Reverend Mr. Wilson passed beside the scaffold, closely muffling his Geneva cloak about him with one arm, and holding the lantern before his breast with the other, the minister could hardly restrain himself from speaking—

"A good evening to you, venerable Father Wilson. Come up hither, I pray you, and pass a pleasant hour with me!"

Good Heavens! Had Mr. Dimmesdale actually spoken? For one instant he believed that these words had passed his lips. But they were uttered only within his imagination. The venerable Father Wilson continued to step slowly onward, looking carefully at the muddy pathway before his feet, and never once turning his head towards the guilty platform. When the light of the glimmering lantern had faded quite away, the minister discovered, by the faintness which came over him, that the last few moments had been a crisis of terrible anxiety, although his mind had made an involuntary effort to relieve itself by a kind of lurid playfulness.

Shortly afterwards, the like grisly sense of the humorous again stole in among the solemn phantoms of his thought. He felt his limbs growing stiff with the unaccustomed chilliness of the night, and doubted whether he should be able to descend the steps of the scaffold. Morning would break and find him there. The neighbourhood would begin to rouse itself. The earliest riser, coming forth in the dim twilight, would perceive a vaguely-defined figure aloft on the place of shame; and half-crazed betwixt alarm and curiosity, would go knocking from door to door, summoning all the people to behold the ghost—as he needs must think it—of some defunct transgressor. A dusky tumult would flap its wings from one house to another. Then—the morning light still waxing stronger—old patriarchs would rise up in great haste, each in his flannel gown, and matronly dames, without pausing to put off their night-gear. The whole tribe of decorous personages, who had never heretofore been seen with a single hair of their heads awry, would start into public view with the disorder of a nightmare in their aspects. Old Governor Bellingham would come grimly forth, with his King James' ruff fastened askew, and Mistress Hibbins, with some twigs of the forest clinging to her skirts, and looking sourer than ever, as having hardly got a wink of sleep after her night ride; and good Father Wilson too, after spending half the night at a death-bed, and liking ill to be disturbed, thus early, out of his dreams about the glorified saints. Hither, likewise, would come the elders and deacons of Mr. Dimmesdale's church, and the young virgins who so idolized their minister, and had made a shrine for him in their white bosoms, which now, by-the-bye, in their hurry and confusion, they would scantly have given themselves time to cover with their kerchiefs. All people, in a word, would come stumbling over their thresholds, and turning up their amazed and horror-stricken visages around the scaffold. Whom would they discern there, with the red eastern light upon his brow? Whom, but the Reverend Arthur Dimmesdale, half-frozen to death, overwhelmed with shame, and standing where Hester Prynne had stood!

Carried away by the grotesque horror of this picture, the minister, unawares, and to his own infinite alarm, burst into a great peal of laughter. It was immediately responded to by a light, airy, childish laugh, in which, with a thrill of the heart—but he knew not whether of exquisite pain, or pleasure as acute—he recognised the tones of little Pearl.

"Pearl! Little Pearl!" cried he, after a moment's pause; then, suppressing his voice—"Hester! Hester Prynne! Are you there?"

"Yes; it is Hester Prynne!" she replied, in a tone of surprise; and the minister heard her footsteps approaching from the side-walk, along which she had been passing. "It is I, and my little Pearl."

"Whence come you, Hester?" asked the minister. "What sent you hither?"

"I have been watching at a death-bed," answered Hester Prynne "at Governor Winthrop's death-bed, and have taken his measure for a robe, and am now going homeward to my dwelling."

"Come up hither, Hester, thou and Little Pearl," said the Reverend Mr. Dimmesdale. "Ye have both been here before, but I was not with you. Come up hither once again, and we will stand all three together."

She silently ascended the steps, and stood on the platform, holding little Pearl by the hand. The minister felt for the child's other hand, and took it. The moment that he did so, there came what seemed a tumultuous rush of new life, other life than his own pouring like a torrent into his heart, and hurrying through all his veins, as if the mother and the child were communicating their vital warmth to his half-torpid system. The three formed an electric chain.

"Minister!" whispered little Pearl.

"What wouldst thou say, child?" asked Mr. Dimmesdale.

"Wilt thou stand here with mother and me, tomorrow noontide?" inquired Pearl.

"Nay; not so, my little Pearl," answered the minister; for, with the new energy of the moment, all the dread of public exposure, that had so long been the anguish of his life, had returned upon him; and he was already trembling at the conjunction in which—with a strange joy, nevertheless—he now found himself—"Not so, my child. I shall, indeed, stand with thy mother and thee one other day, but not to-morrow."

Pearl laughed, and attempted to pull away her hand. But the minister held it fast.

"A moment longer, my child!" said he.

"But wilt thou promise," asked Pearl, "to take my hand, and mother's hand, to-morrow noontide?"

"Not then, Pearl," said the minister; "but another time."

"And what other time?" persisted the child.

"At the great judgment day," whispered the minister; and, strangely enough, the sense that he was a professional teacher of the truth impelled him to answer the child so. "Then, and there, before the judgment-seat, thy mother, and thou, and I must stand together. But the daylight of this world shall not see our meeting!"

Pearl laughed again.

But before Mr. Dimmesdale had done speaking, a light gleamed far and wide over all the muffled sky. It was doubtless caused by one of those meteors, which the night-watcher may so often observe burning out to waste, in the vacant regions of the atmosphere. So powerful was its radiance, that it thoroughly illuminated the dense medium of cloud betwixt the sky and earth. The great vault brightened, like the dome of an immense lamp. It showed the familiar scene of the street with the distinctness of mid-day, but also with the awfulness that is always imparted to familiar objects by an unaccustomed light. The wooden houses, with their jutting storeys and quaint gable-peaks; the doorsteps and thresholds with the early grass springing up about them; the garden-plots, black with freshly-turned earth; the wheel-track, little worn, and even in the market-place margined with green on either side—all were visible, but with a singularity of aspect that seemed to give another moral interpretation to the things of this world than they had ever borne before. And there stood the minister, with his hand over his heart; and Hester Prynne, with the embroidered letter glimmering on her bosom; and little Pearl, herself a symbol, and the connecting link between those two. They stood in the noon of that strange and solemn splendour, as if it were the light that is to reveal all secrets, and the daybreak that shall unite all who belong to one another.

There was witchcraft in little Pearl's eyes; and her face, as she glanced upward at the minister, wore that naughty smile which made its expression frequently so elvish. She withdrew her hand from Mr. Dimmesdale's, and pointed across the street. But he clasped both his hands over his breast, and cast his eyes towards the zenith.

Nothing was more common, in those days, than to interpret all meteoric appearances, and other natural phenomena that occured with less regularity than the rise and set of sun and moon, as so many revelations from a supernatural source. Thus, a blazing spear, a sword of flame, a bow, or a sheaf of arrows seen in the midnight sky, prefigured Indian warfare. Pestilence was known to have been foreboded by a shower of crimson light. We doubt whether any marked event, for good or evil, ever befell New England, from its settlement down to revolutionary times, of which the inhabitants had not been previously warned by some spectacle of its nature. Not seldom, it had been seen by multitudes. Oftener, however, its credibility rested on the faith of some lonely eye-witness, who beheld the wonder through the coloured, magnifying, and distorted medium of his imagination, and shaped it more distinctly in his after-thought. It was, indeed, a majestic idea that the destiny of nations should be revealed, in these awful hieroglyphics, on the cope of heaven. A scroll so wide might not be deemed too expensive for Providence to write a people's doom upon. The belief was a favourite one with our forefathers, as betokening that their infant commonwealth was under a celestial guardianship of peculiar intimacy and strictness. But what shall we say, when an individual discovers a revelation addressed to himself alone, on the same vast sheet of record. In such a case, it could only be the symptom of a highly disordered mental state, when a man, rendered morbidly self-contemplative by long, intense, and secret pain, had extended his egotism over the whole expanse of nature, until the firmament itself should appear no more than a fitting page for his soul's history and fate.

We impute it, therefore, solely to the disease in his own eye and heart that the minister, looking upward to the zenith, beheld there the appearance of an immense letter—the letter A—marked out in lines of dull red light. Not but the meteor may have shown itself at that point, burning duskily through a veil of cloud, but with no such shape as his guilty imagination gave it, or, at least, with so little definiteness, that another's guilt might have seen another symbol in it.

There was a singular circumstance that characterised Mr. Dimmesdale's psychological state at this moment. All the time that he gazed upward to the zenith, he was, nevertheless, perfectly aware that little Pearl was pointing her finger towards old Roger Chillingworth, who stood at no great distance from the scaffold. The minister appeared to see him, with the same glance that discerned the miraculous letter. To his feature as to all other objects, the meteoric light imparted a new expression; or it might well be that the physician was not careful then, as at all other times, to hide the malevolence with which he looked upon his victim. Certainly, if the meteor kindled up the sky, and disclosed the earth, with an awfulness that admonished Hester Prynne and the clergyman of the day of judgment, then might Roger Chillingworth have passed with them for the arch-fiend, standing there with a smile and scowl, to claim his own. So vivid was the expression, or so intense the minister's perception of it, that it seemed still to remain painted on the darkness after the meteor had vanished, with an effect as if the street and all things else were at once annihilated.

"Who is that man, Hester?" gasped Mr. Dimmesdale, overcome with terror. "I shiver at him! Dost thou know the man? I hate him, Hester!"

She remembered her oath, and was silent.

"I tell thee, my soul shivers at him!" muttered the minister again. "Who is he? Who is he? Canst thou do nothing for me? I have a nameless horror of the man!"

"Minister," said little Pearl, "I can tell thee who he is!"

"Quickly, then, child!" said the minister, bending his ear close to her lips. "Quickly, and as low as thou canst whisper."

Pearl mumbled something into his ear that sounded, indeed, like human language, but was only such gibberish as children may be heard amusing themselves with by the hour together. At all events, if it involved any secret information in regard to old Roger Chillingworth, it was in a tongue unknown to the erudite clergyman, and did but increase the bewilderment of his mind. The elvish child then laughed aloud.

"Dost thou mock me now?" said the minister.

"Thou wast not bold! —thou wast not true!" answered the child. "Thou wouldst not promise to take my hand, and mother's hand, to-morrow noon-tide!"

"Worthy sir," answered the physician, who had now advanced to the foot of the platform—"Pious Master Dimmesdale! can this be you? Well, well, indeed! We men of study, whose heads are in our books, have need to be straitly looked after! We dream in our waking moments, and walk in our sleep. Come, good sir, and my dear friend, I pray you let me lead you home!"

"How knewest thou that I was here?" asked the minister, fearfully.

"Verily, and in good faith," answered Roger Chillingworth, "I knew nothing of the matter. I had spent the better part of the night at the bedside of the worshipful Governor Winthrop, doing what my poor skill might to give him ease. He, going home to a better world, I, likewise, was on my way homeward, when this light shone out. Come with me, I beseech you, Reverend sir, else you will be poorly able to do Sabbath duty to-morrow. Aha! see now how they trouble the brain—these books! —these books! You should study less, good sir, and take a little pastime, or these night whimsies will grow upon you."

"I will go home with you," said Mr. Dimmesdale.

With a chill despondency, like one awakening, all nerveless, from an ugly dream, he yielded himself to the physician, and was led away.

The next day, however, being the Sabbath, he preached a discourse which was held to be the richest and most powerful, and the most replete with heavenly influences, that had ever proceeded from his lips. Souls, it is said, more souls than one, were brought to the truth by the efficacy of that sermon, and vowed within themselves to cherish a holy gratitude towards Mr. Dimmesdale throughout the long hereafter. But as he came down the pulpit steps, the grey-bearded sexton met him, holding up a black glove, which the minister recognised as his own.

"It was found," said the Sexton, "this morning on the scaffold where evil-doers are set up to public shame. Satan dropped it there, I take it, intending a scurrilous jest against your reverence. But, indeed, he was blind and foolish, as he ever and always is. A pure hand needs no glove to cover it!"

"Thank you, my good friend," said the minister, gravely, but startled at heart; for so confused was his remembrance, that he had almost brought himself to look at the events of the past night as visionary. "Yes, it seems to be my glove, indeed!"

"And, since Satan saw fit to steal it, your reverence must needs handle him without gloves henceforward," remarked the old sexton, grimly smiling. "But did your reverence hear of the portent that was seen last night? a great red letter in the sky—the letter A, which we interpret to stand for Angel. For, as our good Governor Winthrop was made an angel this past night, it was doubtless held fit that there should be some notice thereof!"

"No," answered the minister; "I had not heard of it."

CHAPTER XXIII THE REVELATION

The eloquent voice, on which the souls of the listening audience had been borne aloft as on the swelling waves of the sea, at length came to a pause. There was a momentary silence, profound as what should follow the utterance of oracles. Then ensued a murmur and half-hushed tumult, as if the auditors, released from the high spell that had transported them into the region of another's mind, were returning into themselves, with all their awe and wonder still heavy on them. In a moment more the crowd began to gush forth from the doors of the church. Now that there was an end, they needed more breath, more fit to support the gross and earthly life into which they relapsed, than that atmosphere which the preacher had converted into words of flame, and had burdened with the rich fragrance of his thought.

In the open air their rapture broke into speech. The street and the market-place absolutely babbled, from side to side, with applauses of the minister. His hearers could not rest until they had told one another of what each knew better than he could tell or hear. According to their united testimony, never had man spoken in so wise, so high, and so holy a spirit, as he that spake this day; nor had inspiration ever breathed through mortal lips more evidently than it did through his. Its influence could be seen, as it were, descending upon him, and possessing him, and continually lifting him out of the written discourse that lay before him, and filling him with ideas that must have been as marvellous to himself as to his audience. His subject, it appeared, had been the relation between the Deity and the communities of mankind, with a special reference to the New England which they were here planting in the wilderness. And, as he drew towards the close, a spirit as of prophecy had come upon him, constraining him to its purpose as mightily as the old prophets of Israel were constrained, only with this difference, that, whereas the Jewish seers had denounced judgments and ruin on their country, it was his mission to foretell a high and glorious destiny for the newly gathered people of the Lord. But, throughout it all, and through the whole discourse, there had been a certain deep, sad undertone of pathos, which could not be interpreted otherwise than as the natural regret of one soon to pass away. Yes; their minister whom they so loved—and who so loved them all, that he could not depart heavenward without a sigh—had the foreboding of untimely death upon him, and would soon leave them in their tears. This idea of his transitory stay on earth gave the last emphasis to the effect which the preacher had produced; it was if an angel, in his passage to the skies, had shaken his bright wings over the people for an instant—at once a shadow and a splendour—and had shed down a shower of golden truths upon them.

Thus, there had come to the Reverend Mr. Dimmesdale—as to most men, in their various spheres, though seldom recognised until they see it far behind them—an epoch of life more brilliant and full of triumph than any previous one, or than any which could hereafter be. He stood, at this moment, on the very proudest eminence of superiority, to which the gifts or intellect, rich lore, prevailing eloquence, and a reputation of whitest sanctity, could exalt a clergyman in New England's earliest days, when the professional character was of itself a lofty pedestal. Such was the position which the minister occupied, as he bowed his head forward on the cushions of the pulpit at the close of his Election Sermon. Meanwhile Hester Prynne was standing beside the scaffold of the pillory, with the scarlet letter still burning on her breast!

Now was heard again the clamour of the music, and the measured tramp of the military escort issuing from the church door. The procession was to be marshalled thence to the town hall, where a solemn banquet would complete the ceremonies of the day.

Once more, therefore, the train of venerable and majestic fathers were seen moving through a broad pathway of the people, who drew back reverently, on either side, as the Governor and magistrates, the old and wise men, the holy ministers, and all that were eminent and renowned, advanced into the midst of them. When they were fairly in the marketplace, their presence was greeted by a shout. This—though doubtless it might acquire additional force and volume from the child-like loyalty which the age awarded to its rulers—was felt to be an irrepressible outburst of enthusiasm kindled in the auditors by that high strain of eloquence which was yet reverberating in their ears. Each felt the impulse in himself, and in the same breath, caught it from his neighbour. Within the church, it had hardly been kept down; beneath the sky it pealed upward to the zenith. There were human beings enough, and enough of highly wrought and symphonious feeling to produce that more impressive sound than the organ tones of the blast, or the thunder, or the roar of the sea; even that mighty swell of many voices, blended into one great voice by the universal impulse which makes likewise one vast heart out of the many. Never, from the soil of New England had gone up such a shout! Never, on New England soil had stood the man so honoured by his mortal brethren as the preacher!

How fared it with him, then? Were there not the brilliant particles of a halo in the air about his head? So etherealised by spirit as he was, and so apotheosised by worshipping admirers, did his footsteps, in the procession, really tread upon the dust of earth?

As the ranks of military men and civil fathers moved onward, all eyes were turned towards the point where the minister was seen to approach among them. The shout died into a murmur, as one portion of the crowd after another obtained a glimpse of him. How feeble and pale he looked, amid all his triumph! The energy—or say, rather, the inspiration which had held him up, until he should have delivered the sacred message that had brought its own strength along with it from heaven—was withdrawn, now that it had so faithfully performed its office. The glow, which they had just before beheld burning on his cheek, was extinguished, like a flame that sinks down hopelessly among the late decaying embers. It seemed hardly the face of a man alive, with such a death-like hue: it was hardly a man with life in him, that tottered on his path so nervously, yet tottered, and did not fall!

One of his clerical brethren—it was the venerable John Wilson—observing the state in which Mr. Dimmesdale was left by the retiring wave of intellect and sensibility, stepped forward hastily to offer his support. The minister tremulously, but decidedly, repelled the old man's arm. He still walked onward, if that movement could be so described, which rather resembled the wavering effort of an infant, with its mother's arms in view, outstretched to tempt him forward. And now, almost imperceptible as were the latter steps of his progress, he had come opposite the well-remembered and weather-darkened scaffold, where, long since, with all that dreary lapse of time between, Hester Prynne had encountered the world's ignominious stare. There stood Hester, holding little Pearl by the hand! And there was the scarlet letter on her breast! The minister here made a pause; although the music still played the stately and rejoicing march to which the procession moved. It summoned him onward—inward to the festival! —but here he made a pause.

Bellingham, for the last few moments, had kept an anxious eye upon him. He now left his own place in the procession, and advanced to give assistance judging, from Mr. Dimmesdale's aspect that he must otherwise inevitably fall. But there was something in the latter's expression that warned back the magistrate, although a man not readily obeying the vague intimations that pass from one spirit to another. The crowd, meanwhile, looked on with awe and wonder. This earthly faintness, was, in their view, only another phase of the minister's celestial strength; nor would it have seemed a miracle too high to be wrought for one so holy, had he ascended before their eyes, waxing dimmer and brighter, and fading at last into the light of heaven!

He turned towards the scaffold, and stretched forth his arms.

"Hester," said he, "come hither! Come, my little Pearl!"

It was a ghastly look with which he regarded them; but there was something at once tender and strangely triumphant in it. The child, with the bird-like motion, which was one of her characteristics, flew to him, and clasped her arms about his knees. Hester Prynne—slowly, as if impelled by inevitable fate, and against her strongest will—likewise drew near, but paused before she reached him. At this instant old Roger Chillingworth thrust himself through the crowd—or, perhaps, so dark, disturbed, and evil was his look, he rose up out of some nether region—to snatch back his victim from what he sought to do! Be that as it might, the old man rushed forward, and caught the minister by the arm.

"Madman, hold! what is your purpose?" whispered he. "Wave back that woman! Cast off this child! All shall be well! Do not blacken your fame, and perish in dishonour! I can yet save you! Would you bring infamy on your sacred profession?"

"Ha, tempter! Methinks thou art too late!" answered the minister, encountering his eye, fearfully, but firmly. "Thy power is not what it was! With God's help, I shall escape thee now!"

He again extended his hand to the woman of the scarlet letter.

"Hester Prynne," cried he, with a piercing earnestness, "in the name of Him, so terrible and so merciful, who gives me grace, at this last moment, to do what—for my own heavy sin and miserable agony—I withheld myself from doing seven years ago, come hither now, and twine thy strength about me! Thy strength, Hester; but let it be guided by the will which God hath granted me! This wretched and wronged old man is opposing it with all his might! —with all his own might, and the fiend's! Come, Hester—come! Support me up yonder scaffold."

The crowd was in a tumult. The men of rank and dignity, who stood more immediately around the clergyman, were so taken by surprise, and so perplexed as to the purport of what they saw—unable to receive the explanation which most readily presented itself, or to imagine any other—that they remained silent and inactive spectators of the judgement which Providence seemed about to work. They beheld the minister, leaning on Hester's shoulder, and supported by her arm around him, approach the scaffold, and ascend its steps; while still the little hand of the sin-born child was clasped in his. Old Roger Chillingworth followed, as one intimately connected with the drama of guilt and sorrow in which they had all been actors, and well entitled, therefore to be present at its closing scene.

"Hadst thou sought the whole earth over," said he looking darkly at the clergyman, "there was no one place so secret—no high place nor lowly place, where thou couldst have escaped me—save on this very scaffold!"

"Thanks be to Him who hath led me hither!" answered the minister.

Yet he trembled, and turned to Hester, with an expression of doubt and anxiety in his eyes, not the less evidently betrayed, that there was a feeble smile upon his lips.

"Is not this better," murmured he, "than what we dreamed of in the forest?"

"I know not! I know not!" she hurriedly replied "Better? Yea; so we may both die, and little Pearl die with us!"

"For thee and Pearl, be it as God shall order," said the minister; "and God is merciful! Let me now do the will which He hath made plain before my sight. For, Hester, I am a dying man. So let me make haste to take my shame upon me!"

Partly supported by Hester Prynne, and holding one hand of little Pearl's, the Reverend Mr. Dimmesdale turned to the dignified and venerable rulers; to the holy ministers, who were his brethren; to the people, whose great heart was thoroughly appalled yet overflowing with tearful sympathy, as knowing that some deep life-matter—which, if full of sin, was full of anguish and repentance likewise—was now to be laid open to them. The sun, but little past its meridian, shone down upon the clergyman, and gave a distinctness to his figure, as he stood out from all the earth, to put in his plea of guilty at the bar of Eternal Justice.

"People of New England!" cried he, with a voice that rose over them, high, solemn, and majestic—yet had always a tremor through it, and sometimes a shriek, struggling up out of a fathomless depth of remorse and woe—"ye, that have loved me! —ye, that have deemed me holy! —behold me here, the one sinner of the world! At last—at last! —I stand upon the spot where, seven years since, I should have stood, here, with this woman, whose arm, more than the little strength wherewith I have crept hitherward, sustains me at this dreadful moment, from grovelling down upon my face! Lo, the scarlet letter which Hester wears! Ye have all shuddered at it! Wherever her walk hath been—wherever, so miserably burdened, she may have hoped to find repose—it hath cast a lurid gleam of awe and horrible repugnance round about her. But there stood one in the midst of you, at whose brand of sin and infamy ye have not shuddered!"

It seemed, at this point, as if the minister must leave the remainder of his secret undisclosed. But he fought back the bodily weakness—and, still more, the faintness of heart—that was striving for the mastery with him. He threw off all assistance, and stepped passionately forward a pace before the woman and the child.

"It was on him!" he continued, with a kind of fierceness; so determined was he to speak out tile whole. "God's eye beheld it! The angels were for ever pointing at it! (The Devil knew it well, and fretted it continually with the touch of his burning finger!) But he hid it cunningly from men, and walked among you with the mien of a spirit, mournful, because so pure in a sinful world! —and sad, because he missed his heavenly kindred! Now, at the death-hour, he stands up before you! He bids you look again at Hester's scarlet letter! He tells you, that, with all its mysterious horror, it is but the shadow of what he bears on his own breast, and that even this, his own red stigma, is no more than the type of what has seared his inmost heart! Stand any here that question God's judgment on a sinner[11]! Behold! Behold, a dreadful witness of it!"

With a convulsive motion, he tore away the ministerial band from before his breast. It was revealed! But it were irreverent to describe that revelation. For an instant, the gaze of the horror-stricken multitude was concentrated on the ghastly miracle; while the minister stood, with a flush of triumph in his face, as one who, in the crisis of acutest pain, had won a victory. Then, down he sank upon the scaffold! Hester partly raised him, and supported his head against her bosom. Old Roger Chillingworth knelt down beside him, with a blank, dull countenance, out of which the life seemed to have departed.

"Thou hast escaped me!" he repeated more than once. "Thou hast escaped me!"

"May God forgive thee!" said the minister. "Thou, too, hast deeply sinned!"

He withdrew his dying eyes from the old man, and fixed them on the woman and the child. "My little Pearl," said he, feebly and there was a sweet and gentle smile over his face, as of a spirit sinking into deep repose; nay, now that the burden was removed, it seemed almost as if he would be sportive with the child—"dear little Pearl, wilt thou kiss me now? Thou wouldst not, yonder, in the forest! But now thou wilt?"

Pearl kissed his lips. A spell was broken. The great scene of grief, in which the wild infant bore a part had developed all her sympathies; and as her tears fell upon her father's cheek, they were the pledge that she would grow up amid human joy and sorrow, nor forever do battle with the world, but be a woman in it. Towards her mother, too, Pearl's errand as a messenger of anguish was fulfilled.

"Hester," said the clergyman, "farewell!"

"Shall we not meet again?" whispered she, bending her face down close to his. "Shall we not spend our immortal life together? Surely, surely, we have ransomed one another, with all this woe! Thou lookest far into eternity, with those bright dying eyes! Then tell me what thou seest!"

"Hush, Hester—hush!" said he, with tremulous solemnity. "The law we broke! —the sin here awfully revealed! —let these alone be in thy thoughts! I fear! I fear! It may be, that, when we forgot our God—when we violated our reverence each for the other's soul—it was thenceforth vain to hope that we could meet hereafter, in an everlasting and pure reunion. God knows; and He is merciful! He hath proved his mercy, most of all, in my afflictions. By giving me this burning torture to bear upon my breast! By sending yonder dark and terrible old man, to keep the torture always at red-heat! By bringing me hither, to die this death of triumphant ignominy before the people! Had either of these agonies been wanting[12], I had been lost for ever! Praised be His name! His will be done! Farewell!"

That final word came forth with the minister's expiring breath. The multitude, silent till then, broke out in a strange, deep voice of awe and wonder, which could not as yet find utterance, save in this murmur that rolled so heavily after the departed spirit.

三、人物解析

《红字》是霍桑的第一部长篇小说，也是他的代表作。小说取材于1642—1649年间发生在北美殖民地新英格兰地区波士顿的故事。英国妇女海斯特·白兰只身来到波士顿，与年轻牧师亚瑟·丁梅斯迪尔产生恋情，并有了爱情的结晶——女儿珠儿。按照清教的法规，触犯通奸罪要被处死。为了教育白兰和警示众人，白兰被罚在绞刑台上站三个小时，并终身佩戴一个耻辱标志“A(英文单词Adultery的第一个字母)”。白兰罚站之时她的丈夫罗杰·齐灵渥斯医生也来到波士顿。为了查清谁是珠儿的父亲，齐灵渥斯使用各种计谋，分别与白兰和丁梅斯迪尔谈话，并跟踪他们。在知晓内情之后，齐灵渥斯并未将实情公布于众，而是继续试探和折磨白兰和丁梅斯迪尔。最终，丁梅斯迪尔忍受不了来自外部和内部的双重折磨，在绞刑台上当众宣布自己是珠儿的父亲，随后死在白兰的怀里。不久齐灵渥斯离开人世，临死前他将自己的丰厚财产留给珠儿。后来珠儿嫁到欧洲，白兰则一人住在波士顿海边，直至终老。

中外学者从多种视角解读《红字》：既分析单个人物形象白兰，也分析四个主要人物形象名字的寓意；既分析小说的结构，又剖析小说的意象和象征意蕴；既从女权主义视角，又从历史和传记视角加以剖析。但是，从四个主要人物之间的关系来探讨小说的主题思想也是个不错的选择。

小说的第2章和第3章、第12章、第23章让四个主要人物全部在场。因此，以这几章为“支点”剖析他们之间的关系对我们了解小说的主题思想十分有意义。

第一，分析白兰和齐灵渥斯的关系。他们在法律上是夫妻关系，但没有感情基础。白兰根本不爱齐灵渥斯，但齐灵渥斯似乎爱白兰。齐灵渥斯人到中年，而白兰年轻、靓丽、善良。他们的结合本身是个错误。而且齐灵渥斯为人冷漠而伪善。他似乎兼顾了“情”与“法”(当时的清教思想就是法律)。白兰的选择则更为复杂。当白兰选择“情”时同时听说丈夫葬身大海，或者死于印第安人之手，她认为自己这样做并无过错。他们夫妻关系的破裂究竟是谁之过？二人都有错，也都没有错。

第二，分析齐灵渥斯和丁梅斯迪尔的关系。他们可称为“同事”，共同肩负将波士顿建设成“山巅之城”之重任。他们俩都是波士顿民众仰慕和尊重的对象：牧师负责净化人们的心灵，医生负责牧师的身体健康。结果呢？他们各自走向“邪路”，触犯戒律。一个死于被折磨，一个死于孤独。但是，不知是相互的默契还是一方对另一方的感染，抑或自我道德和良心的发现，抑或清教力量的强大，他们又先后走向了“善”——丁梅斯迪尔用生命践行清教的法规，换取人们的宽宥，为他人树立榜样；齐灵渥斯将财产留给与自己毫无关系的珠儿，希望用善行洗刷自己的恶行。白兰将他们俩连在一起，波士顿将他们俩连在一起，清教将他们俩连在一起。他们是朋友？还是敌人？或许二者兼有。

第三，分析白兰和丁梅斯迪尔的关系。他们是情人关系、真正意义上的恋人关系。但同时又是清教(丁梅斯迪尔)与世俗思想(白兰)的关系，不过，清教之中杂有世俗，世俗之中有清教；他们的关系也是情感与法律(伦理道德)之间的对话。他们的关系违背了伦理道德，但得到作者和读者的同情，甚至认同。他们的关系引发读者对清教传统的反思、对人性的向往、对美好爱情的憧憬。但同时，人们也应该遵守道德法规，否则社会不能成为社会。从这个意义上讲，丁梅斯迪尔代表理性，白兰则是感性的化身。然而，作者有意让白兰先到美国，让齐灵渥斯死里逃生，并最终也来到美国。这是否暗示丁梅斯迪尔应该从他们的婚姻中退出？作者是否在影射当时的社会？

第四，分析丁梅斯迪尔和珠儿的关系。从血缘关系上讲他们是父女关系。丁梅斯迪尔心里清楚，他对珠儿没有尽到一份责任。但他心有余而力不足，只能暗暗地为珠儿祈祷和祝福。在第12章，丁梅斯迪尔、白兰、珠儿第一次站在一起。牧师握着珠儿的手时感到“一股新生命的激流注入他的心胸，涌遍他全身的血管”。他强烈地感受到了一股亲情的力量。然而，这一切只能发生在黑夜里。其间，珠儿一直在追寻父爱，但始终未果。小说第23章中，牧师再次与白兰和珠儿站在一起，并当众宣布自己是珠儿的父亲。父女最终团聚了。珠儿不再是上帝和波士顿社区的弃儿，她成为“这个世界中的一个妇女”。牧师的行为也是在“情”与“法”之间做出选择。不过，这里的“情”是“亲情”。他首先选择了“法”而隐藏了“情”，但他最终舍弃了“法”，即甘愿受到“法”的惩罚而选择了“亲情”。

第五，分析齐灵渥斯和珠儿的关系。此项工作将交给读者去完成。

四、难点注释

1. an Antinomian, a Quaker：一位唯信仰论者、一位贵格派的教友。前者指的是摒弃社会道德规范的人，认为人的灵魂不能通过行善，而是需要上帝的恩惠才能得到拯救。后者又称“教友派”或“公谊会”，基督教宗派之一，宣称教会和《圣经》都不是绝对的权威，反对设立牧师，不举行宗教仪式，反对一切战争。
2. Elizabeth：英国女王伊丽莎白一世，在位时间为1558—1603年。

3. gossip：原意为“流言飞语”，此处意为“女同事”。
4. not so much…as…：不是……而是……
5. … that the world was only the darker for this woman's beauty, and the more lost for the infant that she had borne：世界因为这个女人的美丽而更加黑暗，因为她生下的婴儿而更加迷茫。
6. Daniel：先知但以理，相传是《旧约·但以理书》的作者，曾为迦勒底王详解“泥足巨人”的梦和揭示墙上的字句之谜。
7. Governor Bellingham：理查德·贝林汉姆(Richard Bellingham)，英国人，分别于1641年、1654年、1665—1672年担任马萨诸塞湾殖民地的总督。
8. … accomplishing so much, precisely because it imagined and hoped so little：他们取得如此卓越的成就，恰恰是因为他们没有想入非非，没有好高骛远。
9. second：作动词用，表示“赞成或支持”。
10. Governor Winthrop：约翰·温斯诺普(John Winthrop)，英国人，是(1630年)马萨诸塞湾殖民地的创始人和第一任总督。
11. Stand any here that question God's judgment on a sinner?：站在这里的人们，有谁怀疑上帝对一个罪人的审判？
12. wanting：缺乏的。

五、延伸阅读与批评

《年轻的古德曼·布朗》发表于1835年，是读者最喜爱阅读和评析的霍桑的作品之一。我们从人物关系入手能够很好地分析他们的言行和性格特征以及小说的思想主旨。小说中，丈夫布朗和妻子费丝经历了“三聚”和“三离”。“三聚”和“三离”指代什么？从文本可以看出：“三聚”是指他们新婚之时情感笃深，黑夜森林中布朗看到妻子费丝的红丝带(暗指费丝在场)，他们俩离开森林重新回家。“三离”是指布朗告别费丝独自参加魔鬼的集会，集会完毕后他们俩各自回家，布朗抑郁而死、永远地离开了费丝。每一次的“聚”与“离”对他们俩的心态和言行产生不同的影响，给他们的命运也带来迥异的结局。它们是小说情节内容，也是主题思想的一部分。他俩为何要“聚”？为何要“离”？这两个问题值得读者去思考。

Chapter 2 The Adventures of Huckleberry Finn

by Mark Twain

(*Excerpts*)

一、作者简介

马克·吐温(1835—1910)，美国著名的小说家和幽默大师。他的小说有《傻子国外旅行记》(1869)、《镀金时代》(1873)、《汤姆·索亚历险记》(1876)、《王子和贫儿》(1881)、《密西西比河上》(1883)、《哈克贝利·费恩历险记》(1884)、《在亚瑟王朝廷里的康涅狄格州美国人》(1889)、《贞德传》(1896)，等等。他的中短篇小说与长篇小说同样齐名。另外，他著有长篇论文《人是怎么回事?》(1906)、《神秘的来客》(1916)以及《自传》(1924)等。他出生于密苏里州，12岁丧父后辍学，先后当过报童、印刷所学徒、水手、士兵、矿工和商人等。丰富的人生履历使他对美国社会有了深刻的认识，为他的作品增加了思想深度。

马克·吐温是出生在密西西比河西部的第一个文学巨人，他也被称为美国著名的地域作家。密西西比河两岸的风土人情和社会万象是他主要作品的创作源泉。然而，他并未止步于个体和区域性的表达，而是通过个性描述反映人类共有的思想体验。他对美国现实社会的关注为美国文学作出巨大的贡献。他对美国文学的另一贡献是他独特的语言风格：鲜活而清新的西部口语和讽刺幽默的风格。而且，他的许多作品结构完整、构思巧妙，作品的形式和内容结合完美。

马克·吐温的创作大致分为前期的浪漫与憧憬、中期的不满与失望和后期的幻灭与悲观三个阶段。他是美国的一部分，与美国一道，从天真走向经验，从迷恋"美国梦"到对"美国梦"的失望。他是美国最伟大的热爱者和憎恨者。小说家豪威尔斯称他是"美国文学中的林肯"。

马克·吐温的小说开创了美国小说语言口语化之先河，对美国文学产生了深远的影响。海明威说："全部现代美国文学起源于马克·吐温的一本名叫《哈克贝利·费恩历险记》的书……这是我们所有的书中最好的一本。"福克纳说："我认为马克·吐温是第一个真正的美国作家，我们大家都是他的后继人。我们是他的胄裔。"这些评价值得读者去体会和思考。

二、文本选读

The Adventures of Huckleberry Finn

CHAPTER VIII

The sun was up so high when I waked that I judged it was after eight o'clock. I laid there in the grass and the cool shade thinking about things, and feeling rested and ruther comfortable and satisfied. I could see the sun out at one or two holes, but mostly it was big trees all about, and gloomy in there amongst them. There was freckled places on the ground where the light sifted down through the leaves, and the freckled places swapped about a little, showing there was a little breeze up there. A couple of squirrels set on a limb and jabbered at me very friendly.

I was powerful lazy and comfortable—didn't want to get up and cook breakfast. Well, I was dozing off again when I thinks I hears a deep sound of "boom!" away up the river. I rouses up, and rests on my elbow and listens; pretty soon I hears it again. I hopped up, and went and looked out at a hole in the leaves, and I see a bunch of smoke laying on the water a long ways up—about abreast the ferry. And there was the ferryboat full of people floating along down. I knowed what was the matter now. "Boom!" I see the white smoke squirt out of the ferryboat's side. You see, they was firing cannon over the water, trying to make my carcass come to the top.

I was pretty hungry, but it warn't going to do for me to start a fire, because they might see the smoke. So I set there and watched the cannon-smoke and listened to the boom. The river was a mile wide there, and it always looks pretty on a summer morning—so I was having a good enough time seeing them hunt for my remainders if I only had a bite to eat. Well, then I happened to think how they always put quicksilver in loaves of bread and float them off, because they always go right to the drownded carcass and stop there. So, says I, I'll keep a lookout, and if any of them's floating around after me I'll give them a show[1]. I changed to the Illinois edge of the island to see what luck I could have, and I warn't disappointed. A big double loaf come along, and I most got it with a long stick, but my foot slipped and she floated out further. Of course I was where the current set in the closest to the shore—I knowed enough for that. But by and by along comes another one, and this time I won. I took out the plug and shook out the little dab of quicksilver, and set my teeth in. It was "baker's bread"—what the quality eat; none of your low-down corn-pone.

I got a good place amongst the leaves, and set there on a log, munching the bread and watching the ferry-boat, and very well satisfied. And then something struck me. I says, now I reckon the widow or the parson or somebody prayed that this bread would find me, and here it has gone and done it. So there ain't no doubt but there is something in that thing—that is, there's something in it when a body like the widow or the parson prays, but it don't work for me, and I reckon it don't work for only just the right kind.

I lit a pipe and had a good long smoke, and went on watching. The ferryboat was floating with the current, and I allowed[2] I'd have a chance to see who was aboard when she come along, because she would come in close, where the bread did. When she'd got pretty well along down towards me, I put out my pipe and went to where I fished out the bread, and laid down behind a log on the bank in a little open place. Where the log forked I could peep through.

By and by she come along, and she drifted in so close that they could a run out a plank and walked ashore. Most everybody was on the boat. Pap, and Judge Thatcher, and Bessie Thatcher, and Jo Harper, and Tom Sawyer, and his old Aunt Polly, and Sid and Mary, and plenty more. Everybody was talking about the murder, but the captain broke in and says:

"Look sharp, now; the current sets in the closest here, and maybe he's washed ashore and got tangled amongst the brush at the water's edge. I hope so, anyway."

I didn't hope so. They all crowded up and leaned over the rails, nearly in my face, and kept still, watching with all their might. I could see them first-rate, but they couldn't see me. Then the captain sung out: "Stand away!" and the cannon let off such a blast right before me that it made me deaf with the noise and pretty near blind with the smoke, and I judged I was gone. If they'd 'a' had some bullets in, I reckon they'd 'a' got the corpse they was after. Well, I see I warn't hurt, thanks to goodness. The boat floated on and went out of sight around the shoulder of the island. I could hear the booming now and then, further and further off, and by and by, after an hour, I didn't hear it no more. The island was three mile long. I judged they had got to the foot, and was giving it up. But they didn't yet awhile. They turned around the foot of the island and started up the channel on the Missouri side, under steam, and booming once in a while as they went. I crossed over to that side and watched them. When they got abreast the head of the island they quit shooting and dropped over to the Missouri shore and went home to the town.

I knowed I was all right now. Nobody else would come a-hunting after me. I got my traps out of the canoe and made me a nice camp in the thick woods. I made a kind of a tent out of my blankets to put my things under so the rain couldn't get at them. I catched a catfish and haggled him open with my saw, and towards sundown I started my camp fire and had supper. Then I set out a line to catch some fish for breakfast.

When it was dark I set by my camp fire smoking, and feeling pretty well satisfied; but by and by it got sort of lonesome, and so I went and set on the bank and listened to the current swashing along, and counted the stars and drift logs and rafts that come down, and then went to bed; there ain't no better way to put in time[3] when you are lonesome; you can't stay so, you soon get over it.

And so for three days and nights. No difference—just the same thing. But the next day I went exploring around down through the island. I was boss of it; it all belonged to me, so to say, and I wanted to know all about it; but mainly I wanted to put in the time. I found plenty strawberries, ripe and prime; and green summer grapes, and green razberries; and the green blackberries was just beginning to show. They would all come handy by and by, I judged.

Well, I went fooling along in the deep woods till I judged I warn't far from the foot of the island. I had my gun along, but I hadn't shot nothing; it was for protection; thought I would kill some game nigh home. About this time I mighty near stepped on a good-sized snake, and it went sliding off through the grass and flowers, and I after it, trying to get a shot at it. I clipped along, and all of a sudden I bounded right on to the ashes of a camp fire that was still smoking.

My heart jumped up amongst my lungs. I never waited for to look further, but uncocked my gun and went sneaking back on my tiptoes as fast as ever I could. Every now and then I stopped a second amongst the thick leaves and listened, but my breath come so hard I couldn't hear nothing else. I slunk along another piece further, then listened again; and so on, and so on. If I see a stump, I took it for a man; if I trod on a stick and broke it, it made me feel like a person had cut one of my breaths in two and I only got half, and the short half, too.

When I got to camp I wasn't feeling very brash, there wasn't much sand in my craw; but I says, this ain't no time to be fooling around. So I got all my traps into my canoe again so as to have them out of sight, and I put out the fire and scattered the ashes around to look like an old last year's camp, and then clumb a tree.

I reckon I was up in the tree two hours; but I didn't see nothing, I didn't hear nothing—I only *thought* I heard and seen as much as a thousand things. Well, I couldn't stay up there forever; so at last I got down, but I kept in the thick woods and on the lookout all the time. All I could get to eat was berries and what was left over from breakfast.

By the time it was night I was pretty hungry. So when it was good and dark I slid out from shore before moonrise and paddled over to the Illinois bank—about a quarter of a mile. I went out in the woods and cooked a supper, and I had about made up my mind I would stay there all night when I hear a *plunkety-plunk*, *plunkety-plunk*, and says to myself, horses coming; and next I hear people's voices. I got everything into the canoe as quick as I could, and then went creeping through the woods to see what I could find out. I hadn't got far when I hear a man say:

"We better camp here if we can find a good place; the horses is about beat out. Let's look around."

I didn't wait, but shoved out and paddled away easy. I tied up in the old place, and reckoned I would sleep in the canoe.

I didn't sleep much. I couldn't, somehow, for thinking. And every time I waked up I thought somebody had me by the neck. So the sleep didn't do me no good. By and by I says to myself, I can't live this way; I'm a-going to find out who it is that's here on the island with me; I'll find it out or bust. Well, I felt better right off.

So I took my paddle and slid out from shore just a step or two, and then let the canoe drop along down amongst the shadows. The moon was shining, and outside of the shadows it made it most as light as day. I poked along well on to an hour, everything still as rocks and sound asleep. Well, by this time I was most down to the foot of the island. A little ripply, cool breeze begun to blow, and that was as good as saying the night was about done. I give her a turn with the paddle and brung her nose to shore; then I got my gun and slipped out and into the edge of the woods. I sat down there on a log, and looked out through the leaves. I see the moon go off watch, and the darkness begin to blanket the river. But in a little while I see a pale streak over the treetops, and knowed the day was coming. So I took my gun and slipped off towards where I had run across that camp fire, stopping every minute or two to listen. But I hadn't no luck somehow; I couldn't seem to find the place. But by and by, sure enough, I catched a glimpse of fire away through the trees. I went for it, cautious and slow. By and by I was close enough to have a look, and there laid a man on the ground. It most give me the fantods. He had a blanket around his head, and his head was nearly in the fire. I set there behind a clump of bushes in about six foot of him, and kept my eyes on him steady. It was getting gray daylight now. Pretty soon he gapped and stretched himself and hove off the blanket, and it was Miss Watson's Jim! I bet I was glad to see him. I says: "Hello, Jim!" and skipped out.

He bounced up and stared at me wild. Then he drops down on his knees, and puts his hands together and says:

"Doan' hurt me—don't! I hain't ever done no harm to a ghos'. I awluz liked dead people, en done all I could for'em. You go en git in de river agin, whah you b'longs, en doan' do nuffn to Ole Jim, 'at' uz awluz yo 'fren'."

Well, I warn't long making him understand I warn't dead. I was ever so glad to see Jim. I warn't lonesome now. I told him I warn't afraid of *him* telling the people where I was. I talked along, but he only set there and looked at me; never said nothing. Then I says:

"It's good daylight. Le's get breakfast. Make up your camp-fire good."

"What's de use er makin' up de camp fire to cook strawbries en sich truck? But you got a gun, hain't you? Den we kin git sumfn better den strawbries."

"Strawberries and such truck," I says. "Is that what you live on?"

"I couldn' git nuffn else," he says.

"Why, how long you been on the island, Jim?"

"I come heah de night arter you's killed."

"What, all that time?"

"Yes—indeedy."

"And ain't you had nothing but that kind of rubbage to eat?"

"No, sah—nuffn else."

"Well, you must be most starved, ain't you?"

"I reck'n I could eat a hoss. I think I could. How long you ben on de islan'?"

"Since the night I got killed."

"No! W'y, what has you lived on? But you got a gun. Oh, yes, you got a gun. Dat's good. Now you kill sumfn en I'll make up de fire."

So we went over to where the canoe was, and while he built a fire in a grassy open place amongst the trees, I fetched meal and bacon and coffee, and coffee-pot and frying-pan, and sugar and tin cups, and the nigger was set back considerable, because he reckoned it was all done with witchcraft. I catched a good big catfish, too, and Jim cleaned him with his knife, and fried him.

When breakfast was ready we lolled on the grass and eat it smoking hot. Jim laid it in with all his might, for he was most about starved. Then when we had got pretty well stuffed, we laid off and lazied.

By and by Jim says:

"But looky here, Huck, who wuz it dat 'uz killed in dat shanty ef it warn't you?"

Then I told him the whole thing, and he said it was smart. He said Tom Sawyer couldn't get up no better plan than what I had. Then I says:

"How do you come to be here, Jim, and how'd you get here?"

He looked pretty uneasy, and didn't say nothing for a minute. Then he says:

"Maybe I better not tell."

"Why, Jim?"

"Well, dey's reasons. But you wouldn' tell on me ef I uz to tell you, would you, Huck?"

"Blamed if I would, Jim."

"Well, I b'lieve you, Huck. I—*run off.*"

"Jim!"

"But mind, you said you wouldn' tell—you know you said you wouldn' tell, Huck."

"Well, I did. I said I wouldn't, and I'll stick to it. Honest *injun*[4], I will. People would call me a low-down Abolitionist and despise me for keeping mum—but that don't make no difference. I ain't a-going to tell, and I ain't a-going back there, anyways. So, now, le's know all about it."

"Well, you see, it 'uz dis way. Ole missus—dat's Miss Watson—she pecks on me all de time, en treats me pooty rough, but she awluz said she wouldn' sell me down to Orleans. But I noticed dey wuz a nigger trader roun' de place considable lately, en I begin to git oneasy. Well, one night I creeps to de do' pooty late, en de do' warn't quite shet, en I hear old missus tell de widder she gwyne to sell me down to Orleans, but she didn' want to, but she could git eight hund'd dollars for me, en it 'uz sich a big stack o' money she couldn' resis'. De widder she try to git her to say she wouldn' do it, but I never waited to hear de res'. I lit out mighty quick, I tell you.

"I tuck out en shin down de hill, en 'spec to steal a skift 'long de sho' som'ers 'bove de town, but dey wuz people a-stirring yit, so I hid in de ole tumble-down cooper-shop on de bank to wait for everybody to go 'way. Well, I wuz dah all night. Dey wuz somebody roun' all de time. 'Long 'bout six in de mawnin' skifts begin to go by, en 'bout eight er nine every skift dat went 'long wuz talkin' 'bout how yo' pap come over to de town en say you's killed. Dese las' skifts wuz full o'ladies en genlmen a-goin' over for to see de place. Sometimes dey'd pull up at de sho' en take a res' b'fo' dey started acrost, so by de talk I got to know all 'bout de killin'. I 'uz powerful sorry you's killed, Huck, but I ain't no mo' now.

"I laid dah under de shavin's all day. I 'uz hungry, but I warn't afeard; bekase I knowed ole missus en de widder wuz goin' to start to de camp-meet'n' right arter breakfas' en be gone all day, en dey knows I goes off wid de cattle 'bout daylight, so dey wouldn' 'spec to see me roun' de place, en so dey wouldn' miss me tell arter dark in de evenin'. De yuther servants wouldn' miss me, kase dey'd shin out en take holiday soon as de ole folks 'uz out'n de way.

"Well, when it come dark I tuck out up de river road, en went 'bout two mile er more to whah dey warn't no houses. I'd made up my mine 'bout what I's agwyne to do. You see, ef I kep' on tryin' to git away afoot, de dogs 'ud track me; ef I stole a skift to cross over, dey'd miss dat skift, you see, en dey'd know 'bout whah I'd lan' on de yuther side, en whah to pick up my track. So I says, a raff is what I's arter; it doan' *make* no track.

"I see a light a-comin' roun' de p'int bymeby, so I wade' in en shove' a log ahead o' me en swum more'n half way acrost de river, en got in 'mongst de drift-wood, en kep' my head down low, en kinder swum agin de current tell de raff come along. Den I swum to de stern uv it en tuck a-holt. It clouded up en 'uz pooty dark for a little while. So I clumb up en laid down on de planks. De men 'uz all 'way yonder in de middle, whah de lantern wuz. De river wuz a-risin', en dey wuz a good current; so I reck'n'd 'at by fo' in de mawnin' I'd be twenty-five mile down de river, en den I'd slip in jis b'fo' daylight en swim asho', en take to de woods on de Illinois side.

"But I didn' have no luck. When we 'uz mos' down to de head er de islan' a man begin to come aft wid de lantern, I see it warn't no use fer to wait, so I slid overboard en struck out fer de islan'. Well, I had a notion I could lan' mos' anywhers, but I couldn't—bank too bluff. I 'uz mos' to de foot er de islan' b'fo' I found' a good place. I went into de woods en jedged I wouldn' fool wid raffs no mo', long as dey move de lantern roun' so. I had my pipe en a plug er dog-leg, en some matches in my cap, en dey warn't wet, so I 'uz all right."

"And so you ain't had no meat nor bread to eat all this time? Why didn't you get mud-turkles?"

"How you gwyne to git 'm? You can't slip up on um en grab um; en how's a body gwyne to hit um wid a rock? How could a body do it in de night? En I warn't gwyne to show mysef on de bank in de daytime."

"Well, that's so. You've had to keep in the woods all the time, of course. Did you hear 'em shooting the cannon?"

"Oh, yes. I knowed dey was arter you. I see um go by heah—watched um thoo de bushes."

Some young birds come along, flying a yard or two at a time and lighting. Jim said it was a sign it was going to rain. He said it was a sign when young chickens flew that way, and so he reckoned it was the same way when young birds done it. I was going to catch some of them, but Jim wouldn't let me. He said it was death. He said his father laid mighty sick once, and some of them catched a bird, and his old granny said his father would die, and he did.

And Jim said you mustn't count the things you are going to cook for dinner, because that would bring bad luck. The same if you shook the table-cloth after sundown. And he said if a man owned a beehive and that man died, the bees must be told about it before sun-up next morning, or else the bees would all weaken down and quit work and die. Jim said bees wouldn't sting idiots; but I didn't believe that, because I had tried them lots of times myself, and they wouldn't sting me.

I had heard about some of these things before, but not all of them. Jim knowed all kinds of signs. He said he knowed most everything. I said it looked to me like all the signs was about bad luck, and so I asked him if there warn't any good-luck signs. He says:

"Mighty few—an' *dey* ain't no use to a body. What you want to know when good luck's a-comin' for? Want to keep it off?" And he said: "Ef you's got hairy arms en a hairy breas', it's a sign dat you's agwyne to be rich. Well, dey's some use in a sign like dat, 'kase it's so fur ahead. You see, maybe you's got to be po' a long time fust, en so you might git discourage' en kill yo'sef 'f you didn' know by de sign dat you gwyne to be rich bymeby."

"Have you got hairy arms and a hairy breast, Jim?"

"What's de use to ax dat question? Don't you see I has?"

"Well, are you rich?"

"No, but I ben rich wunst, and gwyne to be rich agin. Wunst I had foteen dollars, but I tuck to specalat'n', en got busted out."

"What did you speculate in, Jim?"

"Well, fust I tackled stock."

"What kind of stock?"

"Why, live stock—cattle, you know. I put ten dollars in a cow. But I ain' gwyne to resk no mo' money in stock. De cow up 'n' died on my han's."

"So you lost the ten dollars."

"No, I didn't lose it all. I on'y los' 'bout nine of it. I sole de hide en taller for a dollar en ten cents."

"You had five dollars and ten cents left. Did you speculate any more?"

"Yes. You know that one-laigged nigger dat b'longs to old Misto Bradish? Well, he sot up a bank, en say anybody dat put in a dollar would git fo' dollars mo' at de en' er de year. Well, all de niggers went in, but dey didn't have much. I wuz de on'y one dat had much. So I stuck out for mo' dan fo' dollars, en I said 'f I didn' git it I'd start a bank mysef. Well, o' course dat nigger want' to keep me out er de business, bekase he says dey warn't business 'nough for two banks, so he say I could put in my five dollars en he pay me thirty-five at de en' er de year[5].

"So I done it. Den I reck'n'd I'd inves' de thirty-five dollars right off en keep things a-movin'. Dey wuz a nigger name' Bob, dat had ketched a wood-flat, en his marster didn' know it; en I bought it off'n him en told him to take de thirty-five dollars when de en' er de year come; but somebody stole de wood-flat dat night, en nex day de one-laigged nigger say de bank's busted. So dey didn' none uv us git no money."

"What did you do with the ten cents, Jim?"

"Well, I 'uz gwyne to spen' it, but I had a dream, en de dream tole me to give it to a nigger name' Balum—Balum's Ass dey call him for short; he's one er dem chuckleheads, you know. But he's lucky, dey say, en I see I warn't lucky. De dream say let Balum inves' de ten cents en he'd make a raise for me. Well, Balum he tuck de money, en when he wuz in church he hear de preacher say dat whoever give to de po' len' to de Lord[6], en boun' to git his money back a hund'd times. So Balum he tuck en give de ten cents to de po', en laid low to see what wuz gwyne to come of it."

"Well, what did come of it, Jim?"

"Nuffn never come of it. I couldn' manage to k'leck dat money no way; en Balum he couldn'. I ain' gwyne to len' no mo' money 'dout I see de security. Boun' to git yo' money back a hund'd times, de preacher says! Ef I could git de ten *cents* back, I'd call it squah, en be glad er de chanst."

"Well, it's all right anyway, Jim, long as you're going to be rich again some time or other."

"Yes; en I's rich now, come to look at it. I owns mysef, en I's wuth eight hund'd dollars. I wisht I had de money, I wouldn' want no mo'."

CHAPTER XV

We judged that three nights more would fetch us to Cairo, at the bottom of Illinois, where the Ohio River comes in, and that was what we was after. We would sell the raft and get on a steamboat and go way up the Ohio amongst the free States, and then be out of trouble.

Well, the second night a fog begun to come on, and we made for a towhead to tie to, for it wouldn't do to try to run in a fog; but when I paddled ahead in the canoe, with the line to make fast, there warn't anything but little saplings to tie to. I passed the line around one of them right on the edge of the cut bank, but there was a stiff current, and the raft come booming down so lively she tore it out by the roots and away she went. I see the fog closing down, and it made me so sick and scared I couldn't budge for most a half a minute it seemed to me—and then there warn't no raft in sight; you couldn't see twenty yards. I jumped into the canoe and run back to the stern, and grabbed the paddle and set her back a stroke. But she didn't come. I was in such a hurry I hadn't untied her. I got up and tried to untie her, but I was so excited my hands shook so I couldn't hardly do anything with them.

As soon as I got started I took out after the raft, hot and heavy, right down the towhead. That was all right as far as it went, but the towhead warn't sixty yards long, and the minute I flew by the foot of it I shot out into the solid white fog, and hadn't no more idea which way I was going than a dead man.

Thinks I, it won't do to paddle; first I know I'll run into the bank or a towhead or something; I got to set still and float, and yet it's mighty fidgety business to have to hold your hands still at such a time. I whooped and listened. Away down there somewheres I hears a small whoop, and up comes my spirits. I went tearing after it, listening sharp to hear it again. The next time it come I see I warn't heading for it, but heading away to the right of it. And the next time I was heading away to the left of it—and not gaining on it much either, for I was flying around, this way and that and t'other, but it was going straight ahead all the time.

I did wish the fool would think to beat a tin pan, and beat it all the time, but he never did, and it was the still places between the whoops that was making the trouble for me. Well, I fought along, and directly I hears the whoop *behind* me. I was tangled good now. That was somebody else's whoop, or else I was turned around.

I throwed the paddle down. I heard the whoop again; it was behind me yet, but in a different place; it kept coming, and kept changing its place, and I kept answering, till by and by it was in front of me again, and I knowed the current had swung the canoe's head down-stream, and I was all right if that was Jim and not some other raftsman hollering. I couldn't tell nothing about voices in a fog, for nothing don't look natural nor sound natural in a fog.

The whooping went on, and in about a minute I come a-booming down on a cut bank with smoky ghosts of big trees on it, and the current throwed me off to the left and shot by, amongst a lot of snags that fairly roared, the currrent was tearing by them so swift.

In another second or two it was solid white and still again. I set perfectly still then, listening to my heart thump, and I reckon I didn't draw a breath while it thumped a hundred.

I just give up then. I knowed what the matter was. That cut bank was an island, and Jim had gone down t'other side of it. It warn't no towhead that you could float by in ten minutes. It had the big timber of a regular island; it might be five or six miles long and more than half a mile wide.

I kept quiet, with my ears cocked, about fifteen minutes, I reckon. I was floating along, of course, four or five miles an hour; but you don't ever think of that. No, you *feel* like you are laying dead still on the water; and if a little glimpse of a snag slips by you don't think to yourself how fast *you're* going, but you catch your breath and think, my! how that snag's tearing along. If you think it ain't dismal and lonesome out in a fog that way by yourself in the night, you try it once—you'll see.

Next, for about a half an hour, I whoops now and then; at last I hears the answer a long ways off, and tries to follow it, but I couldn't do it, and directly I judged I'd got into a nest of towheads, for I had little dim glimpses of them on both sides of me—sometimes just a narrow channel between, and some that I couldn't see I knowed was there because I'd hear the wash of the current against the old dead brush and trash that hung over the banks. Well, I warn't long loosing the whoops down amongst the towheads; and I only tried to chase them a little while, anyway, because it was worse than chasing a Jack-o'-lantern[7]. You never knowed a sound dodge around so, and swap places so quick and so much.

I had to claw away from the bank pretty lively four or five times, to keep from knocking the islands out of the river; and so I judged the raft must be butting into the bank every now and then, or else it would get further ahead and clear out of hearing—it was floating a little faster than what I was.

Well, I seemed to be in the open river again by and by, but I couldn't hear no sign of a whoop nowheres. I reckoned Jim had fetched up on a snag, maybe, and it was all up with him. I was good and tired, so I laid down in the canoe and said I wouldn't bother no more. I didn't want to go to sleep, of course; but I was so sleepy I couldn't help it; so I thought I would take jest one little cat-nap.

But I reckon it was more than a cat-nap, for when I waked up the stars was shining bright, the fog was all gone, and I was spinning down a big bend stern first. First I didn't know where I was; I thought I was dreaming; and when things began to come back to me they seemed to come up dim out of last week.

It was a monstrous big river here, with the tallest and the thickest kind of timber on both banks; just a solid wall, as well as I could see by the stars. I looked away down-stream, and seen a black speck on the water. I took after it; but when I got to it it warn't nothing but a couple of sawlogs made fast together. Then I see another speck, and chased that; then another, and this time I was right. It was the raft.

When I got to it Jim was setting there with his head down between his knees, asleep, with his right arm hanging over the steering-oar. The other oar was smashed off, and the raft was littered up with leaves and branches and dirt. So she'd had a rough time.

I made fast and laid down under Jim's nose on the raft, and began to gap, and stretch my fists out against Jim, and says:

"Hello, Jim, have I been asleep? Why didn't you stir me up?"

"Goodness gracious, is dat you, Huck? En you ain' dead—you ain' drownded—you's back agin? It's too good for true, honey, it's too good for true. Lemme look at you chile, lemme feel o' you. No, you ain' dead! you's back agin, 'live en soun', jis de same ole Huck—de same ole Huck, thanks to goodness!"

"What's the matter with you, Jim? You been a-drinking?"

"Drinkin'? Has I ben a-drinkin'? Has I had a chance to be a-drinkin'?"

"Well, then, what makes you talk so wild?"

"How does I talk wild?"

"*How*? Why, hain't you been talking about my coming back, and all that stuff, as if I'd been gone away?"

"Huck—Huck Finn, you look me in de eye; look me in de eye. *Hain't* you ben gone away?"

"Gone away? Why, what in the nation do you mean? *I* hain't been gone anywheres. Where would I go to?"

"Well, looky here, boss, dey's sumf'n wrong, dey is. Is I *me*, or who *is* I? Is I heah, or whah *is* I? Now dat's what I wants to know."

"Well, I think you're here, plain enough, but I think you're a tangle-headed old fool, Jim."

"I is, is I? Well, you answer me dis: Didn't you tote out de line in de canoe fer to make fas' to de tow-head?"

"No, I didn't. What tow-head? I hain't see no tow-head."

"You hain't seen no towhead? Looky here, didn't de line pull loose en de raf' go a-hummin' down de river, en leave you en de canoe behine in de fog?"

"What fog?"

"Why, *de* fog! —de fog dat's been aroun' all night. En didn't you whoop, en didn't I whoop, tell we got mix' up in de islands en one un us got los' en t'other one was jis' as good as los', 'kase he didn' know whah he wuz? En didn't I bust up agin a lot er dem islands en have a turrible time en mos' git drownded? Now ain' dat so, boss—ain't it so? You answer me dat."

"Well, this is too many for me, Jim. I hain't seen no fog, nor no islands, nor no troubles, nor nothing. I been setting here talking with you all night till you went to sleep about ten minutes ago, and I reckon I done the same. You couldn't a got drunk in that time, so of course you've been dreaming."

"Dad fetch it, how is I gwyne to dream all dat in ten minutes?"

"Well, hang it all, you did dream it, because there didn't any of it happen."

"But, Huck, it's all jis' as plain to me as—"

"It don't make no difference how plain it is; there ain't nothing in it. I know, because I've been here all the time."

Jim didn't say nothing for about five minutes, but set there studying over it. Then he says:

"Well, den, I reck'n I did dream it, Huck; but dog my cats ef it ain't de powerfullest dream I ever see. En I hain't ever had no dream b'fo' dat's tired me like dis one."

"Oh, well, that's all right, because a dream does tire a body like everything sometimes. But this one was a staving dream; tell me all about it, Jim."

So Jim went to work and told me the whole thing right through, just as it happened, only he painted it up considerable. Then he said he must start in and "'terpret" it, because it was sent for a warning. He said the first towhead stood for a man that would try to do us some good, but the current was another man that would get us away from him. The whoops was warnings that would come to us every now and then, and if we didn't try hard to make out to understand them they'd just take us into bad luck, 'stead of keeping us out of it. The lot of towheads was troubles we was going to get into with quarrelsome people and all kinds of mean folks, but if we minded our business and didn't talk back and aggravate them, we would pull through and get out of the fog and into the big clear river, which was the free States, and wouldn't have no more trouble.

It had clouded up pretty dark just after I got on to the raft, but it was clearing up again now.

"Oh, well, that's all interpreted well enough as far as it goes, Jim," I says; "but what does *these* things stand for?"

It was the leaves and rubbish on the raft and the smashed oar. You could see them first-rate now.

Jim looked at the trash, and then looked at me, and back at the trash again. He had got the dream fixed so strong in his head that he couldn't seem to shake it loose and get the facts back into its place again right away. But when he did get the thing straightened around he looked at me steady without ever smiling, and says:

"What do dey stan' for? I'se gwyne to tell you. When I got all wore out wid work, en wid de callin' for you, en went to sleep, my heart wuz mos' broke bekase you wuz los', en I didn' k'yer no' mo' what become er me en de raf'. En when I wake up en fine you back agin, all safe en soun', de tears come, en I could a got down on my knees en kiss yo' foot, I's so thankful. En all you wuz thinkin' 'bout wuz how you could make a fool uv ole Jim wid a lie. Dat truck dah is *trash*;

en trash is what people is dat puts dirt on de head er dey fren's en makes 'em ashamed."

Then he got up slow and walked to the wigwam, and went in there without saying anything but that. But that was enough. It made me feel so mean I could almost kissed *his* foot to get him to take it back.

It was fifteen minutes before I could work myself up to go and humble myself to a nigger; but I done it, and I warn't ever sorry for it afterwards, neither. I didn't do him no more mean tricks, and I wouldn't done that one if I'd 'a' knowed it would make him feel that way.

CHAPTER XVI

We sleptmost all day, and started out at night, a little ways behind a monstrous long raft that was as long going by as a procession. She had four long sweeps at each end, so we judged she carried as many as thirty men, likely. She had five big wigwams aboard, wide apart, and an open camp fire in the middle, and a tall flag-pole at each end. There was a power of style about her. It *amounted* to something[8] being a raftsman on such a craft as that.

We went drifting down into a big bend, and the night clouded up and got hot. The river was very wide, and was walled with solid timber on both sides; you couldn't see a break in it hardly ever, or a light. We talked about Cairo, and wondered whether we would know it when we got to it. I said likely we wouldn't, because I had heard say there warn't but about a dozen houses there, and if they didn't happen to have them lit up, how was we going to know we was passing a town? Jim said if the two big rivers joined together there, that would show. But I said maybe we might think we was passing the foot of an island and coming into the same old river again. That disturbed Jim—and me too. So the question was, what to do? I said, paddle ashore the first time a light showed, and tell them pap was behind, coming along with a trading-scow, and was a green hand at the business, and wanted to know how far it was to Cairo. Jim thought it was a good idea, so we took a smoke on it and waited.

There warn't nothing to do now but to look out sharp for the town, and not pass it without seeing it. He said he'd be mighty sure to see it, because he'd be a free man the minute he seen it, but if he missed it he'd be in a slave country again and no more show for freedom. Every little while he jumps up and says:

"Dah she is?"

But it warn't. It was Jack-o'-lanterns, or lightning bugs; so he set down again, and went to watching, same as before. Jim said it made him all over trembly and feverish to be so close to freedom. Well, I can tell you it made me all over trembly and feverish, too, to hear him, because I begun to get it through my head that he *was* most free—and who was to blame for it? Why, *me.* I couldn't get that out of my conscience, no how nor no way. It got to troubling me so I couldn't rest; I couldn't stay still in one place. It hadn't ever come home to me before, what this thing was that I was doing. But now it did; and it stayed with me, and scorched me more and more. I tried to make out to myself that *I* warn't to blame, because *I* didn't run Jim off from his rightful owner;

but it warn't no use, conscience up and says, every time, "But you knowed he was running for his freedom, and you could a paddled ashore and told somebody." That was so—I couldn't get around that noway. That was where it pinched. Conscience says to me, "What had poor Miss Watson done to you that you could see her nigger go off right under your eyes and never say one single word? What did that poor old woman do to you that you could treat her so mean? Why, she tried to learn you your book, she tried to learn you your manners[9], she tried to be good to you every way she knowed how. *That's* what she done."

I got to feeling so mean and so miserable I most wished I was dead. I fidgeted up and down the raft, abusing myself to myself, and Jim was fidgeting up and down past me. We neither of us could keep still. Every time he danced around and says, "Dah's Cairo!" it went through me like a shot, and I thought if it *was* Cairo I reckoned I would die of miserableness.

Jim talked out loud all the time while I was talking to myself. He was saying how the first thing he would do when he got to a free State he would go to saving up money and never spend a single cent, and when he got enough he would buy his wife, which was owned on a farm close to where Miss Watson lived; and then they would both work to buy the two children, and if their master wouldn't sell them, they'd get an Ab'litionist to go and steal them.

It most froze me to hear such talk. He wouldn't ever dared to talk such talk in his life before. Just see what a difference it made in him the minute he judged he was about free. It was according to the old saying, "Give a nigger an inch and he'll take an ell." Thinks I, this is what comes of my not thinking. Here was this nigger, which I had as good as helped to run away, coming right out flat-footed and saying he would steal his children—children that belonged to a man I didn't even know; a man that hadn't ever done me no harm.

I was sorry to hear Jim say that, it was such a lowering of him. My conscience got to stirring me up hotter than ever, until at last I says to it, "Let up on me—it ain't too late yet—I'll paddle ashore at the first light and tell." I felt easy and happy and light as a feather right off. All my troubles was gone. I went to looking out sharp for a light, and sort of singing to myself. By and by one showed. Jim sings out:

"We's safe, Huck, we's safe! Jump up and crack yo' heels! Dat's de good ole Cairo at las', I jis knows it!"

I says:

"I'll take the canoe and go and see, Jim. It mightn't be, you know."

He jumped and got the canoe ready, and put his old coat in the bottom for me to set on, and give me the paddle; and as I shoved off, he says:

"Pooty soon I'll be a-shout'n' for joy, en I'll say, it's all on accounts o' Huck; I's a free man, en I couldn't ever ben free ef it hadn' ben for Huck; Huck done it. Jim won't ever forgit you, Huck; you's de bes' fren' Jim's ever had; en you's de *only* fren' ole Jim's got now."

I was paddling off, all in a sweat to tell on him; but when he says this, it seemed to kind of take the tuck all out of me. I went along slow then, and I warn't right down certain whether I was glad I started or whether I warn't. When I was fifty yards off, Jim says:

"Dah you goes, de ole true Huck; de on'y white genlman dat ever kep' his promise to ole Jim."

Well, I just felt sick. But I says, I *got* to do it—I can't get *out* of it. Right then along comes a skiff with two men in it with guns, and they stopped and I stopped. One of them says:

"What's that yonder?"

"A piece of a raft," I says.

"Do you belong on it?"

"Yes, sir."

"Any men on it?"

"Only one, sir."

"Well, there's five niggers run off to-night up yonder, above the head of the bend. Is your man white or black?"

I didn't answer up prompt. I tried to, but the words wouldn't come. I tried for a second or two to brace up and out with it, but I warn't man enough—hadn't the spunk of a rabbit. I see I was weakening; so I just give up trying, and up and says:

"He's white."

"I reckon we'll go and see for ourselves."

"I wish you would," says I, "because it's pap that's there, and maybe you'd help me tow the raft ashore where the light is. He's sick—and so is mam and Mary Ann."

"Oh, the devil! we're in a hurry, boy. But I s'pose we've got to. Come, buckle to your paddle, and let's get along."

I buckled to my paddle and they laid to their oars. When we had made a stroke or two, I says:

"Pap'll be mighty much obleeged to you, I can tell you. Everybody goes away when I want them to help me tow the raft ashore, and I can't do it by myself."

"Well, that's infernal mean. Odd, too. Say, boy, what's the matter with your father?"

"It's the—a—the—well, it ain't anything much."

They stopped pulling. It warn't but a mighty little ways to the raft now. One says:

"Boy, that's a lie. What *is* the matter with your pap? Answer up square now, and it'll be the better for you."

"I will, sir, I will, honest—but don't leave us, please. It's the—the—Gentlemen, if you'll only pull ahead, and let me heave you the headline, you won't have to come a-near the raft—please do."

"Set her back, John, set her back!" says one. They backed water. "Keep away, boy—keep to looard. Confound it, I just expect the wind has blowed it to us. Your pap's got the small-pox, and you know it precious well. Why didn't you come out and say so? Do you want to spread it all over?"

"Well," says I, a-blubbering, "I've told everybody before, and they just went away and left us."

"Poor devil, there's something in that. We are right down sorry for you, but we—well, hang it, we don't want the small-pox, you see. Look here, I'll tell you what to do. Don't you try to land by yourself, or you'll smash everything to pieces. You float along down about twenty miles, and you'll come to a town on the left-hand side of the river. It will be long after sun-up then, and when you ask for help you tell them your folks are all down with chills and fever. Don't be a fool again, and let people guess what is the matter. Now we're trying to do you a kindness; so you just put twenty miles between us, that's a good boy. It wouldn't do any good to land yonder where the light is—it's only a wood-yard. Say, I reckon your father's poor, and I'm bound to say he's in pretty hard luck. Here, I'll put a twenty-dollar gold piece on this board, and you get it when it floats by. I feel mighty mean to leave you; but my kingdom! it won't do to fool with small-pox, don't you see?"

"Hold on, Parker," says the other man, "here's a twenty to put on the board for me. Good-bye, boy; you do as Mr. Parker told you, and you'll be all right."

"That's so, my boy—good-bye, good-bye. If you see any runaway niggers you get help and nab them, and you can make some money by it."

"Good-bye, sir," says I; "I won't let no runaway niggers get by me if I can help it."

They went off and I got aboard the raft, feeling bad and low, because I knowed very well I had done wrong, and I see it warn't no use for me to try to learn to do right; a body that don't get *started* right when he's little ain't got no show—when the pinch comes there ain't nothing to back him up and keep him to his work, and so he gets beat. Then I thought a minute, and says to myself, hold on; s'pose you'd a done right and give Jim up, would you felt better than what you do now? No, says I, I'd feel bad—I'd feel just the same way I do now. Well, then, says I, what's the use you learning to do right when it's troublesome to do right and ain't no trouble to do wrong, and the wages is just the same? I was stuck. I couldn't answer that. So I reckoned I wouldn't bother no more about it, but after this always do whichever come handiest at the time.

I went into the wigwam; Jim warn't there. I looked all around; he warn't anywhere. I says:

"Jim!"

"Here I is, Huck. Is dey out o' sight yit? Don't talk loud."

He was in the river under the stern oar, with just his nose out. I told him they were out of sight, so he come aboard. He says:

"I was a-listenin' to all de talk, en I slips into de river en was gwyne to shove for sho' if dey come aboard. Den I was gwyne to swim to de raf' agin when dey was gone. But lawsy, how you did fool 'em, Huck! Dat *wuz* de smartes' dodge! I tell you, chile, I 'spec it save' ole Jim—ole Jim ain't going to forgit you for dat, honey."

Then we talked about the money. It was a pretty good raise—twenty dollars apiece. Jim said we could take deck passage on a steamboat now, and the money would last us as far as we wanted to go in the free States. He said twenty mile more warn't far for the raft to go, but he wished we was already there.

Towards daybreak we tied up, and Jim was mighty particular about hiding the raft good. Then he worked all day fixing things in bundles, and getting all ready to quit rafting.

That night about ten we hove in sight of the lights of a town away down in a left-hand bend. I went off in the canoe to ask about it. Pretty soon I found a man out in the river with a skiff, setting a trot-line. I ranged up and says:

"Mister, is that town Cairo?"

"Cairo? no. You must be a blame' fool."

"What town is it, mister?"

"If you want to know, go and find out. If you stay here botherin' around me for about a half a minute longer you'll get something you won't want."

I paddled to the raft. Jim was awful disappointed, but I said never mind, Cairo would be the next place, I reckoned.

We passed another town before daylight, and I was going out again; but it was high ground, so I didn't go. No high ground about Cairo, Jim said. I had forgot it. We laid up for the day on a towhead tolerable close to the left-hand bank. I begun to suspicion something. So did Jim. I says:

"Maybe we went by Cairo in the fog that night."

He says:

"Doan' le's talk about it, Huck. Po' niggers can't have no luck. I awluz 'spected dat rattlesnake-skin warn't done wid its work."

"I wish I'd never seen that snake-skin, Jim—I do wish I'd never laid eyes on it."

"It ain't yo' fault, Huck; you didn' know. Don't you blame yo'self 'bout it."

When it was daylight, here was the clear Ohio water inshore, sure enough, and outside was the old regular Muddy! So it was all up with Cairo.

We talked it all over. It wouldn't do to take to the shore; we couldn't take the raft up the stream, of course. There warn't no way but to wait for dark, and start back in the canoe and take the chances. So we slept all day amongst the cottonwood thicket, so as to be fresh for the work, and when we went back to the raft about dark the canoe was gone!

We didn't say a word for a good while. There warn't anything to say. We both knowed well enough it was some more work of the rattlesnake-skin; so what was the use to talk about it? It would only look like we was finding fault, and that would be bound to fetch more bad luck—and keep on fetching it, too, till we knowed enough to keep still.

By and by we talked about what we better do, and found there warn't no way but just to go along down with the raft till we got a chance to buy a canoe to go back in. We warn't going to borrow it when there warn't anybody around, the way pap would do, for that might set people after us.

So we shoved out after dark on the raft.

Anybody that don't believe yet that it's foolishness to handle a snake-skin, after all that that snake-skin done for us, will believe it now if they read on and see what more it done for us.

The place to buy canoes is off of rafts laying up at shore. But we didn't see no rafts laying up; so we went along during three hours and more. Well, the night got gray and ruther thick, which is the next meanest thing to fog. You can't tell the shape of the river, and you can't see no distance. It got to be very late and still, and then along comes a steamboat up the river. We lit the lantern, and judged she would see it. Up-stream boats didn't generly come close to us; they go out and follow the bars and hunt for easy water under the reefs; but nights like this they bull right up the channel against the whole river.

We could hear her pounding along, but we didn't see her good till she was close. She aimed right for us. Often they do that and try to see how close they can come without touching; sometimes the wheel bites off a sweep, and then the pilot sticks his head out and laughs, and thinks he's mighty smart. Well, here she comes, and we said she was going to try and shave us; but she didn't seem to be sheering off a bit. She was a big one, and she was coming in a hurry, too, looking like a black cloud with rows of glow-worms around it; but all of a sudden she bulged out, big and scary, with a long row of wide-open furnace doors shining like red-hot teeth, and her monstrous bows and guards hanging right over us. There was a yell at us, and a jingling of bells to stop the engines, a powwow of cussing, and whistling of steam—and as Jim went overboard on one side and I on the other, she come smashing straight through the raft.

I dived—and I aimed to find the bottom, too, for a thirty-foot wheel had got to go over me, and I wanted it to have plenty of room. I could always stay under water a minute; this time I reckon I stayed under a minute and a half. Then I bounced for the top in a hurry, for I was nearly busting. I popped out to my armpits and blowed the water out of my nose, and puffed a bit. Of course there was a booming current; and of course that boat started her engines again ten seconds after she stopped them, for they never cared much for raftsmen; so now she was churning along up the river, out of sight in the thick weather, though I could hear her.

I sung out for Jim about a dozen times, but I didn't get any answer; so I grabbed a plank that touched me while I was "treading water," and struck out for shore, shoving it ahead of me. But I made out to see that the drift of the current was towards the left-hand shore, which meant that I was in a crossing; so I changed off and went that way.

It was one of these long, slanting, two-mile crossings; so I was a good long time in getting over. I made a safe landing, and clumb up the bank. I couldn't see but a little ways, but I went poking along over rough ground for a quarter of a mile or more, and then I run across a big old-fashioned double log-house before I noticed it. I was going to rush by and get away, but a lot of dogs jumped out and went to howling and barking at me, and I knowed better than to move another peg[10].

三、人物解析

《哈克贝利·费恩历险记》是马克·吐温的杰出代表作。小说有两个主要人物：白人男孩哈克和黑奴吉姆。哈克对"白人教化"不感兴趣，更不能忍受酗酒父亲的折磨，便逃出家门。黑奴吉姆听说自己的主人要把他卖掉，也逃了出来。他们相逢在密西西比河畔，并决定一起乘木筏沿着河流漂流，经过密苏里州、伊利诺伊州、俄亥俄州。途中，他们遭遇各种人物，如门户之争、强盗、骗子等；经受各种考验，如吉姆被抓和成功获救等。最后，在哈克的帮助下吉姆获得人身自由，他的主人在遗嘱中宣布吉姆为自由人。

通过两人的流浪和见闻，小说真实地反映了美国社会现实：白人的虚伪、种族歧视、白人和黑人之间的矛盾、道德的选择、对自由的追求和对美好事物的憧憬，等等。关于对该小说的解读，现存的观点主要包括以下几种：小说是儿童读物，但又不全是；小说反映两个世界之间的对话——大人眼中的孩子世界，孩子眼中的大人世界；一部"成长小说"(initiation story)；一部浪漫小说；一部充满象征的小说；反映美国社会的虚伪和黑暗的批判性小说。如此多样的解析充分说明该小说具有丰富的思想魅力。

作为主题思想一部分的故事人物的性格特征，基本上是通过人物的言行表现出来的。言和行直接表露人物的内心世界和思想活动。哈克和吉姆的言行充分展示各自的性格特征和对外部世界的认知。小说第8章：哈克刚见到吉姆时，吉姆下跪，求哈克别杀他。接着，小说给予吉姆大段的篇幅，让他向哈克细数自己出逃的全部内情——出逃的原因和逃亡路上的辛酸等。第15章：吉姆称哈克为"孩子""主人"，吉姆对哈克的安全回来异常高兴。第16章：吉姆认为在哈克的帮助下自己已成为一个"自由人"，并视哈克为自己唯一的朋友。吉姆的言行表现出几个鲜明的特点：目标集中、反抗被奴役的命运、憧憬美好未来、为人友善。"自由"一直是吉姆心中的向往。他敢于冲破桎梏，追求自由；他对白人感到敬畏——这是种族歧视的结果；他心怀善心，追求平等——对哈克关心，如同父亲关心儿子，把哈克当朋友，一起同甘共苦。可见，透过吉姆的言行，读者可以了解当时的社会现实，对吉姆的认识不断加深。这些既是人物的性格特征，也是小说的思想主旨。

同理，在关注哈克的所言、所行、所思之后，读者发现哈克的思想和性格特征。面对吉姆的陈述，哈克立刻思考如下严肃的问题：吉姆出逃跟自己的关系，自己知情不报的后果，是否把吉姆交出去。这些问题——既有道德层面的，更有社会制度层面的——对年轻的哈克而言似乎太宏大、太沉重。然而，他一边思考(包括第31章)，一边保护吉姆。为什么？因为他发现吉姆是个好人，所以吉姆理应受到平等和公正的待遇。他们相依为命，相互帮助，彼此交往不断深入，双方的感情进一步加深。最后，吉姆的真情打动了哈克，哈克对社会的不公有了更深的认识，他决定：哪怕是"下地狱"也不出卖吉姆。哈克帮助吉姆圆了一个现实与理想交织在一起的"自由"之梦。这个梦究竟是什么？它既是哈克的梦、哈克赋予吉姆的梦、作者赋予哈克的梦，也是吉姆的梦、所有黑人的梦、作者本人的梦。

四、难点注释

1. give somebody a show：给某人机会。

2. allow：认为。
3. put in time：打发时间。
4. Honest *injun*：绝对不假。
5. at de en' er de year：正规的表达是 at the end of the year。
6. to de po' len' to de Lord：正规的表达是 to the poor lend to the Lord。
7. Jack-o'-lantern：鬼火。
8. amount to something：有意义。
9. … learn you your book…learn you your manners：……教你书本知识……教你行为礼仪。
10. peg：(口语)足；腿。

五、延伸阅读与批评

《卡拉维拉斯县有名的跳蛙》发表于1865年，是马克·吐温早期的短篇小说名篇，经常被收入美国文学教材。小说结构完整，语言清晰、活泼、幽默。小说分三个部分：故事的叙述者“我”应朋友之邀去拜访他；他向“我”讲述了“跳蛙”的故事；故事讲完了，我有事离开了朋友的家。小说的精彩之处是描写叙述者的朋友斯迈利和一位陌生者的对话及其“赛蛙”的场景。前者的言行与后者的言行全然不同。作者在描写两位人物时采取了不同的言语策略，不同的策略导致不同的结局。不同策略的内容是什么？是怎样的不同结局？读完小说后，读者在忍俊不禁之余又能从中获得怎样的启示？这些答案都“隐藏”在两位人物各自的话语和行动之中，请仔细思索。

Chapter 3　Billy Budd

by Herman Melville

(*Excerpts*)

一、作者简介

赫尔曼·麦尔维尔(1819—1891)，美国19世纪杰出的小说家、诗人、哲学家。他的长篇小说有《泰比》(1846)、《奥穆》(1847)、《玛迪》(1849)、《雷德伯恩》(1849)、《白鲸》(1851)、《皮埃尔》(1852)、《伊兹莱尔·波特》(1855)、《骗子》(1857)，中短篇小说有《巴特比》(1853)、《贝尼托·切莱诺》(1855)、《水手比利·巴德》(1924)等。他的诗作包括《战争诗集》(1866)和《克拉勒尔》(1876)等。其中，《白鲸》被公认为作者的代表作，他去世后出版的中篇小说《比利·巴德》同样具有极高的思想价值和艺术魅力。

麦尔维尔12岁丧父，家道开始衰落。他先后当过银行职员、店员、教师、农场工人、海关检查员等。他从1839年至1844年一直当水手，饱尝生活的艰辛和社会的冷酷。这些经历成为他日后创作的丰富源泉。

人与自然的关系、人性善与恶的本质、社会政治与个人自由、对资本主义本质的思考是麦尔维尔作品触及的中心话题。他将个人命运与社会时代的发展结合起来，从社会、宗教、政治等视角审视社会本身存在的种种问题、人与自然的对立和斗争、社会政治权威与个人自由意志之间的冲突等。这些问题包含哲学意蕴，使他的作品具有深刻的思想意义。对天真的质疑、对人性与社会中罪恶的揭示是他众多作品共有的核心议题。麦尔维尔的作品语言华丽而庄严，结构安排巧妙，善用修辞，喜欢引经据典，常用象征和暗喻。这些创作风格增强了其作品的思想深度和艺术魅力，读者因此可以将他的某些小说(如《白鲸》等)当做寓言来阅读。同时，这些写作手法也在挑战读者的阅读和理解能力。

麦尔维尔生前默默无闻，文学创作生涯曲折而坎坷，晚年穷困潦倒。他虽然是霍桑的朋友，但远不及霍桑出名。到了20世纪20年代，人们才发现他的文学才华。如今，麦尔维尔已被视为一位世界文坛的巨匠。

二、文本选读

Billy Budd

CHAPTER 1

In the time before steamships, or then more frequently than now, a stroller along the docks of any considerable sea-port would occasionally have his attention arrested by a group of bronzed mariners, man-of-war's men or merchant-sailors in holiday attire ashore on liberty. In certain instances they would flank, or, like a body-guard quite surround some superior figure of their own class, moving along with them like Aldebaran[1] among the lesser lights of his constellation. That signal object was the "Handsome Sailor" of the less prosaic time alike of the military and merchant navies. With no perceptible trace of the vainglorious about him, rather with the off-hand unaffectedness of natural regality, he seemed to accept the spontaneous homage of his shipmates.

A somewhat remarkable instance recurs to me. In Liverpool, now half a century ago, I saw under the shadow of the great dingy street—wall of Prince's Dock (an obstruction long since removed) a common sailor, so intensely black that he must needs have been a native African of the unadulterate blood of Ham. A symmetric figure much above the average height. The two ends of a gay silk handkerchief thrown loose about the neck danced upon the displayed ebony of his chest; in his ears were big hoops of gold, and a Scotch Highland bonnet with a tartan band set off his shapely head. It was a hot noon in July; and his face, lustrous with perspiration, beamed with barbaric good humor. In jovial sallies right and left, his white teeth flashing into he rollicked along, the centre of a company of his shipmates. These were made up of such an assortment of tribes and complexions as would have well fitted them to be marched up by Anacharsis Cloots before the bar of the first French Assembly as Representatives of the Human Race. At each spontaneous tribute rendered by the wayfarers to this black pagod of a fellow—the tribute of a pause and stare, and less frequent an exclamation, —the motley retinue showed that they took that sort of pride in the evoker of it which the Assyrian priests doubtless showed for their grand sculptured Bull when the faithful prostrated themselves.

To return. If in some cases a bit of a nautical Murat in setting forth his person ashore, the Handsome Sailor of the period in question evinced nothing of the dandified Billy-be-Damn, an amusing character all but extinct now, but occasionally to be encountered, and in a form yet more amusing than the original, at the tiller of the boats on the tempestuous Erie Canal or, more likely, vaporing in the groggeries along the tow-path. Invariably a proficient in his perilous calling, he was also more or less of a mighty boxer or wrestler. It was strength and beauty. Tales of his prowess were recited. Ashore he was the champion; afloat the spokesman; on every suitable occasion always foremost. Close-reefing top-sails in a gale, there he was, astride the weather yard-arm-end, foot in the Flemish horse as "stirrup," both hands tugging at the "earring" as at a bridle, in very much the attitude of young Alexander curbing the fiery Bucephalus. A superb figure, tossed up as by the horns of Taurus against the thunderous sky, cheerily hallooing to the strenuous file along the spar.

The moral nature was seldom out of keeping with the physical make. Indeed, except as toned by the former, the comeliness and power, always attractive in masculine conjunction, hardly could have drawn the sort of honest homage the Handsome Sailor in some examples received from his less gifted associates.

Such a cynosure, at least in aspect, and something such too in nature, though with important variations made apparent as the story proceeds, was welkin-eyed Billy Budd, or Baby Budd, as more familiarly under circumstances hereafter to be given he at last came to be called, aged twenty-one, a foretopman of the British fleet toward the close of the last decade of the eighteenth century. It was not very long prior to the time of the narration that follows that he had entered the King's Service, having been impressed on the Narrow Seas from a homeward-bound English merchantman into a seventy-four[2] outward-bound, H. M. S. *Bellipotent*; which ship, as was not unusual in those hurried days, having been obliged to put to sea short of her proper complement of men. Plump upon Billy at first sight in the gangway the boarding officer Lieutenant Ratcliff pounced, even before the merchantman's crew was formally mustered on the quarter-deck for his deliberate inspection. And him only he elected. For whether it was because the other men when ranged before him showed to ill advantage after Billy, or whether he had some scruples in view of the merchantman being rather short-handed, however it might be, the officer contented himself with his first spontaneous choice. To the surprise of the ship's company, though much to the Lieutenant's satisfaction, Billy made no demur. But, indeed, any demur would have been as idle as the protest of a goldfinch popped into a cage.

Noting this uncomplaining acquiescence, all but cheerful one might say, the shipmates turned a surprised glance of silent reproach at the sailor. The Shipmaster was one of those worthy mortals found in every vocation, even the humbler ones—the sort of person whom everybody agrees in calling "a respectable man." And—nor so strange to report as it may appear to be—though a ploughman of the troubled waters, life-long contending with the intractable elements, there was nothing this honest soul at heart loved better than simple peace and quiet. For the rest, he was fifty or thereabouts, a little inclined to corpulence, a prepossessing face, unwhiskered, and of an agreeable color—a rather full face, humanely intelligent in expression. On a fair day with a fair wind and all going well, a certain musical chime in his voice seemed to be the veritable unobstructed outcome of the innermost man. He had much prudence, much conscientiousness, and there were occasions when these virtues were the cause of overmuch disquietude in him. On a passage, so long as his craft was in any proximity to land, no sleep for Captain Graveling. He took to heart those serious responsibilities not so heavily borne by some shipmasters.

Now while Billy Budd was down in the forecastle getting his kit together, the *Bellipotent*'s Lieutenant, burly and bluff, nowise disconcerted by Captain Graveling's omitting to proffer the customary hospitalities on an occasion so unwelcome to him, an omission simply caused by preoccupation of thought, unceremoniously invited himself into the cabin, and also to a flask from the spirit-locker, a receptacle which his experienced eye instantly discovered. In fact he was one of those sea-dogs in whom all the hardship and peril of naval life in the great prolonged wars of his time never impaired the natural instinct for sensuous enjoyment. His duty he always faithfully did; but duty is sometimes a dry obligation, and he was for irrigating its aridity, whensoever possible, with a fertilizing decoction of strong waters. For the cabin's proprietor there was nothing left but to play the part of the enforced host with whatever grace and alacrity were practicable. As necessary adjuncts to the flask, he silently placed tumbler and water-jug before the irrepressible guest. But excusing himself from partaking just then, he dismally watched the unembarrassed officer deliberately diluting his grog a little, then tossing it off in three swallows, pushing the empty tumbler away, yet not so far as to be beyond easy reach, at the same time settling himself in his seat and smacking his lips with high satisfaction, looking straight at the host.

These proceedings over, the Master broke the silence; and there lurked a rueful reproach in the tone of his voice: "Lieutenant, you are going to take my best man from me, the jewel of 'em."

"Yes, I know," rejoined the other, immediately drawing back the tumbler preliminary to a replenishing; "Yes, I know. Sorry."

"Beg pardon, but you don't understand, Lieutenant. See here now. Before I shipped that young fellow, my forecastle was a rat-pit of quarrels. It was black times, I tell you, aboard the Rights here. I was worried to that degree my pipe had no comfort for me. But Billy came; and it was like a Catholic priest striking peace in an Irish shindy. Not that he preached to them or said or did anything in particular; but a virtue went out of him, sugaring the sour ones. They took to him like hornets to treacle; all but the buffer of the gang, the big shaggy chap with the fire-red whiskers. He indeed out of envy, perhaps, of the newcomer, and thinking such a 'sweet and pleasant fellow,' as he mockingly designated him to the others, could hardly have the spirit of a game-cock, must needs bestir himself in trying to get up an ugly row with him. Billy forebore with him and reasoned with him in a pleasant way—he is something like myself, Lieutenant, to whom aught like a quarrel is hateful—but nothing served. So, in the second dog-watch one day the Red Whiskers in presence of the others, under pretence of showing Billy just whence a sirloin steak was cut—for the fellow had once been a butcher—insultingly gave him a dig under the ribs. Quick as lightning Billy let fly his arm. I dare say he never meant to do quite as much as he did, but anyhow he gave the burly fool a terrible drubbing. It took about half a minute, I should think. And, lord bless you, the lubber was astonished at the celerity. And will you believe it, Lieutenant, the Red Whiskers now really loves Billy—loves him, or is the biggest hypocrite that ever I heard of. But they all love him. Some of 'em do his washing, darn his old trousers for him; the carpenter is at odd times making a pretty little chest of drawers for him. Anybody will do anything for Billy Budd; and it's the happy family here. But now, Lieutenant, if that young fellow goes—I know how it will be aboard the Rights. Not again very soon shall I, coming up from dinner, lean over the capstan smoking a quiet pipe—no, not very soon again, I think. Ay, Lieutenant, you are going to take away the jewel of 'em; you are going to take away my peacemaker!" And with that the good soul had really some ado in checking a rising sob.

"Well," said the officer who had listened with amused interest to all this, and now waxing merry with his tipple; "Well, blessed are the peacemakers, especially the fighting peacemakers! And such are the seventy-four beauties some of which you see poking their noses out of the port-holes of yonder war-ship lying-to for me," pointing thro' the cabin window at the *Bellipotent*. "But courage! don't look so downhearted, man. Why, I pledge you in advance the royal approbation. Rest assured that His Majesty will be delighted to know that in a time when his hard tack is not sought for by sailors with such avidity as should be; a time also when some shipmasters privily resent the borrowing from them a tar or two for the service; His Majesty, I say, will be delighted to learn that one shipmaster at least cheerfully surrenders to the King, the flower of his flock, a sailor who with equal loyalty makes no dissent. —But where's my beauty? Ah," looking through the cabin's open door, "Here he comes; and, by Jove—lugging along his chest—Apollo with his portmanteau! —My man," stepping out to him, "you can't take that big box aboard a war-ship. The boxes there are mostly shot-boxes. Put your duds in a bag, lad. Boot and saddle for the cavalryman, bag and hammock for the man-of-war's man."

The transfer from chest to bag was made. And, after seeing his man into the cutter and then following him down, the Lieutenant pushed off from the *Rights-of-Man*. That was the merchant-ship's name; tho' by her master and crew abbreviated in sailor fashion into the *Rights*. The hard-headed Dundee owner was a staunch admirer of Thomas Paine[3] whose book in rejoinder to Burke's arraignment of the French Revolution had then been published for some time and had gone everywhere. In christening his vessel after the title of Paine's volume, the man of Dundee was something like his contemporary shipowner, Stephen Girard of Philadelphia, whose sympathies, alike with his native land and its liberal philosophers, he evinced by naming his ships after Voltaire, Diderot, and so forth.

But now, when the boat swept under the merchantman's stern, and officer and oarsmen were noting—some bitterly and others with a grin, —the name emblazoned there; just then it was that the new recruit jumped up from the bow where the coxswain had directed him to sit, and waving his hat to his silent shipmates sorrowfully looking over at him from the taffrail, bade the lads a genial good-bye. Then, making a salutation as to the ship herself, "And good-bye to you too, old *Rights-of-Man*."

"Down, Sir!" roared the Lieutenant, instantly assuming all the rigour of his rank, though with difficulty repressing a smile.

To be sure, Billy's action was a terrible breach of naval decorum. But in that decorum he had never been instructed; in consideration of which the Lieutenant would hardly have been so energetic in reproof but for the concluding farewell to the ship. This he rather took as meant to convey a covert sally on the new recruit's part, a sly slur at impressment in general, and that of himself in especial. And yet, more likely, if satire it was in effect, it was hardly so by intention, for Billy, tho' happily endowed with the gayety of high health, youth, and a free heart, was yet by no means of a satirical turn. The will to it and the sinister dexterity were alike wanting. To deal in double meanings and insinuations of any sort was quite foreign to his nature.

As to his enforced enlistment, that he seemed to take pretty much as he was wont to take any vicissitude of weather. Like the animals, though no philosopher, he was, without knowing it, practically a fatalist. And, it may be, that he rather liked this adventurous turn in his affairs, which promised an opening into novel scenes and martial excitements.

Aboard the Indomitable our merchant-sailor was forthwith rated as an able-seaman and assigned to the starboard watch of the fore-top. He was soon at home in the service, not at all disliked for his unpretentious good looks and a sort of genial happy-go-lucky air. No merrier man in his mess: in marked contrast to certain other individuals included like himself among the impressed portion of the ship's company; for these when not actively employed were sometimes, and more particularly in the last dog-watch when the drawing near of twilight induced revery, apt to fall into a saddish mood which in some partook of sullenness. But they were not so young as our foretopman, and no few of them must have known a hearth of some sort; others may have had wives and children left, too probably, in uncertain circumstances, and hardly any but must have had acknowledged kith and kin, while for Billy, as will shortly be seen, his entire family was practically invested in himself.

CHAPTER 2

Though our new-made foretopman was well received in the top and on the gun decks, hardly here was he that cynosure he had previously been among those minor ship's companies of the merchant marine, with which companies only had he hitherto consorted.

He was young; and despite his all but fully developed frame, in aspect looked even younger than he really was, owing to a lingering adolescent expression in the as yet smooth face, all but feminine in purity of natural complexion, but where, thanks to his seagoing, the lily was quite suppressed and the rose had some ado visibly to flush through the tan.

To one essentially such a novice in the complexities of factitious life, the abrupt transition from his former and simpler sphere to the ampler and more knowing world of a great war-ship; this might well have abashed him had there been any conceit or vanity in his composition. Among her miscellaneous multitude, the *Bellipotent* mustered several individuals who, however inferior in grade, were of no common natural stamp, sailors more signally susceptive of that air which continuous martial discipline and repeated presence in battle can in some degree impart even to the average man. As the Handsome Sailor, Billy Budd's position aboard the seventy-four was something analogous to that of a rustic beauty transplanted from the provinces and brought into competition with the highborn dames of the court. But this change of circumstances he scarce noted. As little did he observe that something about him provoked an ambiguous smile in one or two harder faces among the blue-jackets. Nor less unaware was he of the peculiar favorable effect his person and demeanour had upon the more intelligent gentlemen of the quarter-deck. Nor could this well have been otherwise. Cast in a mould peculiar to the finest physical examples of those Englishmen in whom the Saxon[4] strain would seem not at all to partake of any Norman or other admixture, he showed in face that humane look of reposeful good nature which the Greek sculptor in some instances gave to his heroic strong man, Hercules. But this again was subtly modified by another and pervasive quality. The ear, small and shapely, the arch of the foot, the curve in mouth and nostril, even the indurated hand dyed to the orange-tawny of the toucan's bill, a hand telling alike of the halyards and tar-bucket; but, above all, something in the mobile expression, and every chance attitude and movement, something suggestive of a mother eminently favored by Love and the Graces[5]; all this strangely indicated a lineage in direct contradiction to his lot. The mysteriousness here became less mysterious through a matter-of-fact elicited when Billy, at the capstan, was being formally mustered into the service. Asked by the officer, a small brisk little gentleman, as it chanced among other questions, his place of birth, he replied, "Please, Sir, I don't know."

"Don't know where you were born? —Who was your father?"

"God knows, Sir."

Struck by the straightforward simplicity of these replies, the officer next asked, "Do you know anything about your beginning?"

"No, Sir. But I have heard that I was found in a pretty silklined basket hanging one morning from the knocker of a good man's door in Bristol."

"*Found*, say you? Well," throwing back his head and looking up and down the new recruit; "Well, it turns out to have been a pretty good find. Hope they'll find some more like you, my man; the fleet sadly needs them."

Yes, Billy Budd was a foundling, a presumable by-blow, and, evidently, no ignoble one. Noble descent was as evident in him as in a blood horse.

For the rest, with little or no sharpness of faculty or any trace of the wisdom of the serpent, nor yet quite a dove[6], he possessed that kind and degree of intelligence going along with the unconventional rectitude of a sound human creature, one to whom not yet has been proffered the questionable apple of knowledge. He was illiterate; he could not read, but he could sing, and like the illiterate nightingale was sometimes the composer of his own song.

Of self-consciousness he seemed to have little or none, or about as much as we may reasonably impute to a dog of Saint Bernard's breed.

Habitually living with the elements and knowing little more of the land than as a beach, or, rather, that portion of the terraqueous globe providentially set apart for dance-houses, doxies and tapsters, in short what sailors call a "fiddlers'-green," his simple nature remained unsophisticated by those moral obliquities which are not in every case incompatible with that manufacturable thing known as respectability. But are sailors, frequenters of "fiddlers'-greens," without vices? No; but less often than with landsmen do their vices, so called, partake of crookedness of heart, seeming less to proceed from viciousness than exuberance of vitality after long constraint; frank manifestations in accordance with natural law. By his original constitution aided by the cooperating influences of his lot, Billy in many respects was little more than a sort of upright barbarian, much such perhaps as Adam presumably might have been ere the urbane Serpent wriggled himself into his company.

And here be it submitted that apparently going to corroborate the doctrine of man's fall, a doctrine now popularly ignored, it is observable that where certain virtues pristine and unadulterate peculiarly characterize anybody in the external uniform of civilization, they will upon scrutiny seem not to be derived from custom or convention, but rather to be out of keeping with these, as if indeed exceptionally transmitted from a period prior to Cain's city[7] and citified man. The character marked by such qualities has to an unvitiated taste an untampered—with flavor like that of berries, while the man thoroughly civilized, even in a fair specimen of the breed, has to the same moral palate a questionable smack as of a compounded wine. To any stray inheritor of these primitive qualities found, like Caspar Hauser[8], wandering dazed in any Christian capital of our time, the good-natured poet's famous invocation, near two thousand years ago, of the good rustic out of his latitude in the Rome of the Cesars, still appropriately holds.

"Honest and poor, faithful in word and thought,
What has thee, Fabian, to the city brought?"

Though our Handsome Sailor had as much of masculine beauty as one can expect anywhere to see; nevertheless, like the beautiful woman in one of Hawthorne's minor tales, there was just one thing amiss in him. No visible blemish, indeed, as with the lady; no, but an occasional liability to a vocal defect. Though in the hour of elemental uproar or peril he was everything that a sailor should be, yet under sudden provocation of strong heart-feeling, his voice otherwise singularly musical, as if expressive of the harmony within, was apt to develop an organic hesitancy, in fact, more or less of a stutter or even worse. In this particular Billy was a striking instance that the arch interferer, the envious marplot of Eden[9], still has more or less to do with every human consignment to this planet of earth. In every case, one way or another he is sure to slip in his little card, as much as to remind us—I too have a hand here.

The avowal of such an imperfection in the Handsome Sailor should be evidence not alone that he is not presented as a conventional hero, but also that the story in which he is the main figure is no romance.

CHAPTER 3

At the time of Billy Budd's arbitrary enlistment into the *Bellipotent* that ship was on her way to join the Mediterranean fleet. No long time elapsed before the 'unction was effected. As one of that fleet the seventy-four participated in its movements, tho' at times, on account of her superior sailing qualities, in the absence of frigates, despatched on separate duty as a scout and at times on less temporary service. But with all this the story has little concernment, restricted as it is to the inner life of one particular ship and the career of an individual sailor.

It was the summer of 1797. In the April of that year had occurred the commotion at Spithead followed in May by a second and yet more serious outbreak in the fleet at the Nore. The latter is known, and without exaggeration in the epithet, as the Great Mutiny. It was indeed a demonstration more menacing to England than the contemporary manifestoes and conquering and proselyting armies of the French Directory. To the British Empire the Nore Mutiny was what a strike in the fire-brigade would be to London threatened by general arson. In a crisis when the kingdom might well have anticipated the famous signal that some years later published along the naval line of battle what it was that upon occasion England expected of Englishmen; *that* was the time when at the mast-heads of the three-deckers and seventy-fours moored in her own roadstead—a fleet, the right arm of a Power then all but the sole free conservative one of the Old World—the blue-jackets, to be numbered by thousands, ran up with huzzas the British colors with the union and cross wiped out; by that cancellation transmuting the flag of founded law and freedom defined, into the enemy's red meteor of unbridled and unbounded revolt. Reasonable discontent growing out of practical grievances in the fleet had been ignited into irrational combustion, as by live cinders blown across the Channel from France in flames.

The event converted into irony for a time those spirited strains of Dibdin—as a song-writer no mean auxiliary to the English Government at the European conjuncture—strains celebrating, among other things, the patriotic devotion of the British tar: "And as for my life, 'tis the King's!"

Such an episode in the Island's grand naval story her naval historians naturally abridge; one of them (G. P. R. James) candidly acknowledging that fain would he pass it over did not "impartiality forbid fastidiousness." And yet his mention is less a narration than a reference, having to do hardly at all with details. Nor are these readily to be found in the libraries. Like some other events in every age befalling states everywhere, including America, the Great Mutiny was of such character that national pride along with views of policy would fain shade it off into the historical background. Such events can not be ignored, but there is a considerate way of historically treating them. If a well-constituted individual refrains from blazoning aught amiss or calamitous in his family, a nation in the like circumstance may without reproach be equally discreet.

Though after parleyings between Government and the ringleaders, and concessions by the former as to some glaring abuses, the first uprising—that at Spithead—with difficulty was put down, or matters for the time pacified; yet at the Nore the unforeseen renewal of insurrection on a yet larger scale, and emphasized in the conferences that ensued by demands deemed by the authorities not only inadmissible but aggressively insolent, indicated—if the Red Flag did not sufficiently do so—what was the spirit animating the men. Final suppression, however, there was; but only made possible perhaps by the unswerving loyalty of the marine corps and voluntary resumption of loyalty among influential sections of the crews.

To some extent the Nore Mutiny may be regarded as analogous to the distempering irruption of contagious fever in a frame constitutionally sound, and which anon throws it off.

At all events, of these thousands of mutineers were some of the tars who not so very long afterwards—whether wholly prompted thereto by patriotism, or pugnacious instinct, or by both, —helped to win a coronet for Nelson at the Nile, and the naval crown of crowns for him at Trafalgar[10]. To the mutineers those battles, and especially Trafalgar, were a plenary absolution and a grand one: For all that goes to make up scenic naval display, heroic magnificence in arms, those battles, especially Trafalgar, stand unmatched in human annals.

三、人物解析

《比利·巴德》是麦尔维尔晚年创作的最后一部小说，直到1924年才出版。小说主要讲述三个英国人在“永胜号”船上的故事。比利·巴德被强征到英国战舰上，当了一名前桅水手。他为人正直敬业，受到船长和船员的一致喜爱。一天，他从同事丹斯克尔那里获悉兵器教官克拉加德对自己怀有恶意，但他不以为然。后来，克拉加德在船长威尔面前诬告比利试图谋反。为辨别真伪，船长叫他们二人当面对质。比利气愤之极，加之有口吃毛病，无法辩驳，竟然一拳打死了克拉加德。当时正值英法军队交战时期，为整肃军规和防止不测，比利被船长处以绞刑。

比利是小说的主要人物之一。小说的前两章集中介绍了比利的情况，特别描述了他的外貌特征，这对故事情节的发展和人物的命运变化起了铺垫作用。小说开篇便称比利是“我们中的佼佼者”，是“英俊的水手”、人们关注的焦点人物。他是一个强有力的拳击手或摔跤手，是“力与美”的结合；他只有21岁，被称为“宝贝·巴德”、“人中的珠宝”；他又是“和平的使者”；他年轻，发育完全成熟，但看上去比实际年龄更年轻；他有一张女人般的脸，天然而纯净；他像是从英国人最优秀的模子里铸造出来的；他的脸透露出恬静的善意和充满人性的表情，那就是希腊雕刻家手下英雄大力神赫拉克勒斯的神情。当问及自己的出生地和父亲是谁时，比利回答说“不知道”。但他听说，他是在一只垫着丝绸衬底的篮子里被发现的，篮子被挂在一个好人的门环上，他身上有贵族血统；他又有点像与撒旦见面之前的亚当；尽管比利散发着阳刚之美，但就像霍桑故事中的美女一样也有缺点——他有时有口吃的毛病。小说的第18章视比利为“堕落之前年轻亚当的裸体雕像”。

小说对比利·巴德的外貌描写充满赞美之词，这些词语为读者理解小说的内涵提供了许多暗示性的信息。我们可以从以下五个方面解析比利的外貌特征及其蕴涵的意义。第一，从“人性恶”的宗教角度上讲，比利的“美貌”必遭同行妒忌。因此，他的“英俊”最终酿成他的悲剧。他如同伊甸园的亚当，天真无邪，但也逃不过撒旦的诱惑，落入克拉加德的陷阱，后者露出其固有的“恶”。第二，从一般的人性上讲，比利有女人味——女人往往是非理性和激情的化身，这预示了他在船长和克拉加德面前采取不理智的行为；同时，一个人无论多么完美，他总有缺点。比利的短处是口吃。在关键时刻，他的口吃导致他诉诸暴力，酿成命案，他最终为此付出生命的代价。第三，从社会政治角度上看，他是同伴心中的偶像，享受同伴的敬意，又是“和平制造者”，他理当为同伴作出贡献。他单身一人，没有牵挂，所以为同伴献身也在情理之中。第四，从基督教角度看，有关他不知其父和不知自己出身的身世也让人联想到代替人类赎罪的耶稣基督。这些解读方式正好契合小说富含多层面的主题思想。第五，从文学视角看，小说将比利的外表与神话或宗教人物联系起来，让读者觉得比利既是一个真实的人物，也是一个符号、一个象征。此举赋予比利更多的含义，也增强了作品的思想深度。

四、难点注释

1. Aldebaran：金牛星。
2. seventy-four：指的是配备七十四门炮火的“战力号(Bellipotent)”军舰。
3. Thomas Paine：托马斯·潘恩(1737—1809)，美国独立战争时期的政治家和资产阶级民主主义者，其作品《常识》号召北美殖民地人民反抗英国统治；他曾参加北美独立战争，著有《人的权利》和《理性时代》等。在小说《水手比利·巴德》中，水手比利·巴德以前服役的船只名称为“人的权利号(Rights-of-Man)”，表明作者麦尔维尔崇尚人的自然权利。
4. Saxon：撒克逊人，英国人。
5. Love and the Graces：(希腊和罗马神话)爱神(丘比特)和美惠三女神(灿烂、欢乐、花朵)。
6. quite a dove：像鸽子一样温顺。
7. Cain's city：该隐的城市。《创世记》(4：13-17)记载，该隐杀死哥哥亚伯后被上帝驱逐，被迫离家，最后在伊甸园东部的诺得之地建起另一座城市。
8. Caspar Hauser：卡斯帕尔·豪斯尔(1812？—1833)，一个富有传奇色彩的德国青年。有人说他有王室血统，又有人说他是个江湖骗子。他遭人囚禁，一直生活在一个黑暗的地窖里面，完全与世隔绝，后被人刺死。小说引用他旨在说明他的生活方式具有原生态特点。
9. marplot of Eden：伊甸园的捣乱者，即撒旦。
10. at Trafalgar：特指特拉法尔加战役。1805年英国海军统帅纳尔逊率领英国皇家海军在西班牙西南部的特拉法尔加角海战中大败法国和西班牙联合舰队，进一步巩固了英国海军的海上霸主地位。在这场战役中纳尔逊本人身受重伤而亡，他因此被称为“海军皇冠上最璀璨的明珠”(the naval crown of crowns)。纳尔逊是英国历史上最伟大的战争英雄之一。

五、延伸阅读与批评

《白鲸》被公认为麦尔维尔的代表作。小说对船长亚伯的外部形象描写给读者留下深刻的印象，而且该形象具有多重含义。第16、19、28章集中描述亚伯：从整体到局部、从上到下，甚至从内到外，特别是对他的眼神、一只假腿、脸部特征的描述更加细致。它们全方位地展示了亚伯的特征。这些文字合成的亚伯“画像”引发读者思考：他是一个人、超人的神，还是一个魔鬼？或者，他是一个人与神(上帝或上帝之子耶稣)、人与动物(白鲸)、人与魔鬼(怪物)的“混合物”？再者，那些用来修饰亚伯的词语背后也有丰富的联想意义。在第28章，小说特别提到亚伯“出场”的时间(圣诞节期间)和当时的天气情况，这是不是作者有意安排的？综上所述，亚伯的人物形象特征对读者理解他本人的命运走向、他与其他人物的关系、小说的主题思想等都有暗示和启示作用。

Chapter 4 A Father-To-Be

by Saul Bellow

一、作者简介

索尔·贝娄(1915—2005)，美国20世纪最杰出的小说家之一，1976年获得诺贝尔文学奖。他的创作生涯长达半个世纪，代表性的小说有《晃来晃去的人》(1944)、《受害者》(1947)、《奥吉·马奇历险记》(1953)、《只争朝夕》(1956)、《雨王汉德森》(1959)、《赫索格》(1964)、《塞姆勒先生的行星》(1970)、《洪堡的礼物》(1975)、《院长的十二月》(1982)、《更多的人死于心碎》(1987)，两部中篇小说是《盗窃》(1989)和《贝拉罗莎的亲戚》(1989)。他还写了短篇小说集《他的洋相》(1984)，论文集《我们走向何方》(1956)和《它全加起来》(1994)以及剧本《最后的分析》等。

贝娄出生在加拿大，父母都是来自俄国的犹太移民，后来举家迁往芝加哥。他是美国犹太文学的代表人物。他学过法语、英语、依第绪语和希伯来语，先后就读芝加哥大学、西北大学，攻读社会学和人类学，而且他对心理学也很感兴趣。后来他到《大不列颠百科全书》编辑部工作。第二次世界大战后贝娄曾在明尼苏达大学、纽约大学和普林斯顿大学教书。因此，贝娄是一个博学多识的学者型作家。

自由、爱(情)、家庭的破裂与性关系、成功与失败、权力与死亡等是贝娄的长篇小说经常探讨的话题。他的作品往往通过刻画有学问的犹太知识分子来反映美国社会现实中人类的共同问题：人与社会的关系、心理与现实的关系；人在精神上的压抑、心理上的挫伤和生活中的孤独感；对“自我”和人性的追寻。他希望通过作品表达出自己的心声：人要有尊严；人与人之间要相互沟通、同情、理解；世界需要爱和人性的回归。1976年诺贝尔文学奖颁奖词这样评价贝娄的作品：“他的作品中融合了对人性的理解和对当代文化的精湛分析。”

贝娄在创作手法上将现代主义文学的心理描写和现实主义的客观细致描写结合起来。他对人物内心世界的剖析有思想深度，有时甚至上升到哲学层面。他对心理现实和物质现实双重世界的描写将现实主义文学推向新的高度。

二、文本选读

A Father-To-Be

The strangest notions had a way of forcing themselves into Rogin's mind. Just thirty-one and passable-looking, with short black hair, small eyes, but a high, open forehead, he was a research chemist, and his mind was generally serious and dependable. But on a snowy Sunday evening while this stocky man, buttoned to the chin in a Burberry coat and walking in his preposterous gait—feet turned outward—was going toward the subway, he fell into a peculiar state[1].

He was on his way to have supper with his fiancée. She had phoned him a short while ago and said, "You'd better pick up a few things on the way."

"What do we need?"

"Some roast beef, for one thing. I bought a quarter of a pound coming home from my aunt's."

"Why a quarter of a pound, Joan?" said Rogin, deeply annoyed. "That's just about enough for one good sandwich."

"So you have to stop at a delicatessen. I had no more money."

He was about to ask, "What happened to the thirty dollars I gave you on Wednesday?" but he knew that would not be right.

"I had to give Phyllis money for the cleaning woman," said Joan.

Phyllis, Joan's cousin, was a young divorcee, extremely wealthy. The two women shared an apartment.

"Roast beef," he said, "and what else?"

"Some shampoo, sweetheart. We've used up all the shampoo. And hurry, darling, I've missed you all day."

"And I've missed you," said Rogin, but to tell the truth he had been worrying most of the time. He had a younger brother whom he was putting through college[2], and his mother, whose annuity wasn't quite enough in these days of inflation and high taxes, needed money, too. Joan had debts he was helping her to pay, for she wasn't working. She was looking for something suitable to do. Beautiful, well-educated, aristocratic in her attitude, she couldn't clerk in a dime store, she couldn't model clothes (Rogin thought this made girls vain and stiff, and he didn't want her to); she couldn't be a waitress or a cashier. What could she be? Well, something would turn up, and meantime Rogin hesitated to complain. He paid her bills—the dentist, the department store, the osteopath, the doctor, the psychiatrist. At Christmas, Rogin almost went mad. Joan bought him a velvet smoking jacket with frog fasteners, a beautiful pipe, and a pouch. She bought Phyllis a garnet brooch, an Italian silk umbrella, and a gold cigarette holder. For other friends, she bought Dutch pewter and Swedish glassware. Before she was through[3], she had spent five hundred dollars of Rogin's money. He loved her too much to show his suffering. He believed she had a far better nature than his. She didn't worry about money. She had a marvelous character, always cheerful, and she really didn't need a psychiatrist at all. She went to one because Phyllis did and it made her curious. She tried too much to keep up with her cousin, whose father had mad millions in the rug business.

While the woman in the drugstore was wrapping the shampoo bottle a clear idea suddenly arose in Rogin's thoughts. Money surrounds you in life as the earth does in death. Superimposition[4] is the universal law. Who is free? No one is free. Who has no burdens? Everyone is under pressure. The very rocks, the waters of the earth, beasts, men, children—everyone has some weight to carry. This idea was extremely clear to him at first. Soon it became rather vague, but it had a great effect nevertheless, as if someone had given him a valuable gift. (Not like the velvet smoking jacket he couldn't bring himself to wear, or the pipe it choked him to smoke.) The notion that all were under pressure and affliction, instead of saddening him, had the opposite influence. It put him in a wonderful mood. It was extraordinary how happy he became and, in addition, clear-sighted. His eyes all at once were opened to what was around him. He was with delight how the druggist and the woman who wrapped the shampoo bottle were smiling and flirting, how the lines of worry in her face went over into lines of cheer and the druggist's receding gums did not hinder his kidding and friendliness. And in the delicatessen, also, it was amazing how much Rogin noted and what happiness it gave him simply to be there.

Delicatessens on Sunday night, when all other stores are shut, will overcharge you ferociously, and Rogin would normally have been on guard, but he was not tonight, or scarcely so. Smells of pickle, sausage, mustard, and smoked fish overjoyed him. He pitied the people who would buy the chicken salad and chopped herring; they could do it only because their sight was too dim to see what they were getting—the fat flakes of pepper on the chicken, the soppy herring, mostly vinegar-soaked stale bread. Who would buy them? Late risers, people living alone, waking up in the darkness of the afternoon, finding their refrigerators empty, or people whose gaze was turned inward. The roast beef looked not bad, and Rogin ordered a pound.

While the storekeeper was slicing the meat, he yelled at a Puerto Rican kid who was reaching for a bag of chocolate cookies. "Hey, you want to pull me down the whole display on yourself? You, chico, wait a half a minute." This storekeeper, though he looked like one of Pancho Villa's bandits, the kind that smeared their enemies with syrup and staked them down on anthills, a man with toadlike eyes and stout hands made to clasp pistols hung around his belly, was not so bad. He was a New York man, thought Rogin—who was from Albany himself—a New York man toughened by every abuse of the city, trained to suspect everyone. But in his own realm, on the board behind the counter, there was justice. Even clemency.

The Puerto Rican kid wore a complete cowboy outfit—a green hat with white braid, guns, chaps, spurs, boots, and gauntlets—but he couldn't speak any English. Rogin unhooked the cellophane bag of hard circular cookies and gave it to him. The boy tore the cellophane with his teeth and began to chew one of those dry chocolate discs. Rogin recognized his state—the energetic dream of childhood. Once, he, too, had found these dry biscuits delicious. It would have bored him now to eat one.

What else would Joan like? Rogin thought fondly. Some strawberries? "Give me some frozen strawberries. No, raspberries, she likes those better. And heavy cream. And some rolls, cream cheese, and some of those rubber-looking gherkins."

"What rubber?"

"Those deep green, with eyes. Some ice cream might be in order, too."

He tried to think of a compliment, a good comparison, an endearment, for Joan when she'd open the door. What about her complexion? There was really nothing to compare her sweet, small, daring, shapely, timid, defiant, loving face to. How difficult she was[5], and how beautiful!

As Rogin went down into the stony, odorous, metallic, captive air of the subway, he was diverted by an unusual confession made by a man to his friend. These were two very tall men, shapeless in their winter clothes, as if their coats concealed suits of chain mail.

"So, how long have you known me?" said one.

"Twelve years."

"Well, I have an admission to make," he said. "I've decided that I might as well. For years I've been a heavy drinker. You didn't know. Practically an alcoholic."

But his friend was not surprised, and he answered immediately, "Yes, I did know."

"You knew? Impossible! How could you?"

Why, thought Rogin, as if it could be a secret! Look at that long, austere, alcohol-washed face, that drink-ruined nose, the skin by his ears like turkey wattles, and those whiskey-saddened eyes.

"Well, I did know, though."

"You couldn't have. I can't believe it." He was upset, and his friend didn't seem to want to soothe him. "But it's all right now," he said. "I've been going to a doctor and taking pills, a new revolutionary Danish discovery. It's a miracle. I'm beginning to believe they can cure you of anything and everything. You can't beat the Danes in science. They do everything. They turned a man into a woman."

"That isn't how they stop you from drinking, is it?"

"No. I hope not. This is only like aspirin. It's super-aspirin. They call it the aspirin of the future. But if you use it, you have to stop drinking."

Rogin's illuminated mind asked of itself while the human tides of the subway swayed back and forth, and cars linked and transparent like fish bladders raced under the streets: How come he thought nobody would know what everybody couldn't help knowing[6]? And, as a chemist, he asked himself what kind of compound this new Danish drug might be, and started thinking about various inventions of his own, synthetic albumen, a cigarette that lit itself, a cheaper motor fuel. Ye gods, but he needed money! As never before. What was to be done? His mother was growing more and more difficult. On Friday night, she had neglected to cut up his meat for him, and he was hurt. She had sat at the table motionless, with her long-suffering face, severe, and let him cut his own meat, a thing she almost never did. She had always spoiled him and made his brother envy him. but what she expected now! Oh, Lord, how he had to pay, and it had never even occurred to him formerly that these things might have a price.

Seated, one of the passengers, Rogin recovered his calm, happy, even clairvoyant state of mind. To think of money was to think as the world wanted you to think; then you'd never be your own master. When people said they wouldn't do something for love or money, they meant that love and money were opposite passions and one the enemy of the other. He went on to reflect how little people knew about this, how they slept through life, how small a light the light of consciousness was. Rogin's clean, snub-nosed face shone while his heart was torn with joy at these deeper thoughts of our ignorance. You might take this drunkard as an example, who for long years thought his closest friends never suspected he drank. Rogin looked up and down the aisle for this remarkable knightly symbol, but he was gone.

However, there was no lack of things to see. There was a small girl with a new white muff; into the muff a doll's head was sewn, and the child was happy and affectionately vain of it, while her old man, stout and grim, with a huge scowling nose, kept picking her up and resettling her in the seat, as if he were trying to change her into something else. Then another child, led by her mother, boarded the car, and this other child carried the very same doll-faced muff, and this greatly annoyed both parents. The woman, who looked like a difficult, contentious woman, took her daughter away. It seemed to Rogin that each child was in love with its own muff and didn't even see the other, but it was one of his foibles to think he understood the hearts of little children.

A foreign family next engaged his attention. They looked like Central Americans to him. on one side the mother, quite old, dark-faced, white-haired, and worn out; on the other a son with the whitened, porous hands of a dishwasher. But what was the dwarf who sat between them—a son or a daughter? The hair was long and wavy and the cheeks smooth, but the shirt and tie were masculine. The overcoat was feminine, but the shoes—the shoes were a puzzle. A pair of brown oxfords[7] with an outer seam like a man's, but Baby Louis heels like a woman's—a plain toe like a man's, but a strap across the instep like a woman's. No stockings. That didn't help much. The dwarf's fingers were beringed, but without a wedding band. There were small grim dents in the cheeks. The eyes were puffy and concealed, but Rogin did not doubt that they could reveal strange things if they chose and that this was a creature of remarkable understanding. He had for many years owned De la Mare's *Memoirs of a Midget*. Now he took a resolve; he would read it. As soon as he had decided, he was free from his consuming curiosity as to the dwarf's sex and was able to look at the person who sat beside him.

Thoughts very often grow fertile in the subway, because of the motion, the great company, the subtlety of the rider's state as he rattles under streets and rivers, under the foundations of great buildings, and Rogin's mind had already been strangely stimulated. Clasping the bag of groceries from which there rose odors of bread and pickle spice, he was following a train of reflections first about the chemistry of sex determination, the X and Y chromosomes, hereditary linkages, the uterus, afterward about his brother as tax exemption. He recalled two dreams of the night before. In one, an undertaker had offered to cut his hair and he had refused. In another he had been carrying a woman on his head. Sad dreams both! Very sad! Which was the woman—Joan or Mother? and the undertaker—his lawyer? He gave a deep sigh, and by force of habit began to put together his synthetic albumen that was to revolutionize the entire egg industry.

Meanwhile, he had not interrupted his examination of the passengers and had fallen into a study of the man next to him. This was a man whom he had never in his life seen before but with whom he now suddenly felt linked through all existence. He was middle-aged, sturdy, with clear skin and blue eyes. His hands were clean, well formed, but Rogin did not approve of them. The coat he wore was a fairly expensive blue check such as Rogin would never have chosen for himself. He would not have worn blue suede shoes, either, or such a faultless hat, a cumbersome felt animal of a hat encircled by a high, fat ribbon. There are all kinds of dandies, not all of them are of the flaunting kind; some are dandies of respectability, and Rogin's fellow passenger was one of these. His straight-nosed profile was handsome, yet he had betrayed his gift, for he was flat-looking. But in his flat way he seemed to warn people that he wanted no difficulties with them, he wanted nothing to do with them. Wearing such blue suede shoes, he could not afford to have people treading on his feet, and he seemed to draw about himself a circle of privilege, notifying all others to mind their own business and let him read his paper. He was holding a *Tribune*, and perhaps it would be overstatement to say that he was reading. He was holding it.

His clear skin and blue eyes, his straight and purely Roman nose—even the way he sat—all strongly suggested one person to Rogin: Joan. He tried to escape the comparison, but it couldn't be helped. This man not only looked like Joan's father, whom Rogin detested; he looked like Joan herself. Forty years hence, a son of hers, provided she had one, might be like this. A son of hers? Of such a son, he himself, Rogin, would be the father. Lacking in dominant traits as compared with Joan, his heritage would not appear. Probably the children would resemble her. Yes, think forty years ahead, and a man like this, who sat by him knee to knee in the hurtling car among their fellow creatures, unconscious participants in a sort of great carnival of transit—such a man would carry forward what had been Rogin.

This was why he felt bound to him through all existence. What were forty years reckoned against eternity! Forty years were gone, and he was gazing at his own son. Here he was. Rogin was frightened and moved. "My son! My son!" he said to himself, and the pity of it almost made him burst into tears. The holy and frightful work of the masters of life and death brought this about. We were their instruments. We worked toward ends we thought were our own. But no! The whole thing was so unjust. To suffer, to labor, to toil and force your way through the spikes of life, to crawl through its darkest caverns, to push through the worst, to struggle under the weight of economy, to make money—only to become the father of a fourth-rate man of the world like this, so flat-looking, with his ordinary, clean, rosy, uninteresting, self-satisfied, fundamentally bourgeois face. What a curse to have a dull son! A son like this, who could never understand his father. They had absolutely nothing, but nothing, in common, he and this neat, chubby, blue-eyed man. He was so pleased, though Rogin, with all he owned and all he did and all he was that he could hardly unfasten his lip[8]. Look at that lip, sticking up at the tip like a little thorn or egg tooth. He wouldn't give anyone the time of day[9]. Would this perhaps be general forty years from now? Would personalities be chillier as the world aged and grew colder? The inhumanity of the next generation incensed Rogin. Father and son had no sign[10] to make to each other. Terrible! Inhuman! What a vision of existence it gave him. Man's personal aims were nothing, illusion. The life force occupied each of us in turn in its progress toward its own fulfillment, trampling on our individual humanity, using us for its own ends like mere dinosaurs or bees, exploiting love heartlessly, making us engage in the social process, labor, struggle for money, and submit to the law of pressure, the universal law of layers, superimposition!

What the blazes am I getting into? Rogin thought. To be the father of a throwback to her father[11]. The image of this white-haired, gross, peevish old man with his ugly selfish blue eyes revolted Rogin. This was how his grandson would look. Joan, with whom Rogin was now more and more displeased, could not help that. For her, it was inevitable. But did it have to be inevitable for him? Well, then, Rogin, you fool, don't be a damned instrument. Get out of the way!

But it was too late for this, because he had already experienced the sensation of sitting next to his own son, his son and Joan's. He kept staring at him, waiting for him to say something, but the presumptive son remained coldly silent though he must have been aware of Rogin's scrutiny. They even got out at the same stop—Sheridan Square. When they stepped to the platform the man, without even looking at Rogin, went away in a different direction in his detestable blue-checked coat, with his rosy, nasty face.

The whole thing upset Rogin very badly. When he approached Joan's door and heard Phyllis's little dog Henri barking even before he could knock, his face was very tense. "I won't be used," he declared to himself. "I have my own right to exist." Joan had better watch out. She had a light way of bypassing grave questions he had given earnest thought to. She always assumed no really disturbing thing would happen. He could not afford the luxury of such a care-free, debonair attitude himself, because he had to work hard and earn money so that disturbing things would not happen. Well, at the moment this situation could not be helped, and he really did not mind the money if he could feel that she was not necessarily the mother of such a son as his subway son or entirely the daughter of that awful, obscene father of hers. After all, Rogin was not himself so much like either of his parents, and quite different from his brother.

Joan came to the door, wearing one of Phyllis's expensive housecoats. It suited her very well. At first sight of her happy face, Rogin was brushed by the shadow of resemblance; the touch of it was extremely light, almost figmentary, but it made his flesh tremble.

She began to kiss him, saying, "Oh, my baby. You're covered with snow. Why didn't you wear your hat? It's all over its little head"—her favorite third-person endearment.

"Well, let me put down this bag of stuff. Let me take off my coat," grumbled Rogin, and escaped from her embrace. Why couldn't she wait making up to him[12]? "It's so hot in here. My face is burning. Why do you keep this place at this temperature? And that damned dog keeps barking. If you didn't keep it cooped up, it wouldn't be so spoiled and noisy. Why doesn't anybody ever walk him?"

"Oh, it's not really so hot here! You've just come in from the cold. Don't you think this housecoat fits me better than Phyllis? Especially across the hips. She thinks so, too. She may sell it to me."

"I hope not," Rogin almost exclaimed.

She brought a towel to dry the melting snow from his short black hair. The flurry of rubbing excited Henri intolerably, and Joan locked him up in the bedroom, where he jumped persistently against the door with a rhythmic sound of claws on the wood.

Joan said, "Did you bring the shampoo?"

"Here it is."

"Then I'll wash your hair before dinner. Come."

"I don't want it washed."

"Oh, come on," she said, laughing.

Her lack of consciousness of guilt amazed him. he did not see how it could be. And the carpeted, furnished, lamplit, curtained room seemed to stand against his vision. So that he felt accusing and angry, his spirit sore and bitter, but it did not seem fitting to say why. Indeed, he began to worry lest the reason for it all slip away from him.

They took off his coat and his shirt in the bathroom, and she filled the sink. Rogin was full of his troubled emotions; now that his chest was bare he could feel them even more distinctly inside, and he said to himself, I'll have a thing or two to tell her pretty soon. I'm not letting them get away with it. "Do you think," he was going to tell her, "that I alone was made to carry the burden of the whole world on me? Do you think I was born just to be taken advantage of and sacrificed? Do you think I'm just a natural resource like a coal mine, or oil well, or fishery, or the like? Remember, that I'm a man is no reason why I should be loaded down. I have a soul in me no bigger or stronger than yours.

"Take away the external, like the muscles, deeper voice, and so forth, and what remains? A pair of spirits, practically alike[13]. So why shouldn't there also be equality? I can't always be the strong one."

"Sit here," said Joan bringing up a kitchen stool to the sink. "Your hair's gotten all matted."

He sat with his breast against the cool enamel, his chin on the edge of the basin, the green hot radiant water reflecting the glass and the tile, and the sweet, cool fragrant juice of the shampoo poured on his head. She began to wash him.

"You have the healthiest-looking scalp," she said. "It's all pink."

He answered, "Well, it should be white. There must be something wrong with me."

"But there's absolutely nothing wrong with you," she said and pressed against him from behind, surrounding him, pouring the water gently over him until it seemed to him that the water came from within him, it was the warm fluid of his own secret loving spirit overflowing into the sink, green and foaming and the words he had rehearsed he forgot, and his anger at his son-to-be disappeared altogether, and he sighed, and said to her from the water-filled hollow of the sink, "You always have such wonderful ideas, Joan. You know? You have a kind of instinct, a regular gift."

三、人物解析

《未来的爸爸》发表于 1955 年，是贝娄的短篇小说代表作之一。小说讲述了 31 岁的化学家罗金准备到未婚妻琼的家里吃晚饭的故事。琼要求罗金在路上买点洗发水、烤牛排、草莓等东西。罗金首先来到一家熟食店购物。期间他想到自己的母亲和未婚妻，想到自己身上的经济压力，想到自由和压力是人类的普遍规律。在地铁车站，罗金听到两个朋友谈论酗酒的话题后想到爱情和金钱的关系。在地铁车厢里，他看到一个人的长相既像琼的父亲，也像琼本人。而且罗金不喜欢此人。罗金由此引发联想：如果自己未来的儿子长得如此模样，那将是十分糟糕的。他的思绪进一步滋长，想到人性和未来的父子关系，想到人的尊严和自由等。他为此感到不安和愤怒，并准备向琼宣布"我有自己的生存权"。然而，到了琼的家里以后，罗金在琼面前彻底改变了言行。琼对罗金嘘寒问暖，还帮他洗头。她的柔情蜜意融化和俘虏了罗金的心。

小说对罗金的心理活动描写有什么特点？为什么说它是读者理解作品主题的关键？其中的三个场景及其引发的思考为什么尤其值得读者注意？

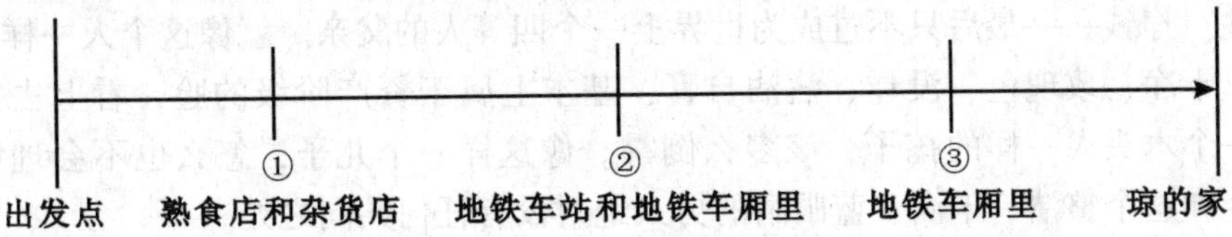

下面一一列举每个场景对应罗金的心理活动内容。

第一个场景：熟食店和杂货店。

罗金想到在通货膨胀和高税收时期母亲的养老金不够用；未婚妻不仅不工作，而且花钱大方，她完全不为钱操心。圣诞节期间罗金气得要发疯了，琼给他买了一件天鹅绒的带有蛙式纽扣的吸烟服、一个漂亮的烟斗和一个烟荷包，可是罗金因为太爱她而无法表露痛苦。于是他开始思考：人活着的时候金钱压在你的周围，就像死后大地压在你的周围一样。负担过重是普遍的规律。谁能逃得了？谁也逃不了。谁没有负担？每个人都有压力。岩石、地球上的水域、野兽、男人、孩子——每个人都要负载一些重量。这个想法开始时特别清晰，但立刻变得相当模糊，但它对他仍然有很大的作用，就好像有人给了他一个珍贵的礼物。(不像那件天鹅绒吸烟服，他实在无法穿它，也不像那个烟斗，一抽烟呛得他透不过气来。)想到一切都要承受压力和遭受折磨，他非但没有感到悲哀，反倒心情舒畅起来。

第二个场景：地铁车站和地铁车厢里。

在地铁车站，罗金听到两个朋友的谈话：一个酗酒男以为他的朋友不知道他是个酒鬼，但其实后者早已知晓。酗酒男对此十分诧异，并感到难过。因为他当此是秘密。不过，酗酒男已开始服用丹麦人开的药丸，准备戒酒了。他相信此药，认为它能治百病。丹麦人的科学无人可以企及，甚至能把男人变成女人。罗金对酗酒男的长相印象深刻：因长期嗜酒而老气横秋，消瘦的脸变得苍白，长着一个酒糟鼻子，耳朵旁边的皮像火鸡的垂肉，眼睛也因喝威士忌酒变得黯然无神。罗金由此受到启发，想起自己的职业和种种发明。而这些都需要金钱。坐上火车，罗金从酗酒男的无知中产生了一个清晰的想法：人们常说他们不会干某一件事，不管是为了爱情还是为了金钱。他们视爱情和金钱为两种敌对的欲望。他接着想到，人们对这件事是多么地无知，糊里糊涂地过一辈子，知觉之光能照亮多小的圈子啊。罗金的深刻思想与人们的无知形成鲜明对比，他为此欣喜不已。

第三个场景：地铁车厢里。

罗金注意到坐在他旁边的中年男人：体格健壮，皮肤光亮洁净，眼睛碧蓝，手很干净，长得匀称。但他不喜欢这些。突然，他发现此人的相貌酷似琼的父亲和琼本人。他的思维顿时活跃起来。他在想，如果琼有了儿子，四十年后，就是这个样子。那是她的儿子，罗金就是这儿子的父亲。罗金觉得自己的整个存在都与这个人相关。与永恒相比，四十年又算得上什么？四十年过去，他正在凝视自己的儿子。儿子就在眼前，罗金既恐惧又感动。他暗暗地说："我的儿子！我的儿子！"他的哀怜之情几乎使他失声痛哭。他觉得这个结果是主宰生死的造物主所做的神圣而可怕的工作造成的。我们都是他手里的工具。我们以为是向着自己的目标努力前进。但是不是！这整个事情是如此地不公平。受苦，受累，受难，勉强挨过人生的坎坷。慢慢爬过最黑暗的洞穴，度过最坏的时刻，在经济的压力下挣扎。挣钱——最后只不过成为世界上一个四等人的父亲。就像这个人一样，长着一张平庸、干净、玫瑰色、没趣、沾沾自喜，基本上属于资产阶级的脸，看上去是那样木讷。有一个木头人一样的孩子，该多么倒霉。像这样一个儿子，怎么也不会理解他的父亲。罗金和这个整洁、丰满、蓝眼睛的男人绝对没有任何共同之处。

罗金用自己的思维方式感知和解读现实的世界。其解读方式既有总结、提炼和升华(关于第一个和第二个地点)，也有认同和层进(关于第三个地点)。然而，一切的心理活动在最终的现实面前(琼本人和琼的家里)戛然而止。

我们可以从以下四个方面分析罗金几次心理活动所蕴涵的意义。第一，由熟食店和杂货店购物以及无意间听到两位朋友对话引发的思想活动表明心理现实(世界)对客观现实(世界)的超越。总的来说，罗金对自己的心理活动表示满意，他的思想超越了现实，他也从中找到了暂时的自我。并且，他对现实的思考有相当强的说服力，值得读者沿着他的思路做进一步思索。第二，对金钱和爱情关系之思考是物质的享乐世界与精神的自由世界之间的对话。尽管罗金对母亲的生活状况以及琼的不工作和慷慨花钱行为表示忧虑和不满，但他最终无法跨越和战胜现实。他用思想的触角探寻生活的前方之路，在苦恼中获得了平静；但平静之中增添新的苦恼。他享受着他自己精神世界里的自由和快乐，同时又对不得不立足和生活在物质世界里感到郁闷。他似乎戴着物质世界的"枷锁"跳着自由的精神世界之"舞"。这也许就是他的生活和思想方式。第三，对自己未来"儿子"的思考反映罗金对人类意义和价值的追寻。人们在辛苦中忍受和前行究竟为了什么？人的命运是天定抑或自定？这类哲学命题实际上也是读者需要思考的问题。第四，罗金对母亲的关心和对未婚妻的爱恨交加表明他对待爱和爱情的态度。他或许徘徊在性别歧视思想和"俄狄浦斯情结”之间：对母亲充满关怀；对未婚妻既恨又爱。他渴望家庭和爱情的温馨，乃至性爱的满足。他在自己的精神世界感到孤独，期望呼吸由爱带来的温暖而愉悦的空气。

总之，该小说的突出特色就是：通过客观而细致地刻画现实世界引发对人物心理活动想象式描写，从而实现两个世界的交融。它印证了贝娄的观点：艺术与生活关系密切。

四、难点注释

1. he fell into a peculiar state：他脑子里有奇怪的想法。
2. putting through college：供(某人)上大学。put somebody through college/university 是一个词组。
3. through：be through：完成(购物)；用完(钱)。
4. superimposition：压力/负担过重；重压。
5. How difficult she was：她一派凛然、难以取悦的模样。
6. How come he thought nobody would know what everybody couldn't help knowing?：人人都会知道的，可这个人怎么会觉得没有人知道呢?
7. oxford：牛津鞋(系带的浅帮鞋)。
8. unfasten his lip：说话。
9. give anyone the time of day：与人谈话。
10. make a sign：做手势；打招呼。
11. What the blazes am I getting into? Rogin thought. To be the father of a throwback to her father：我多么倒霉啊！罗金想，成为一个像她父亲一样的父亲。what the blazes：到底在搞什么。
12. make up to：讨好；奉承。
13. A pair of spirits, practically alike：极其相似的一对灵魂，指的是罗金和他的未婚妻。

五、延伸阅读与批评

《寻找格林先生》是贝娄写于20世纪40年代的作品，选自他早期的短篇小说集《莫斯比的回忆及其他》，表现了作者存在主义的思想倾向。小说的主人公乔治·格里布是个白人，他的工作是在黑人区送救济金支票。他历经辛苦也找不到格林。最终，他找到一个女人，她替格林先生收下了支票。小说采用第三人称的叙述方式，经常描写格里布的内心世界。在寻找格林的途中，格里布穿过黑乎乎的经济公寓，目睹黑人的简陋生活，看到墙上随意涂画的线条和字迹，他因此想到人类起源时期洞穴上的涂鸦。他最终也没有见到格林先生。他对格林的种种想象代表什么？他对原始社会洞穴的想象有什么现实意义或者历史意义？在格里布看来，寻找格林先生是有寓意的，那个寓意又是什么？

Chapter 5 A Good Man Is Hard to Find

by Flannery O'Connor

一、作者简介

弗兰纳里·奥康纳(1925—1964)，20世纪美国杰出的小说家，美国南方哥特文学的杰出代表，被誉为“南方的文学先知”。她的作品包括两部长篇小说——《智血》(1952)和《暴力夺取》(1960)，以及两部短篇小说集——《好人难寻》(1955)和《上升的必将汇合》(1965)。

奥康纳生于乔治亚州一个典型的天主教家庭，童年时期便展现出不凡的绘画和写作天赋。在她十五岁时，其父因红斑狼疮而病逝，备受呵护的童年就此结束。她在乔治亚州立女子大学攻读文学时一直为校刊供稿，当时就展现出过人的洞察力与讽刺天赋。1947年硕士毕业后奥康纳开始进入创作生涯的第一个高峰期，她的首部小说《智血》一出版就反响不俗，获得了爱荷华州小说奖。然而不久后她自己也被确诊患有家族性红斑狼疮，只得随母亲搬迁至农场养病并一直留在那里直至1964年病逝，时年三十九岁。然而在农场养病的日子里她也从未停止创作，通过与菲茨杰拉德夫妇和哥顿等文学家的频繁书信交流，她一直同文学界保持着密切的联系。1955—1960年她迎来了创作的第二个辉煌期，《好人难寻》《善良的乡下人》《流离失所的人》等短篇小说杰作为她赢得了数次欧·亨利文学奖，临终前她的最后一篇短篇小说《启示》荣获欧·亨利文学奖第一名。美国评论界称她的早逝是“自弗朗西斯·菲茨杰拉德去世以来美国文坛最重大的损失”，她短暂而灿烂的创作生涯为世界留下了宝贵的文学遗产。

奥康纳是一个虔诚的天主教徒，强烈的宗教信念是她创作的中心和源泉。因此她对上帝的恩典与救赎以及基督的存在与再生所进行的探索与思考构成了其作品的重要思想内容。

奥康纳的创作基本取材于其所生活的美国南方乡村，她采用现实主义的手法，描写具体生动，语言幽默睿智。虽然她多从精神和心理角度来刻画人物，但她的写作仍表现出对自己所处时代敏锐的现实关怀。作为宗教作家，奥康纳与霍桑一样坚信要彰显上帝的存在与恩典就必须创造不寻常的人物与情景。她借鉴了霍桑对传奇的运用，并在此基础上纳入怪诞和扭曲的叙事手法，从而深刻地展现世人隐藏的原罪和堕落的本性。在奥康纳笔下，带来天惠时刻(moment of grace)的并不是圣徒，而是形形色色的怪人、罪犯、畸形和残疾人，这成为她小说创作的一大特征，也是读者理解她作品的重要关注点。

二、文本选读

A Good Man Is Hard to Find

The grandmother didn't want to go to Florida. She wanted to visit some of her connections in east Tennessee and she was seizing at every chance to change Bailey's mind. Bailey was the son she lived with, her only boy. He was sitting on the edge of his chair at the table, bent over the orange sports section of the Journal. "Now look here, Bailey," she said, "see here, read this," and she stood with one hand on her thin hip and the other rattling the newspaper at his bald head. "Here this fellow that calls himself The Misfit is aloose from the Federal Pen[1] and headed toward Florida and you read here what it says he did to these people. Just you read it. I wouldn't take my children in any direction with a criminal like that aloose in it. I couldn't answer to my conscience if I did."

Bailey didn't look up from his reading so she wheeled around then and faced the children's mother, a young woman in slacks, whose face was as broad and innocent as a cabbage and was tied around with a green head-kerchief that had two points on the top like rabbit's ears. She was sitting on the sofa, feeding the baby his apricots out of a jar. "The children have been to Florida before," the old lady said. "You all ought to take them somewhere else for a change so they would see different parts of the world and be broad. They never have been to east Tennessee."

The children's mother didn't seem to hear her but the eight-year-old boy, John Wesley, a stocky child with glasses, said, "If you don't want to go to Florida, why dontcha[2] stay at home?" He and the little girl, June Star, were reading the funny papers on the floor.

"She wouldn't stay at home to be queen for a day," June Star said without raising her yellow head.

"Yes and what would you do if this fellow, The Misfit, caught you?" the grandmother asked.

"I'd smack his face," John Wesley said.

"She wouldn't stay at home for a million bucks," June Star said. "Afraid she'd miss something. She has to go everywhere we go."

"All right, Miss," the grandmother said. "Just remember that the next time you want me to curl your hair."

June Star said her hair was naturally curly.

The next morning the grandmother was the first one in the car, ready to go. She had her big black valise[3] that looked like the head of a hippopotamus in one corner, and underneath it she was hiding a basket with Pitty Sing, the cat, in it. She didn't intend for the cat to be left alone in the house for three days because he would miss her too much and she was afraid he might brush against one of the gas burners and accidentally asphyxiate[4] himself. Her son, Bailey, didn't like to arrive at a motel with a cat.

She sat in the middle of the back seat with John Wesley and June Star on either side of her.

Bailey and the children's mother and the baby sat in front and they left Atlanta at eight forty-five with the mileage on the car at 55890. The grandmother wrote this down because she thought it would be interesting to say how many miles they had been when they got back. It took them twenty minutes to reach the outskirts of the city.

The old lady settled herself comfortably, removing her white cotton gloves and putting them up with her purse on the shelf in front of the back window. The children's mother still had on slacks and still had her head tied up in a green kerchief[5], but the grandmother had on a navy blue straw sailor hat with a bunch of white violets on the brim and a navy blue dress with a small white dot in the print. Her collars and cuffs[6] were white organdy[7] trimmed with lace and at her neckline she had pinned a purple spray of cloth violets containing a sachet. In case of an accident, anyone seeing her dead on the highway would know at once that she was a lady.

She said she thought it was going to be a good day for driving, neither too hot nor too cold, and she cautioned Bailey that the speed limit was fifty-five miles an hour and that the patrolmen hid themselves behind billboards and small clumps of trees and sped out after you before you had a chance to slow down. She pointed out interesting details of the scenery: Stone Mountain; the blue granite that in some places came up to both sides of the highway; the brilliant red clay banks slightly streaked with purple; and the various crops that made rows of green lace-work on the ground. The trees were full of silver-white sunlight and the meanest of them sparkled. The children were reading comic magazines and their mother had gone back to sleep.

"Let's go through Georgia fast so we won't have to look at it much," John Wesley said.

"If I were a little boy," said the grandmother, "I wouldn't talk about my native state that way. Tennessee has the mountains and Georgia has the hills."

"Tennessee is just a hillbilly dumping ground," John Wesley said, "and Georgia is a lousy state too."

"You said it," June Star said.

"In my time," said the grandmother, folding her thin veined fingers, "children were more respectful of their native states and their parents and everything else. People did right then. Oh look at the cute little pickaninny[8]!" she said and pointed to a Negro child standing in the door of a shack. "Wouldn't that make a picture, now?" she asked and they all turned and looked at the little Negro out of the back window. He waved.

"He didn't have any britches[9] on," June Star said.

"He probably didn't have any," the grandmother explained. "Little niggers in the country don't have things like we do. If I could paint, I'd paint that picture," she said.

The children exchanged comic books.

The grandmother offered to hold the baby and the children's mother passed him over the front seat to her. She set him on her knee and bounced him and told him about the things they were passing. She rolled her eyes and screwed up her mouth and stuck her leathery thin face into his smooth bland one. Occasionally he gave her a faraway smile. They passed a large cotton field with five or six graves fenced in the middle of it, like a small island. "Look at the graveyard!" the grandmother said, pointing it out. "That was the old family burying ground. That belonged to the plantation."

"Where's the plantation?" John Wesley asked.

"Gone With the Wind," said the grandmother. "Ha. Ha."

When the children finished all the comic books they had brought, they opened the lunch and ate it. The grandmother ate a peanut butter sandwich and an olive and would not let the children throw the box and the paper napkins out the window. When there was nothing else to do they played a game by choosing a cloud and making the other two guess what shape it suggested. John Wesley took one the shape of a cow and June Star guessed a cow and John Wesley said, no, an automobile, and June Star said he didn't play fair, and they began to slap each other over the grandmother.

The grandmother said she would tell them a story if they would keep quiet. When she told a story, she rolled her eyes and waved her head and was very dramatic. She said once when she was a maiden lady she had been courted by a Mr. Edgar Atkins Teagarden from Jasper, Georgia. She said he was a very good-looking man and a gentleman and that he brought her a watermelon every Saturday afternoon with his initials cut in it, E. A. T. Well, one Saturday, she said, Mr. Teagarden brought the watermelon and there was nobody at home and he left it on the front porch and returned in his buggy to Jasper, but she never got the watermelon, she said, because a nigger boy ate it when he saw the initials, E. A. T.! This story tickled John Wesley's funny bone and he giggled and giggled but June Star didn't think it was any good. She said she wouldn't marry a man that just brought her a watermelon on Saturday. The grandmother said she would have done well to marry Mr. Teagarden because he was a gentleman and had bought Coca-Cola stock when it first came out and that he had died only a few years ago, a very wealthy man.

They stopped at The Tower for barbecued sandwiches. The Tower was a part stucco and part wood filling station and dance hall set in a clearing outside of Timothy. A fat man named Red Sammy Butts ran it and there were signs stuck here and there on the building and for miles up and down the highway saying, TRY RED SAMMY'S FAMOUS BARBECUE. NONE LIKE FAMOUS RED SAMMY'S! RED SAM! THE FAT BOY WITH THE HAPPY LAUGH. A VETERAN! RED SAMMY'S YOUR MAN!

Red Sammy was lying on the bare ground outside The Tower with his head under a truck while a gray monkey about a foot high, chained to a small chinaberry tree, chattered nearby. The monkey sprang back into the tree and got on the highest limb as soon as he saw the children jump out of the car and run toward him.

Inside, The Tower was a long dark room with a counter at one end and tables at the other and dancing space in the middle. They all sat down at a board table next to the nickelodeon and Red Sam's wife, a tall burnt-brown woman with hair and eyes lighter than her skin, came and took their order. The children's mother put a dime in the machine and played "The Tennessee Waltz," and the grandmother said that tune always made her want to dance. She asked Bailey if he would like to dance but he only glared at her. He didn't have a naturally sunny disposition like she did and trips made him nervous. The grandmother's brown eyes were very bright. She swayed her head from side to side and pretended she was dancing in her chair. June Star said play something she could tap to so the children's mother put in another dime and played a fast number and June Star stepped out onto the dance floor and did her tap routine.

"Ain't she cute?" Red Sam's wife said, leaning over the counter. "Would you like to come be my little girl?"

"No I certainly wouldn't," June Star said. "I wouldn't live in a broken-down place like this for a minion bucks!" and she ran back to the table.

"Ain't she cute?" the woman repeated, stretching her mouth politely.

"Arn't you ashamed?" hissed the grandmother.

Red Sam came in and told his wife to quit lounging on the counter and hurry up with these people's order. His khaki trousers reached just to his hip bones and his stomach hung over them like a sack of meal swaying under his shirt. He came over and sat down at a table nearby and let out a combination sigh and yodel[10]. "You can't win," he said. "You can't win," and he wiped his sweating red face off with a gray handkerchief. "These days you don't know who to trust," he said. "Ain't that the truth?"

"People are certainly not nice like they used to be," said the grandmother.

"Two fellers[11] come in here last week," Red Sammy said, "driving a Chrysler. It was a old beat-up car but it was a good one and these boys looked all right to me. Said they worked at the mill and you know I let them fellers charge the gas they bought? Now why did I do that?"

"Because you're a good man!" the grandmother said at once.

"Yes'm, I suppose so," Red Sam said as if he were struck with this answer.

His wife brought the orders, carrying the five plates all at once without a tray, two in each hand and one balanced on her arm. "It isn't a soul in this green world of God's that you can trust," she said. "And I don't count nobody out of that, not nobody," she repeated, looking at Red Sammy.

"Did you read about that criminal, The Misfit, that's escaped?" asked the grandmother.

"I wouldn't be a bit surprised if he didn't attact this place right here," said the woman. "If he hears about it being here, I wouldn't be none surprised to see him. If he hears it's two cent in the cash register, I wouldn't be a tall surprised if he..."

"That'll do," Red Sam said. "Go bring these people their Co'-Colas," and the woman went off to get the rest of the order.

"A good man is hard to find," Red Sammy said. "Every-thing is getting terrible. I remember the day you could go off and leave your screen door unlatched. Not no more."

He and the grandmother discussed better times. The old lady said that in her opinion Europe was entirely to blame for the way things were now. She said the way Europe acted you would think we were made of money and Red Sam said it was no use talking about it, she was exactly right. The children ran outside into the white sunlight and looked at the monkey in the lacy chinaberry tree. He was busy catching fleas on himself and biting each one carefully between his teeth as if it were a delicacy.

They drove off again into the hot afternoon. The grand-mother took cat naps and woke up every few minutes with her own snoring. Outside of Toombsboro she woke up and recalled an old plantation that she had visited in this neighborhood once when she was a young lady. She said the house had six white columns across the front and that there was an avenue of oaks leading up to it and two little wooden trellis arbors on either side in front where you sat down with your suitor after a stroll in the garden. She recalled exactly which road to turn off to get to it. She knew that Bailey would not be willing to lose any time looking at an old house, but the more she talked about it, the more she wanted to see it once again and find out if the little twin arbors were still standing. "There was a secret panel in this house," she said craftily, not telling the truth but wishing that she were, "and the story went that all the family silver was hidden in it when Sherman came through but it was never found..."

"Hey!" John Wesley said. "Let's go see it! We'll find it! We'll poke all the woodwork and find it! Who lives there? Where do you turn off at? Hey Pop, can't we turn off there?"

"We never have seen a house with a secret panel!" June Star shrieked. "Let's go to the house with the secret panel! Hey Pop, can't we go see the house with the secret panel!"

"It's not far from here, I know," the grandmother said. "It wouldn't take over twenty minutes."

Bailey was looking straight ahead. His jaw was as rigid as a horseshoe. "No," he said.

The children began to yell and scream that they wanted to see the house with the secret panel. John Wesley kicked the back of the front seat and June Star hung over her mother's shoulder and whined desperately into her ear that they never had any fun even on their vacation, that they could never do what THEY wanted to do. The baby began to scream and John Wesley kicked the back of the seat so hard that his father could feel the blows in his kidney.

"All right!" he shouted and drew the car to a stop at the side of the road. "Will you all shut up? Will you all just shut up for one second? If you don't shut up, we won't go anywhere."

"It would be very educational for them," the grandmother murmured.

"All right," Bailey said, "but get this: this is the only time we're going to stop for anything like this. This is the one and only time."

"The dirt road that you have to turn down is about a mile back," the grandmother directed. "I marked it when we passed."

"A dirt road," Bailey groaned.

After they had turned around and were headed toward the dirt road, the grandmother recalled other points about the house, the beautiful glass over the front doorway and the candle-lamp in the hall. John Wesley said that the secret panel was probably in the fireplace.

"You can't go inside this house," Bailey said. "You don't know who lives there."

"While you all talk to the people in front, I'll run around behind and get in a window," John Wesley suggested.

"We'll all stay in the car," his mother said. They turned onto the dirt road and the car raced roughly along in a swirl of pink dust. The grandmother recalled the times when there were no paved roads and thirty miles was a day's journey. The dirt road was hilly and there were sudden washes in it and sharp curves on dangerous embankments. All at once they would be on a hill, looking down over the blue tops of trees for miles around, then the next minute, they would be in a red depression with the dust-coated trees looking down on them.

"This place had better turn up in a minute," Bailey said, "or I'm going to turn around."

The road looked as if no one had traveled on it in months.

"It's not much farther," the grandmother said and just as she said it, a horrible thought came to her. The thought was so embarrassing that she turned red in the face and her eyes dilated and her feet jumped up, upsetting her valise in the corner. The instant the valise moved, the newspaper top she had over the basket under it rose with a snarl and Pitty Sing, the cat, sprang onto Bailey's shoulder.

The children were thrown to the floor and their mother, clutching the baby, was thrown out the door onto the ground; the old lady was thrown into the front seat. The car turned over once and landed right-side-up in a gulch off the side of the road. Bailey remained in the driver's seat with the cat-gray-striped with a broad white face and an orange nose-clinging to his neck like a caterpillar.

As soon as the children saw they could move their arms and legs, they scrambled out of the car, shouting, "We've had an ACCIDENT!" The grandmother was curled up under the dashboard, hoping she was injured so that Bailey's wrath[12] would not come down on her all at once. The horrible thought she had had before the accident was that the house she had remembered so vividly was not in Georgia but in Tennessee.

Bailey removed the cat from his neck with both hands and flung it out the window against the side of a pine tree. Then he got out of the car and started looking for the children's mother. She was sitting against the side of the red gutted ditch, holding the screaming baby, but she only had a cut down her face and a broken shoulder. "We've had an ACCIDENT!" the children screamed in a frenzy of delight.

"But nobody's killed," June Star said with disappointment as the grandmother limped out of the car, her hat still pinned to her head but the broken front brim standing up at a jaunty angle and the violet spray hanging off the side. They all sat down in the ditch, except the children, to recover from the shock. They were all shaking.

"Maybe a car will come along," said the children's mother hoarsely.

"I believe I have injured an organ," said the grandmother, pressing her side, but no one answered her. Bailey's teeth were clattering. He had on a yellow sport shirt with bright blue parrots designed in it and his face was as yellow as the l shirt. The grandmother decided that she would not mention that the house was in Tennessee.

The road was about ten feet above and they could see only the tops of the trees on the other side of it. Behind the ditch they were sitting in there were more woods, tall and dark and deep. In a few minutes they saw a car some distance away on top of a hill, coming slowly as if the occupants were watching them. The grandmother stood up and waved both arms dramatically to attract their attention. The car continued to come on slowly, disappeared around a bend and appeared again, moving even slower, on top of the hill they had gone over. It was a big black battered hearse-like[13] automobile. There were three men in it.

It came to a stop just over them and for some minutes, the driver looked down with a steady expressionless gaze to where they were sitting, and didn't speak. Then he turned his head and muttered something to the other two and they got out. One was a fat boy in black trousers and a red sweat shirt with a silver stallion embossed on the front of it. He moved around on the right side of them and stood staring, his mouth partly open in a kind of loose grin. The other had on khaki pants and a blue striped coat and a gray hat pulled down very low, hiding most of his face. He came around slowly on the left side. Neither spoke.

The driver got out of the car and stood by the side of it, looking down at them. He was an older man than the other two. His hair was just beginning to gray and he wore silver-rimmed spectacles that gave him a scholarly look. He had a long creased face and didn't have on any shirt or undershirt. He had on blue jeans that were too tight for him and was holding a black hat and a gun. The two boys also had guns.

"We've had an ACCIDENT!" the children screamed.

The grandmother had the peculiar feeling that the bespectacled man was someone she knew. His face was as familiar to her as if she had known him au her life but she could not recall who he was. He moved away from the car and began to come down the embankment, placing his feet carefully so that he wouldn't slip. He had on tan and white shoes and no socks, and his ankles were red and thin. "Good afternoon," he said. "I see you all had you a little spill."

"We turned over twice!" said the grandmother.

"Once", he corrected. "We seen it happen. Try their car and see will it run, Hiram," he said quietly to the boy with the gray hat.

"What you got that gun for?" John Wesley asked. "Whatcha gonna do with that gun?"

"Lady," the man said to the children's mother, "would you mind calling them children to sit down by you? Children make me nervous. I want all you all to sit down right together there where you're at."

"What are you telling US what to do for?" June Star asked.

Behind them the line of woods gaped like a dark open mouth. "Come here," said their mother.

"Look here now," Bailey began suddenly, "we're in a predicament! We're in. . ."

The grandmother shrieked. She scrambled to her feet and stood staring. "You're The Misfit!" she said. "I recognized you at once!"

"Yes'm," the man said, smiling slightly as if he were pleased in spite of himself to be known, "but it would have been better for all of you, lady, if you hadn't of reckernized me."

Bailey turned his head sharply and said something to his mother that shocked even the children. The old lady began to cry and The Misfit reddened.

"Lady," he said, "don't you get upset. Sometimes a man says things he don't mean. I don't reckon he meant to talk to you that away."

"You wouldn't shoot a lady, would you?" the grandmother said and removed a clean handkerchief from her cuff and began to slap at her eyes with it.

The Misfit pointed the toe of his shoe into the ground and made a little hole and then covered it up again. "I would hate to have to," he said.

"Listen," the grandmother almost screamed, "I know you're a good man. You don't look a bit like you have com-mon blood. I know you must come from nice people!"

"Yes mam," he said, "finest people in the world." When he smiled he showed a row of strong white teeth. "God never made a finer woman than my mother and my daddy's heart was pure gold," he said. The boy with the red sweat shirt had come around behind them and was standing with his gun at his hip. The Misfit squatted[14] down on the ground. "Watch them children, Bobby Lee," he said. "You know they make me nervous." He looked at the six of them huddled together in front of him and he seemed to be embarrassed as if he couldn't think of anything to say. "Ain't a cloud in the sky," he remarked, looking up at it. "Don't see no sun but don't see no cloud neither."

"Yes, it's a beautiful day," said the grandmother. "Listen," she said, "you shouldn't call yourself The Misfit because I know you're a good man at heart. I can just look at you and tell."

"Hush!" Bailey yelled. "Hush! Everybody shut up and let me handle this!" He was squatting in the position of a runner about to sprint forward but he didn't move.

"I prechate that, lady,"[15] The Misfit said and drew a little circle in the ground with the butt of his gun.

"It'll take a half a hour to fix this here car," Hiram called, looking over the raised hood of it.

"Well, first you and Bobby Lee get him and that little boy to step over yonder with you," The Misfit said, pointing to Bailey and John Wesley. "The boys want to ast you some-thing," he said to Bailey. "Would you mind stepping back in them woods there with them?"

"Listen," Bailey began, "we're in a terrible predicament! Nobody realizes what this is," and his voice cracked. His eyes were as blue and intense as the parrots in his shirt and he remained perfectly still.

The grandmother reached up to adjust her hat brim as if she were going to the woods with him but it came off in her hand. She stood staring at it and after a second she let it fall on the ground.

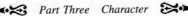

Hiram pulled Bailey up by the arm as if he were assisting an old man. John Wesley caught hold of his father's hand and Bobby Lee followed. They went off toward the woods and just as they reached the dark edge, Bailey turned and supporting himself against a gray naked pine trunk, he shouted, "I'll be back in a minute, Mamma, wait on me!"

"Come back this instant!" his mother shrilled but they all disappeared into the woods.

"Bailey Boy!" the grandmother called in a tragic voice but she found she was looking at The Misfit squatting on the ground in front of her. "I just know you're a good man," she said desperately. "You're not a bit common!"

"Nome, I ain't a good man," The Misfit said after a second as if he had considered her statement carefully, "but I ain't the worst in the world neither. My daddy said I was a different breed of dog from my brothers and sisters. 'You know,' Daddy said, 'it's some that can live their whole life out without asking about it and it's others has to know why it is, and this boy is one of the latters. He's going to be into every-thing!'" He put on his black hat and looked up suddenly and then away deep into the woods as if he were embarrassed again. "I'm sorry I don't have on a shirt before you ladies," he said, hunching his shoulders slightly. "We buried our clothes that we had on when we escaped and we're just making do until we can get better. We borrowed these from some folks we met," he explained.

"That's perfectly all right," the grandmother said. "Maybe Bailey has an extra shirt in his suitcase."

"I'll look and see terrectly," The Misfit said.

"Where are they taking him?" the children's mother screamed.

"Daddy was a card himself," The Misfit said. "You couldn't put anything over on him. He never got in trouble with the Authorities though. Just had the knack of handling them."

"You could be honest too if you'd only try," said the grandmother. "Think how wonderful it would be to settle down and live a comfortable life and not have to think about some-body chasing you all the time."

The Misfit kept scratching in the ground with the butt of his gun as if he were thinking about it. "Yes'm, somebody is always after you," he murmured.

The grandmother noticed how thin his shoulder blades were just behind-his hat because she was standing up looking down on him. "Do you ever pray?" she asked.

He shook his head. All she saw was the black hat wiggle between his shoulder blades. "Nome," he said.

There was a pistol shot from the woods, followed closely by another. Then silence. The old lady's head jerked around. She could hear the wind move through the tree tops like a long satisfied insuck of breath. "Bailey Boy!" she called.

"I was a gospel singer for a while," The Misfit said. "I been most everything. Been in the arm service, both land and sea, at home and abroad, been twict married, been an undertaker, been with the railroads, plowed Mother Earth, been in a tornado, seen a man burnt alive oncet[16]," and he looked up at the children's mother and the little girl who were sitting close together, their faces white and their eyes glassy; "I even seen a woman flogged," he said.

"Pray, pray," the grandmother began, "pray, pray. . ."

"I never was a bad boy that I remember of," The Misfit said in an almost dreamy voice, "but somewheres along the line I done something wrong and got sent to the penitentiary. I was buried alive," and he looked up and held her attention to him by a steady stare.

"That's when you should have started to pray," she said "What did you do to get sent to the penitentiary that first time?"

"Turn to the right, it was a wall," The Misfit said, looking up again at the cloudless sky. "Turn to the left, it was a wall. Look up it was a ceiling, look down it was a floor. I forget what I done, lady. I set there and set there, trying to remember what it was I done and I ain't recalled it to this day. Oncet in a while, I would think it was coming to me, but it never come."

"Maybe they put you in by mistake," the old lady said vaguely.

"Nome," he said. "It wasn't no mistake. They had the papers on me."

"You must have stolen something," she said.

The Misfit sneered slightly. "Nobody had nothing I wanted," he said. "It was a head-doctor at the penitentiary said what I had done was kill my daddy but I known that for a lie. My daddy died in nineteen ought nineteen of the epidemic flu and I never had a thing to do with it. He was buried in the Mount Hopewell Baptist churchyard and you can go there and see for yourself."

"If you would pray," the old lady said, "Jesus would help you."

"That's right," The Misfit said.

"Well then, why don't you pray?" she asked trembling with delight suddenly.

"I don't want no hep," he said. "I'm doing all right by myself."

Bobby Lee and Hiram came ambling back from the woods. Bobby Lee was dragging a yellow shirt with bright blue parrots in it.

"Thow me that shirt, Bobby Lee," The Misfit said. The shirt came flying at him and landed on his shoulder and he put it on. The grandmother couldn't name what the shirt reminded her of. "No, lady," The Misfit said while he was buttoning it up, "I found out the crime don't matter. You can do one thing or you can do another, kill a man or take a tire off his car, because sooner or later you're going to forget what it was you done and just be punished for it."

The children's mother had begun to make heaving noises as if she couldn't get her breath. "Lady," he asked, "would you and that little girl like to step off yonder with Bobby Lee and Hiram and join your husband?"

"Yes, thank you," the mother said faintly. Her left arm dangled helplessly and she was holding the baby, who had gone to sleep, in the other. "Hep that lady up, Hiram," The Misfit said as she struggled to climb out of the ditch, "and Bobby Lee, you hold onto that little girl's hand."

"I don't want to hold hands with him," June Star said. "He reminds me of a pig."

The fat boy blushed and laughed and caught her by the arm and pulled her off into the woods after Hiram and her mother.

Alone with The Misfit, the grandmother found that she had lost her voice. There was not a cloud in the sky nor any sun. There was nothing around her but woods. She wanted to tell him that he must pray. She opened and closed her mouth several times before anything came out. Finally she found herself saying, "Jesus. Jesus," meaning, Jesus will help you, but the way she was saying it, it sounded as if she might be cursing.

"Yes'm," The Misfit said as if he agreed. "Jesus shown everything off balance. It was the same case with Him as with me except He hadn't committed any crime and they could prove I had committed one because they had the papers on me. Of course," he said, "they never shown me my papers. That's why I sign myself now. I said long ago, you get you a signature and sign everything you do and keep a copy of it. Then you'll know what you done and you can hold up the crime to the punishment and see do they match and in the end you'll have something to prove you ain't been treated right. I call myself The Misfit," he said, "because I can't make what all I done wrong fit what all I gone through in punishment."

There was a piercing scream from the woods, followed closely by a pistol report. "Does it seem right to you, lady, that one is punished a heap and another ain't punished at all?"

"Jesus!" the old lady cried. "You've got good blood! I know you wouldn't shoot a lady! I know you come from nice people! Pray! Jesus, you ought not to shoot a lady. I'll give you all the money I've got!"

"Lady," The Misfit said, looking beyond her far into the woods, "there never was a body that give the undertaker a tip."

There were two more pistol reports and the grandmother raised her head like a parched old turkey hen crying for water and called, "Bailey Boy, Bailey Boy!" as if her heart would break.

"Jesus was the only One that ever raised the dead," The Misfit continued, "and He shouldn't have done it. He shown everything off balance. If He did what He said, then it's nothing for you to do but thow away everything and follow Him, and if He didn't, then it's nothing for you to do but enjoy the few minutes you got left the best way you can—by killing somebody or burning down his house or doing some other meanness to him. No pleasure but meanness," he said and his voice had become almost a snarl.

"Maybe He didn't raise the dead," the old lady mumbled, not knowing what she was saying and feeling so dizzy that she sank down in the ditch with her legs twisted under her.

"I wasn't there so I can't say He didn't," The Misfit said. "I wisht I had of been there," he said, hitting the ground with his fist. "It ain't right I wasn't there because if I had of been there I would of known. Listen lady," he said in a high voice, "if I had of been there I would of known and I wouldn't be like I am now." His voice seemed about to crack and the grandmother's head cleared for an instant. She saw the man's face twisted close to her own as if he were going to cry and she murmured, "Why you're one of my babies. You're one of my own children!" She reached out and touched him on the shoulder. The Misfit sprang back as if a snake had bitten him and shot her three times through the chest. Then he put his gun down on the ground and took off his glasses and began to clean them.

Hiram and Bobby Lee returned from the woods and stood over the ditch, looking down at the grandmother who half sat and half lay in a puddle of blood with her legs crossed under her like a child's and her face smiling up at the cloudless sky.

Without his glasses, The Misfit's eyes were red-rimmed and pale and defenseless-looking. "Take her off and thow her where you shown the others," he said, picking up the cat that was rubbing itself against his leg.

"She was a talker, wasn't she?" Bobby Lee said, sliding down the ditch with a yodel.

"She would of been a good woman," The Misfit said, "if it had been somebody there to shoot her every minute of her life."

"Some fun!" Bobby Lee said.

"Shut up, Bobby Lee" The Misfit said. "It's no real pleasure in life."

三、人物解析

《好人难寻》是奥康纳的短篇小说杰作，故事生动，语言简洁，寓意深刻。小说描述了一个传统的南方家庭在驱车度假途中的遭遇。故事以祖母与家人之间关于度假地点的争执为开端，以一个名为"不合时宜者"的杀人犯从佛罗里达州逃脱的事件作为伏线将读者带入了一个令人窒息的噩梦。祖母利用凶犯越狱事件编造借口令家人改变计划，于是一家人转而开往田纳西州，途中意外翻车，所幸伤势不重。此时，另一辆车却不期而至，车上正是那群令人胆战心惊的逃犯，等待这家人的不是救援之手而是杀身之祸。故事的矛盾冲突围绕着祖母与逃犯"不合时宜者"二人之间的对立关系层层深化，并在冷血的枪杀中达到高潮。随即，小说在血腥的杀戮和祖母临终前的顿悟中戛然而止，使读者在挥之不去的震惊中不得不反思南方守旧传统与荒诞现实之间难容的矛盾和尖锐的冲突。

《好人难寻》采取了第三人称叙事视角，主要围绕祖母这个人物来展开叙述。人物塑造与叙事方式有机结合、相辅相成，从而循序渐进地传达出其创作主旨。奥康纳运用了直接和间接塑造相结合的手法来呈现祖母这个复杂的人物，并通过人物的塑造来突出原罪、恩典与救赎的主题。

整篇小说中祖母的名字从未出现过，而其他人物都有其具体的名字。祖母是一种身份，也是一种相对关系代号。祖母这个人物正是通过她与小说中其他人物之间的相对关系和互动而逐渐变得丰满立体。作者除了通过对祖母的衣着言行、心理活动等进行直接描述来凸显祖母身上的原罪，同时还运用其他人物对祖母的回应以及矛盾对立来折射出祖母这个人物所代表的世人堕落的本质和救赎的需要。

在衣着外表上，除了祖母以外，小说中所有人物都衣着随意，只有祖母一人坚持在出行路上也必须穿戴隆重，目的在于即使不幸遇难，外人也能从她的衣着判断出她的尊贵的出身。这种对自我身份认同近乎夸张的执念体现了祖母的骄傲原罪。文中详尽地描写了她如何刻意搭配繁复老派的服饰以炫耀其地位；"白色手套，蕾丝花边，紫罗兰佩饰"等无一不是奢侈而多余的装饰，然而，路边的黑人儿童却衣衫褴褛，祖母不仅没有半点怜悯之心，反而轻蔑地称之为“小黑鬼”，并对孙子灌输“一无所有的乡下黑人怎比得上自家衣食无忧”的种族歧视观念，甚至幸灾乐祸地表示如果她会画画，一定把这黑人的惨状画来留念。祖母对自己的衣着装扮近乎挑剔，因为在她心中体面的外表显示出她高人一等。然而面对衣不蔽体的黑人小孩她却收起对自己的这套标尺，反而毫不掩饰地张扬其冷酷的种族观念，这一矛盾反映出祖母的价值观和道德标准具有双重性与利己性，其骄傲和虚荣的原罪一览无遗。

在言行上，祖母一面自诩虔诚忠实，一面编制各种谎言、借口来操纵摆布家人以满足一己私欲。作者除了直接利用祖母与其他人物之间的表里不一的对话，还绘声绘色地描述了孩子们与祖母对话时用词粗鲁、毫无敬意的幽默场景，从侧面影射出祖母的自以为是和虚荣伪善。祖母在这种自我满足的催眠中逐渐忘却了上帝的存在和对恩典的需求。

祖母的堕落本质在她与“不合时宜者”这个凶犯的对立中得到最充分的展现，作者通过对这两个对立人物的塑造传达出上帝对堕落灵魂的救赎和天惠降临时所必经的死亡关口。表面上“不合时宜者”是残忍的杀人犯，然而他却是整篇小说中唯一表里如一的人物。在他与祖母间断断续续的对话中，读者可知他没有犯罪却被投入监牢，甚至被活埋。作者通过《圣经》典故暗示“不合时宜者”和基督一样为了他人的罪而承受十字架，在象征意义上“不合时宜者”的原型就是基督。当祖母在极度恐惧中面对杀人犯“不合时宜者”陈述不公待遇时，她本能地呼唤耶稣之名，似乎想对“不合时宜者”说耶稣会救他，但她的呼声听起来却像是诅咒，她依然没有意识到自己的原罪，因而无法获得恩典与救赎。这时“不合时宜者”对祖母说“只有耶稣能使死者重生，耶稣让一切都不再平衡”。他告诫祖母如果相信耶稣的救赎就应该放下一切去跟随耶稣。可祖母却依然有所怀疑耶稣是否能使死者重生，直到死亡即将来临的一刹那，祖母终于有所顿悟。

祖母骄傲自私、虚荣伪善，她自诩为虔诚的信徒，却忘了骄傲本是七宗罪之首。她无视自己的原罪，从未觉悟到自己有被救赎的必要。直到她的生命将被“不合时宜者”剥夺时自我蒙蔽的祖母才意识到自己的堕落本质，认真地看待自己的灵魂在面临死亡时所经历的改变，从而获得上帝的恩典与灵魂的救赎。小说结尾处正当祖母有所顿悟地触碰“不合时宜者”时，对方像被蛇咬一样对着她当胸连发三枪。作者通过祖母的结局传达出死亡是接受恩典的必经关口，正如“不合时宜者”所说：“如果每时每刻都有个人枪毙她的话，她一定会是个好女人。”

四、难点注释

1. Federal Pen：联邦监狱。
2. dontcha：don't you 暗示南方口音。
3. valise：小旅行包。
4. asphyxiate：使窒息；闷死。
5. kerchief：方巾，天主教徒在头上佩戴方巾表示对上帝的服从。
6. cuffs：袖口。
7. organdy：蝉翼纱；泡泡蝉翼绉。

8. pickaninny：黑人小孩，也写为 piccaninny。
9. britches：马裤。
10. yodel：约德尔唱法(以瑞士传统的真假嗓音交替歌唱)。
11. feller：采伐者；伐木者。
12. wrath：愤怒；怒气。
13. hearse-like：灵车般的，此处作者运用 foreshadow 为祖母及家人的遇害埋下伏笔。
14. squat：蹲；蹲坐；非法占用。
15. “I pre-chate that, lady”：相当于“I appreciate that, Lady”，暗示“不合时宜者”这个人物教育程度低，语句不符合语法习惯。
16. oncet：once 的变体，为美国南部和中南部方言。

五、延伸阅读与批评

奥康纳的短篇小说《流离失所的人》讲述了一个波兰难民雇工惨死于美国南方农场的故事。小说的标题取自冷战时期的法令 *Displaced Persons Act*，这一法令允许欧洲难民移民到美国，这也是美国前总统杜鲁门迫于压力才颁布的法令。种族主义是这篇小说的核心主题，故事中的美国南方农场与“二战”时欧洲的死亡集中营有着相同的本质，冷战时期美国的排外分子把来自东欧的白人难民视作“部分有色人种”和“第二肤色威胁”。表面上，流离失所的人指的是逃亡异乡的波兰难民古扎克先生；实质上奥康纳通过象征揭示出真正在心灵上流离失所的是那被放逐于“恩典”与“救赎”之外的人们——麦金太尔太太和肖特利夫妇。奥康纳在这篇小说中并没有描述太多死亡和血腥的场面，反而通过塑造两个同样在社会底层挣扎求存却还歧视迫害波兰难民古扎克的小人物——肖特利夫妇来揭示冷战时期依然存在的白人至上论的种族主义。《流离失所的人》中作者如何通过塑造人物的复杂本性和原罪来突出其创作主题？肖特利夫妇和波兰难民古扎克先生之间的关系与《好人难寻》中的祖母和“不合时宜者”之间的关系是否具有可比性？

（张文撰写，甘文平审校）

Part Four

Theme

“主题”就是作者在文学作品中表达的观点或想法，是作者对作品中人物的言行举止或事件做出的伦理、道德、美学评判，是作品的“中心思想”。它是作家的心声和思想的表露，是需要读者去挖掘、了解和掌握的信息。它很少由作者直接表达，往往蕴涵在作品之内，通过多种手段展现出来。事实上，前面的三章都不同程度地涉及了主题。

“主题”可谓一个文学作品的灵魂，没有主题的文学作品基本上是不存在的。文学作品一般有两种“主题”：文本之内的主题和文本之外的主题。前者是作品本身的主题，后者指由前者引申出来的具有“普适性”的主题。文学作品的主题大多是一个统一的思想体系。一部优秀的文学作品往往有多个主题，它们之间可以是平行关系，可以是互补或递进关系，也可以是对立或矛盾关系。

本部分选取四部小说和一部剧本，它们分别从人物言行分析、文本之内和文本之外的主题、结构的特殊设计、场景变换与人物对话方式、夹叙与夹议相结合几个方面表现主题思想。“延伸阅读与批评”部分说明叙事视角、意象(或象征)、图像等都与主题密切相关，读者借此可以从多种视角更好地把握作品的主题思想。

Chapter 1 The Great Gatsby

by Francis Fitzgerald

(*An Excerpt*)

一、作者简介

弗朗西斯·菲茨杰拉德(1896—1940)，美国20世纪杰出的小说家。他的长篇小说有《人间天堂》(1920)、《美与丑》(1922)、《了不起的盖茨比》(1925)、《夜色温柔》(1934)、《最后的一个巨头》(1941)、《崩溃》(1945)。此外，他还出版了四部短篇小说集：《时髦女与哲学家》(1921)、《爵士时代的故事》(1922)、《所有痛苦的年轻人》(1926)、《雷维尔的节拍声》(1935)。他的短篇小说与长篇小说一样齐名。《了不起的盖茨比》是他的代表作。

菲茨杰拉德出身贵族家庭，但父母并不富有。他年轻时便显露文学创作才华。追求生活奢华的美女泽尔妲并与之结婚是他创作并且获得成功的动力，他因此享受了一段富贵和享乐的婚姻。然而，过度的挥霍和夫妻的争吵使他们的婚姻陷入窘境：妻子得了精神病，菲茨杰拉德的身体因劳累、孤独、饮酒而迅速恶化，直至1940年英年早逝。

菲茨杰拉德是美国20世纪20年代"迷惘的一代"的代表人物之一，是"爵士乐时代"(又称为"喧嚣的20年代")的代言人。他用小说的方式再现自己的生活，而他个人的生活方式正是当时美国社会的真实写照。因此，小说是连接作者的个体生活现实和整个美国社会现实的媒介和桥梁。这就是作者展现给时代和读者的独特魅力。追求"美国梦"(成名、金钱、美女)和"美国梦"的破灭是他小说的主题。他笔下的主人公往往怀揣美好的梦想，而且坚定不移，令人佩服。但是，在物质繁荣、精神空虚、金钱与地位至上的社会里，他们的梦想不切实际，即使目标坚定，但个人力量渺小，因而只能以悲剧告终。行文流畅、文字优美、运用意象和象征、现实与浪漫相结合、戏剧中含有讽刺、美丽和自信中透露出忧郁和悲伤是菲茨杰拉德作品的主要艺术特征。

《了不起的盖茨比》被美国兰登书屋评为20世纪百部最佳小说之一，是年轻人必读的经典小说。菲茨杰拉德被称为与海明威和福克纳并肩齐名的美国作家。

二、文本选读

The Great Gatsby

Chapter 3

There was music from my neighbor's house through the summer nights. In his blue gardens men and girls came and went like moths among the whisperings and the champagne and the stars. At high tide in the afternoon I watched his guests diving from the tower of his raft, or taking the sun on the hot sand of his beach while his two motor-boats slit the waters of the Sound, drawing aquaplanes over cataracts of foam. On week-ends his Rolls-Royce became an omnibus, bearing parties to and from the city between nine in the morning and long past midnight, while his station wagon scampered like a brisk yellow bug to meet all trains. And on Mondays eight servants, including an extra gardener, toiled all day with mops and scrubbing-brushes and hammers and garden-shears, repairing the ravages of the night before.

Every Friday five crates of oranges and lemons arrived from a fruiterer in New York—every Monday these same oranges and lemons left his back door in a pyramid of pulpless halves. There was a machine in the kitchen which could extract the juice of two hundred oranges in half an hour if a little button was pressed two hundred times by a butler's thumb.

At least once a fortnight a corps of caterers came down with several hundred feet of canvas and enough colored lights to make a Christmas tree of Gatsby's enormous garden. On buffet tables, garnished with glistening hors-d'oeuvre[1], spiced baked hams crowded against salads of harlequin designs and pastry pigs and turkeys bewitched to a dark gold. In the main hall a bar with a real brass rail was set up, and stocked with gins and liquors and with cordials so long forgotten that most of his female guests were too young to know one from another.

By seven o'clock the orchestra has arrived, no thin five-piece affair[2], but a whole pitful of oboes and trombones and saxophones and viols and cornets and piccolos, and low and high drums. The last swimmers have come in from the beach now and are dressing upstairs; the cars from New York are parked five deep in the drive, and already the halls and salons and verandas are gaudy with primary colors, and hair shorn in strange new ways, and shawls beyond the dreams of Castile. The bar is in full swing, and floating rounds of cocktails permeate the garden outside, until the air is alive with chatter and laughter, and casual innuendo and introductions forgotten on the spot, and enthusiastic meetings between women who never knew each other's names.

The lights grow brighter as the earth lurches away from the sun, and now the orchestra is playing yellow cocktail music, and the opera of voices pitches a key higher. Laughter is easier minute by minute, spilled with prodigality, tipped out at a cheerful word. The groups change more swiftly, swell with new arrivals, dissolve and form in the same breath; already there are wanderers, confident girls who weave here and there among the stouter and more stable, become for a sharp, joyous moment the centre of a group, and then, excited with triumph, glide on through the sea-change of faces and voices and color under the constantly changing light.

Suddenly one of the gypsies, in trembling opal, seizes a cocktail out of the air, dumps it down for courage and, moving her hands like Frisco[3], dances out alone on the canvas platform. A momentary hush; the orchestra leader varies his rhythm obligingly for her, and there is a burst of chatter as the erroneous news goes around that she is Gilda Gray's[4] understudy from the *Follies*. The party has begun.

I believe that on the first night I went to Gatsby's house I was one of the few guests who had actually been invited. People were not invited—they went there. They got into automobiles which bore them out to Long Island, and somehow they ended up at Gatsby's door. Once there they were introduced by somebody who knew Gatsby, and after that they conducted themselves according to the rules of behavior associated with an amusement park. Sometimes they came and went without having met Gatsby at all, came for the party with a simplicity of heart that was its own ticket of admission.

I had been actually invited. A chauffeur in a uniform of robin's-egg blue crossed my lawn early that Saturday morning with a surprisingly formal note from his employer: the honor would be entirely Gatsby's, it said, if I would attend his "little party." that night. He had seen me several times, and had intended to call on me long before, but a peculiar combination of circumstances had prevented it—signed Jay Gatsby, in a majestic hand.

Dressed up in white flannels I went over to his lawn a little after seven, and wandered around rather ill at ease among swirls and eddies of people I didn't know—though here and there was a face I had noticed on the commuting train. I was immediately struck by the number of young Englishmen dotted about; all well dressed, all looking a little hungry, and all talking in low, earnest voices to solid and prosperous Americans. I was sure that they were selling something: bonds or insurance or automobiles. They were at least agonizingly aware of the easy money in the vicinity and convinced that it was theirs for a few words in the right key.

As soon as I arrived I made an attempt to find my host, but the two or three people of whom I asked his whereabouts stared at me in such an amazed way, and denied so vehemently any knowledge of his movements, that I slunk off in the direction of the cocktail table—the only place in the garden where a single man could linger without looking purposeless and alone.

I was on my way to get roaring drunk from sheer embarrassment when Jordan Baker came out of the house and stood at the head of the marble steps, leaning a little backward and looking with contemptuous interest down into the garden.

Welcome or not, I found it necessary to attach myself to someone before I should begin to address cordial remarks to the passers-by.

"Hello!" I roared, advancing toward her. My voice seemed unnaturally loud across the garden.

"I thought you might be here," she responded absently as I came up. "I remembered you lived next door to—"

She held my hand impersonally, as a promise that she'd take care of me in a minute, and gave ear to two girls in twin yellow dresses, who stopped at the foot of the steps.

"Hello!" they cried together. "Sorry you didn't win."

That was for the golf tournament. She had lost in the finals the week before.

"You don't know who we are," said one of the girls in yellow, "but we met you here about a month ago."

"You've dyed your hair since then," remarked Jordan, and I started, but the girls had moved casually on and her remark was addressed to the premature moon, produced like the supper, no doubt, out of a caterer's basket. With Jordan's slender golden arm resting in mine, we descended the steps and sauntered about the garden. A tray of cocktails floated at us through the twilight, and we sat down at a table with the two girls in yellow and three men, each one introduced to us as Mr. Mumble[5].

"Do you come to these parties often?" inquired Jordan of the girl beside her.

"The last one was the one I met you at," answered the girl, in an alert confident voice. She turned to her companion: "Wasn't it for you, Lucille?"

It was for Lucille, too.

"I like to come," Lucille said. "I never care what I do, so I always have a good time. When I was here last I tore my gown on a chair, and he asked me my name and address—inside of a week I got a package from Croirier's with a new evening gown in it."

"Did you keep it?" asked Jordan.

"Sure I did. I was going to wear it tonight, but it was too big in the bust and had to be altered. It was gas blue with lavender beads. Two hundred and sixty-five dollars."

"There's something funny about a fellow that'll do a thing like that," said the other girl eagerly. "He doesn't want any trouble with anybody."

"Who doesn't?" I inquired.

"Gatsby. Somebody told me—"

The two girls and Jordan leaned together confidentially.

"Somebody told me they thought he killed a man once."

A thrill passed over all of us. The three Mr. Mumbles bent forward and listened eagerly.

"I don't think it's so much *THAT*," argued Lucille sceptically; "it's more that he was a German spy during the war."

One of the men nodded in confirmation.

"I heard that from a man who knew all about him, grew up with him in Germany," he assured us positively.

"Oh, no," said the first girl, "it couldn't be that, because he was in the American army during the war." As our credulity switched back to her she leaned forward with enthusiasm. "You look at him sometimes when he thinks nobody's looking at him. I'll bet he killed a man."

She narrowed her eyes and shivered. Lucille shivered. We all turned and looked around for Gatsby. It was testimony to the romantic speculation he inspired that there were whispers about him from those who had found little that it was necessary to whisper about in this world.

The first supper—there would be another one after midnight—was now being served, and Jordan invited me to join her own party, who were spread around a table on the other side of the garden. There were three married couples and Jordan's escort, a persistent undergraduate given to violent innuendo, and obviously under the impression that sooner or later Jordan was going to yield him up her person to a greater or lesser degree. Instead of rambling, this party had preserved a dignified homogeneity, and assumed to itself the function of representing the staid nobility of the countryside—East Egg condescending to West Egg[6], and carefully on guard against its spectroscopic gaiety.

"Let's get out," whispered Jordan, after a somehow wasteful and inappropriate half-hour; "this is much too polite for me."

We got up, and she explained that we were going to find the host: "I had never met him," she said, "and it was making me uneasy." The undergraduate nodded in a cynical, melancholy way.

The bar, where we glanced first, was crowded, but Gatsby was not there. She couldn't find him from the top of the steps, and he wasn't on the veranda. On a chance we tried an important-looking door, and walked into a high Gothic library, panelled with carved English oak, and probably transported complete from some ruin overseas.

A stout, middle-aged man, with enormous owl-eyed spectacles, was sitting somewhat drunk on the edge of a great table, staring with unsteady concentration at the shelves of books. As we entered he wheeled excitedly around and examined Jordan from head to foot.

"What do you think?" he demanded impetuously.

"About what?"

He waved his hand toward the book-shelves.

"About that. As a matter of fact you needn't bother to ascertain. I ascertained. They're real."

"The books?"

He nodded.

"Absolutely real—have pages and everything. I thought they'd be a nice durable cardboard. Matter of fact, they're absolutely real. Pages and—Here! Lemme show you."

Taking our scepticism for granted, he rushed to the bookcases and returned with Volume One of the "*Stoddard Lectures*."

"See!" he cried triumphantly. "It's a bona-fide piece of printed matter. It fooled me. This fella's a regular Belasco. It's a triumph. What thoroughness! What realism! Knew when to stop, too—didn't cut the pages. But what do you want? What do you expect?"

He snatched the book from me and replaced it hastily on its shelf, muttering that if one brick was removed the whole library was liable to collapse.

"Who brought you?" he demanded. "Or did you just come? I was brought. Most people were brought."

Jordan looked at him alertly, cheerfully, without answering.

"I was brought by a woman named Roosevelt," he continued. "Mrs. Claud Roosevelt. Do you know her? I met her somewhere last night. I've been drunk for about a week now, and I thought it might sober me up to sit in a library."

"Has it?"

"A little bit, I think. I can't tell yet. I've only been here an hour. Did I tell you about the books? They're real. They're—"

"You told us."

We shook hands with him gravely and went back outdoors.

There was dancing now on the canvas in the garden; old men pushing young girls backwards in eternal graceless circles, superior couples holding each other tortuously, fashionably, and keeping in the corners—and a great number of single girls dancing individualistically or relieving the orchestra for a moment of the burden of the banjo or the traps. By midnight the hilarity had increased. A celebrated tenor had sung in Italian, and a notorious contralto had sung in jazz, and between the numbers people were doing "stunts." all over the garden, while happy, vacuous bursts of laughter rose toward the summer sky. A pair of stage twins, who turned out to be the girls in yellow, did a baby act in costume, and champagne was served in glasses bigger than finger-bowls. The moon had risen higher, and floating in the Sound was a triangle of silver scales, trembling a little to the stiff, tinny drip of the banjoes on the lawn.

I was still with Jordan Baker. We were sitting at a table with a man of about my age and a rowdy little girl, who gave way upon the slightest provocation to uncontrollable laughter. I was enjoying myself now. I had taken two fingerbowls of champagne, and the scene had changed before my eyes into something significant, elemental, and profound.

At a lull in the entertainment the man looked at me and smiled.

"Your face is familiar," he said, politely. "Weren't you in the Third Division during the war?"

"Why, yes. I was in the Twenty eighth Infantry."

"I was in the Sixteenth Infantry until June nineteen-eighteen. I knew I'd seen you somewhere before."

We talked for a moment about some wet, grey little villages in France. Evidently he lived in this vicinity, for he told me that he had just bought a hydroplane, and was going to try it out in the morning.

"Want to go with me, old sport? Just near the shore along the Sound."

"What time?"

"Any time that suits you best."

It was on the tip of my tongue to ask his name when Jordan looked around and smiled.

"Having a gay time now?" she inquired.

"Much better." I turned again to my new acquaintance. "This is an unusual party for me. I haven't even seen the host. I live over there—" I waved my hand at the invisible hedge in the distance, "and this man Gatsby sent over his chauffeur with an invitation."

For a moment he looked at me as if he failed to understand.

"I'm Gatsby," he said suddenly.

"What!" I exclaimed. "Oh, I beg your pardon."

"I thought you knew, old sport[7]. I'm afraid I'm not a very good host."

He smiled understandingly—much more than understandingly. It was one of those rare smiles with a quality of eternal reassurance in it, that you may come across four or five times in life. It faced—or seemed to face—the whole external world for an instant, and then concentrated on *you* with an irresistible prejudice in your favor. It understood you just as far as you wanted to be understood, believed in you as you would like to believe in yourself, and assured you that it had precisely the impression of you that, at your best, you hoped to convey. Precisely at that point it vanished—and I was looking at an elegant young roughneck, a year or two over thirty, whose elaborate formality of speech just missed being absurd. Sometime before he introduced himself I'd got a strong impression that he was picking his words with care.

Almost at the moment when Mr. Gatsby identified himself, a butler hurried towards him with the information that Chicago was calling him on the wire. He excused himself with a small bow that included each of us in turn.

"If you want anything just ask for it, old sport," he urged me. "Excuse me. I will rejoin you later."

When he was gone I turned immediately to Jordan—constrained to assure her of my surprise. I had expected that Mr. Gatsby would be a florid and corpulent person in his middle years.

"Who is he?" I demanded. "Do you know?"

"He's just a man named Gatsby."

"Where is he from, I mean? And what does he do?"

"Now *you're* started on the subject," she answered with a wan smile. "Well, he told me once he was an Oxford man[8]."

A dim background started to take shape behind him, but at her next remark it faded away.

"However, I don't believe it."

"Why not?"

"I don't know," she insisted, "I just don't think he went there."

Something in her tone reminded me of the other girl's "I think he killed a man," and had the effect of stimulating my curiosity. I would have accepted without question the information that Gatsby sprang from the swamps of Louisiana or from the lower East Side of New York[9]. That was comprehensible. But young men didn't—at least in my provincial inexperience I believed they didn't—drift coolly out of nowhere and buy a palace on Long Island Sound.

"Anyhow, he gives large parties," said Jordan, changing the subject with an urbane taste for the concrete. "And I like large parties. They're so intimate. At small parties there isn't any privacy."

There was the boom of a bass drum, and the voice of the orchestra leader rang out suddenly above the echolalia of the garden.

"Ladies and gentlemen," he cried. "At the request of Mr. Gatsby we are going to play for you Mr. Vladimir Tostoff's latest work, which attracted so much attention at Carnegie Hall last

May. If you read the papers, you know there was a big sensation." He smiled with jovial condescension, and added: "Some sensation!" Whereupon everybody laughed.

"The piece is known," he concluded lustily, "as Vladimir Tostoff's *Jazz History of the World*."

The nature of Mr. Tostoff's composition eluded me, because just as it began my eyes fell on Gatsby, standing alone on the marble steps and looking from one group to another with approving eyes. His tanned skin was drawn attractively tight on his face and his short hair looked as though it were trimmed every day. I could see nothing sinister about him. I wondered if the fact that he was not drinking helped to set him off from his guests, for it seemed to me that he grew more correct as the fraternal hilarity increased. When the *Jazz History of the World* was over, girls were putting their heads on men's shoulders in a puppyish, convivial way, girls were swooning backward playfully into men's arms, even into groups, knowing that some one would arrest their falls—but no one swooned backward on Gatsby, and no French bob[10] touched Gatsby's shoulder, and no singing quartets were formed with Gatsby's head for one link.

"I beg your pardon."

Gatsby's butler was suddenly standing beside us.

"Miss Baker?" he inquired. "I beg your pardon, but Mr. Gatsby would like to speak to you alone."

"With me?" she exclaimed in surprise.

"Yes, madame."

She got up slowly, raising her eyebrows at me in astonishment, and followed the butler towards the house. I noticed that she wore her evening-dress, all her dresses, like sports clothes—there was a jauntiness about her movements as if she had first learned to walk upon golf courses on clean, crisp mornings.

I was alone and it was almost two. For some time confused and intriguing sounds had issued from a long, many-windowed room which overhung the terrace. Eluding Jordan's undergraduate, who was now engaged in an obstetrical conversation with two chorus girls, and who implored me to join him, I went inside.

The large room was full of people. One of the girls in yellow was playing the piano, and beside her stood a tall, red-haired young lady from a famous chorus, engaged in song. She had drunk a quantity of champagne, and during the course of her song she had decided, ineptly, that everything was very, very sad—she was not only singing, she was weeping too. Whenever there was a pause in the song she filled it with gasping, broken sobs, and then took up the lyric again in a quavering soprano. The tears coursed down her cheeks—not freely, however, for when they came into contact with her heavily beaded eyelashes they assumed an inky color, and pursued the rest of their way in slow black rivulets. A humorous suggestion was made that she sing the notes on her face, whereupon she threw up her hands, sank into a chair, and went off into a deep vinous sleep.

"She had a fight with a man who says he's her husband," explained a girl at my elbow.

I looked around. Most of the remaining women were now having fights with men said to be their husbands. Even Jordan's party, the quartet from East Egg, were rent asunder by dissension. One of the men was talking with curious intensity to a young actress, and his wife, after attempting to laugh at the situation in a dignified and indifferent way, broke down entirely and resorted to flank attacks—at intervals she appeared suddenly at his side like an angry diamond, and hissed: "You promised!" into his ear.

The reluctance to go home was not confined to wayward men. The hall was at present occupied by two deplorably sober men and their highly indignant wives. The wives were sympathizing with each other in slightly raised voices.

"Whenever he sees I'm having a good time he wants to go home."

"Never heard anything so selfish in my life."

"We're always the first ones to leave."

"So are we."

"Well, we're almost the last tonight," said one of the men sheepishly. "The orchestra left half an hour ago."

In spite of the wives' agreement that such malevolence was beyond credibility, the dispute ended in a short struggle, and both wives were lifted, kicking, into the night.

As I waited for my hat in the hall the door of the library opened and Jordan Baker and Gatsby came out together. He was saying some last word to her, but the eagerness in his manner tightened abruptly into formality as several people approached him to say goodbye.

Jordan's party were calling impatiently to her from the porch, but she lingered for a moment to shake hands.

"I've just heard the most amazing thing," she whispered. "How long were we in there?"

"Why, about an hour."

"It was ... simply amazing," she repeated abstractedly. "But I swore I wouldn't tell it and here I am tantalizing you." She yawned gracefully in my face: "Please come and see me... Phone book ... Under the name of Mrs. Sigourney Howard... My aunt ..." She was hurrying off as she talked—her brown hand waved a jaunty salute as she melted into her party at the door.

Rather ashamed that on my first appearance I had stayed so late, I joined the last of Gatsby's guests, who were clustered around him. I wanted to explain that I'd hunted for him early in the evening and to apologize for not having known him in the garden.

"Don't mention it," he enjoined me eagerly. "Don't give it another thought, old sport." The familiar expression held no more familiarity than the hand which reassuringly brushed my shoulder. "And don't forget we're going up in the hydroplane to-morrow morning, at nine o'clock."

Then the butler, behind his shoulder:

"Philadelphia wants you on the phone, sir."

"All right, in a minute. Tell them I'll be right there... Good night."

"Good night."

"Good night." He smiled—and suddenly there seemed to be a pleasant significance in having been among the last to go, as if he had desired it all the time. "Good night, old sport... Good night."

But as I walked down the steps I saw that the evening was not quite over. Fifty feet from the door a dozen headlights illuminated a bizarre and tumultuous scene. In the ditch beside the road, right side up, but violently shorn of one wheel, rested a new coupe which had left Gatsby's drive not two minutes before. The sharp jut of a wall accounted for the detachment of the wheel, which was now getting considerable attention from half a dozen curious chauffeurs. However, as they had left their cars blocking the road, a harsh, discordant din from those in the rear had been audible for some time, and added to the already violent confusion of the scene.

A man in a long duster had dismounted from the wreck and now stood in the middle of the road, looking from the car to the tire and from the tire to the observers in a pleasant, puzzled way.

"See!" he explained. "It went in the ditch."

The fact was infinitely astonishing to him, and I recognized first the unusual quality of wonder, and then the man—it was the late patron of Gatsby's library.

"How'd it happen?"

He shrugged his shoulders.

"I know nothing whatever about mechanics," he said decisively.

"But how did it happen? Did you run into the wall?"

"Don't ask me," said Owl Eyes, washing his hands of the whole matter. "I know very little about driving—next to nothing. It happened, and that's all I know."

"Well, if you're a poor driver you oughtn't to try driving at night."

"But I wasn't even trying," he explained indignantly, "I wasn't even trying."

An awed hush fell upon the bystanders.

"Do you want to commit suicide?"

"You're lucky it was just a wheel! A bad driver and not even *trying*!"

"You don't understand," explained the criminal. "I wasn't driving. There's another man in the car."

The shock that followed this declaration found voice in a sustained "Ah-h-h!" as the door of the coupé swung slowly open. The crowd—it was now a crowd—stepped back involuntarily, and when the door had opened wide there was a ghostly pause. Then, very gradually, part by part, a pale, dangling individual stepped out of the wreck, pawing tentatively at the ground with a large uncertain dancing shoe.

Blinded by the glare of the headlights and confused by the incessant groaning of the horns, the apparition stood swaying for a moment before he perceived the man in the duster.

"Wha's matter?" he inquired calmly. "Did we run outa gas?"

"Look!"

Half a dozen fingers pointed at the amputated wheel—he stared at it for a moment, and then looked upward as though he suspected that it had dropped from the sky.

"It came off," some one explained.

He nodded.

"At first I din' notice we'd stopped."

A pause. Then, taking a long breath and straightening his shoulders, he remarked in a determined voice:

"Wonder'ff tell me where there's a gas'line station?"

At least a dozen men, some of them little better off than he was, explained to him that wheel and car were no longer joined by any physical bond.

"Back out," he suggested after a moment. "Put her in reverse."

"But the *wheel's* off!"

He hesitated.

"No harm in trying," he said.

The caterwauling horns had reached a crescendo and I turned away and cut across the lawn towards home. I glanced back once. A wafer of a moon was shining over Gatsby's house, making the night fine as before, and surviving the laughter and the sound of his still glowing garden. A sudden emptiness seemed to flow now from the windows and the great doors, endowing with complete isolation the figure of the host, who stood on the porch, his hand up in a formal gesture of farewell.

Reading over what I have written so far, I see I have given the impression that the events of three nights several weeks apart were all that absorbed me. On the contrary, they were merely casual events in a crowded summer, and, until much later, they absorbed me infinitely less than my personal affairs.

Most of the time I worked. In the early morning the sun threw my shadow westward as I hurried down the white chasms of lower New York to the Probity Trust. I knew the other clerks and young bond-salesmen by their first names, and lunched with them in dark, crowded restaurants on little pig sausages and mashed potatoes and coffee. I even had a short affair with a girl who lived in Jersey City and worked in the accounting department, but her brother began throwing mean looks in my direction, so when she went on her vacation in July I let it blow quietly away.

I took dinner usually at the Yale Club—for some reason it was the gloomiest event of my day—and then I went upstairs to the library and studied investments and securities for a conscientious hour. There were generally a few rioters around, but they never came into the library, so it was a good place to work. After that, if the night was mellow, I strolled down Madison Avenue past the old Murray Hill Hotel, and over 33rd Street to the Pennsylvania Station.

I began to like New York, the racy, adventurous feel of it at night, and the satisfaction that the constant flicker of men and women and machines gives to the restless eye. I liked to walk up Fifth Avenue and pick out romantic women from the crowd and imagine that in a few minutes I was going to enter into their lives, and no one would ever know or disapprove. Sometimes, in my mind, I followed them to their apartments on the corners of hidden streets, and they turned and smiled back at me before they faded through a door into warm darkness. At the enchanted metropolitan twilight I felt a haunting loneliness sometimes, and felt it in others—poor young clerks who loitered in front of windows waiting until it was time for a solitary restaurant dinner—young clerks in the dusk, wasting the most poignant moments of night and life.

Again at eight o'clock, when the dark lanes of the Forties were lined five deep with throbbing taxi-cabs, bound for the theatre district, I felt a sinking in my heart. Forms leaned together in the taxis as they waited, and voices sang, and there was laughter from unheard jokes, and lighted cigarettes made unintelligible circles inside. Imagining that I, too, was hurrying towards gaiety and sharing their intimate excitement, I wished them well.

For a while I lost sight of Jordan Baker, and then in midsummer I found her again. At first I was flattered to go places with her, because she was a golf champion, and every one knew her name. Then it was something more. I wasn't actually in love, but I felt a sort of tender curiosity. The bored haughty face that she turned to the world concealed something—most affectations conceal something eventually, even though they don't in the beginning—and one day I found what it was. When we were on a house-party together up in Warwick, she left a borrowed car out in the rain with the top down, and then lied about it—and suddenly I remembered the story about her that had eluded me that night at Daisy's. At her first big golf tournament there was a row that nearly reached the newspapers—a suggestion that she had moved her ball from a bad lie in the semi-final round. The thing approached the proportions of a scandal—then died away. A caddy retracted his statement, and the only other witness admitted that he might have been mistaken. The incident and the name had remained together in my mind.

Jordan Baker instinctively avoided clever, shrewd men, and now I saw that this was because she felt safer on a plane where any divergence from a code[11] would be thought impossible. She was incurably dishonest. She wasn't able to endure being at a disadvantage and, given this unwillingness, I suppose she had begun dealing in subterfuges when she was very young in order to keep that cool, insolent smile turned to the world and yet satisfy the demands of her hard, jaunty body.

It made no difference to me. Dishonesty in a woman is a thing you never blame deeply—I was casually sorry, and then I forgot. It was on that same house-party that we had a curious conversation about driving a car. It started because she passed so close to some workmen that our fender flicked a button on one man's coat.

"You're a rotten driver," I protested. "Either you ought to be more careful, or you oughtn't to drive at all."

"I am careful."

"No, you're not."

"Well, other people are," she said lightly.

"What's that got to do with it?"

"They'll keep out of my way," she insisted. "It takes two to make an accident."

"Suppose you met somebody just as careless as yourself."

"I hope I never will," she answered. "I hate careless people. That's why I like you."

Her gray, sun-strained eyes stared straight ahead, but she had deliberately shifted our relations, and for a moment I thought I loved her. But I am slow-thinking and full of interior rules that act as brakes on my desires[12], and I knew that first I had to get myself definitely out of that tangle back home. I'd been writing letters once a week and signing them: "Love, Nick," and all I could think of was how, when that certain girl played tennis, a faint mustache of perspiration appeared on her upper lip. Nevertheless there was a vague understanding that had to be tactfully broken off before I was free.

Every one suspects himself of at least one of the cardinal virtues, and this is mine: I am one of the few honest people that I have ever known.

三、主题解析

《了不起的盖茨比》的情节围绕叙述者尼克·卡洛威展开。来自中西部的尼克为了追逐潮流，到东部的纽约经营股票。他是故事的主人公——杰伊·盖茨比的邻居。盖茨比看上美女黛西，但因自己太穷，无法拥有她。黛西投入富人汤姆·布坎南的怀抱。后来盖茨比通过非法手段盈利致富。他经常举办宴席舞会，期望召回黛西的芳心。而且无需邀请，几乎任何人都可以到场把酒狂欢。然而，物是人非，眼前的黛西与以前的她已是判若两人。盖茨比的富有和诚心几乎打动了黛西，但是她的丈夫对盖茨比展开强势回击。夹在两个男人中的黛西心情十分糟糕，开车时撞死了自己丈夫的情人马尔特·威尔逊。为了保全自己，汤姆告诉威尔逊说杀害马尔特的凶手是盖茨比。威尔逊潜入盖茨比家中，开枪打死盖茨比后开枪自杀。最后，只有尼克、盖茨比的父亲和几个仆人出席了盖茨比的葬礼。东部之行让尼克对大都市社会冷漠的人际关系有了深刻的认识，他最终决定回到中西部。

通过分析主要人物的性格特征来获得作品的主题思想几乎是读者最常用的分析方式。如果分析盖茨比，就该关注他的所思和所想以及所言和所行，考察他的行为是否合理和切合实际，以及它们带来的后果。他一心想将过去变成现实——获得黛西的真爱；他挥金如土，指望用行动打动黛西；他实现从穷到富的蜕变；他甚至愿意帮黛西承担撞死马尔特的责任。然而，他的一切举动不切实际。第一，黛西不是从前的黛西："她的声音充满了金钱"(第七章)，"她所做的决定一定是通过某种力量——爱、金钱、毫无疑问的实用性来完成的"(第八章)。第二，好多人都知道他的致富手段是非法的，而且据传他杀过人(第三章)。第三，他的"情敌"比他更富有、更有侵略性、更狡猾，因此盖茨比不是他的对手。综上所述，盖茨比的思想和行为的每一个环节都有问题，他的悲剧当然不可避免。

本文是小说的第三章。它通过数字、细节列举(海陆空交通工具并用、众多仆人忙碌、水果琳琅满目、声光色混杂)等手法充分彰显盖茨比举行舞会和宴会的奢华场面。但是豪华的背后蕴藏着讽刺和暗示。读者(包括到场的"客人")不禁要问：这家主人真有钱，他是做什么的？其次，尽管宾客盈门，但应邀者甚少。为什么？他们中的大多数根本不认识盖茨比，只是过来行乐和享乐的。再者，他们都对盖茨比感到好奇，都想目睹这位大款的尊容，但有关他的负面传闻早已传开，例如有人听说盖茨比曾经"杀过人"。这为盖茨比后来的命运走向埋下伏笔。最后，直到该部分的中间，盖茨比才露面。读者可能和当时在场的宾客(包括叙述者尼克)一样，想了解盖茨比的身世，想知晓他为何经常举办如此盛大的舞会。透过人潮涌动的舞会、宴会的喧闹声，读者感受到一个社会的缩影：享乐至上、世态炎凉、人情冷漠。总之，该部分为小说的情节发展提供若干信息，为人物的命运和人物之间的关系起到铺垫作用。同时，小说的主题思想——"美国梦"的主要内涵在此也略见一斑。

四、难点注释

1. hors-d'oeuvre：〈法语〉餐前或餐间的开胃小吃。
2. no thin five-piece affair：不是简单的五人小乐队。
3. Frisco：〈俚语〉快而有力地；San Francisco 的简称。
4. Gilda Gray：当时轰动一时的纽约舞星。
5. Mr. Mumble：指说话咕噜或声音低沉的人。
6. East Egg condescending to West Egg：East Egg 和 West Egg 分别指东卵和西卵，前者是富人居住区，后者是盖茨比的居住区。
7. sport：〈俚语〉朋友；老兄。
8. Oxford man：求学牛津大学的人。
9. lower East Side of New York：纽约东城的贫民窟。
10. French bob：姑娘的(时髦)短发。
11. code：规范；道德标准。
12. ... full of interior rules that act as brakes on my desires：内心充满了清规戒律，它们限制着我的欲望。词组 act as a brake (brakes) on 表示"约束；控制"。

五、延伸阅读与批评

《一颗像里兹饭店一样大的钻石》是菲茨杰拉德的短篇小说代表作，也是描写和反映"美国梦"的主题，但其内涵与《了不起的盖茨比》中"美国梦"的内涵不同。

故事发生在20世纪30年代美国经济大萧条时期，讲述了就读大学预科的约翰随同班同学帕西一起访问他家乡的经历。经过一番近似神奇之旅，他们俩来到被称为钻石山的地方——帕西的家——一座比世上最富的皇宫还要富、依山而建的宫殿。山上到处都是钻石，宫殿里随处可见世间珍奇饰品，高科技运用在生活的各个方面。约翰在惊讶之余享受了一段梦幻般的生活。帕西的父亲神通广大，几乎无所不能，甚至能买通上帝。他们都过着衣来伸手和饭来张口的生活。后来宫殿被毁灭，所有的钻石化为灰烬。约翰和帕西的两个姐姐逃离宫殿，保全性命。

然而，帕西的家庭成员对待钻石和生活的态度各异。通过他们各自的言行和思想活动，读者发现他们的内心世界各不相同。例如，帕西的姐姐贾斯米不顾父亲的反对，邀请外面的姑娘来玩，而且这些姑娘将被她的父亲处死。为什么？与帕西相比，约翰和帕西的家世有天壤之别，可为什么帕西的姐姐贾斯米冒着父亲反对的危险，仍然爱上约翰，甚至想与之私奔？逃跑途中，贾斯米说："自由而又贫穷，多有趣！"她为何有如此想法？她又说："我以前从来没有注意过星星。我总以为它们是属于一个什么人的很大很大的钻石。可是现在它们使我害怕。它们使我感到这一切全是一场梦，我的全部青春是一场梦。"约翰对此深表认同。这些表达小说中心思想的句子的内涵究竟是什么？这个问题令人关注。

Chapter 2 Death of a Salesman

by Arthur Miller

(An Excerpt)

一、作者简介

阿瑟·米勒(1915—2005)，美国现当代著名的剧作家。他的作品很多，主要的剧本包括《鸿运高照的人》(1944)、《全是我的儿子》(1947)、《推销员之死》(1949)、《炼狱》(1953)、《两个星期一的回忆》(1955)、《桥头眺望》(1955)、《不合时宜的人》(1961)、《堕落之后》(1964)、《创世记及其他》(1972)、《大主教的天花板》(1977)、《某种爱情》(1982)和《破玻璃》(1994)等。此外，他还出版了《米勒戏剧论文集》(1978)。代表作《推销员之死》与奥尼尔的《进入黑夜的漫长旅程》和威廉斯的《欲望号街车》并称为美国最杰出的三部戏剧。米勒出生在一个犹太移民家庭。父亲的生意破产将全家抛入经济拮据的窘境，米勒开始接触生活底层，体验普通人民的生活并与戏剧结下不解之缘。当时著名的影星玛丽莲·梦露是米勒的第二任妻子，他们的婚姻被称为世上最美的思想和最美的肉体的结合。

米勒的创作大致分为两个时期。第一时期主要描写美国社会中低层市民的现实生活状况，揭示社会的丑恶现象和人物的悲惨命运，表现作者反抗强权压迫如20世纪50年代的麦卡锡主义和坚持正义的斗争精神。《全是我的儿子》和《推销员之死》是该时期的代表作。后期作品主要表达对宗教思想(清教主义的原罪说)的思考。在表现手法上，米勒著书立说，大胆尝试戏剧创作的新理念。他认为普通的小人物也是值得书写的悲剧式英雄人物，将现实主义、现代主义、表现主义和心理分析等手法融为一体，为美国戏剧的进一步繁荣作出重要贡献。他因此成为继尤金·奥尼尔之后与田纳西·威廉斯齐名的美国戏剧大师。1965年以来他两次担任国际笔会主席，1984年获得华盛顿肯尼迪艺术中心奖。

米勒也是中国读者熟知和喜爱的作家。1979年米勒的《中国奇遇》和《推销员在北京》分别记录了他于1978年访问中国和1983年抵京亲自执导《推销员之死》的经历。当时扮演剧中男主角的英若诚先生还亲自将《推销员之死》译成中文(2011年出版)。这真是中国读者的福气!

二、文本选读

Death of a Salesman

ACT Ⅱ (Excerpt)

Music is heard, gay and bright. The curtain rises as the music fades away. Willy[1]*, in shirt sleeves,* *is sitting at the kitchen table, sipping coffee, his hat in his lap. Linda is filling his cup when she can.*

WILLY: Wonderful coffee. Meal in itself.

LINDA: Can I make you some eggs?

WILLY: No. Take a breath.

LINDA: You look so rested, dear.

WILLY: I slept like a dead one. First time in months. Imagine, sleeping till ten on a Tuesday morning. Boys left nice and early, heh?

LINDA: They were out of here by eight o'clock.

WILLY: Good work!

LINDA: It was so thrilling to see them leaving together. I can't get over the shaving lotion in this house[2]!

WILLY, *smiling*: Mmm...

LINDA: Biff was very changed this morning. His whole attitude seemed to be hopeful. He couldn't wait to get downtown to see Oliver.

WILLY: He's heading for a change. There's no question, there simply are certain men that take longer to get-solidified[3]. How did he dress?

LINDA: His blue suit. He's so handsome in that suit. He could be a—anything in that suit!

Willy gets up from the table. Linda holds his jacket for him.

WILLY: There's no question, no question at all. Gee, on the way home tonight I'd like to buy some seeds.

LINDA, *laughing*: That'd be wonderful. But not enough sun gets back there. Nothing'll grow any more.

WILLY: You wait, kid, before it's all over we're gonna get a little place out in the country, and I'll raise some vegetables, a couple of chickens...

LINDA: You'll do it yet, dear.

Willy walks out of his jacket. Linda follows him.

WILLY: And they'll get married, and come for a weekend. I'd build a little guest house. 'Cause I got so many fine tools, all I'd need would be a little lumber and some peace of mind.

LINDA, *joyfully*: I sewed the lining...

WILLY: I could build two guest houses, so they'd both come. Did he decide how much he's going to ask Oliver for?

LINDA, *getting him into the jacket*: He didn't mention it, but I imagine ten or fifteen thousand. You going to talk to Howard today?

WILLY: Yeah. I'll put it to him straight and simple. He'll just have to take me off the road[4].

LINDA: And Willy, don't forget to ask for a little advance, because we've got the insurance premium. It's the grace period now.

WILLY: That's a hundred... ?

LINDA: A hundred and eight, sixty-eight. Because we're a little short again.

WILLY: Why are we short?

LINDA: Well, you had the motor job on the car[5]...

WILLY: That goddam Studebaker!

LINDA: And you got one more payment on the refrigerator...

WILLY: But it just broke again!

LINDA: Well, it's old, dear.

WILLY: I told you we should've bought a well-advertised machine. Charley bought a General Electric and it's twenty years old and it's still good, that son-of-a-bitch.

LINDA: But, Willy...

WILLY: Whoever heard of a Hastings refrigerator? Once in my life I would like to own something outright before it's broken! I'm always in a race with the junkyard! I just finished paying for the car and it's on its last legs[6]. The refrigerator consumes belts like a goddam maniac. They time those things. They time them so when you finally paid for them, they're used up.

LINDA, *buttoning up his jacket as he unbuttons it*: All told, about two hundred dollars would carry us, dear. But that includes the last payment on the mortgage. After this payment, Willy, the house belongs to us.

WILLY: It's twenty-five years!

LINDA: Biff was nine years old when we bought it.

WILLY: Well, that's a great thing. To weather a twenty-five year mortgage is...

LINDA: It's an accomplishment.

WILLY: All the cement, the lumber, the reconstruction I put in this house! There ain't a crack to be found in it any more.

LINDA: Well, it served its purpose.

WILLY: What purpose? Some stranger'll come along, move in, and that's that. If only Biff would take this house, and raise a family...*He starts to go*. Good-by, I'm late.

LINDA, *suddenly remembering*: Oh, I forgot! You're supposed to meet them for dinner.

WILLY: Me?

LINDA: At Frank's Chop House on Forty-eighth near Sixth Avenue.

WILLY: Is that so! How about you?

LINDA: No, just the three of you. They're gonna blow you to a big meal[7]!

WILLY: Don't say! Who thought of that?

LINDA: Biff came to me this morning, Willy, and he said, "tell Dad, we want to blow him to a big meal." Be there six o'clock. You and your two boys are going to have dinner.

WILLY: Gee whiz! That's really somethin'. I'm gonna knock Howard for a loop[8], kid. I'll get an advance, and I'll come home with a New York job. Goddammit, now I'm gonna do it!

LINDA: Oh, that's the spirit, Willy!

WILLY: I will never get behind a wheel[9] the rest of my life!

LINDA: It's changing. Willy, I can feel it changing!

WILLY: Beyond a question. G'by, I'm late. *He starts to go again.*

LINDA, *calling after him as she runs to the kitchen table for a handkerchief*: You got your glasses?

WILLY, *feels for them, then comes back in*: Yeah, yeah, got my glasses.

LINDA, *giving him the handkerchief*: And a handkerchief.

WILLY: Yeah, handkerchief.

LINDA: And your saccharine?

WILLY: Yeah, my saccharine.

LINDA: Be careful on the subway stairs.

She kisses him, and a silk stocking is seen hanging from her hand. Willy notices it.

WILLY: Will you stop mending stockings? At least while I'm in the house. It gets me nervous. I can't tell you. Please.

Linda hides the stocking in her hand as she follows Willy across the forestage in front of the house.

LINDA: Remember, Frank's Chop House.

WILLY, *passing the apron*[10]: Maybe beets would grow out there.

LINDA, *laughing*: But you tried so many times.

WILLY: Yeah. Well, don't work hard today. *He disappears around the right corner of the house.*

LINDA: Be careful!

As Willy vanishes, Linda waves to him. Suddenly the phone rings. She runs across the stage and into the kitchen and lifts it.

LINDA: Hello? Oh, Biff. I'm so glad you called, I just… Yes, sure, I just told him. Yes, he'll be there for dinner at six o'clock, I didn't forget. Listen, I was just dying to tell you. You know that little rubber pipe[11] I told you about? That he connected to the gas heater? I finally decided to go down the cellar this morning and take it away and destroy it. But it's gone! Imagine? He took it away himself, it isn't there! *She listens.* When? Oh, then you took it. Oh—nothing, it's just that I'd hoped he'd taken it away himself. Oh, I'm not worried, darling, because this morning he left in such high spirits, it was like the old days! I'm not afraid any more. Did Mr. Oliver see you? … Well, you wait there then. And make a nice impression on him, darling. Just don't perspire too much before you see him. And have a nice time with Dad. He may have big news too! … That's right, a New York job. And be sweet to him tonight, dear. Be loving to him. Because he's only a little boat looking for a harbor. *She is trembling with sorrow and joy.* Oh, that's wonderful, Biff, you'll save his life. Thanks, darling. Just put your arm around him when he comes into the restaurant. Give him a smile. That's the boy… Good-by, dear. You got your comb? … That's fine. Good-by, Biff dear.

In the middle of her speech, Howard Wagner, thirty-six, wheels on a small typewriter table on which is a wire-recording machine and proceeds to plug it in. This is on the left forestage. Light slowly fades on Linda as it rises on Howard. Howard is intent on threading the machine and only glances over his shoulder as Willy appears.

WILLY: Pst! Pst!

HOWARD: Hello, Willy, come in.

WILLY: Like to have a little talk with you, Howard.

HOWARD: Sorry to keep you waiting. I'll be with you in a minute.

WILLY: What's that, Howard?

HOWARD: Didn't you ever see one of these? Wire recorder.

WILLY: Oh. Can we talk a minute?

HOWARD: Records things. Just got delivery yesterday. Been driving me crazy, the most terrific machine I ever saw in my life. I was up all night with it.

WILLY: What do you do with it?

HOWARD: I bought it for dictation, but you can do anything with it. Listen to this. I had it home last night. Listen to what I picked up. The first one is my daughter. Get this. *He flicks the switch and "Roll out the Barrel" is heard being whistled.* Listen to that kid whistle.

WILLY: That is lifelike, isn't it?

HOWARD: Seven years old. Get that tone.

WILLY: Ts, ts. Like to ask a little favor if you...

The whistling breaks off, and the voice of Howard's daughter is heard.

HIS DAUGHTER: "Now you, Daddy."

HOWARD: She's crazy for me! *Again the same song is whistled.* That's me! Ha! *He winks.*

WILLY: You're very good!

The whistling breaks off again. The machine runs silent for a moment.

HOWARD: Sh! Get this now, this is my son.

HIS SON: "The capital of Alabama is Montgomery; the capital of Arizona is Phoenix; the capital of Arkansas is Little Rock; the capital of California is Sacramento..." *and on, and on.*

HOWARD, *holding up five fingers*: Five years old. Willy!

WILLY: He'll make an announcer some day!

HIS SON, *continuing*: "the capital..."

HOWARD: Get that—alphabetical order! *The machine breaks off suddenly.* Wait a minute. The maid kicked the plug out.

WILLY: It certainly is a...

HOWARD: Sh, for God's sake!

HIS SON: "It's nine o'clock, Bulova watch time[12]. So I have to go to sleep."

WILLY: That really is...

HOWARD: Wait a minute! The next is my wife.

They wait.

HOWARD'S VOICE: "Go on, say something." *Pause.* "Well, you gonna talk?"

HIS WIFE: "I can't think of anything."

HOWARD'S VOICE: "Well, talk—it's turning."

HIS WIFE, *shyly*, *beaten*: "Hello." *Silence.* "Oh, Howard, I can't talk into this..."

HOWARD, *snapping the machine off*: That was my wife.

WILLY: That is a wonderful machine. Can we—

HOWARD: I tell you, Willy, I'm gonna take my camera, and my bandsaw, and all my hobbies, and out they go. This is the most fascinating relaxation I ever found.

WILLY: I think I'll get one myself.

HOWARD: Sure, they're only a hundred and a half. You can't do without it. Supposing you wanna hear Jack Benny, see? But you can't be at home at that hour. So you tell the maid to turn the radio on when Jack Benny comes on, and this automatically goes on with the radio...

WILLY: And when you come home you...

HOWARD: You can come home twelve o'clock, one o'clock, any time you like, and you get yourself a Coke and sit yourself down, throw the switch, and there's Jack Benny's program in the middle of the night!

WILLY: I'm definitely going to get one. Because lots of times I'm on the road, and I think to myself, what I must be missing on the radio!

HOWARD: Don't you have a radio in the car?

WILLY: Well, yeah, but who ever thinks of turning it on?

HOWARD: Say, aren't you supposed to be in Boston?

WILLY: That's what I want to talk to you about, Howard. You got a minute? *He draws a chair in from the wing.*

HOWARD: What happened? What're you doing here?

WILLY: Well...

HOWARD: You didn't crack up again, did you?

WILLY: Oh, no. No...

HOWARD: Geez, you had me worried there for a minute. What's the trouble?

WILLY: Well, tell you the truth, Howard. I've come to the decision that I'd rather not travel any more.

HOWARD: Not travel! Well, what'll you do?

WILLY: Remember, Christmas time, when you had the party here? You said you'd try to think of some spot for me here in town.

HOWARD: With us?

WILLY: Well, sure.

HOWARD: Oh, yeah, yeah. I remember. Well, I couldn't think of anything for you, Willy.

WILLY: I tell ya, Howard. The kids are all grown up, y'know. I don't need much any more. If I could take home—well, sixty-five dollars a week, I could swing[13] it.

HOWARD: Yeah, but Willy, see I...

WILLY: I tell ya why. Howard. Speaking frankly and between the two of us, y'know—I'm just a little tired.

HOWARD: Oh, I could understand that, Willy. But you're a road man, Willy, and we do a road business. We've only got a half-dozen salesmen on the floor here.

WILLY: God knows, Howard. I never asked a favor of any man. But I was with the firm when your father used to carry you in here in his arms.

HOWARD: I know that, Willy, but...

WILLY: Your father came to me the day you were born and asked me what I thought of the name of Howard, may he rest in peace.

HOWARD: I appreciate that, Willy, but there just is no spot here for you. If I had a spot I'd slam you right in, but I just don't have a single solitary spot.

He looks for his lighter. Willy has picked it up and gives it to him. Pause.

WILLY, *with increasing anger*: Howard, all I need to set my table is fifty dollars a week.

HOWARD: But where am I going to put you, kid?

WILLY: Look, it isn't a question of whether I can sell merchandise, is it?

HOWARD: No, but it's a business, kid, and everybody's gotta pull his own weight[14].

WILLY, *desperately*: Just let me tell you a story. Howard...

HOWARD: 'Cause you gotta admit, business is business.

WILLY, *angrily*: Business is definitely business, but just listen for a minute. You don't understand this. When I was a boy—eighteen, nineteen—I was already on the road. And there was a question in my mind as to whether selling had a future for me. Because in those days I had a yearning to go to Alaska. See, there were three gold strikes in one month in Alaska, and I felt like going out. Just for the ride, you might say.

HOWARD, *barely interested*: Don't say.

WILLY: Oh, yeah, my father lived many years in Alaska. He was an adventurous man. We've got quite a little streak of self-reliance in our family. I thought I'd go out with my older brother and try to locate him, and maybe settle in the North with the old man. And I was almost decided to go, when I met a salesman in the Parker House. His name was Dave Singleman. And he was eighty-four years old, and he'd drummed merchandise in thirty-one states. And old Dave, he'd go up to his room, y'understand, put on his green velvet slippers—I'll never forget—and pick up his phone and call the buyers, and without ever leaving his room, at the age of eighty-four, he made his living. And when I saw that, I realized that selling was the greatest career a man could want. 'Cause what could be more satisfying than to be able to go, at the age of eighty-four, into twenty or thirty different cities, and pick up a phone, and be remembered and loved and helped by so many different people? Do you know? When he died—and by the way he died the death of a salesman, in his green velvet slippers in the smoker of the New York, New Haven and Hartford, going into Boston—when he died, hundreds of salesmen and buyers were at his funeral. Things were sad on a lotta trains for months after that. *He stands up. Howard has not looked at him.* In those days there was personality in it, Howard. There was respect, and comradeship, and gratitude in it. Today, it's all cut and dried, and there's no chance for bringing friendship to bear—or personality. You see what I mean? They don't know me any more.

HOWARD, *moving away, to the right*: That's just the thing, Willy.

WILLY: If I had forty dollars a week—that's all I'd need. Forty dollars, Howard.

HOWARD: Kid, I can't take blood from a stone, I…

WILLY, *desperation is on him now*: Howard, the year Al Smith was nominated, your father came to me and…

HOWARD, *starting to go off*: I've got to see some people, kid.

WILLY, *stopping him.* I'm talking about your father! There were promises made across this desk! You mustn't tell me you've got people to see—I put thirty-four years into this firm, Howard, and now I can't pay my insurance! You can't eat the orange and throw the peel away—a man is not a piece of fruit! *After a pause.* Now pay attention. Your father—in 1928 I had a big year. I averaged a hundred and seventy dollars a week in commissions.

HOWARD, *impatiently*: Now, Willy, you never averaged…

WILLY, *banging his hand on the desk*: I averaged a hundred and seventy dollars a week in the year of 1928! And your father came to me—or rather, I was in the office here—it was right over this desk—and he put his hand on my shoulder…

HOWARD, *getting up*: You'll have to excuse me, Willy, I gotta see some people. Pull yourself together. *Going out.* I'll be back in a little while.

On Howard's exit, the light on his chair grows very bright and strange.

WILLY: Pull myself together! What the hell did I say to him? My God, I was yelling at him! How could I? *Willy breaks off, staring at the light, which occupies the chair, animating it. He approaches this chair, standing across the desk from it.* Frank, Frank, don't you remember what you told me that time? How you put your hand on my shoulder, and Frank… *He leans on the desk and as he speaks the dead man's name he accidentally switches on the recorder, and instantly*

HOWARD'S SON: "… of New York is Albany. The capital of Ohio is Cincinnati, the capital of Rhode Island is…" *The recitation continues.*

WILLY, *leaping away with fright, shouting*: Ha, Howard! Howard! Howard!

HOWARD, *rushing in*: What happened?

WILLY, *pointing at the machine, which continues nasally, childishly, with the capital cities*: Shut it off! Shut it off!

HOWARD, *pulling the plug out*: Look, Willy...

WILLY, *pressing his hands to his eyes*: I gotta get myself some coffee. I'll get some coffee...

Willy starts to walk out. Howard stops him.

HOWARD, *rolling up the cord*: Willy, look...

WILLY: I'll go to Boston.

HOWARD: Willy, you can't go to Boston for us.

WILLY: Why can't I go?

HOWARD: I don't want you to represent us. I've been meaning to tell you for a long time now.

WILLY: Howard, are you firing me?

HOWARD: I think you need a good long rest, Willy.

WILLY: Howard...

HOWARD: And when you feel better, come back, and we'll see if we can work something out.

WILLY: But I gotta earn money, Howard. I'm in no position to...

HOWARD: Where are your sons? Why don't your sons give you a hand?

WILLY: They're working on a very big deal.

HOWARD: This is no time for false pride, Willy. You go to your sons and you tell them that you're tired. You've got two great boys, haven't you?

WILLY: Oh, no question, no question, but in the meantime...

HOWARD: Then that's that, heh?

WILLY: All right, I'll go to Boston tomorrow.

HOWARD: No, no.

WILLY: I can't throw myself on my sons. I'm not a cripple!

HOWARD: Look, kid, I'm busy this morning.

WILLY, *grasping Howard's arm*: Howard, you've got to let me go to Boston!

HOWARD, *hard, keeping himself under control*: I've got a line of people to see this morning. Sit down, take five minutes, and pull yourself together, and then go home, will ya? I need the office, Willy. *He starts to go, turns, remembering the recorder, starts to push off the table holding the recorder.* Oh, yeah. Whenever you can this week, stop by and drop off the samples. You'll feel better, Willy, and then come back and we'll talk. Pull yourself together, kid, there's people outside. *Howard exits, pushing the table off left. Willy stares into space, exhausted. Now the music is heard—Ben's music—first distantly, then closer, closer. As Willy speaks, Ben enters from the right. He carries valise and umbrella.*

WILLY: Oh, Ben, how did you do it? What is the answer? Did you wind up the Alaska deal already?

BEN: Doesn't take much time if you know what you're doing. Just a short business trip. Boarding ship in an hour. Wanted to say good-by.

WILLY: Ben, I've got to talk to you.

BEN, *glancing at his watch*: Haven't the time, William.

WILLY, *crossing the apron to Ben*: Ben, nothing's working out. I don't know what to do.

BEN: Now, look here, William. I've bought timberland in Alaska and I need a man to look after things for me.

WILLY: God, timberland! Me and my boys in those grand outdoors?

BEN: You've a new continent at your doorstep, William. Get out of these cities, they're full of talk and time payments and courts of law[15]. Screw on your fists and you can fight for a fortune up there.

WILLY: Yes, yes! Linda, Linda!

Linda enters as of old[16], *with the wash.*

LINDA: Oh, you're back?

BEN: I haven't much time.

WILLY: No, wait! Linda, he's got a proposition for me in Alaska.

LINDA: But you've got... *To Ben*: He's got a beautiful job here.

WILLY: But in Alaska, kid, I could...

LINDA: You're doing well enough, Willy!

BEN, *to Linda*: Enough for what, my dear?

LINDA, *frightened of Ben and angry at him*: Don't say those things to him! Enough to be happy right here, right now. *To Willy, while Ben laughs*: Why must everybody conquer the world? You're well liked, and the boys love you, and someday—*To Ben*—why, old man Wagner told him just the other day that if he keeps it up he'll be a member of the firm, didn't he, Willy?

WILLY: Sure, sure. I am building something with this firm, Ben, and if a man is building something he must be on the right track, mustn't he?

BEN: What are you building? Lay your hand on it. Where is it?

WILLY, *hesitantly*: That's true, Linda, there's nothing.

LINDA: Why? *To Ben*: There's a man eighty-four years old.

WILLY: That's right, Ben, that's right. When I look at that man I say, what is there to worry about?

BEN: Bah!

WILLY: It's true, Ben. All he has to do is go into any city, pick up the phone, and he's making his living and you know why?

BEN, *picking up his valise*: I've got to go.

WILLY, *holding Ben back*: Look at this boy!

Biff, in his high school sweater, enters carrying suitcase. Happy carries Biffs shoulder guards[17]*, gold helmet, and football pants.*

WILLY: Without a penny to his name, three great universities are begging for him, and from there the sky's the limit, because it's not what you do, Ben. It's who you know and the smile on your face! It's contacts, Ben, contacts! The whole wealth of Alaska passes over the lunch table at the Commodore Hotel, and that's the wonder, the wonder of this country, that a man can end with diamonds here on the basis of being liked! *He turns to Biff.* And that's why when you get out on that field today it's important. Because thousands of people will be rooting for you and loving you. *To Ben, who has again begun to leave.* And Ben! When he walks into a business office his name will sound out like a bell and all the doors will open to him! I've seen it, Ben, I've seen it a thousand times! You can't feel it with your hand like timber, but it's there!

BEN: Good-by, William.

WILLY: Ben, am I right? Don't you think I'm right? I value your advice.

BEN: There's a new continent at your doorstep, William. You could walk out rich. Rich! *He is gone.*

WILLY: We'll do it here, Ben! You hear me? We're gonna do it here!

Young Bernard rushes in. The gay music of the Boys is heard.

BERNARD: Oh, gee, I was afraid you left already!

WILLY: Why? What time is it?

BERNARD: It's half-past one!

WILLY: Well, come on, everybody! Ebbets Field next stop! Where's the pennants? *He rushes through the wall-line of the kitchen and out into the living room.*

LINDA, *to Biff*: Did you pack fresh underwear?

BIFF, *who has been limbering up*: I want to go!

BERNARD: Biff, I'm carrying your helmet, ain't I?

HAPPY: No, I'm carrying the helmet.

BERNARD: Oh, Biff, you promised me.

HAPPY: I'm carrying the helmet.

BERNARD: How am I going to get in the locker room?

LINDA: Let him carry the shoulder guards. *She puts her coat and hat on in the kitchen.*

BERNARD: Can I, Biff? 'Cause I told everybody I'm going to be in the locker room.

HAPPY: In Ebbets Field it's the clubhouse.

BERNARD: I meant the clubhouse. Biff!

HAPPY: Biff!

BIFF, *grandly, after a slight pause*: Let him carry the shoulder guards.

HAPPY, *as he gives Bernard the shoulder guards*: Stay close to us now.

Willy rushes in with the pennants.

WILLY, *handing them out*: Everybody wave when Biff comes out on the field. *Happy and Bernard run off.* You set now, boy?

The music has died away.

BIFF: Ready to go, Pop. Every muscle is ready.

WILLY, *at the edge of the apron*: You realize what this means?

BIFF: That's right, Pop.

WILLY, *feeling Biffs muscles*: You're comin' home this afternoon captain of the All-Scholastic Championship Team of the City of New York.

BIFF: I got it, Pop. And remember, pal, when I take off my helmet, that touchdown[18] is for you.

WILLY: Let's go! *He is starting out, with his arm around Biff, when Charley enters, as of old, in knickers.* I got no room for you, Charley.

CHARLEY: Room? For what?

WILLY: In the car.

CHARLEY: You goin' for a ride? I wanted to shoot some casino.

WILLY, *furiously*: Casino! *Incredulously.* Don't you realize what today is?

LINDA: Oh, he knows, Willy. He's just kidding you.

WILLY: That's nothing to kid about!

CHARLEY: No, Linda, what's goin on?

LINDA: He's playing in Ebbets Field.

CHARLEY: Baseball in this weather?

WILLY: Don't talk to him. Come on, come on! *He is pushing them out.*

CHARLEY: Wait a minute, didn't you hear the news?

WILLY: What?

CHARLEY: Don't you listen to the radio? Ebbets Field just blew up.

WILLY: You go to hell! *Charley laughs. Pushing them out*: Come on, come on! We're late.

CHARLEY, *as they go*: Knock a homer, Biff, knock a homer!

WILLY, *the last to leave, turning to Charley*: I don't think that was funny, Charley. This is the greatest day of his life.

CHARLEY: Willy, when are you going to grow up?

WILLY: Yeah, heh? When this game is over, Charley, you'll be laughing out of the other side of your face. They'll be calling him another Red Grange[19]. Twenty-five thousand a year.

CHARLEY, *kidding*: Is that so?

WILLY: Yeah, that's so.

CHARLEY: Well, then, I'm sorry, Willy. But tell me something.

WILLY: What?

CHARLEY: Who is Red Grange?

WILLY: Put up your hands. Goddam you, put up your hands!

Charley, chuckling, shakes his head and walks away, around the left comer of the stage. Willy follows him. The music rises to a mocking frenzy.

WILLY: Who the hell do you think you are, better than everybody else? You don't know every thing, you big, ignorant, stupid... Put up your hands!

Light rises, on the right side of the forestage, on a small table in the reception room of Charley's office. Traffic sounds are heard. Bernard, now mature, sits whistling to himself. A pair of tennis rackets and an overnight bag are on the floor beside him.

WILLY, *offstage*: What are you walking away for? Don't walk away! If you're going to say something say it to my face! I know you laugh at me behind my back. You'll laugh out of the other side of your goddam face after this game. Touchdown! Touch-down! Eighty thousand people! Touchdown! Right between the goal posts.

Bernard is a quiet, earnest, but self-assured young man. Willy's voice is coming from right upstage now. Bernard lowers his feet off the table and listens. Jenny, his father's secretary, enters.

JENNY, *distressed*: Say, Bernard, will you go out in the hall?

BERNARD: What is that noise? Who is it?

JENNY: Mr. Loman. He just got off the elevator.

BERNARD, *getting up*: Who's he arguing with?

JENNY: Nobody. There's nobody with him. I can't deal with him any more, and your father gets all upset every time he comes. I've got a lot of typing to do, and your father's waiting to sign it. Will you see him?

WILLY, *entering*: Touchdown! Touch—*He sees Jenny*. Jenny, Jenny, good to see you. How're ya? Workin'? Or still honest?

JENNY: Fine. How've you been feeling?

WILLY: Not much any more, Jenny. Ha, ha! *He is surprised to see the rackets.*

BERNARD: Hello, Uncle Willy.

WILLY, *almost shocked*: Bernard! Well, look who's here! *He comes quickly, guiltily, to Bernard and warmly shakes his hand.*

BERNARD: How are you? Good to see you.

WILLY: What are you doing here?

BERNARD: Oh, just stopped by to see Pop. Get off my feet till my train leaves. I'm going to Washington in a few minutes.

WILLY: Is he in?

BERNARD: Yes, he's in his office with the accountant. Sit down.

WILLY, *sitting down*: What're you going to do in Washington?

BERNARD: Oh, just a case I've got there, Willy.

WILLY: That so? *Indicating the rackets*. You going to play tennis there?

BERNARD: I'm staying with a friend who's got a court.

WILLY: Don't say. His own tennis court. Must be fine people, I bet.

BERNARD: They are, very nice. Dad tells me Biffs in town.

WILLY, *with a big smile*: Yeah, Biffs in. Working on a very big deal, Bernard.

BERNARD: What's Biff doing?

WILLY: Well, he's been doing very big things in the West. But he decided to establish himself here. Very big. We're having dinner. Did I hear your wife had a boy?

BERNARD: That's right. Our second.

WILLY: Two boys! What do you know!

BERNARD: What kind of a deal has Biff got?

WILLY: Well, Bill Oliver—very big sporting-goods man—he wants Biff very badly. Called him in from the West. Long distance, carte blanche[20], special deliveries. Your friends have their own private tennis court?

BERNARD: You still with the old firm, Willy?

WILLY, *after a pause*: I'm—I'm overjoyed to see how you made the grade, Bernard, overjoyed. It's an encouraging thing to see a young man really—really—Looks very good for Biff—very—*He breaks off, then*. Bernard—*He is so full of emotion, he breaks off again.*

BERNARD: What is it, Willy?

WILLY, *small and alone*: What—what's the secret?

BERNARD: What secret?

WILLY: How—how did you? Why didn't he ever catch on?

BERNARD: I wouldn't know that, Willy.

WILLY, *confidentially*, *desperately*: You were his friend, his boyhood friend. There's something I don't understand about it. His life ended after that Ebbets Field game. From the age of seventeen nothing good ever happened to him.

BERNARD: He never trained himself for anything.

WILLY: But he did, he did. After high school he took so many correspondence courses. Radio mechanics; television; God knows what, and never made the slightest mark.

BERNARD, *taking off his glasses*: Willy, do you want to talk candidly?

WILLY, *rising*, *faces Bernard*: I regard you as a very brilliant man, Bernard. I value your advice.

BERNARD: Oh, the hell with the advice, Willy. I couldn't advise you. There's just one thing I've always wanted to ask you. When he was supposed to graduate, and the math teacher flunked him—

WILLY: Oh, that son-of-a-bitch ruined his life.

BERNARD: Yeah, but, Willy, all he had to do was go to summer school and make up that subject.

WILLY: That's right, that's right.

BERNARD: Did you tell him not to go to summer school?

WILLY: Me? I begged him to go. I ordered him to go!

BERNARD: Then why wouldn't he go?

WILLY: Why? Why! Bernard, that question has been trailing me like a ghost for the last fifteen years. He flunked the subject, and laid down and died like a hammer hit him!

BERNARD: Take it easy, kid.

WILLY: Let me talk to you—I got nobody to talk to. Bernard, Bernard, was it my fault? Y'see? It keeps going around in my mind, maybe I did something to him. I got nothing to give him.

BERNARD: Don't take it so hard.

WILLY: Why did he lay down? What is the story there? You were his friend!

BERNARD: Willy, I remember, it was June, and our grades came out. And he'd flunked math.

WILLY: That son-of-a-bitch!

BERNARD: No, it wasn't right then. Biff just got very angry, I remember, and he was ready to enroll in summer school.

WILLY, *surprised*: He was?

BERNARD: He wasn't beaten by it at all. But then, Willy, he disappeared from the block for almost a month. And I got the idea that he'd gone up to New England to see you. Did he have a talk with you then?

Willy stares in silence.

BERNARD: Willy?

WILLY, *with a strong edge of resentment in his voice*: Yeah, he came to Boston. What about it?

BERNARD: Well, just that when he came back—I'll never forget this, it always mystifies me. Because I'd thought so well of Biff, even though he'd always taken advantage of me. I loved him, Willy, y' know? And he came back after that month and took his sneakers—remember those sneakers with "University of Virginia" printed on them? He was so proud of those, wore them every day. And he took them down in the cellar, and burned them up in the furnace. We had a fist fight. It lasted at least half an hour. Just the two of us, punching each other down the cellar, and crying right through it. I've often thought of how strange it was that I knew he'd given up his life. What happened in Boston, Willy?

Willy looks at him as at an intruder.

BERNARD: I just bring it up because you asked me.

WILLY, *angrily*: Nothing. What do you mean, "What happened?" What's that got to do with anything?

BERNARD: Well, don't get sore.

WILLY: What are you trying to do, blame it on me? If a boy lays down is that my fault?

BERNARD: Now, Willy, don't get—

WILLY: Well, don't—don't talk to me that way! What does that mean, "What happened?"

Charley enters. He is in his vest, and he carries a bottle of bourbon.

CHARLEY: Hey; you're going to miss that train. *He waves the bottle.*

BERNARD: Yeah, I'm going. *He takes the bottle.* Thanks, Pop. *He picks up his rackets and bag.* Good-by, Willy, and don't worry about it. You know, "If at first you don't succeed..."

WILLY: Yes, I believe in that.

BERNARD: But sometimes, Willy, it's better for a man just to walk away.

WILLY: Walk away?

BERNARD: That's right.

WILLY: But if you can't walk away?

BERNARD, *after a slight pause*: I guess that's when it's tough. *Extending his hand*: Good-by, Willy.

WILLY, *shaking Bernard's hand*: Good-by, boy.

CHARLEY, *an arm on Bernard's shoulder*: How do you like this kid? Gonna argue a case in front of the Supreme Court.

BERNARD, *protesting*: Pop!

WILLY, *genuinely shocked, pained, and happy*: No! The Supreme Court!

BERNARD: I gotta run. 'By, Dad!

CHARLEY: Knock 'em dead, Bernard!

Bernard goes off.

WILLY, *as Charley takes out his wallet*: The Supreme Court! And he didn't even mention it!

CHARLEY, *counting out money on the desk*: He don't have to—he's gonna do it.

WILLY: And you never told him what to do, did you? You never took any interest in him.

CHARLEY: My salvation is that I never took any interest in anything. There's some money—fifty dollars. I got an accountant inside.

WILLY: Charley, look... *With difficulty*: I got my insurance to pay. If you can manage it—I need a hundred and ten dollars.

Charley doesn't reply for a moment; merely stops moving.

WILLY: I'd draw it from my bank but Linda would know, and I...

CHARLEY: Sit down, Willy.

WILLY, *moving toward the chair*: I'm keeping an account of everything, remember. I'll pay every penny back. *He sits.*

CHARLEY: Now listen to me, Willy.

WILLY: I want you to know I appreciate...

CHARLEY, *sitting down on the table*: Willy, what're you doin'? What the hell is going on in your head?

WILLY: Why? I'm simply...

CHARLEY: I offered you a job. You make fifty dollars a week, and I won't send you on the road.

WILLY: I've got a job.

CHARLEY: Without pay? What kind of a job is a job without pay? *He rises.* Now, look, kid, enough is enough. I'm no genius but I know when I'm being insulted.

WILLY: Insulted!

CHARLEY: Why don't you want to work for me?

WILLY: What's the matter with you? I've got a job.

CHARLEY: Then what're you walkin' in here every week for?

WILLY, *getting up*: Well, if you don't want me to walk in here—

CHARLEY: I'm offering you a job.

WILLY: I don't want your goddam job!

CHARLEY: When the hell are you going to grow up?

WILLY, *furiously*: You big ignoramus, if you say that to me again I'll rap you one! I don't care how big you are! *He's ready to fight.*

Pause.

CHARLEY, *kindly, going to him*: How much do you need, Willy?

WILLY: Charley, I'm strapped. I'm strapped. I don't know what to do. I was just fired.

CHARLEY: Howard fired you?

WILLY: That snotnose. Imagine that? I named him. I named him Howard.

CHARLEY: Willy, when're you gonna realize that them things don't mean anything? You named him Howard, but you can't sell that. The only thing you got in this world is what you can sell. And the funny thing is that you're a salesman, and you don't know that.

WILLY: I've always tried to think otherwise, I guess. I always felt that if a man was impressive, and well liked, that nothing—

CHARLEY: Why must everybody like you? Who liked J. P. Morgan? Was he impressive? In a Turkish bath he'd look like a butcher. But with his pockets on he was very well liked. Now listen, Willy, I know you don't like me, and nobody can say I'm in love with you, but I'll give you a job because—just for the hell of it, put it that way. Now what do you say?

WILLY: I—I just can't work for you, Charley.

CHARLEY: What're you, jealous of me?

WILLY: I can't work for you, that's all, don't ask me why.

CHARLEY, *angered, takes out more bills*: You been jealous of me all your life, you damned fool! Here, pay your insurance. *He puts the money in Willy's hand.*

WILLY: I'm keeping strict accounts.

CHARLEY: I've got some work to do. Take care of yourself. And pay your insurance.

WILLY, *moving to the right*: Funny, y'know? After all the highways, and the trains, and the appointments, and the years, you end up worth more dead than alive[21].

CHARLEY: Willy, nobody's worth nothin' dead. *After a slight pause.* Did you hear what I said?

Willy stands still, dreaming.

CHARLEY: Willy!

WILLY: Apologize to Bernard for me when you see him. I didn't mean to argue with him. He's a fine boy. They're all fine boys, and they'll end up big—all of them. Someday they'll all play tennis together. Wish me luck, Charley. He saw Bill Oliver today.

CHARLEY: Good luck.

WILLY, *on the verge of tears*: Charley, you're the only friend I got. Isn't that a remarkable thing?

He goes out.

CHARLEY: Jesus! …

三、主题解析

《推销员之死》讲述一个普通的旅行推销员在金钱至上的资本主义社会里的悲剧故事。已年过六旬的威利一生贫穷，当了 34 年的“房奴”。可是他一直恪守一个成功哲学：靠自己的人品和魅力就可以赢得事业上的一片天空，但是结果总是事与愿违。他年事已高，希望换一个轻松的工作，却被老板解雇。他用自己的成功哲学要求两个儿子，希望他们成功和成名，但仍未成功。大儿子 30 多岁仍一事无成，而且父子间经常吵架。大儿子是威利的翻版，盲目自大。威利的哥哥本恩则是靠无情竞争获得成功的实业家，与威利构成鲜明对照。尽管如此，威利仍未清醒。他在还清房款的当年开车自杀，为儿子留下一笔人寿保险金，指望他们继续追寻自己尚未实现的美梦。大儿子终于从父亲之死中悟出生活的道理：“他错就错在他那些梦想。全部都错了。”大儿子决定子承父业，继续奋斗。威利用生命换回儿子的醒悟，这也许是对威利生命的安慰吧。

剧本共分两幕。第一幕是剧情介绍，包括剧中人物和人物之间的关系以及主要人物的谈论话题，为第二幕做铺垫。第二幕是情节的推进、高潮和结局。剧本主要通过虚实结合、场景转换和先扬后抑的对话等艺术手法表现人物的内心世界、思想特征和行为走向，并最终指向剧本的思想主题。

本章选自剧本第二幕的前半部分。它涵盖了以上几种表现手法。第一，运用虚实结合和场景转换，表达人物的内心现实，将情节推向前进。现实中的威利经常进入记忆的世界。他与已故哥哥本恩的对话带领读者穿越在不同的时空中。威利一方面做着现实与将来的梦：希望和相信两个儿子能够出人头地；希望自己不再外出奔波，做一份轻松的工作享受晚年。另一方面，他不断地回忆过去，回忆那个美好但未实现的梦：跟随哥哥到阿拉斯加发财。第二个例子是比夫和哈皮请爸爸吃饭时比夫想到爸爸的风流韵事，将父子的矛盾冲突及其原因揭示出来，也道出比夫数学不及格的真正原因。威利的思想总是忙碌着，但似乎很少用双眼关注眼前的残酷现实。虚实之间的场景变换展现了剧本的时空宽度，暴露了人物的思想活动及其背后的意义，为情节走向高潮和结局起到重要的推动作用。

第二，抑扬变化的对话设计几乎随处可见。威利去见老板霍华德前后的心理活动展示威利对美梦的执著追求以及现实与梦想的差距。在跟老板见面之前，他们夫妻二人设计了美丽“台词”，他们认为霍华德会满足威利预支工资和调换工作的要求。然而霍华德对威利几乎是视而不见，不但没有听取他的要求和请求，反而解雇了他。威利最终彻底失败。另一个例子是，比夫向爸爸威利说明他见过奥利弗的真实情形之前，威利的欣喜情绪与他得知真情以后的悲伤心情形成强烈反差。此番安排再次证明威利在经历一系列挫折之后仍然执迷不悟，一心一意地坚守自己对儿子成名的幻想。第三个例子是威利与邻居查利的对话。查利对威利的看法与比夫对父亲的看法是否存在某些类同点？威利认为，事业的成功靠人格的魅力和长相。你对此如何评价？查利如何看待威利的成功哲学？

四、难点注释

1. Willy：Willy Loman，威利·洛曼，剧本的男主人公。在此按出场的顺序一并介绍“节选”的其他主要人物。

   Linda：Linda Loman，琳达，威利的妻子。

   Oliver：Bill Oliver，比尔·奥利弗，体育用品商，威利一直希望大儿子比夫成为奥利弗的推销员。

   Howard：Howard Wagner，霍华德·瓦格纳，36 岁，威利所在的瓦格纳公司老板。

   Charley：查利，威利的邻居。

   Biff：比夫，威利和琳达的大儿子。

   Frank：Frank Wagner，弗兰克·瓦格纳，霍华德的父亲，瓦格纳公司的前任老板，也是威利过去的老板。

   Ben：本恩，威利已故的哥哥，在威利回忆往事时出现。

   Bernard：伯纳德，邻居查利之子。

   Happy：哈皮，威利的次子。
2. I can't get over the shaving lotion in this house!：满屋子都是刮胡膏的味道，我真闻不够。意思是说威利喜欢两个儿子出门时外表清爽的样子。
3. take longer to get-solidified：大器晚成。
4. He'll just have to take me off the road：他不能让我再跑销售了。
5. You had the motor job on the car：汽车马达的修理费。
6. it's on its last legs：濒临死亡，此处的意思是汽车要散架了。
7. blow you to a big meal：请你吃大餐。
8. knock Howard for a loop：knock somebody for a loop 意为“把……击倒；使……大为震惊”。此处的意思是狠狠地敲打霍华德。
9. behind a wheel：在驾驶。此处指开车到处跑。
10. apron：舞台的台口。
11. rubber pipe：橡皮管，暗指威利想用煤气自杀。
12. Bulova watch time：中标公司的广告用语。
13. swing：维持。
14. pull his (one's) own weight：干好本职工作。
15. they're full of talk and time payments and courts of law：他们光会说空话、分期付款和打

官司。

16. as of old：像过去的样子。
17. shoulder guards：护肩。
18. touchdown：(美式足球)底线得分。下文的 knock a homer 是棒球术语，意为“跑个全垒”。
19. Red Grange：美国足球明星格兰奇。
20. carte blanche：〈法语〉自由处理权。意思是条件由比夫挑。
21. you end up worth more dead than alive：你的结果是死了比活着值钱。暗指威利为了骗取保险金将选择撞车自杀。

五、延伸阅读与批评

《榆树下的欲望》发表于1924年，是诺贝尔文学奖获得者剧作家尤金·奥尼尔早期很有分量的作品。他通过书写乱伦和对财产的占有欲对家庭的危害，描写了一部现代社会里既令人同情又让人震惊和恐惧的悲剧。

儿子伊本对老父伊弗雷姆怀恨在心，因为他认为是父亲占有了他死去的母亲的农场。年轻的爱碧嫁给伊弗雷姆，意图得到他的农庄。她设计勾引伊本，两人产生恋情，并生下一子。父亲认为自己老年得子，欣喜若狂，声称要将农场留给幼子。而且老父告诉伊本，爱碧亦有此想法。伊本闻此大为恼怒，认为继母对他的爱全是骗局。为表达对伊本的真爱，继母杀死了他们的儿子，并把真相告诉了伊弗雷姆。伊本再次为情所动。他最终主动投案，表示愿意与爱碧一起承担罪名。

自由、美梦、物质占有欲和性欲是该剧表达的三大主题。剧作的思想厚度和历史深度在于：第一是借古讽今。它虽然描写的19世纪中期美国新英格兰地区的历史，但对物质占有的描写反映了美国现代社会的现实。第二是将古希腊神话人物形象“嵌入”剧中人物，丰富人物的思想内涵，增强了剧作的悲剧意蕴。

俄狄浦斯、菲德拉和美迪亚三位希腊神话人物分别对应该剧中的哪些人物？他们之间有何相似点？有人说，“榆树”是女性的象征；也有人说，“榆树”象征着几乎令人窒息的清教主义环境。你认为呢？

Chapter 3 Invisible Man

by Ralph Ellison

(An Excerpt)

一、作者简介

拉尔夫·艾里森(1914—1994),美国当代著名的小说家、文学评论家。他的作品不多,但对美国文学影响颇深。1952年出版的《看不见的人》是艾里森的第一部小说,出版后便引起轰动,他一举成名。1960年艾里森开始创作第二部小说,部分内容在杂志上连载。但是一场大火将其余的手稿烧尽,直到作者去世,他的第二部小说也未能付梓。2010年美国现代图书馆将艾里森所有未完成的小说原稿结集出版,题目为《拍摄的前三天》。

1964年艾里森出版了论文集《影子和行动》,收集了作者20年间的论文作品,记录了他作为文学和社会批评家到被公认为严肃小说家的成长史。该论文集包含三部分的内容:文学和民间传说的关系、黑人音乐——爵士乐和布鲁斯音乐的表达、黑人亚文化和作为整体的北美之间的关系。1986年他出版了第二部论文集《走向领域》,其中收录他的部分论文和讲稿,集中反映了作者对作为整体的美国文化和黑人文化之间的关系、作为美国黑人的思考、种族问题等的深入思考。

艾里森多才多艺。他不仅熟读欧美文学书籍,而且精通音乐,将黑人的爵士乐和布鲁斯音乐融入文学创作是他作品的一大特色。在纽约期间,他结识了当时杰出的黑人作家理查德·赖特和兰斯顿·休斯,并在他们的鼓励下开始文学创作。艾里森为传承和发展美国黑人文学作出了杰出的贡献。

整体上的美国文化和黑人文化的关系、黑人作家的文学和社会意识、种族问题、对自我的追寻是艾里森关心的主要问题。特别是,对黑人命运以及包括黑人和白人在内的作为一个普通个体命运的双重关注使他成为黑人和白人读者关注和讨论的焦点。《看不见的人》除了采用传统的现实主义手法,还运用了象征、讽刺、表现主义、超现实主义、音乐文本与文字文本相结合的手法等,这些特征使得该小说具有浓厚的现代主义文学色彩。

二、文本选读

Invisible Man

Prologue[1]

I am an invisible man. No, I am not a spook like those who haunted Edgar Allan Poe; nor am I one of your Hollywood-movie ectoplasms. I am a man of substance, of flesh and bone, fiber and liquids—and I might even be said to possess a mind. I am invisible, understand, simply because people refuse to see me. Like the bodiless heads you see sometimes in circus sideshows, it is as though I have been surrounded by mirrors of hard, distorting glass. When they approach me they see only my surroundings, themselves, or figments of their imagination—indeed, everything and anything except me.

Nor is my invisibility exactly a matter of a bio-chemical accident to my epidermis. That invisibility to which I refer occurs because of a peculiar disposition of the eyes of those with whom I come in contact. A matter of the construction of their *inner eyes*, those eyes with which they look through their physical eyes upon reality. I am not complaining, nor am I protesting either. It is sometimes advantageous to be unseen, although it is most often rather wearing on the nerves[2]. Then too, you're constantly being bumped against by those of poor vision. Or again, you often doubt if you really exist. You wonder whether you aren't simply a phantom in other people's minds. Say, a figure in a nightmare which the sleeper tries with all his strength to destroy. It's when you feel like this that, out of resentment, you begin to bump people back. And, let me confess, you feel that way most of the time. You ache with the need to convince yourself that you do exist in the real world, that you're a part of all the sound and anguish, and you strike out with your fists, you curse and you swear to make them recognize you. And, alas, it's seldom successful.

One night I accidentally bumped into a man, and perhaps because of the near darkness he saw me and called me an insulting name. I sprang at him, seized his coat lapels and demanded that he apologize. He was a tall blond man, and as my face came close to his he looked insolently out of his blue eyes and cursed me, his breath hot in my face as he struggled. I pulled his chin down sharp upon the crown of my head, butting him as I had seen the West Indians do, and I felt his flesh tear and the blood gush out, and I yelled, "Apologize! Apologize!" But he continued to curse and struggle, and I butted him again and again until he went down heavily, on his knees, profusely bleeding. I kicked him repeatedly, in a frenzy because he still uttered insults though his lips were frothy with blood. Oh yes, I kicked him! And in my outrage I got out my knife and prepared to slit his throat, right there beneath the lamplight in the deserted street, holding him by the collar with one hand, and opening the knife with my teeth—when it occurred to me that the man had not seen me, actually; that he, as far as he knew, was in the midst of a walking nightmare! And I stopped the blade, slicing the air as I pushed him away, letting him fall back to the street. I stared at him hard as the lights of a car stabbed through the darkness. He lay there, moaning on the asphalt; a man almost killed by a phantom. It unnerved me. I was both disgusted and ashamed. I was like a drunken man myself, wavering about on weakened legs. Then I was amused. Something in this man's thick head had sprung out and beaten him within an inch of his life. I began to laugh at this crazy discovery. Would he have awakened at the point of death? Would Death himself have freed him for wakeful living? But I didn't linger. I ran away into the dark, laughing so hard I feared I might rupture myself. The next day I saw his picture in the *Daily News*, beneath a caption stating that he had been "mugged[3]". Poor fool, poor blind fool, I thought with sincere compassion, mugged by an invisible man!

Most of the time (although I do not choose as I once did to deny the violence of my days by ignoring it) I am not so overtly violent. I remember that I am invisible and walk softly so as not to awaken the sleeping ones. Sometimes it is best not to awaken them; there are few things in the world as dangerous as sleepwalkers. I learned in time though that it is possible to carry on a fight against them without their realizing it. For instance, I have been carrying on a fight with Monopolated Light & Power[4] for some time now. I use their service and pay them nothing at all, and they don't know it. Oh, they suspect that power is being drained off, but they don't know where. All they know is that according to the master meter back there in their power station a hell of a lot of free current is disappearing somewhere into the jungle of Harlem. The joke, of course, is that I don't live in Harlem but in a border area. Several years ago (before I discovered the advantage of being invisible) I went through the routine process of buying service and paying their outrageous rates. But no more. I gave up all that, along with my apartment, and my old way of life: That way based upon the fallacious assumption that I, like other men, was visible. Now, aware of my invisibility, I live rent-free in a building rented strictly to whites, in a section of the basement that was shut off and forgotten during the nineteenth century, which I discovered when I was trying to escape in the night from Ras the Destroyer[5]. But that's getting too far ahead of the story, almost to the end, although the end is in the beginning and lies far ahead.

The point now is that I found a home—or a hole in the ground, as you will. Now don't jump to the conclusion that because I call my home a "hole" it is damp and cold like a grave; there are cold holes and warm holes. Mine is a warm hole. And remember, a bear retires to his hole for the winter and lives until spring; then he comes strolling out like the Easter chick breaking from its shell. I say all this to assure you that it is incorrect to assume that, because I'm invisible and live in a hole, I am dead. I am neither dead nor in a state of suspended animation. Call me Jack-the-Bear, for I am in a state of hibernation.

My hole is warm and full of light. Yes, full of light. I doubt if there is a brighter spot in all New York than this hole of mine, and I do not exclude Broadway. Or the Empire State Building on a photographer's dream night. But that is taking advantage of you. Those two spots are among the darkest of our whole civilization—pardon me, out whole culture (an important distinction I've heard)—which might sound like a hoax, or a contradiction, but that (by contradiction, I mean) is how the world moves: Not like an arrow, but a boomerang[6]. (Beware of those who speak of the spiral of history; they are preparing a boomerang. Keep a steel helmet handy.) I know; I have been boomeranged across my head so much that I now can see the darkness of lightness. And I love light. Perhaps you'll think it strange that an invisible man should need light, desire light, love light. But maybe it is exactly because I am invisible. Light confirms my reality, gives birth to my form. A beautiful girl once told me of a recurring nightmare in which she lay in the center of a large dark room and felt her face expand until it filled the whole room, becoming a formless mass while her eyes ran in bilious jelly up the chimney. And so it is with me. Without light I am not only invisible, but formless as well; and to be unaware of one's form is to live a death. I myself, after existing some twenty years, did not become alive until I discovered my invisibility.

That is why I fight my battle with Monopolated Light & Power. The deeper reason, I mean: It allows me to feel my vital aliveness. I also fight them for taking so much of my money before I learned to protect myself. In my hole in the basement there are exactly 1,369 lights. I've wired the entire ceiling, every inch of it. And not with fluorescent bulbs, but with the older, more-expensive-to-operate kind, the filament type. An act of sabotage, you know. I've already begun to wire the wall. A junk man I know, a man of vision, has supplied me with wire and sockets. Nothing, storm or flood, must get in the way of our need for light and ever more and brighter light. The truth is the light and light is the truth[7]. When I finish all four walls, then I'll start on the floor. Just how that will go, I don't know. Yet when you have lived invisible as long as I have you develop a certain ingenuity. I'll solve the problem. And maybe I'll invent a gadget to place my coffeepot on the fire while I lie in bed, and even invent a gadget to warm my bed—like the fellow I saw in one of the picture magazines who made himself a gadget to warm his shoes! Though invisible, I am in the great American tradition of tinkers. That makes me kin to Ford, Edison and Franklin. Call me, since I have a theory and a concept, a "thinker-tinker". Yes, I'll warm my shoes; they need it they're usually full of holes. I'll do that and more.

Now I have one radio-phonograph; I plan to have five. There is a certain acoustical deadness in my hole, and when I have music I want to feel its vibration, not only with my ear but with my whole body. I'd like to hear five recordings of Louis Armstrong[8] playing and singing "What Did I Do to Be so Black and Blue"—all at the same time. Sometimes now I listen to Louis while I have my favorite dessert of vanilla ice cream and sloe gin. I pour the red liquid over the white mound, watching it glisten and the vapor rising as Louis bends that military instrument into a beam of lyrical sound. Perhaps I like Louis Armstrong because he's made poetry out of being invisible. I think it must be because he's unaware that he is invisible. And my own grasp of invisibility aids me to understand his music. Once when I asked for a cigarette, some jokers gave me a reefer[9], which I lighted when I got home and sat listening to my phonograph. It was a strange evening. Invisibility, let me explain, gives one a slightly different sense of time, you're never quite on the beat. Sometimes you're ahead and sometimes behind. Instead of the swift and imperceptible flowing of time, you are aware of its nodes, those points where time stands still or from which it leaps ahead. And you slip into the breaks and look around. That's what you hear vaguely in Louis' music.

三、主题解析

《看不见的人》被公认为美国黑人文学和美国当代文学的一部杰作。1965 年，美国著名的评论杂志《每周书评》(*Book Week*)召集 200 名评论家、作家和编辑，推荐第二次世界大战以来"最出色的一部作品"，艾里森的《看不见的人》荣膺桂冠。

小说共有 25 章，另加一个"序言"和"尾声"，1981 年作者又为它增加了一个"前言"。

“序言”接着“尾声”，使小说形成一个环形。小说叙述了一个无名黑人青年从南方到北方“寻找自我”的故事。主人公在中学毕业典礼上因展现其演说才华，而被邀请到当地白人显赫人物的集会上做同样的主题发言，并同样取得成功。他因此获准就读州立黑人学院，但因带领一个白人校董参观了不体面的地方而被开除。他从此踏上“北上”的“自我追寻”征程。在纽约，他先后在“自由油漆公司”当工人和锅炉工助手。在一次事故中他差点丢了性命，经过医院治疗后他来到纽约的黑人集中地——哈莱姆。在那里他因慷慨陈词，痛斥白人歧视黑人行为而受到黑人进步组织“兄弟会”的青睐，被吸收为会员，且成为该组织的发言人。然而，他与该组织领导的意见不合。后来，在与“兄弟会”作对的黑人民族主义者的追捕下他东躲西藏，最后逃到一个检修口，在一个地下煤库里躲起来，成为一个彻底的看不见的人。在地下室，他点亮1369个灯泡，让地下室通明，以证明自己是一个看得见的活生生的人。

种族歧视是小说的一个鲜明主题。无论南方还是北方，话语权始终掌握在白人手中，黑人始终处于社会的边缘，成为美国社会里看不见的人。为什么？因为在南方，白人头面人物和大学的白人校董都是权力的控制者和使用者；在北方，纽约的白人阔佬、医院的白人医生、“兄弟会”的白人领袖等都可以对黑人指手画脚。因此，在这样的环境里，小说的主人公找不到“自我”，成为一个“看不见的人”。不仅如此，主人公在黑人眼中也是一个“看不见的人”。和他一起玩耍的黑孩子、大学的黑人校长、附近的黑人居民、酒吧里的黑人老板、黑人退伍士兵、工厂里的黑人师傅和工会会员、“兄弟会”的黑人兄弟、黑人民族主义者，全部与他为敌，在他竭力证明自己的存在和价值时都与他作对，使之遭遇不幸。综上所述，这个“看不见”的黑人在白人社会和黑人社会的“双重语境”中都找不到“自我”，无法证明自己的存在价值。小说在表现一个个体黑人“身份”遭遇的同时，蜕除其“黑色之皮”，为他“植入”其他肤色，使之成为一个“普遍之人”，反映他在美国现代复杂社会里不同文化的交流与碰撞过程中以及人与人之间的复杂关系中如何寻找和确立“自我身份”的“普适性”主题。再者，无论何人，在文化差异的环境以及人与人的交往中都会面临“自我身份”定位——在自我立足的同时实现自我价值的问题。这是《看不见的人》的另一个重要的主题。

四、难点注释

1. prologue：序言。
2. wearing on the nerves：词组 wear on somebody's nerves 表示“折磨某人的神经”。
3. mugged：(俚语)袭击并抢劫。
4. Monopolated Light & Power：电力专利公司。
5. Ras the Destroyer：毁灭者拉斯，是小说的主要人物之一，纽约市黑人民族主义者领导人。主人公就是在他的追逐下躲进地下室的。
6. boomerang：回飞镖。
7. The truth is the light and light is the truth：这句话中的light对理解小说的主题起到重要作用。它是“灯光”的意思，但可以将它与“白色”联系起来。“白色”的对立面是“黑色”，因此又让人想到“白人”和“黑人”。

8. Louis Armstrong：路易·阿姆斯特朗（1900—1971），美国著名的黑人爵士乐演奏家。
9. reefer：（俚语）大麻烟卷。

五、延伸阅读与批评

我们沿着美国黑人小说创作的脉络，告别艾里森的《看不见的人》，来看一看20世纪70年代另一位著名黑人作家——托尼·莫里森的《所罗门之歌》（1977）。评论家们认为，《所罗门之歌》是继赖特的《土生子》和艾里森的《看不见的人》之后最好的黑人小说。稍作比较，我们发现《看不见的人》和《所罗门之歌》在主题方面有鲜明的相似点和不同点，非常值得关注。

两部小说的相似点：主人公都是黑人男性，同样在追寻自己的身份（identity）。它们的不同点：前者主人公的行踪是从美国南方到美国北方，后者主人公的行踪是从北方到南方，二者刚好相反。由是引发下列问题：第一部小说中"南方"和"北方"的含义是否与第二部小说中"南方"和"北方"的含义相同？如果不同，它们分别代表什么？两位主人公的身份追寻路线恰好相反，说明什么？上述问题对探析小说的主题思想有何帮助？两位主人公的身份追寻对我们有什么启示？如果把这些问题放在自美国内战以来的美国历史和美国黑人文学两大语境中思考，也许就比较容易找到答案了。

Chapter 4 Everyday Use

by Alice Walker

一、作者简介

艾丽丝·沃克(1944—)，美国当代最著名的黑人女作家之一。她的著作包括短篇小说、长篇小说、诗歌、论文集。短篇小说集包括《爱情与麻烦：黑人妇女的故事》(1973)、《你不能压制一个好女人》(1982)，诗集有《一度》(1968)，长篇小说有《格兰奇·科普兰的第三次生命》(1970)、《梅丽迪恩》(1976)、《紫色》(1982)、《我熟悉的一切之神庙》(1989)、《由于我父亲的微笑》(1998)，论文集包括《寻找我们母亲的花园》(1983)、《靠词汇活着》(1988)。此外，她还担任过当时女权主义组织杂志《女士》的编辑。

《紫色》是沃克的长篇小说代表作，获得美国文学作品的三个大奖：普利策奖、国家图书奖、全国书评家奖。沃克因此成为第一个获得普利策奖的黑人女作家。《寻找我们母亲的花园》充分地肯定了美国“哈莱姆文艺复兴”时期黑人作家，尤其是黑人女作家的文学成就和社会贡献，是研究现当代美国黑人文学的重要文献。

沃克出身在美国南方的一个黑人佃农家庭，从小承担家务劳动。她8岁时弄瞎了一只眼睛。读大学时曾因偶然怀孕而产生自杀念头。黑人，尤其是黑人女性的社会地位问题一直是沃克关注的中心。20世纪60年代以来，她积极投身美国女权主义运动和黑人民权运动，用文字揭示黑人女性的坚强和美丽。沃克第一次提出“妇女主义”观点(既关注黑人女性，又关注其他族裔的女性，还关注整个人类的和谐与平等)，这一观点是读者研读美国黑人文学历史必须了解的学术思想。

种族歧视、黑人与白人的关系、黑人家庭成员之间的关系、黑人女性的爱恨与喜悲，特别是黑人女性的善良与坚强等是沃克作品的思想主题。她采用现实主义和现代主义(书信体创作和第一人称叙述方式)相结合的创作手法，语言朴实流畅，兼用黑人口语。无论是创作形式还是内容表达，沃克对美国黑人文学的传承和发展都作出了杰出的贡献。

二、文本选读

Everyday Use

For Your Grandmamma

I will wait for her in the yard that Maggie and I made so clean and wavy yesterday afternoon. A yard like this is more comfortable than most people know. It is not just a yard. It is like an extended living room. When the hard clay is swept clean as a floor and the fine sand around the edges lined with tiny, irregular grooves, anyone can come and sit and look up into the elm tree and wait for the breezes that never come inside the house.

Maggie will be nervous until after her sister goes: she will stand hopelessly in corners, homely and ashamed of the burn scars down her arms and legs, eying her sister with a mixture of envy and awe. She thinks her sister has held life always in the palm of one hand[1], that "no" is a word the world never learned to say to her.

You've no doubt seen those TV shows where the child who has "made it" is confronted, as a surprise, by her own mother and father, tottering in weakly from backstage. (A pleasant surprise, of course: What would they do if parent and child came on the show only to curse out and insult each other?) On TV mother and child embrace and smile into each other's faces. Sometimes the mother and father weep, the child wraps them in her arms and leans across the table to tell how she would not have made it without their help. I have seen these programs.

Sometimes I dream a dream in which Dee and I are suddenly brought together on a TV program of this sort. Out of a dark and soft-seated limousine I am ushered into a bright room filled with many people. There I meet a smiling, gray, sporty man like Johnny Carson[2] who shakes my hand and tells me what a fine girl I have. Then we are on the stage and Dee is embracing me with tears in her eyes. She pins on my dress a large orchid, even though she has told me once that she thinks orchids are tacky flowers.

In real life I am a large, big-boned woman with rough, man-working hands. In the winter I wear flannel nightgowns to bed and overalls during the day. I can kill and clean a hog as mercilessly as a man. My fat keeps me hot in zero weather. I can work outside all day, breaking ice to get water for washing; I can eat pork liver cooked over the open fire minutes after it comes steaming from the hog. One winter I knocked a bull calf straight in the brain between the eyes with a sledge hammer and had the meat hung up to chill before nightfall. But of course all this does not show on television. I am the way my daughter would want me to be: a hundred pounds lighter, my skin like an uncooked barley pancake. My hair glistens in the hot bright lights. Johnny Carson has much to do to keep up with my quick and witty tongue.

But that is a mistake. I know even before I wake up. Who ever knew a Johnson with a quick tongue? Who can even imagine me looking a strange white man in the eye? It seems to me I have talked to them always with one foot raised in flight, with my head turned in whichever way is farthest from them. Dee, though. She would always look anyone in the eye. Hesitation was no part of her nature.

"How do I look, Mama?" Maggie says, showing just enough of her thin body enveloped in pink skirt and red blouse for me to know she's there, almost hidden by the door.

"Come out into the yard," I say.

Have you ever seen a lame animal, perhaps a dog run over by some careless person rich enough to own a car, sidle up to someone who is ignorant enough to be kind to them? That is the way my Maggie walks. She has been like this, chin on chest, eyes on ground, feet in shuffle, ever since the fire that burned the other house to the ground.

Dee is lighter than Maggie, with nicer hair and a fuller figure. She's a woman now, though sometimes I forget. How long ago was it that the other house burned? Ten, twelve years? Sometimes I can still hear the flames and feel Maggie's arms sticking to me, her hair smoking and her dress falling off her in little black papery flakes. Her eyes seemed stretched open, blazed open by the flames reflected in them. And Dee. I see her standing off under the sweet gum tree she used to dig gum out of; a look of concentration on her face as she watched the last dingy gray board of the house fall in toward the red-hot brick chimney. Why don't you do a dance around the ashes? I'd wanted to ask her. She had hated the house that much.

I used to think she hated Maggie, too. But that was before we raised money, the church and me, to send her to Augusta to school. She used to read to us without pity; forcing words, lies, other folks' habits, whole lives upon us two, sitting trapped and ignorant underneath her voice. She washed us in a river of make-believe, burned[3] us with a lot of knowledge we didn't necessarily need to know. Pressed us to her with the serious way she read, to shove us away at just the moment, like dimwits, we seemed about to understand.

Dee wanted nice things. A yellow organdy dress to wear to her graduation from high school; black pumps to match a green suit she'd made from an old suit somebody gave me. She was determined to stare down any disaster in her efforts. Her eyelids would not flicker for minutes at a time. Often I fought off the temptation to shake her. At sixteen she had a style of her own: and knew what style was.

I never had an education myself. After second grade the school was closed down. Don't ask my why: in 1927 colored asked fewer questions than they do now. Sometimes Maggie reads to me. She stumbles along good-naturedly but can't see well. She knows she is not bright. Like good looks and money, quickness passes her by. She will marry John Thomas (who has mossy teeth in an earnest face) and then I'll be free to sit here and I guess just sing church songs to myself. Although I never was a good singer. Never could carry a tune. I was always better at a man's job. I used to love to milk till I was hooked in the side in '49. Cows are soothing and slow and don't bother you, unless you try to milk them the wrong way.

I have deliberately turned my back on the house. It is three rooms, just like the one that burned, except the roof is tin; they don't make shingle roofs any more. There are no real windows, just some holes cut in the sides, like the portholes in a ship, but not round and not square, with rawhide holding the shutters up on the outside. This house is in a pasture, too, like the other one. No doubt when Dee sees it she will want to tear it down. She wrote me once that no matter where we "choose" to live, she will manage to come see us. But she will never bring her friends. Maggie and I thought about this and Maggie asked me, "Mama, when did Dee ever have any friends?"

She had a few. Furtive boys in pink shirts hanging about on washday after school. Nervous girls who never laughed. Impressed with her they worshiped the well-turned phrase, the cute shape, the scalding humor that erupted like bubbles in lye. She read to them.

When she was courting Jimmy T she didn't have much time to pay to us, but turned all her faultfinding power on him. He flew to marry a cheap city girl from a family of ignorant flashy people. She hardly had time to recompose herself.

When she comes I will meet—but there they are!

Maggie attempts to make a dash for the house, in her shuffling way, but I stay her with my hand. "Come back here," I say. And she stops and tries to dig a well in the sand with her toe.

It is hard to see them clearly through the strong sun. But even the first glimpse of leg out of the car tells me it is Dee. Her feet were always neat-looking, as if God himself had shaped them with a certain style. From the other side of the car comes a short, stocky man. Hair is all over his head a foot long and hanging from his chin like a kinky mule tail. I hear Maggie suck in her breath. "Uhnnnh," is what it sounds like. Like when you see the wriggling end of a snake just in front of your foot on the road. "Uhnnnh."

Dee next. A dress down to the ground, in this hot weather. A dress so loud it hurts my eyes. There are yellows and oranges enough to throw back the light of the sun. I feel my whole face warming from the heat waves it throws out. Earrings gold, too, and hanging down to her shoulders. Bracelets dangling and making noises when she moves her arm up to shake the folds of the dress out of her armpits. The dress is loose and flows, and as she walks closer, I like it. I hear Maggie go "Uhnnnh" again. It is her sister's hair. It stands straight up like the wool on a sheep. It is black as night and around the edges are two long pigtails that rope about like small lizards disappearing behind her ears.

"Wa-su-zo-Tean-o[4]!" she says, coming on in that gliding way the dress makes her move. The short stocky fellow with the hair to his navel is all grinning and he follows up with "Asalamalakim, my mother and sister!" He moves to hug Maggie but she falls back, right up against the back of my chair. I feel her trembling there and when I look up I see the perspiration falling off her chin.

"Don't get up," says Dee. Since I am stout it takes something of a push. You can see me trying to move a second or two before I make it. She turns, showing white heels through her sandals, and goes back to the car. Out she peeks next with a Polaroid. She stoops down quickly and lines up picture after picture of me sitting there in front of the house with Maggie cowering behind me. She never takes a shot without making sure the house is included. When a cow comes nibbling around the edge of the yard she snaps it and me and Maggie and the house. Then she puts the Polaroid in the back seat of the car, and comes up and kisses me on the forehead.

Meanwhile Asalamalakim is going through motions with Maggie's hand. Maggie's hand is as limp as a fish, and probably as cold, despite the sweat, and she keeps trying to pull it back. It looks like Asalamalakim wants to shake hands but wants to do it fancy[5]. Or maybe he don't know how people shake hands. Anyhow, he soon gives up on Maggie.

"Well," I say. "Dee."

"No, Mama," she says. "Not 'Dee,' Wangero Leewanika Kemanjo!"

"What happened to 'Dee'?" I wanted to know.

"She's dead," Wangero said. "I couldn't bear it any longer, being named after the people who oppress me."

"You know as well as me you was named after your aunt Dicie," I said. Dicie is my sister. She named Dee. We called her "Big Dee" after Dee was born.

"But who was she named after?" asked Wangero.

"I guess after Grandma Dee," I said.

"And who was *she* named after?" asked Wangero.

"Her mother," I said, and saw Wangero was getting tired. "That's about as far back as I can trace it," I said. Though, in fact, I probably could have carried it back beyond the Civil War through the branches.

"Well," said Asalamalakim, "there you are."

"Uhnnnh," I heard Maggie say.

"There I was not," I said, "before 'Dicie' cropped up in our family, so why should I try to trace it that far back?"

He just stood there grinning, looking down on me like somebody inspecting a Model A car. Every once in a while he and Wangero sent eye signals over my head.

"How do you pronounce this name?" I asked.

"You don't have to call me by it if you don't want to," said Wangero.

"Why shouldn't I?" I asked. "If that's what you want us to call you, we'll call you."

"I know it might sound awkward at first," said Wangero.

"I'll get used to it," I said. "Read it out again."

Well, soon we got the name out of the way. Asalamalakim had a name twice as long and three times as hard[6]. After I tripped over it two or three times he told me to just call him Hakim-a-barber. I wanted to ask him was he a barber, but I didn't really think he was, so I didn't ask.

"You must belong to those beef-cattle peoples down the road," I said. They said "Asalamalakim" when they met you, too, but they didn't shake hands. Always too busy: feeding the cattle, fixing the fences, putting up salt-lick shelters, throwing down hay. When the white folks poisoned some of the herd the men stayed up all night with rifles in their hands. I walked a mile and a half just to see the sight.

Hakim-a-barber said, "I accept some of their doctrines, but farming and raising cattle is not my style." (They didn't tell me, and I didn't ask, whether Wangero (Dee) had really gone and married him.)

We sat down to eat and right away he said he didn't eat collards and pork was unclean. Wangero, though, went on through the chitlins and corn bread, the greens and everything else. She talked a blue streak[7] over the sweet potatoes. Everything delighted her. Even the fact that we still used the benches her daddy made for the table when we couldn't afford to buy chairs.

"Oh, Mama!" she cried. Then turned to Hakim-a-barber. "I never knew how lovely these benches are. You can feel the rump prints," she said, running her hands underneath her and along the bench. Then she gave a sigh and her hand closed over Grandma Dee's butter dish. "That's it!" she said. "I knew there was something I wanted to ask you if I could have." She jumped up from the table and went over in the corner where the churn stood, the milk in it crabber by now. She looked at the churn and looked at it.

"This churn top is what I need," she said. "Didn't Uncle Buddy whittle it out of a tree you all used to have?"

"Yes," I said.

"Un huh," she said happily. "And I want the dasher, too."

"Uncle Buddy whittle that, too?" asked the barber.

Dee (Wangero) looked up at me.

"Aunt Dee's first husband whittled the dash," said Maggie so low you almost couldn't hear her. "His name was Henry, but they called him Stash."

"Maggie's brain is like an elephant's[8]," Wangero said, laughing. "I can use the churn top as a centerpiece for the alcove table," she said, sliding a plate over the churn, "and I'll think of something artistic to do with the dasher."

When she finished wrapping the dasher the handle stuck out. I took it for a moment in my hands. You didn't even have to look close to see where hands pushing the dasher up and down to make butter had left a kind of sink in the wood. In fact, there were a lot of small sinks; you could see where thumbs and fingers had sunk into the wood. It was beautiful light yellow wood, from a tree that grew in the yard where Big Dee and Stash had lived.

After dinner Dee (Wangero) went to the trunk at the foot of my bed and started rifling through it. Maggie hung back in the kitchen over the dishpan. Out came Wangero with two quilts. They had been pieced by Grandma Dee and then Big Dee and me had hung them on the quilt frames on the front porch and quilted them. One was in the Lone Star pattern. The other was Walk Around the Mountain. In both of them were scraps of dresses Grandma Dee had worn fifty and more years ago. Bits and pieces of Grandpa Jarrell's Paisley shirts. And one teeny faded blue piece, about the size of a penny matchbox, that was from Great Grandpa Ezra's uniform that he wore in the Civil War.

"Mama," Wangro said sweet as a bird. "Can I have these old quilts?"

I heard something fall in the kitchen, and a minute later the kitchen door slammed.

"Why don't you take one or two of the others?" I asked. "These old things was just done by me and Big Dee from some tops your grandma pieced before she died."

"No," said Wangero. "I don't want those. They are stitched around the borders by machine."

"That'll make them last better," I said.

"That's not the point," said Wangero. "These are all pieces of dresses Grandma used to wear. She did all this stitching by hand. Imagine!" She held the quilts securely in her arms, stroking them.

"Some of the pieces, like those lavender ones, come from old clothes her mother handed down to her," I said, moving up to touch the quilts. Dee (Wangero) moved back just enough so that I couldn't reach the quilts. They already belonged to her.

"Imagine!" she breathed again, clutching them closely to her bosom.

"The truth is," I said, "I promised to give them quilts to Maggie, for when she marries John Thomas."

She gasped like a bee had stung her.

"Maggie can't appreciate these quilts!" she said. "She'd probably be backward enough to put them to everyday use."

"I reckon she would," I said. "God knows I been saving 'em for long enough with nobody using 'em. I hope she will!" I didn't want to bring up how I had offered Dee (Wangero) a quilt when she went away to college. Then she had told me they were old-fashioned, out of style.

"But they're priceless!" she was saying now, furiously; for she has a temper. "Maggie would put them on the bed and in five years they'd be in rags. Less than that!"

"She can always make some more," I said. "Maggie knows how to quilt."

Dee (Wangero) looked at me with hatred. "You just will not understand. The point is these quilts, these quilts!"

"Well," I said, stumped. "What would you do with them?"

"Hang them," she said. As if that was the only thing you could do with quilts.

Maggie by now was standing in the door. I could almost hear the sound her feet made as they scraped over each other.

"She can have them, Mama," she said, like somebody used to never winning anything, or having anything reserved for her. "I can 'member Grandma Dee without the quilts."

I looked at her hard. She had filled her bottom lip with checkerberry snuff and it gave her face a kind of dopey, hangdog look. It was Grandma Dee and Big Dee who taught her how to quilt herself. She stood there with her scarred hands hidden in the folds of her skirt. She looked at her sister with something like fear but she wasn't mad at her. This was Maggie's portion. This was the way she knew God to work.

When I looked at her like that something hit me in the top of my head and ran down to the soles of my feet. Just like when I'm in church and the spirit of God touches me and I get happy and shout. I did something I never had done before: hugged Maggie to me, then dragged her on into the room, snatched the quilts out of Miss Wangero's hands and dumped them into Maggie's lap. Maggie just sat there on my bed with her mouth open.

"Take one or two of the others," I said to Dee.

But she turned without a word and went out to Hakim-a-barber.

"You just don't understand," she said, as Maggie and I came out to the car.

"What don't I understand?" I wanted to know.

"Your heritage," she said, And then she turned to Maggie, kissed her, and said, "You ought to try to make something of yourself[9], too, Maggie. It's really a new day for us. But from the way you and Mama still live you'd never know it."

She put on some sunglasses that hid everything above the tip of her nose and chin.

Maggie smiled; maybe at the sunglasses. But a real smile, not scared. After we watched the car dust settle I asked Maggie to bring me a dip of snuff. And then the two of us sat there just enjoying, until it was time to go in the house and go to bed.

三、主题解析

《日常家用》收入在《爱情与麻烦：黑人妇女的故事》中，是艾丽丝·沃克的短篇小说名篇。小说讲述一个黑人家庭母女之间的故事。母亲和小女儿在乡村务农。一个下午，生活在城市的大女儿带着男朋友回到农村的老家，希望把家里自制的百纳被带回城市，作为艺术品挂在家中。但母亲不同意，因为她已经答应将被子作为嫁妆留给小女儿。大女儿对母亲的行为表示不满，认为这是对祖辈传统的损坏。最后，大女儿带着家里的其他物品回城。母女俩享受着乡村的夜晚。

美国黑人内部价值观的差异是小说比较明显的主题思想。"被子"及其制作是黑人家庭的祖传，也是黑人文化传统的象征。但是受过大学教育的大女儿与几乎没有文化的母亲和妹妹对"被子"的态度完全不同。大女儿认为，珍惜"被子"的方式应该是将之悬挂起来，供人参观和欣赏。如果日日使用，必将磨损它，直至破旧和消失。但是，母亲和妹妹则要天天使用"被子"。她们认为：珍视它的最好办法就是每日与之接触，用它驱寒取暖，保护自己的身体健康。况且，小女儿已经掌握了制作"被子"的方法。大女儿对母亲和妹妹的做法十分不满，但母亲依然故我。双方不能达成共识。她们对"被子"持有不同的价值观。

该小说在结构安排上有何独特之处？通过关注小说的结构，我们发现小说通过首尾呼应的结构处理表现了另一个主题思想：美国黑人女性知足常乐的乐观生活态度。小说的第一段描写了一幅舒适而美丽的场景。大女儿即将回家，母亲和小女儿心情激动。她们把院子打扫干净，使它比任何院子都舒服；和风吹拂，棕榈树叶轻飘；任何过客皆可坐下小憩。这是一个令人向往的时刻和地点。尽管她俩辛苦劳作，但依然对自己的简陋家园爱护有加。她们没有抱怨命运，而是通过自己的双手建设自己美好的家。她们知足，她们快乐。想到与亲人团聚，她们高兴不已。小女儿既兴奋又不安，不知如何面对姐姐。

随着故事的发展和情节的推动，母亲和大女儿就"被子"展开对话和交锋。后来小女儿也加入她们的对话之中，并希望姐姐拿走"被子"。言谈之中，大女儿认为妹妹"不能欣赏这些被子"。她对母亲也不礼貌，眼神甚至带着恨意。但是，她俩并未用相同方式对待这个"不讲理的人"，而是让她拿走屋里的其他东西。小说结尾，母亲和小女儿的心情并未受到影响。小女儿露出真正的微笑，不再胆怯。母亲抽着鼻烟。她们一起坐在院内，享受院子的舒适和夜晚的美好。末段的"享受"回应了首段的"舒服"，共同表达了"知足常乐”的主题。虽然贫穷、简陋、辛苦，但她们勇敢面对现实。母亲一人可以解决生活中的一切问题，小女儿善良、手巧、善解人意。母女相互依存，共同向前。通过巧妙的结构安排，读者强烈地感受到黑人女性的自立和坚强、善良和乐观。小说闪烁着女权主义的思想光芒。这是作者着力表达的一个重要主题。该主题是对美国黑人文学的发展，是留给读者的新启示。

如果把小说放到美国20世纪60年代黑人民权运动的背景中去考量，它是否表达了小说的叙述者“我”对该运动的漠不关心呢？

四、难点注释

1. in the palm of one hand：在完全控制下。
2. Johnny Carson：20世纪60至70年代美国著名的电视节目主持人。
3. burned：欺骗；使上当。
4. Wa-su-zo-Team-o：打招呼用语。下文的Asalamalakim也是类似的意思。
5. do it fancy：做得出色。
6. Asalamalakim had a name twice as long and three times as hard：他的名字比她的名字长两倍，难记三倍。
7. blue streak：滔滔不绝的一番话。take a blue streak意为“滔滔不绝地说”。
8. Maggie's brain is like an elephant's：梅吉的记性像大象的一样好。
9. make something of yourself：make something of oneself意为“有所成就；做点事业”。

五、延伸阅读与批评

艾丽丝·沃克也是著名的诗人。她的诗歌与小说几乎同样齐名，而且二者在创作内容、主题表达和写作手法方面有诸多相似点。因此阅读她的诗歌可以加深读者对其小说的理解。

《记得吗？》是沃克的代表诗作之一。诗歌采用第一人称“我”与读者的对话形式——“记得我吗？”的问句开始，用“让我们开始吧”结束，形成一个完整的文本。“我”贯穿每一个诗节：“我”是一个受过伤、外貌丑陋、为他人当奴仆的女孩；但是，“我”改变了自己的外貌，成为正常人；“我”是一个女人，要向全人类展示自己追求的唯一“希望”，那就是亲如姊妹的两朵花——“正义”与“希望”。全诗情感饱满、气势磅礴、激情飞扬，读者从中强烈地感受“我”对社会的呐喊和对自己未来的自信。

如果将该诗与《日常家用》做比较，我们发现两者存在鲜明的共同点。诗中的“我”是否就是小说中的梅吉？结合沃克本人的成长经历，作者、梅吉和“我”是否就是同一个人？诗作中“正义”和“希望”的意思是什么？还有，诗作的最后一行“让我们开始吧”中的“我们”指谁：黑人，白人，还是各种肤色的人？“开始”干什么呢？“开始”为实现社会的正义和自由而努力奋斗？

Chapter 5 The Things They Carried

by Tim O'Brien

(An Excerpt)

一、作者简介

梯姆·奥布莱恩(1946—)，美国当代著名的小说家。他创作的小说包括《假如我死在战区，把我装棺运回家》(1973)、《北极光》(1975)、《追寻卡西亚托》(1978)、《核时代》(1985)、《他们携带的东西》(1990)、《林中之湖》(1994)、《恋爱中的托马斯》(1998)、《七月，七月》(2002)，他的短篇小说有《越南在我心中》(1994)和《信仰》等。《追寻卡西亚托》和《他们携带的东西》是他的两部代表作，前者于1978年获得美国国家图书奖。他的其他作品还获得过其他众多的文学奖项。

奥布莱恩读大学时成绩优异，获得政治学学士学位。越南战争爆发后，他于1969至1970年到越南的广义省服役，当过步兵、无线电操作员等，荣获战斗步兵勋章、紫星和铜星勋章等。退伍时获得中士军衔。回国后奥布莱恩在哈佛大学攻读政治学博士学位，但未完成博士论文"美国军事干涉的案例研究"。对社会政治问题的关注和从军的经历极大地影响了他以后的创作题材和主题。

奥布莱恩的绝大部分作品都与越南战争有关。战前和战争期间美国复杂的社会现实、越南战争本身的特点、美国士兵对战争的看法、战争给美国社会和人民造成的创伤等是他作品的主要题材和内容。他采用后现代主义的写作技巧描写和探讨越南战争之中诸多的不确定特征、记忆与现实的关系、现实与想象的关系、士兵的心理真实和现实真实之间的关系、时空颠倒、叙述文本与评论文本并置、小说创作的性质(元小说)等问题。同时，他从新历史主义视角解读越南战争历史中真实性和虚构性之间的关系及其背后的意识形态等。总的说来，他对美国政府发动越南战争持反对态度，他笔下的人物大多是遭受越南战争创伤的美国士兵。

由于奥布莱恩比较全面和系统地处理越南战争题材，并且运用高超的写作技巧，他被约瑟夫·海勒称为"我们最好的作家之一"，也是中外学者和读者讨论最多的书写美国越南战争的作家。

二、文本选读

The Things They Carried

How to Tell a True War Story

This is true.

I had a buddy in Vietnam. His name was Bob Kiley, but everybody called him Rat.

A friend of his gets killed, so about a week later Rat sits down and writes a letter to the guy's sister. Rat tells her what a great brother she had, how together the guy was, a number one pal and comrade. A real soldier's soldier, Rat says. Then he tells a few stories to make the point, how her brother would always volunteer for stuff nobody else would volunteer for in a million years, dangerous stuff, like doing recon or going out on these really badass night patrols. Stainless steel balls, Rat tells her. The guy was a little crazy, for sure, but crazy in a good way, a real daredevil, because he liked the challenge of it, he liked testing himself, just man against gook[1]. A great, great guy, Rat says.

Anyway, it's a terrific letter, very personal and touching. Rat almost bawls writing it. He gets all teary telling about the good times they had together, how her brother made the war seem almost fun, always raising hell and lighting up villes and bringing smoke to bear every which way. A great sense of humor, too. Like the time at this river when he went fishing with a whole damn crate of hand grenades. Probably the funniest thing in world history, Rat says, all that gore, about twenty zillion dead gook fish. Her brother, he had the right attitude. He knew how to have a good time. On Halloween, this real hot spooky night, the dude paints up his body all different colors and puts on this weird mask and hikes over to a ville and goes trick-or-treating almost stark naked, just boots and balls and an M-16. A tremendous human being, Rat says. Pretty nutso sometimes, but you could trust him with your life.

And then the letter gets very sad and serious. Rat pours his heart out. He says he loved the guy. He says the guy was his best friend in the world. They were like soul mates, he says, like twins or something, they had a whole lot in common. He tells the guy's sister he'll look her up when the war's over.

So what happens?

Rat mails the letter. He waits two months. The dumb cooze[2] never writes back.

A true war story is never moral. It does not instruct, nor encourage virtue, nor suggest models of proper human behavior, nor restrain men from doing the things men have always done. If a story seems moral, do not believe it. If at the end of a war story you feel uplifted, or if you feel that some small bit of rectitude has been salvaged from the larger waste, then you have been made the victim of a very old and terrible lie. There is no rectitude whatsoever. There is no virtue. As a first rule of thumb, therefore, you can tell a true war story by its absolute and uncompromising allegiance to obscenity and evil. Listen to Rat Kiley. Cooze, he says. He does not say bitch. He certainly does not say woman, or girl. He says cooze. Then he spits and stares. He's nineteen years old—it's too much for him—so he looks at you with those big sad gentle killer eyes and says cooze, because his friend is dead, and because it's so incredibly sad and true: she never wrote back.

You can tell a true war story if it embarrasses you. If you don't care for obscenity, you don't care for the truth; if you don't care for the truth, watch how you vote. Send guys to war, they come home talking dirty.

Listen to Rat: "Jesus Christ, man, I write this beautiful fuckin' letter, I slave over it, and what happens? The dumb cooze never writes back."

The dead guy's name was Curt Lemon. What happened was, we crossed a muddy river and marched west into the mountains, and on the third day we took a break along a trail junction in deep jungle. Right away, Lemon and Rat Kiley started goofing. They didn't understand about the spookiness. They were kids; they just didn't know. A nature hike, they thought, not even a war, so they went off into the shade of some giant trees—quadruple canopy, no sunlight at all—and they were giggling and calling each other yellow mother[3] and playing a silly game they'd invented. The game involved smoke grenades, which were harmless unless you did stupid things, and what they did was pull out the pin and stand a few feet apart and play catch under the shade of those huge trees. Whoever chickened out was a yellow mother. And if nobody chickened out, the grenade would make a light popping sound and they'd be covered with smoke and they'd laugh and dance around and then do it again.

It's all exactly true.

It happened, to *me*, nearly twenty years ago, and I still remember that trail junction and those giant trees and a soft dripping sound somewhere beyond the trees. I remember the smell of moss. Up in the canopy there were tiny white blossoms, but no sunlight at all, and I remember the shadows spreading out under the trees where Curt Lemon and Rat Kiley were playing catch with smoke grenades. Mitchell Sanders sat flipping his yo-yo[4]. Norman Bowker and Kiowa and Dave Jensen were dozing, or half dozing, and all around us were those ragged green mountains.

Except for the laughter things were quiet.

At one point, I remember, Mitchell Sanders turned and looked at me, not quite nodding, as if to warn me about something, as if he already *knew*, then after a while he rolled up his yo-yo and moved away.

It's hard to tell you what happened next.

They were just goofing. There was a noise, I suppose, which must've been the detonator, so I glanced behind me and watched Lemon step from the shade into bright sunlight. His face was suddenly brown and shining. A handsome kid, really. Sharp gray eyes, lean and narrow-waisted, and when he died it was almost beautiful, the way the sunlight came around him and lifted him up and sucked him high into a tree full of moss and vines and white blossoms.

In any war story, but especially a true one, it's difficult to separate what happened from what seemed to happen. What seems to happen becomes its own happening and has to be told that way. The angles of vision are skewed[5]. When a booby trap explodes, you close your eyes and duck and float outside yourself. When a guy dies, like Curt Lemon, you look away and then look back for a moment and then look away again. The pictures get jumbled; you tend to miss a lot. And then afterward, when you go to tell about it, there is always that surreal seemingness, which makes the story seem untrue, but which in fact represents the hard and exact truth as it *seemed*.

In many cases a true war story cannot be believed. If you believe it, be skeptical. It's a question of credibility. Often the crazy stuff is true and the normal stuff isn't, because the normal stuff is necessary to make you believe the truly incredible craziness.

In other cases you can't even tell a true war story. Sometimes it's just beyond telling.

I heard this one, for example, from Mitchell Sanders. It was near dusk and we were sitting at my foxhole along a wide muddy river north of Quang Ngai[6]. I remember how peaceful the twilight was. A deep pinkish red spilled out on the river, which moved without sound, and in the morning we would cross the river and march west into the mountains. The occasion was right for a good story.

"God's truth," Mitchell Sanders said. "A six-man patrol goes up into the mountains on a basic listening-post operation. The idea's to spend a week up there, just lie low and listen for enemy movement. They've got a radio along, so if they hear anything suspicious—anything—they're supposed to call in artillery or gunships, whatever it takes. Otherwise they keep strict field discipline. Absolute silence. They just listen."

Sanders glanced at me to make sure I had the scenario. He was playing with his yo-yo, dancing it with short, tight little strokes of the wrist.

His face was blank in the dusk.

"We're talking regulation, by-the-book LP. These six guys, they don't say boo for a solid week. They don't got tongues. *All* ears."

"Right," I said.

"Understand me?"

"Invisible."

Sanders nodded.

"Affirm," he said. "Invisible. So what happens is, these guys get themselves deep in the bush, all camouflaged up, and they lie down and wait and that's all they do, nothing else, they lie there for seven straight days and just listen. And man, I'll tell you—it's spooky. This is mountains. You don't *know* spooky till you been there. Jungle, sort of, except it's way up in the clouds and there's always this fog—like rain, except it's not raining—everything's all wet and swirly and tangled up and you can't see jack, you can't find your own pecker to piss with. Like you don't even have a body. Serious spooky. You just go with the vapors—the fog sort of takes you in... And the sounds, man. The sounds carry forever. You hear stuff nobody should *ever* hear."

Sanders was quiet for a second, just working the yo-yo, then he smiled at me.

"So after a couple days the guys start hearing this real soft, kind of wacked-out music. Weird echoes and stuff. Like a radio or something, but it's not a radio, it's this strange gook music that comes right out of the rocks. Faraway, sort of, but right up close, too. They try to ignore it. But it's a listening post, right? So they listen. And every night they keep hearing that crazyass gook concert. All kinds of chimes and xylophones. I mean, this is wilderness—no way, it can't be real—but there it *is*, like the mountains are tuned in to Radio fucking Hanoi. Naturally they get nervous. One guy sticks Juicy Fruit in his ears. Another guy almost flips. Thing is, though, they can't report music. They can't get on the horn and call back to base and say, 'Hey, listen, we need some firepower, we got to blow away this weirdo gook rock band.' They can't do that. It wouldn't go down. So they lie there in the fog and keep their mouths shut. And what makes it extra bad, see, is the poor dudes can't horse around like normal. Can't joke it away. Can't even talk to each other except maybe in whispers, all hush-hush, and that just revs up the willies. All they do is listen."

Again there was some silence as Mitchell Sanders looked out on the river. The dark was coming on hard now, and off to the west I could see the mountains rising in silhouette, all the mysteries and unknowns.

"This next part," Sanders said quietly, "you won't believe."

"Probably not," I said.

"You won't. And you know why?" He gave me a long, tired smile. "Because it happened. Because every word is absolutely dead-on true."

Sanders made a sound in his throat, like a sigh, as if to say he didn't care if I believed him or not. But he did care. He wanted me to feel the truth, to believe by the raw force of feeling. He seemed sad, in a way.

"These six guys," he said, "they're pretty fried out by now, and one night they start hearing voices. Like at a cocktail party. That's what it sounds like, this big swank gook cocktail party somewhere out there in the fog. Music and chitchat and stuff. It's crazy, I know, but they hear the champagne corks. They hear the actual martini glasses. Real hoity-toity, all very civilized, except this isn't civilization. This is Nam.

"Anyway, the guys try to be cool. They just lie there and groove, but after a while they start hearing—you won't believe this—they hear chamber music[7]. They hear violins and cellos. They hear this terrific mama-san soprano. Then after a while they hear gook opera and a glee club and the Haiphong Boys Choir and a barbershop quartet and all kinds of weird chanting and Buddha-Buddha stuff. And the whole time, in the background, there's still that cocktail party going on. All these different voices. Not human voices, though. Because it's the mountains. Follow me? The rock—it's *talking*. And the fog, too, and the grass and the goddamn mongooses. Everything talks. The trees talk politics, the monkeys talk religion. The whole country. Vietnam. The place talks. It talks. Understand? Nam—it truly *talks*.

"The guys can't cope. They lose it. They get on the radio and report enemy movement—a whole army, they say—and they order up the firepower. They get arty and gunships. They call in air strikes. And I'll tell you, they fuckin' crash that cocktail party. All night long, they just smoke those mountains. They make jungle juice. They blow away trees and glee clubs and whatever else there is to blow away. Scorch time. They walk napalm up and down the ridges. They bring in the Cobras and F-4s, they use Willie Peter and HE and incendiaries. It's all fire. They make those mountains burn.

"Around dawn things finally get quiet. Like you never even *heard* quiet before. One of those real thick, real misty days—just clouds and fog, they're off in this special zone—and the mountains are absolutely dead-flat silent. Like *Brigadoon*—pure vapor, you know? Everything's all sucked up inside the fog. Not a single sound, except they still *hear* it.

"So they pack up and start humping. They head down the mountain, back to base camp, and when they get there they don't say diddly. They don't talk. Not a word, like they're deaf and dumb. Later on this fat bird colonel comes up and asks what the hell happened out there. What'd they hear? Why all the ordnance? The man's ragged out, he gets down tight on their case. I mean, they spent six trillion dollars on firepower, and this fatass colonel wants answers, he wants to know what the fuckin' story is.

"But the guys don't say zip. They just look at him for a while, sort of funny like, sort of amazed, and the whole war is right there in that stare. It says everything you can't ever say. It says, man, you got *wax* in your ears. It says, poor bastard, you'll never know—wrong frequency—you don't *even* want to hear this. Then they salute the fucker and walk away, because certain stories you don't ever tell."

You can tell a true war story by the way it never seems to end. Not then, not ever. Not when Mitchell Sanders stood up and moved off into the dark.

It all happened.

Even now, at this instant, I remember that yo-yo. In a way, I suppose, you had to be there, you had to hear it, but I could tell how desperately Sanders wanted me to believe him, his frustration at not quite getting the details right, not quite pinning down the final and definitive truth.

And I remember sitting at my foxhole that night, watching the shadows of Quang Ngai, thinking about the coming day and how we would cross the river and march west into the mountains, all the ways I might die, all the things I did not understand.

Late in the night Mitchell Sanders touched my shoulder. "Just came to me," he whispered. "The moral, I mean. Nobody listens. Nobody hears nothin'. Like that fatass colonel. The politicians, all the civilian types. Your girlfriend. My girlfriend. Everybody's sweet little virgin girlfriend. What they need is to go out on LP. The vapors, man. Trees and rocks—you got to *listen* to your enemy."

And then again, in the morning, Sanders came up to me. The platoon was preparing to move out, checking weapons, going through all the little rituals that preceded a day's march. Already the lead squad had crossed the river and was filing off toward the west.

"I got a confession to make," Sanders said. "Last night, man, I had to make up a few things."

"I know that."

"The glee club. There wasn't any glee club."

"Right."

"No opera."

"Forget it, I understand."

"Yeah, but listen, it's still true. Those six guys, they heard wicked sound out there. They heard sound you just plain won't believe."

Sanders pulled on his rucksack, closed his eyes for a moment, then almost smiled at me. I knew what was coming.

"All right," I said, "what's the moral?"

"Forget it."

"No, go ahead."

For a long while he was quiet, looking away, and the silence kept stretching out until it was almost embarrassing. Then he shrugged and gave me a stare that lasted all day.

"Hear that quiet, man?" he said. "That quiet—just listen. There's your moral."

In a true war story, if there's a moral at all, it's like the thread that makes the cloth. You can't tease it out. You can't extract the meaning without unraveling the deeper meaning. And in the end, really, there's nothing much to say about a true war story, except maybe "Oh."

True war stories do not generalize. They do not indulge in abstraction or analysis.

For example: War is hell. As a moral declaration the old truism seems perfectly true, and yet because it abstracts, because it generalizes, I can't believe it with my stomach. Nothing turns inside.

It comes down to gut instinct. A true war story, if truly told, makes the stomach believe.

This one does it for me. I've told it before—many times, many versions—but here's what actually happened.

We crossed that river and marched west into the mountains. On the third day, Curt Lemon stepped on a booby-trapped 105 round. He was playing catch with Rat Kiley, laughing, and then he was dead. The trees were thick; it took nearly an hour to cut an LZ for the dustoff.

Later, higher in the mountains, we came across a baby VC water buffalo. What it was doing there I don't know—no farms or paddies—but we chased it down and got a rope around it and led it along to a deserted village where we set up for the night. After supper Rat Kiley went over and stroked its nose.

He opened up a can of C rations, pork and beans, but the baby buffalo wasn't interested. Rat shrugged.

He stepped back and shot it through the right front knee. The animal did not make a sound. It went down hard, then got up again, and Rat took careful aim and shot off an ear. He shot it in the hindquarters and in the little hump at its back. He shot it twice in the flanks. It wasn't to kill; it was to hurt. He put the rifle muzzle up against the mouth and shot the mouth away. Nobody said much. The whole platoon stood there watching, feeling all kinds of things, but there wasn't a great deal of pity for the baby water buffalo. Curt Lemon was dead. Rat Kiley had lost his best friend in the world. Later in the week he would write a long personal letter to the guy's sister, who would not write back, but for now it was a question of pain. He shot off the tail. He shot away chunks of meat below the ribs. All around us there was the smell of smoke and filth and deep greenery, and the evening was humid and very hot. Rat went to automatic. He shot randomly, almost casually, quick little spurts in the belly and butt. Then he reloaded, squatted down, and shot it in the left front knee. Again the animal fell hard and tried to get up, but this time it couldn't quite make it. It wobbled and went down sideways. Rat shot it in the nose. He bent forward and whispered something, as if talking to a pet, then he shot it in the throat. All the while the baby buffalo was silent, or almost silent, just a light bubbling sound where the nose had been. It lay very still. Nothing moved except the eyes, which were enormous, the pupils shiny black and dumb.

Rat Kiley was crying. He tried to say something, but then cradled his rifle and went off by himself.

The rest of us stood in a ragged circle around the baby buffalo. For a time no one spoke. We had witnessed something essential, something brand-new and profound, a piece of the world so startling there was not yet a name for it.

Somebody kicked the baby buffalo.

It was still alive, though just barely, just in the eyes.

"Amazing," Dave Jensen said. "My whole life, I never seen anything like it."

"Never?"

"Not hardly. Not once."

Kiowa and Mitchell Sanders picked up the baby buffalo. They hauled it across the open square, hoisted it up, and dumped it in the village well.

Afterward, we sat waiting for Rat to get himself together.

"Amazing," Dave Jensen kept saying. "A new wrinkle. I never seen it before."

Mitchell Sanders took out his yo-yo. "Well, that's Nam[8]," he said. "Garden of Evil. Over here, man, every sin's real fresh and original."

How do you generalize?

War is hell, but that's not the half of it, because war is also mystery and terror and adventure and courage and discovery and holiness and pity and despair and longing and love. War is nasty;

war is fun. War is thrilling; war is drudgery. War makes you a man; war makes you dead.

The truths are contradictory. It can be argued, for instance, that war is grotesque. But in truth war is also beauty. For all its horror, you can't help but gape at the awful majesty of combat. You stare out at tracer rounds[9] unwinding through the dark like brilliant red ribbons. You crouch in ambush as a cool, impassive moon rises over the nighttime paddies. You admire the fluid symmetries of troops on the move, the harmonies of sound and shape and proportion, the great sheets of metal-fire streaming down from a gunship, the illumination rounds[10], the white phosphorus, the purply orange glow of napalm, the rocket's red glare. It's not pretty, exactly. It's astonishing. It fills the eye. It commands you. You hate it, yes, but your eyes do not. Like a killer forest fire, like cancer under a microscope, any battle or bombing raid or artillery barrage has the aesthetic purity of absolute moral indifference—a powerful, implacable beauty—and a true war story will tell the truth about this, though the truth is ugly.

To generalize about war is like generalizing about peace. Almost everything is true. Almost nothing is true. At its core, perhaps, war is just anther name for death, and yet any soldier will tell you, if he tells the truth, that proximity to death brings with it a corresponding proximity to life. After a firefight, there is always the immense pleasure of aliveness. The trees are alive. The grass, the soil—everything. All around you things are purely living, and you among them, and the aliveness makes you tremble. You feel an intense, out-of-the-skin awareness of your living self—your truest self, the human being you want to be and then become by the force of wanting it. In the midst of evil you want to be a good man. You want decency. You want justice and courtesy and human concord, things you never knew you wanted. There is a kind of largeness to it, a kind of godliness. Though it's odd, you're never more alive than when you're almost dead. You recognize what's valuable. Freshly, as if for the first time, you love what's best in yourself and in the world, all that might be lost. At the hour of dusk you sit at your foxhole and look out on a wide river turning pinkish red, and at the mountains beyond, and although in the morning you must cross the river and go into the mountains and do terrible things and maybe die, even so, you find yourself studying the fine colors on the river, you feel wonder and awe at the setting of the sun, and you are filled with a hard, aching love for how the world could be and always should be, but now is not.

Mitchell Sanders was right. For the common soldier, at least, war has the feel—the spiritual texture—of a great ghostly fog, thick and permanent. There is no clarity. Everything swirls. The old rules are no longer binding, the old truths no longer true. Right spills over into wrong. Order blends into chaos, love into hate, ugliness into beauty, law into anarchy, civility into savagery. The vapors suck you in. You can't tell where you are, or why you're there, and the only certainty is overwhelming ambiguity.

In war you lose your sense of the definite, hence your sense of truth itself, and therefore it's safe to say that in a true war story nothing is ever absolutely true.

Often in a true war story there is not even a point, or else the point doesn't hit you until twenty years later, in your sleep, and you wake up and shake your wife and start telling the story to her, except when you get to the end you've forgotten the point again. And then for a long time you lie there watching the story happen in your head. You listen to your wife's breathing. The war's over. You close your eyes. You smile and think, Christ, what's the *point*?

This one wakes me up.

In the mountains that day, I watched Lemon turn sideways. He laughed and said something to Rat Kiley. Then he took a peculiar half step, moving from shade into bright sunlight, and the booby-trapped 105 round blew him into a tree. The parts were just hanging there, so Dave Jensen and I were ordered to shinny up and peel him off. I remember the white bone of an arm. I remember pieces of skin and something wet and yellow that must've been the intestines. The gore was horrible, and stays with me. But what wakes me up twenty years later is Dave Jensen singing "Lemon Tree[11]" as we threw down the parts.

You can tell a true war story by the questions you ask. Somebody tells a story, let's say, and afterward you ask, "Is it true?" and if the answer matters, you've got your answer.

For example, we've all heard this one. Four guys go down a trail. A grenade sails out. One guy jumps on it and takes the blast and saves his three buddies.

Is it true?

The answer matters.

You'd feel cheated if it never happened. Without the grounding reality, it's just a trite bit of puffery, pure Hollywood, untrue in the way all such stories are untrue. Yet even if it did happen—and maybe it did, anything's possible—even then you know it can't be true, because a true war story does not depend upon that kind of truth. Absolute occurrence is irrelevant. A thing may happen and be a total lie; another thing may not happen and be truer than the truth. For example: Four guys go down a trail. A grenade sails out. One guy jumps on it and takes the blast, but it's a killer grenade and everybody dies anyway. Before they die, though, one of the dead guys says, "The fuck you do *that* for?" and the jumper says, "Story of my life[12], man," and the other guy starts to smile but he's dead.

That's a true story that never happened.

Twenty years later, I can still see the sunlight on Lemon's face. I can see him turning, looking back at Rat Kiley, then he laughed and took that curious half step from shade into sunlight, his face suddenly brown and shining, and when his foot touched down, in that instant, he must've thought it was the sunlight that was killing him. It was not the sunlight. It was a rigged 105 round. But if I could ever get the story right, how the sun seemed to gather around him and pick him up and lift him high into a tree, if I could somehow re-create the fatal whiteness of that light, the quick glare, the obvious cause and effect, then you would believe the last thing Curt Lemon believed, which for him must've been the final truth.

Now and then, when I tell this story, someone will come up to me afterward and say she liked it. It's always a woman. Usually it's an older woman of kindly temperament and humane politics. She'll explain that as a rule she hates war stories; she can't understand why people want to wallow in all the blood and gore. But this one she liked. The poor baby buffalo, it made her sad. Sometimes, even, there are little tears. What I should do, she'll say, is put it all behind me. Find new stories to tell.

I won't say it but I'll think it.

I'll picture Rat Kiley's face, his grief, and I'll think, *You dumb cooze.*

Because she wasn't listening.

It *wasn't* a war story. It was a *love* story.

But you can't say that. All you can do is tell it one more time, patiently, adding and subtracting, making up a few things to get at the real truth. No Mitchell Sanders, you tell her. No Lemon, no Rat Kiley. No trail junction. No baby buffalo. No vines or moss or white blossoms. Beginning to end, you tell her, it's all made up. Every goddamn detail—the mountains and the river and especially that poor dumb baby buffalo. None of it happened. None of it. And even of it did happen, it didn't happen in the mountains, it happened in this little village on the Batangan Peninsula, and it was raining like crazy, and one night a guy named Stink Harris woke up screaming with a leech on his tongue. You can tell a true war story if you just keep on telling it.

And in the end, of course, a true war story is never about war. It's about sunlight. It's about the special way that dawn spreads out on a river when you know you must cross the river and march into the mountains and do things you are afraid to do. It's about love and memory. It's about sorrow. It's about sisters who never write back and people who never listen.

三、主题解析

《他们携带的东西》由22个部分组成，采用第一人称叙述方式讲述了“我”的生活经历和越南战争经历、“我”与其他美国士兵在战时的交流、他们给“我”讲述他们自己的生活故事和越南战争经历、“我”对讲故事艺术的看法，但这些内容没有按照时间先后顺序排列。标题中的“东西”在第一部分“他们携带的东西”里做了比较详细的说明，包括从女友的信件、各种枪支的信息、食品罐头到驱蚊剂等。显然，美国士兵携带的“东西”既包括战时的必需品，也包含士兵们对国内亲人的思念以及对参战所持的复杂心态。叙述者“我”是他们中的一员。

一个有趣的现象是，《他们携带的东西》的叙述者也叫“梯姆·奥布莱恩”，而且叙述者奥布莱恩与作者奥布莱恩有诸多相似之处，这使得该作品的文学类型不易界定。有人称之为一部小说，有人视它为一个故事集，还有人说它是一部战争回忆录，甚至是一部自传。作者为什么要这样处理？

“如何讲述一个真实的战争故事”是《他们携带的东西》里最典型的一个章节。它运用夹叙夹议的方式阐明“真实的战争故事”的内涵。该章节的第一句话就明示“我”的观点：“这一切是真的。”然后叙述一个真实的故事——“我”的朋友鲍勃·凯利讲述了一个他亲历的故事。他的好友卡特·莱蒙在一次玩掷手榴弹游戏时被炸死，尸首分家，内脏被炸到树上。鲍勃为此伤心不已，便写了一封感人至深的信寄给卡特的妹妹。可是他妹妹从未回信，因为在她看来这一切太不可信，是假的。在讲述上述故事的中间，“我”提出另一个观点：“一个真实的战争故事是从来没有道德意义的。”接着，“我”又提出一个观点：“在许多情况下一个真实的战争故事不足为信。如果你相信它，就该怀疑它。”该观点的例子是米歇尔·桑德斯的故事。他讲述他们到山中巡逻的经历。他们走进丛林，听到由山、树和岩石发出各种怪异的声音。可是，当问及其中的原因时，他们拒绝回答，因为他们认为对方无法理解他们的故事。第二天，桑德斯承认他杜撰了故事的部分内容。第三个故事是鲍勃射杀一头幼水牛。他一边哭叫一边射中水牛的腿部。他不是要杀死它，而是要打伤它，让它疼痛。之后，“我”又转述桑德斯的故事和卡特之死的细节。该章节的结尾是总结性的叙述：“一个真实的战争故事从来不是关于战争。它是关于阳光……关于爱和记忆。它是关于悲伤。它是关于妹妹们从不回信……”其中的几个“关于”基本对应上述几个故事。一个观点(“议”)对应一个例子(“叙”)。

为何说“真实的战争故事是关于阳光”？卡特死后，部分尸体和器官挂在树上，在阳光的照射下显得格外引人注目，格外令人震惊和难忘。无怪乎士兵们认为是阳光杀死了卡特。尽管卡特之死与真正的战争无关，但他死于战争期间。如果没有战争，卡特不会上战场，不会丢了性命。他们玩游戏是为了打发无聊时光，或是驱散心中的恐惧。从这个意义上说，是战争夺走了卡特的生命，卡特的死成为战争的一部分。综上所述，故事的叙述者“我”认为，士兵的切身感受、心理真实(对战时周围环境的感知、伤痛和恐惧等)、记忆、与战争密切相关的人和事等都是真实战争故事的重要内容。战争故事通常讲述有形的东西，如战场的硝烟和搏杀以及生与死的场面，但是那些无形的东西，如士兵的心理活动和感受等也应引起足够的重视。这就是作者奥布莱恩在“如何讲述一个真实的战争故事”中表达的新型战争文学创作的美学追求。

四、难点注释

1. gook：(贬义词)外国佬，这里指越南人。
2. cooze：(俚语)娘们。
3. yellow mother：胆小鬼。
4. yo-yo：溜溜球。
5. The angles of vision are skewed：视角是偏斜的。意思是不同的人有不同的感受或看法。
6. Quang Ngai：越南的广义省。
7. chamber music：〈古〉室内乐。
8. Nam：Viet Nam 的简称，越南。
9. tracer rounds：曳光弹。
10. illumination rounds：照明弹。

11. Lemon Tree：“柠檬树”，20世纪60年代美国的一首流行歌曲。
12. story of my life：我自己的事情；不告诉你。

五、延伸阅读与批评

《越南在我心中》发表于1994年，是奥布莱恩的短篇小说。小说用日记的方式记载了“我”于1994年重访越南的经历，包括“我”受到越南人民的欢迎、“我”记忆中的越南与眼前现实中的越南、“我”参观昔日的越南战争战场等。小说的叙述者“我”与《他们携带的东西》的叙述者“我”有若干相似之处。而后一个“我”的名字也叫梯姆·奥布莱恩，与小说作者完全同名。那么，上述的两个“我”是否是作者本人？

1968年3月16日，美军在越南广义省一个叫美莱的村子里将504名无辜的老人、妇女和孩子赶到一个沟边用机枪扫射，村民无一生还。这就是越南战争期间最为令人震惊的“美莱大屠杀”。

《越南在我心中》直接引用美国军事法庭审判在越南战争期间制造“美莱大屠杀”的部分美国士兵时审判官提出的问题和受审者的回答，这些证词在奥布莱恩同年出版的小说《林中之湖》中多次出现。作者两次邀请读者“重访”越南战争历史的现场——“美莱大屠杀”和审判现场，旨在提醒读者关注“美莱大屠杀”的性质：究竟是一个小过失，还是美国官兵蓄意为之？读了这些证词，你认为作者奥布莱恩对该事件持什么态度？

Part Five

Figure of Speech

一般说来，“修辞”涵盖语音手段、节奏和韵律、词法和句法手段、比喻和典故的引用四个方面，每个方面又包含若干具体内容。

文学的美学价值和魅力在很大的程度上来自各种修辞手法的运用。文学是语言的艺术，而修辞贯穿语言的各个层面：从语音到字、词、句子，甚至到段落和篇章的设计和安排。优秀的文学作品都是恰到好处地借助各种修辞手段达到打动读者的目的，创造经久不衰的艺术魅力。成功运用修辞的文学作品能够引起读者的联想、想象、憧憬，激发读者思考和回味，给读者带来美的享受，产生净化心灵、愉悦情绪、陶冶精神的效果，并对读者的思想和行为具有指引作用。

该部分包括五个单元：二首诗歌、一篇散文、一篇小说。它们的主要内容如下：运用类比产生形式和内容的对称美，使用夸张和对比制造幽默和讽刺的效果，引经据典拓宽意义的宽度、广度和深度，词法和句法的特殊安排加强表达的气势和力度。这些不同修辞手法的运用为作品创造出多种多样的美学效果。

Chapter 1　To a Waterfowl

by William Cullen Bryant

一、作者简介

威廉·卡伦·布莱恩特(1794—1878)，美国早期著名的浪漫主义诗人，美国第一个土生土长并享有国际声誉的浪漫主义诗人。他是典型的“早慧者”，14 岁便发表诗歌。他的诗集有《泉》(1842)、《白蹄鹿》(1844)、《森林赞歌》(1860)、《似水流年》(1878)。代表性的诗篇有《禁运令》(1808)、《黄色紫罗兰》(1814)、《致水鸟》(1815)、《死亡随想曲》(1817)等。其中《死亡随想曲》往往被视为布莱恩特的代表作。晚年，他还将荷马的《伊利亚德》和《奥德赛》翻译成英语。

布莱恩特 9 岁时便能作诗，并赢得师生的赞扬，后因抨击时局被学校开除。于是他开始告别诗歌，潜心学习法律，并获得律师从业资格。可是他难以抵挡对诗歌的喜爱，他一边从事法律工作，一边写诗。成名诗坛后，布莱恩特放弃了律师职业，转向新闻工作。美国内战时期他十分关心政治和民主，主张废除奴隶制，宣传政治自由主义和普遍的人权，并坚决支持林肯总统。因此，他又被认为“纽约第一市民”、美国的爱国诗人。

人生与死亡、永恒、自然万物是诗人经常关注的题材。然而，他面对死亡时并未表现出悲观与哀伤，而是表现出一种平静和淡定，甚至勇敢与坚强。面对自然的花草和鸟兽，诗人则充满亲近感和无限向往。他认为自然界的万物具有灵性和神性(上帝般的力量)，是真和善的化身，是人类的精神寄托和荡涤心灵的场所。从这种意义上讲，布莱恩特有时被称为美国最早的自然主义诗人之一和“美国的华兹华斯”。

国内学者曾将布莱恩特和他同时代的另一位诗人爱伦·坡进行比较。例如从对待“孤独”而言，布莱恩特认为现实世界虽然充满烦恼和纷争，但艺术家可以通过回归充满神灵的大自然找到自己心灵的寄托；坡则常常从孤独走向变态。就诗歌的审美功能而言，前者认为诗贵在言志、教化、启迪；后者认为诗贵在形式、美感和泻情。这些见解可以帮助我们更好地把握布莱恩特的诗歌主旨。

二、文本选读

To a Waterfowl

Whither[1], midst falling dew,
While glow the heavens with the last steps of day,
Far, through their rosy depths, dost thou pursue
Thy solitary way?

Vainly the fowler's[2] eye
Might mark thy distant flight to do thee wrong[3],
As, darkly seen against the crimson sky,
Thy figure floats along.

Seek'st thou the plashy brink
Of weedy lake, or marge of river wide,
Or where the rocking billows rise and sing
On the chafed ocean-side?

There is a Power whose care
Teaches thy way along that pathless coast,
The desert and illimitable air,
Lone wandering, but not lost.

All day thy wings have fann'd,
At that far height, the cold, thin atmosphere,
Yet stoop[4] not, weary, to the welcome land,
Though the dark night is near.

And soon that toil[5] shall end,
Soon shalt thou find a summer home, and rest,
And scream among thy fellows; reeds shall bend,
Soon, o'er[6] thy sheltered nest.

Thou'rt gone, the abyss of heaven
Hath swallowed up thy form; yet, on my heart
Deeply has sunk the lesson[7] thou hast given,
And shall not soon depart.

He, who, from zone to zone,
Guides through the boundless sky thy certain flight,
In the long way that I must tread alone,
Will lead my steps aright.

三、修辞解析

英国诗人兼批评家马修·阿诺德称赞《致水鸟》是"语言中最完美的短诗",美国诗人兼批评家理查德·威尔伯认为该诗是“美国第一首没有瑕疵的诗”。由此可见这首诗在美国文学乃至世界文学中崇高的地位。该诗是由若干个比喻(明喻、暗喻、拟人、借代等)构成的一个完美的类比。类比属于比较的一种，是比较两个不同对象的若干个侧面，找出它们的相似点，达到整体比较的目的。

黄昏时分，诗人(诗歌的叙述者)的心情十分糟糕，他感到悲伤和绝望，不知人生的方向。就在此时，他看到一只水鸟孤独地在天空中飞翔。他触景生情，想象水鸟飞在回家的路上。水鸟不知疲倦，克难奋进，没有迷途，直奔自己的家园，受到同伴的欢迎。诗人顿生奇想：水鸟一定是得到某种神圣“力量”的帮助才得以回归故园。那“力量”也许来自上帝，也许是上帝将之赋予水鸟，也许水鸟就是上帝的化身。最后，诗人获得灵感和暗示：他自己也将在该“力量”(神灵)或者水鸟本身的指引下找到自己前行的正确方向。

在此，水鸟是自然的化身，诗人从它身上获取慰藉和感悟；诗人将自己和水鸟合二为一，因为二者有若干类似点；水鸟的灵性代表着自然的灵性，上帝“置入”水鸟的神灵也给了诗人力量。用图示表示类比的内容：

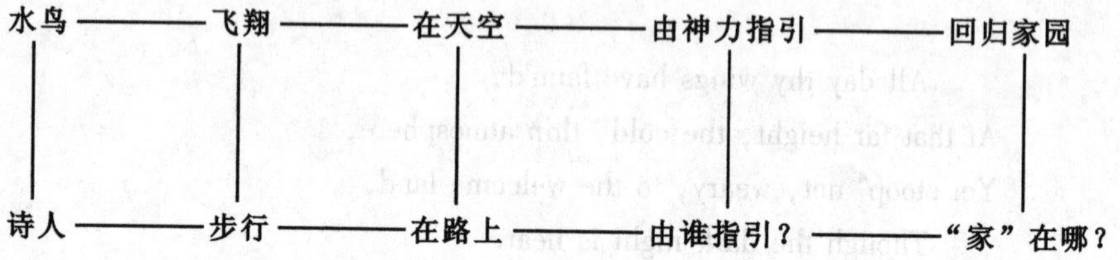

图示中的两个问号是诗人面对的问题。他在寻找答案。最终，他从水鸟那里获得启示，明白前进的方向，找到自己的精神和思想归宿。这个答案是什么？

四、难点注释

1. whither：同 where，去哪里。
2. fowler's：hunter's，猎人的。
3. do thee wrong：捕杀。
4. stoop (to)：俯身；弯腰。另一层意思是“停歇”。
5. toil：(辛苦的)飞行。
6. o'er：为了音节数量的相等而缩写的 over。
7. lesson：启示；启迪。

五、延伸阅读与批评

亨利·朗费罗是与布莱恩特同时代且同样出名的诗人，他的代表性诗作之一《大海的秘密(意义)》也包含一个类比。诗歌的主旨：只有那些勇敢面对各种危险的人才能理解大海的秘密(意义)。诗作将大海比作人生，水手即普通的人，危险就是人生中的各种困难。

大海跟人生一样，既有风雨，也有彩虹。水手在海上航行的过程恰似人们历经生活风浪的过程——二者之间存在若干共同点。下面几个问号的具体内容是什么？

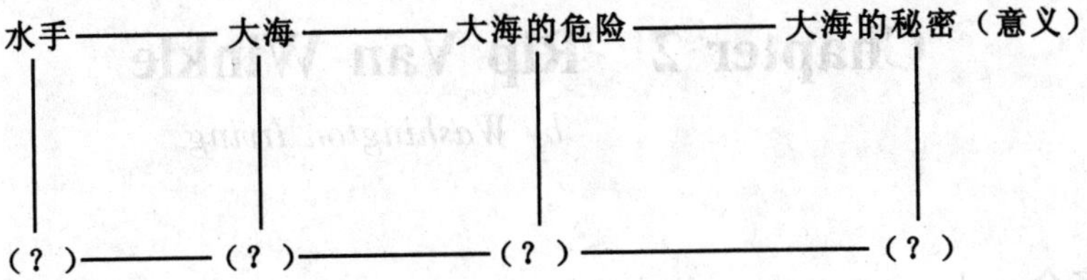

Chapter 2 Rip Van Winkle

by Washington Irving

一、作者简介

华盛顿·欧文(1783—1859)，美国19世纪著名的浪漫主义小说家、美国建国后第一个获得国际声誉的作家，被誉为“美国文学之父”。

他的作品包括短篇小说、散文、杂文、人物传记等：(与人合著)杂文集《萨马根迪》(1808)，喜剧式的历史写作《纽约外史》(1809)，散文、随笔、故事集《见闻札记》(1819—1820)，散文和短篇小说集《布雷斯布里奇田庄》(1822)，故事集《阿尔罕伯拉》(1832)，三卷本的美国西部之旅《克莱杨杂记》(1835)。欧文在晚期完成了三部人物传记：《哥尔德斯密斯传》(1840，1849)、《穆罕默德及其继承者》(1850)、多卷本《华盛顿传》(1855—1859)。《见闻札记》被公认为欧文的代表作，其中收录的短篇小说《瑞普·凡·温克尔》和《睡谷的传说》都是小说名作。欧文旅居欧洲17年，熟悉英国、德国、法国、西班牙等国的历史和风土人情，特别熟悉英国文学；回国后定居在哈德森河畔，钟情于美国的山水。这些经历为作者的文学创作提供了丰富的素材和灵感。

欧美的自然风光、社会历史风情、著名人物的生活是欧文关注的主要对象，不过他的作品大多以欧洲为题材，怀古与怀旧、喜爱自然、抨击殖民者、同情印第安人等是他作品经常表达的主题。他的作品弥漫着浪漫主义气息，兼有中世纪欧洲文学风格；文笔优美，行文流畅，情节生动，幽默和夸张手法的运用恰到好处，为作品增添了令人印象深刻的艺术魅力。

欧文是美国文学史上第一个关注和表现美国历史和风土人情的作家，他创造性地将欧洲的文学写作风格与美国本土的题材结合起来，为独立的美国民族文学诞生，即实现从题材、内容和表现手法都具有美国特色的目标作出了重要贡献。尤其是，他那幽默和夸张的写作风格代代相传，为美国文学注入了持久的艺术魅力，代表性的继承者有马克·吐温、斯蒂芬·克莱恩、西奥多·德莱塞和索尔·贝娄等。

二、文本选读

Rip Van Winkle

Whoever has made a voyage up the Hudson must remember the Kaatskill mountains. They are a dismembered branch of the great Appalachian family, and are seen away to the west of the river, swelling up to a noble height, and lording it over the surrounding country. Every change of season, every change of weather, indeed, every hour of the day, produces some change in the magical hues and shapes of these mountains, and they are regarded by all the good wives, far and near, as perfect barometers. When the weather is fair and settled, they are clothed in blue and purple, and print their bold outlines on the clear evening sky; but, sometimes, when the rest of the landscape is cloudless, they will gather a hood of gray vapors about their summits, which, in the last rays of the setting sun, will glow and light up like a crown of glory.

At the foot of these fairy mountains, the voyager may have descried the light smoke curling up from a village, whose shingle-roofs gleam among the trees, just where the blue tints of the upland melt away into the fresh green of the nearer landscape. It is a little village of great antiquity, having been founded by some of the Dutch colonists, in the early times of the province, just about the beginning of the government of the good Peter Stuyvesant[1], (may he rest in peace!) and there were some of the houses of the original settlers standing within a few years, built of small yellow bricks brought from Holland, having latticed windows and gable fronts, surmounted with weather-cocks.

In that same village, and in one of these very houses (which, to tell the precise truth, was sadly time-worn and weather-beaten), there lived many years since, while the country was yet a province of Great Britain, a simple good-natured fellow of the name of Rip Van Winkle. He was a descendant of the Van Winkles who figured so gallantly in the chivalrous days of Peter Stuyvesant, and accompanied him to the siege of Fort Christina. He inherited, however, but little of the martial character of his ancestors. I have observed that he was a simple good-natured man; he was, moreover, a kind neighbor, and an obedient hen-pecked husband. Indeed, to the latter circumstance might be owing that meekness of spirit which gained him such universal popularity; for those men are most apt to be obsequious and conciliating abroad, who are under the discipline of shrews at home. Their tempers, doubtless, are rendered pliant and malleable in the fiery furnace of domestic tribulation; and a curtain lecture is worth all the sermons in the world for teaching the virtues of patience and long-suffering[2]. A termagant wife may, therefore, in some respects, be considered a tolerable blessing; and if so, Rip Van Winkle was thrice blessed.

Certain it is, that he was a great favorite among all the good wives of the village, who, as usual, with the amiable sex, took his part in all family squabbles; and never failed, whenever they talked those matters over in their evening gossipings, to lay all the blame on Dame Van Winkle. The children of the village, too, would shout with joy whenever he approached. He assisted at their sports, made their playthings, taught them to fly kites and shoot marbles, and told them long stories of ghosts, witches, and Indians. Whenever he went dodging about the village, he was surrounded by a troop of them, hanging on his skirts, clambering on his back, and playing a thousand tricks on him with impunity; and not a dog would bark at him throughout the neighborhood.

The great error in Rip's composition was an insuperable aversion to all kinds of profitable labor. It could not be from the want of assiduity or perseverance; for he would sit on a wet rock, with a rod as long and heavy as a Tartar's lance, and fish all day without a murmur, even though he should not be encouraged by a single nibble. He would carry a fowling-piece on his shoulder for hours together, trudging through woods and swamps, and up hill and down dale, to shoot a few squirrels or wild pigeons. He would never refuse to assist a neighbor even in the roughest toil, and was a foremost man at all country frolics for husking Indian corn, or building stone-fences; the women of the village, too, used to employ him to run their errands, and to do such little odd jobs as their less obliging husbands would not do for them. In a word Rip was ready to attend to anybody's business but his own; but as to doing family duty, and keeping his farm in order, he found it impossible.

In fact, he declared it was of no use to work on his farm; it was the most pestilent little piece of ground in the whole country; every thing about it went wrong, and would go wrong, in spite of him. His fences were continually falling to pieces; his cow would either go astray, or get among the cabbages; weeds were sure to grow quicker in his fields than anywhere else; the rain always made a point of setting in just as he had some out-door work to do; so that though his patrimonial estate had dwindled away under his management, acre by acre, until there was little more left than a mere patch of Indian corn and potatoes, yet it was the worst conditioned farm in the neighborhood.

His children, too, were as ragged and wild as if they belonged to nobody. His son Rip, an urchin begotten in his own likeness, promised to inherit the habits, with the old clothes of his father. He was generally seen trooping like a colt at his mother's heels, equipped in a pair of his father's cast-off galligaskins, which he had much ado to hold up with one hand, as a fine lady does her train in bad weather.

Rip Van Winkle, however, was one of those happy mortals, of foolish, well-oiled dispositions, who take the world easy, eat white bread or brown, whichever can be got with least thought or trouble, and would rather starve on a penny than work for a pound. If left to himself, he would have whistled life away in perfect contentment; but his wife kept continually dinning in his ears about his idleness, his carelessness, and the ruin he was bringing on his family. Morning, noon, and night her tongue was incessantly going, and everything he said or did was sure to produce a torrent of household eloquence[3]. Rip had but one way of replying to all lectures of the kind, and that, by frequent use, had grown into a habit. He shrugged his shoulders, shook his head, cast up his eyes, but said nothing. This, however, always provoked a fresh volley from his wife; so that he was fain to draw off his forces, and take to the outside of the house—the only side which, in truth, belongs to a hen-pecked husband.

Rip's sole domestic adherent was his dog Wolf, who was as much hen-pecked as his master; for Dame Van Winkle regarded them as companions in idleness, and even looked upon Wolf with an evil eye, as the cause of his master's going so often astray. True it is, in all points of spirit befitting an honorable dog, he was as courageous an animal as ever scoured the woods—but what courage can withstand the ever-during and all-besetting terrors of a woman's tongue? The moment Wolf entered the house his crest fell, his tail drooped to the ground, or curled between his legs, he sneaked about with a gallows air, casting many a sidelong glance at Dame Van Winkle, and at the least flourish of a broomstick or ladle, he would fly to the door with yelping precipitation.

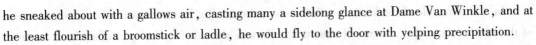

Times grew worse and worse with Rip Van Winkle as years of matrimony rolled on; a tart temper never mellows with age, and a sharp tongue is the only edged tool that grows keener with constant use. For a long while he used to console himself, when driven from home, by frequenting a kind of perpetual club of the sages, philosophers, and other idle personages of the village; which held its sessions on a bench before a small inn, designated by a rubicund portrait of His Majesty George the Third[4]. Here they used to sit in the shade through a long lazy summer's day, talking listlessly over village gossip, or telling endless sleepy stories about nothing. But it would have been worth any statesman's money to have heard the profound discussions that sometimes took place, when by chance an old newspaper fell into their hands from some passing traveler. How solemnly they would listen to the contents, as drawled out by Derrick Van Bummel, the schoolmaster, a dapper learned little man, who was not to be daunted by the most gigantic word in the dictionary; and how sagely they would deliberate upon public events some months after they had taken place.

The opinions of this junto were completely controlled by Nicholas Vedder, a patriarch of the village, and landlord of the inn, at the door of which he took his seat from morning till night, just moving sufficiently to avoid the sun and keep in the shade of a large tree; so that the neighbors could tell the hour by his movements as accurately as by a sundial. It is true he was rarely heard to speak, but smoked his pipe incessantly. His adherents, however (for every great man has his adherents), perfectly understood him, and knew how to gather his opinions. When any thing that was read or related displeased him, he was observed to smoke his pipe vehemently, and to send forth short, frequent and angry puffs; but when pleased, he would inhale the smoke slowly and tranquilly, and emit it in light and placid clouds; and sometimes, taking the pipe from his mouth, and letting the fragrant vapor curl about his nose, would gravely nod his head in token of perfect approbation.

From even this strong-hold the unlucky Rip was at length routed by his termagant wife, who would suddenly break in upon the tranquillity of the assemblage and call the members all to naught[5]; nor was that august personage, Nicholas Vedder himself, sacred from the daring tongue of this terrible virago, who charged him outright with encouraging her husband in habits of idleness.

Poor Rip was at last reduced almost to despair; and his only alternative, to escape from the labor of the farm and clamor of his wife, was to take gun in hand and stroll away into the woods. Here he would sometimes seat himself at the foot of a tree, and share the contents of his wallet with Wolf, with whom he sympathized as a fellow-sufferer in persecution. "Poor Wolf," he would say, "thy mistress leads thee a dog's life of it; but never mind, my lad, whilst I live thou shalt never want a friend to stand by thee!" Wolf would wag his tail, look wistfuly in his master's face, and if dogs can feel pity I verily believe he reciprocated the sentiment with all his heart.

In a long ramble of the kind on a fine autumnal day, Rip had unconsciously scrambled to one of the highest parts of the Kaatskill mountains. He was after his favorite sport of squirrel shooting, and the still solitudes had echoed and reechoed with the reports of his gun. Panting and fatigued, he threw himself, late in the afternoon, on a green knoll, covered with mountain herbage, that crowned the brow of a precipice. From an opening between the trees he could overlook all the lower country for many a mile of rich woodland. He saw at a distance the lordly Hudson, far, far below him, moving on its silent but majestic course, with the reflection of a purple cloud, or the sail of a lagging bark, here and there sleeping on its glassy bosom, and at last losing itself in the blue highlands.

On the other side he looked down into a deep mountain glen, wild, lonely, and shagged, the bottom filled with fragments from the impending cliffs, and scarcely lighted by the reflected rays of the setting sun. For some time Rip lay musing on this scene; evening was gradually advancing; the mountains began to throw their long blue shadows over the valleys; he saw that it would be dark long before he could reach the village, and he heaved a heavy sigh when he thought of encountering the terrors of Dame Van Winkle.

As he was about to descend, he heard a voice from a distance, hallooing, "Rip Van Winkle! Rip Van Winkle!" He looked round, but could see nothing but a crow winging its solitary flight across the mountain. He thought his fancy must have deceived him, and turned again to descend, when he heard the same cry ring through the still evening air; "Rip Van Winkle! Rip Van Winkle!"—at the same time Wolf bristled up his back, and giving a low growl, skulked to his master's side, looking fearfully down into the glen. Rip now felt a vague apprehension stealing over him; he looked anxiously in the same direction, and perceived a strange figure slowly toiling up the rocks, and bending under the weight of something he carried on his back. He was surprised to see any human being in this lonely and unfrequented place, but supposing it to be some one of the neighborhood in need of his assistance, he hastened down to yield it.

On nearer approach he was still more surprised at the singularity of the stranger's appearance. He was a short square-built old fellow, with thick bushy hair, and a grizzled beard. His dress was of the antique Dutch fashion—a cloth jerkin strapped round the waist—several pair of breeches, the outer one of ample volume, decorated with rows of buttons down the sides, and bunches at the knees. He bore on his shoulder a stout keg, that seemed full of liquor, and made signs for Rip to approach and assist him with the load. Though rather shy and distrustful of this new acquaintance, Rip complied with his usual alacrity; and mutually relieving one another, they clambered up a narrow gully, apparently the dry bed of a mountain torrent. As they ascended, Rip every now and then heard long rolling peals, like distant thunder, that seemed to issue out of a deep ravine, or rather cleft, between lofty rocks, toward which their rugged path conducted. He paused for an instant, but supposing it to be the muttering of one of those transient thundershowers which often take place in mountain heights, he proceeded. Passing through the ravine, they came to a hollow, like a small amphitheatre, surrounded by perpendicular precipices, over the brinks of which impending trees shot their branches, so that you only caught glimpses of the azure sky and the bright evening cloud. During the whole time Rip and his companion had labored on in silence; for though the former marvelled greatly what could be the object of carrying a keg of liquor up this wild mountain, yet there was something strange and incomprehensible about the unknown, that inspired awe and checked familiarity.

On entering the amphitheatre, new objects of wonder presented themselves. On a level spot in the centre was a company of odd-looking personages playing at nine-pins. They were dressed in a quaint, outlandish fashion; some wore short doublets, others jerkins, with long knives in their belts, and most of them had enormous breeches, of similar style with that of the guide's. Their visages, too, were peculiar; one had a large beard, broad face, and small piggish eyes: the face of another seemed to consist entirely of nose, and was surmounted by a white sugar-loaf hat set off with a little red cock's tail. They all had beards, of various shapes and colors. There was one who seemed to be the commander. He was a stout old gentleman, with a weather-beaten countenance; he wore a laced doublet, broad belt and hanger, high-crowned hat and feather, red stockings, and high-heeled shoes, with roses in them. The whole group reminded Rip of the figures in an old Flemish painting, in the parlor of Dominie Van Shaick, the village parson, and which had been brought over from Holland at the time of the settlement.

What seemed particularly odd to Rip was, that though these folks were evidently amusing themselves, yet they maintained the gravest faces, the most mysterious silence, and were, withal, the most melancholy party of pleasure he had ever witnessed. Nothing interrupted the stillness of the scene but the noise of the balls, which, whenever they were rolled, echoed along the mountains like rumbling peals of thunder.

As Rip and his companion approached them, they suddenly desisted from their play, and stared at him with such fixed statue-like gaze, and such strange, uncouth, lack-lustre countenances, that his heart turned within him, and his knees smote together. His companion now emptied the contents of the keg into large flagons, and made signs to him to wait upon the company. He obeyed with fear and trembling; they quaffed the liquor in profound silence, and then returned to their game.

By degrees Rip's awe and apprehension subsided. He even ventured, when no eye was fixed upon him, to taste the beverage, which he found had much of the flavor of excellent Hollands. He was naturally a thirsty soul, and was soon tempted to repeat the draught. One taste provoked another; and he reiterated his visits to the flagon so often that at length his senses were overpowered, his eyes swam in his head, his head gradually declined, and he fell into a deep sleep.

On waking, he found himself on the green knoll whence he had first seen the old man of the glen. He rubbed his eyes—it was a bright sunny morning. The birds were hopping and twittering among the bushes, and the eagle was wheeling aloft, and breasting the pure mountain breeze.

"Surely," thought Rip, "I have not slept here all night." He recalled the occurrences before he fell asleep. The strange man with a keg of liquor—the mountain ravine—the wild retreat among the rocks—the woe-begone party at ninepins—the flagon—"Oh! that flagon! that wicked flagon!" thought Rip—"what excuse shall I make to Dame Van Winkle!"

He looked round for his gun, but in place of the clean well-oiled fowling-piece, he found an old firelock lying by him, the barrel incrusted with rust, the lock falling off, and the stock worm-eaten. He now suspected that the grave roysterers of the mountain had put a trick upon him, and having dosed him with liquor, had robbed him of his gun. Wolf, too, had disappeared, but he might have strayed away after a squirrel or partridge. He whistled after him and shouted his name, but all in vain; the echoes repeated his whistle and shout, but no dog was to be seen.

He determined to revisit the scene of the last evening's gambol, and if he met with any of the party, to demand his dog and gun. As he rose to walk, he found himself stiff in the joints, and wanting in his usual activity. "These mountain beds do not agree with me," thought Rip, "and if this frolic should lay me up with a fit of the rheumatism, I shall have a blessed time with Dame Van Winkle." With some difficulty he got down into the glen: he found the gully up which he and his companion had ascended the preceding evening; but to his astonishment a mountain stream was now foaming down it, leaping from rock to rock, and filling the glen with babbling murmurs. He, however, made shift to scramble up its sides, working his toilsome way through thickets of birch, sassafras, and witch-hazel, and sometimes tripped up or entangled by the wild grapevines that twisted their coils or tendrils from tree to tree, and spread a kind of network in his path.

At length he reached to where the ravine had opened through the cliffs to the amphitheatre; but no traces of such opening remained. The rocks presented a highly impenetrable wall over which the torrent came tumbling in a sheet of feathery foam, and fell into a broad deep basin, black from the shadows of the surrounding forest. Here, then, poor Rip was brought to a stand. He again called and whistled after his dog; he was only answered by the cawing of a flock of idle crows, sporting high in air about a dry tree that overhung a sunny precipice; and who, secure in their elevation, seemed to look down and scoff at the poor man's perplexities. What was to be done? the morning was passing away, and Rip felt famished for want of his breakfast. He grieved to give up his dog and gun; he dreaded to meet his wife; but it would not do to starve among the mountains. He shook his head, shouldered the rusty firelock, and, with a heart full of trouble and anxiety, turned his steps homeward.

As he approached the village he met a number of people, but none whom he knew, which somewhat surprised him, for he had thought himself acquainted with every one in the country round. Their dress, too, was of a different fashion from that to which he was accustomed. They all stared at him with equal marks of surprise, and whenever they cast their eyes upon him, invariably stroked their chins. The constant recurrence of this gesture induced Rip, involuntarily, to do the same, when, to his astonishment, he found his beard had grown a foot long!

He had now entered the skirts of the village. A troop of strange children ran at his heels, hooting after him, and pointing at his gray beard. The dogs, too, not one of which he recognized for an old acquaintance, barked at him as he passed. The very village was altered; it was larger and more populous. There were rows of houses which he had never seen before, and those which had been his familiar haunts had disappeared. Strange names were over the doors—strange faces at the windows—every thing was strange. His mind now misgave him; he began to doubt whether both he and the world around him were not bewitched. Surely this was his native village, which he had left but the day before. There stood the Kaatskill mountains—there ran the silver Hudson at a distance—there was every hill and dale precisely as it had always been—Rip was sorely perplexed—"That flagon last night," thought he, "has addled my poor head sadly!"

It was with some difficulty that he found the way to his own house, which he approached with silent awe, expecting every moment to hear the shrill voice of Dame Van Winkle. He found the house gone to decay—the roof fallen in, the windows shattered, and the doors off the hinges. A half-starved dog that looked like Wolf was skulking about it. Rip called him by name, but the cur snarled, showed his teeth, and passed on. This was an unkind cut[6] indeed—"My very dog," sighed poor Rip, "has forgotten me!"

He entered the house, which, to tell the truth, Dame Van Winkle had always kept in neat order. It was empty, forlorn, and apparently abandoned. This desolateness overcame all his connubial fears—he called loudly for his wife and children—the lonely chambers rang for a moment with his voice, and then all again was silence.

He now hurried forth, and hastened to his old resort, the village inn—but it too was gone. A large rickety wooden building stood in its place, with great gaping windows, some of them broken and mended with old hats and petticoats, and over the door was painted, "the Union Hotel, by Jonathan Doolittle." Instead of the great tree that used to shelter the quiet little Dutch inn of yore, there now was reared a tall naked pole, with something on the top that looked like a red night-cap, and from it was fluttering a flag, on which was a singular assemblage of stars and stripes[7]—all this was strange and incomprehensible. He recognized on the sign, however, the ruby face of King George, under which he had smoked so many a peaceful pipe, but even this was singularly metamorphosed. The red coat was changed for one of blue and buff, a sword was held in the hand instead of a sceptre, the head was decorated with a cocked hat, and underneath was painted in large characters, GENERAL WASHINGTON.

There was, as usual, a crowd of folk about the door, but none that Rip recollected. The very character of the people seemed changed. There was a busy, bustling, disputatious tone about it, instead of the accustomed phlegm and drowsy tranquillity. He looked in vain for the sage Nicholas Vedder, with his broad face, double chin, and fair long pipe, uttering clouds of tobacco-smoke instead of idle speeches; or Van Bummel, the schoolmaster, doling forth the contents of an ancient newspaper. In place of these, a lean, bilious-looking fellow, with his pockets full of handbills, was haranguing vehemently about rights of citizens—elections—members of congress—liberty—Bunker's Hill—heroes of seventy-six—and other words, which were a perfect Babylonish jargon[8] to the bewildered Van Winkle.

The appearance of Rip, with his long grizzled beard, his rusty fowling-piece, his uncouth dress, and an army of women and children at his heels, soon attracted the attention of the tavern politicians. They crowded round him, eyeing him from head to foot with great curiosity. The orator bustled up to him, and, drawing him partly aside, inquired "on which side he voted?" Rip stared in vacant stupidity. Another short but busy little fellow pulled him by the arm, and, rising on tiptoe, inquired in his ear, "Whether he was Federal or Democrat?" Rip was equally at a loss to comprehend the question; when a knowing, self-important old gentleman, in a sharp cocked hat, made his way through the crowd, putting them to the right and left with his elbows as he passed, and planting himself before Van Winkle, with one arm akimbo, the other resting on his cane, his keen eyes and sharp hat penetrating as it were, into his very soul demanded in an austere tone, "what brought him to the election with a gun on his shoulder, and a mob at his heels, and whether he meant to breed a riot in the village?"—"Alas! Gentlemen," cried Rip, somewhat dismayed, "I am a poor quiet man, a native of the place, and a loyal subject of the king, God bless him!"

Here a general shout burst from the by-standers—"A Tory[9]! a Tory! a spy! a refugee! hustle him! away with him!" It was with great difficulty that the self-important man in the cocked hat restored order; and, having assumed a tenfold austerity of brow, demanded again of the unknown culprit, what he came there for, and whom he was seeking? The poor man humbly assured him that he meant no harm, but merely came there in search of some of his neighbors, who used to keep about the tavern.

"Well—who are they? —name them."

Rip bethought himself a moment, and inquired, "Where's Nicholas Vedder?"

There was a silence for a little while, when an old man replied, in a thin piping voice, "Nicholas Vedder! why, he is dead and gone these eighteen years! There was a wooden tombstone in the church-yard that used to tell all about him, but that's rotten and gone too."

"Where's Brom Dutcher?"

"Oh, he went off to the army in the beginning of the war; some say he was killed at the storming of Stony Point—others say he was drowned in a squall at the foot of Antony's Nose. I don't know—he never came back again."

"Where's Van Bummel, the schoolmaster?"

"He went off to the wars too, was a great militia general, and is now in congress."

Rip's heart died away at hearing of these sad changes in his home and friends, and finding himself thus alone in the world. Every answer puzzled him too, by treating of such enormous lapses of time, and of matters which he could not understand: war—congress—Stony Point; —he had no courage to ask after any more friends, but cried out in despair, "Does nobody here know Rip Van Winkle?"

"Oh, Rip Van Winkle!" exclaimed two or three, "Oh, to be sure that's Rip Van Winkle yonder, leaning against the tree."

Rip looked, and beheld a precise counterpart of himself[10], as he went up the mountain: apparently as lazy, and certainly as ragged. The poor fellow was now completely confounded. He doubted his own identity, and whether he was himself or another man. In the midst of his bewilderment, the man in the cocked hat demanded who he was, and what was his name?

"God knows," exclaimed he, at his wit's end; "I'm not myself—I'm somebody else—that's me yonder—no—that's somebody else got into my shoes—I was myself last night, but I fell asleep on the mountain, and they've changed my gun, and every thing's changed, and I'm changed, and I can't tell what's my name, or who I am!"

The by-standers began now to look at each other, nod, wink significantly, and tap their fingers against their foreheads. There was a whisper, also, about securing the gun, and keeping the old fellow from doing mischief, at the very suggestion of which the self-important man in the cocked hat retired with some precipitation. At this critical moment a fresh comely woman pressed through the throng to get a peep at the gray-bearded man. She had a chubby child in her arms, which, frightened at his looks, began to cry. "Hush, Rip," cried she, "hush, you little fool; the old man won't hurt you." The name of the child, the air of the mother, the tone of her voice, all awakened a train of recollections in his mind. "What is your name, my good woman?" asked he.

"Judith Gardenier."

"And your father's name?"

"Ah, poor man, Rip Van Winkle was his name, but it's twenty years since he went away from home with his gun, and never has been heard of since—his dog came home without him; but whether he shot himself, or was carried away by the Indians, nobody can tell. I was then but a little girl."

Rip had but one question more to ask; but he put it with a faltering voice:

"Where's your mother?"

"Oh, she too had died but a short time since; she broke a blood-vessel in a fit of passion at a New-England peddler."

There was a drop of comfort, at least, in this intelligence. The honest man could contain[11] himself no longer. He caught his daughter and her child in his arms. "I am your father!" cried he—"Young Rip Van Winkle once—old Rip Van Winkle now! —Does nobody know poor Rip Van Winkle?"

All stood amazed, until an old woman, tottering out from among the crowd, put her hand to her brow, and peering under it in his face for a moment, exclaimed, "Sure enough! it is Rip Van Winkle—it is himself! Welcome home again, old neighbor—Why, where have you been these twenty long years?"

Rip's story was soon told, for the whole twenty years had been to him but as one night. The neighbors stared when they heard it; some were seen to wink at each other, and put their tongues in their cheeks: and the self-important man in the cocked hat, who, when the alarm was over, had returned to the field, screwed down the corners of his mouth, and shook his head—upon which there was a general shaking of the head throughout the assemblage.

It was determined, however, to take the opinion of old Peter Vanderdonk, who was seen slowly advancing up the road. He was a descendant of the historian of that name, who wrote one of the earliest accounts of the province. Peter was the most ancient inhabitant of the village, and well versed in all the wonderful events and traditions of the neighborhood. He recollected Rip at once, and corroborated his story in the most satisfactory manner. He assured the company that it was a fact, handed down from his ancestor the historian, that the Kaatskill mountains had always been haunted by strange beings. That it was affirmed that the great Hendrick Hudson[12], the first discoverer of the river and country, kept a kind of vigil there every twenty years, with his crew of the Half-moon; being permitted in this way to revisit the scenes of his enterprise, and keep a guardian eye upon the river, and the great city called by his name. That his father had once seen them in their old Dutch dresses playing at nine-pins in a hollow of the mountain; and that he himself had heard, one summer afternoon, the sound of their balls, like distant peals of thunder.

To make a long story short, the company broke up, and returned to the more important concerns of the election. Rip's daughter took him home to live with her; she had a snug, well-furnished house, and a stout cheery farmer for a husband, whom Rip recollected for one of the urchins that used to climb upon his back. As to Rip's son and heir, who was the ditto of himself, seen leaning against the tree, he was employed to work on the farm; but evinced an hereditary disposition to attend to anything else but his business.

Rip now resumed his old walks and habits[13]; he soon found many of his former cronies, though all rather the worse for the wear and tear of time; and preferred making friends among the rising generation, with whom he soon grew into great favor.

Having nothing to do at home, and being arrived at that happy age when a man can be idle with impunity, he took his place once more on the bench at the inn door, and was reverenced as one of the patriarchs of the village, and a chronicle of the old times "before the war." It was some time before he could get into the regular track of gossip, or could be made to comprehend the strange events that had taken place during his torpor. How that there had been a revolutionary war—that the country had thrown off the yoke of old England—and that, instead of being a subject of his Majesty George the Third, he was now a free citizen of the United States. Rip, in fact, was no politician; the changes of states and empires made but little impression on him; but there was one species of despotism under which he had long groaned, and that was—petticoat government[14]. Happily that was at an end; he had got his neck out of the yoke of matrimony, and could go in and out whenever he pleased, without dreading the tyranny of Dame Van Winkle. Whenever her name was mentioned, however, he shook his head, shrugged his shoulders, and cast up his eyes; which might pass either for an expression of resignation to his fate, or joy at his deliverance[15].

He used to tell his story to every stranger that arrived at Mr. Doolittle's hotel. He was observed, at first, to vary on some points every time he told it, which was, doubtless, owing to his having so recently awaked. It at last settled down precisely to the tale I have related, and not a man, woman, or child in the neighborhood, but knew it by heart. Some always pretended to doubt the reality of it, and insisted that Rip had been out of his head, and that this was one point on which he always remained flighty. The old Dutch inhabitants, however, almost universally gave it full credit. Even to this day they never hear a thunderstorm of a summer afternoon about the Kaatskill, but they say Hendrick Hudson and his crew are at their game of nine-pins; and it is a common wish of all hen-pecked husbands in the neighborhood, when life hangs heavy on their hands, that they might have a quieting draught out of Rip Van Winkle's flagon.

三、修辞解析

小说的主人公瑞普·凡·温克尔不做家务，也不从事农活，喜欢听村里的老者们闲聊，为此经常受到妻子的唠叨。后来他终因不堪忍受妻子的“管教”而与自己的爱犬一起离家，走入森林。林中，他碰到一群陌生人，并偷饮了对方的酒。之后他陷于沉睡，一睡就是二十年。醒后回到村里，温克尔发现时过境迁，原来的一切早已物是人非。美国已经摆脱英国殖民者的统治，村民正忙于选举。他和已经结婚生子的女儿相认，并得知妻子已过世。他们三代人一起生活，温克尔适应了村子的新生活，安享晚年。

面对时代变化带来的困难、从无知到成熟、劳动与休闲的冲突、逃避责任、自我的丧失和追寻、女性形象的丑化、男女主人公的原型形象及其在美国文学中的变迁等是学者们从该故事中解读出的各种主题。幽默、夸张和讽刺是该小说最显著的艺术效果。下面对三个例子进行具体分析：对狗(名叫伍尔夫)的描写、对校长德里克·凡·巴梅尔的刻画、温克尔与狗的对话。作者针对不同的对象分别采用不同的修辞方式，将这些对象刻画得栩栩如生，达到令人忍俊不禁而又难忘的效果。

首先是对狗的描写。作者采用拟人的手法，将温克尔的狗比做人，细致地描绘它的各种动作和神态，并透过行为直指它的内心世界。一般人难以了解动物的喜怒哀乐，但是当作家把动物比做人，并赐予它们人类的情感时，人和动物的距离才被拉近。温克尔得了“妻管严”，他唯一的伙伴——伍尔夫也是如此。不管它在外面多么风光，但每当它进门时就变成另一副模样。小说如此描绘它的形象：它的脊背下弯，尾巴下垂到接触地面，或者弯曲在两腿中间。他潜行着，神态像一个即将被处决的罪犯。他一边走，一边斜视着温克尔夫人。只要是扫帚或长柄锅稍有动静，伍尔夫便一边惨叫，一边朝着门口飞奔。读完这段，读者在发笑之余对伍尔夫的不幸遭遇表示同情，对温克尔夫人的残暴表示敬畏和不满。伍尔夫走路的样子、眼神和对环境的警觉充分表露出它对女主人的屈从和恐惧，因为女主人经常用扫帚和长柄锅打它。因此，家对伍尔夫来说意味着危险和伤痛。伍尔夫和温克尔一样，几乎整天游手好闲；而温克尔夫人忙里忙外，是劳动者的化身。二者形成强烈的反差。

其次，对校长巴梅尔的刻画。作者运用词语的对比手法，寥寥数笔，将校长的形象栩栩如生地表现出来。他个子矮小，衣冠楚楚，有学问。但是，他官腔十足，讲话时严肃而认真。他喜欢用字典里最大的词语，而且用起来得心应手，毫无惧色。他对发生在数月前的事情的解读如此深刻而有哲理。校长外形矮小，可能成为旁观者取笑的对象；可是他学识渊博，神情严肃，是思想的巨人。听完他的高论，读者只会对他肃然起敬，而绝无嘲笑之意。此番幽默的效果正是通过一“小”和一“大”的对比以及对他的外貌描摹来实现的。另一个对比是，作者对校长的“扬”为他对温克尔夫人的“抑”形成对照。温克尔夫人是“悍妇”和“泼妇”，她敢训斥村里的族长，自然不把校长放在眼里。在他们村里，温克尔夫人的形象最“高大”，只不过在村民和作者看来她的“高大”带有讽刺意味罢了。为什么？

再次，描写温克尔和狗的对话。作者在用词和神态描写两方面将幽默和讽刺的效果展示出来。穷途末路的温克尔不忘关怀伍尔夫。他对它说：“可怜的伍尔夫，你的女主人让你过着狗一般的生活。不过没关系，老弟，只要我活着，我将永远是站在你身边的朋友。”伍尔夫听懂了他的话，摇着尾巴，依依不舍地望着他主人的脸。温克尔自己走投无路，但他的心情似乎未受影响。他用古英语 thy 和 thee 表达“你的”和“你”，而不用现代英语中对应的 your 和 you。这似乎揭示了温克尔的怀旧心情——留恋过去饱食终日、无所事事的日子。再者，他视狗为兄弟，而非狗，说明他心中有善，有同情心，有博爱。他究竟是在拔高狗的形象，还是贬低他自己的形象？还有，妻子和狗在他心中的地位孰轻孰重？这些问题对温克尔本人来说可能没有答案，也可能有。读者在帮助温克尔寻找这些答案的同时对他的态度是既同情又可气和可笑。

小说对村里族长的描述和对温克尔太太“大闹会议现场”的描述同样是小说的精彩之笔。它们的幽默表现在哪些方面？是通过什么途径来实现的？答案也许在前面的分析中。

四、难点注释

1. Peter Stuyvesant：彼得·斯泰福山特(1602—1682)，荷兰人，1647 年任纽约曼哈顿岛总督。
2. in the fiery furnace of domestic tribulation; and a curtain lecture ...and long suffering：在家庭磨难的熊熊火炉里(受过锻炼)，枕边说教。curtain lecture 的意思是床帏拉上后的讲话，即妻子私下对丈夫的责备管教。
3. a torrent of household eloquence：一连贯的唠叨。同一段落里的 a volley 指的是一阵连珠炮似的责骂。作者频繁使用隐喻，达到幽默讽刺的效果。
4. His Majesty George the Third：乔治三世陛下(1738—1820)，美国革命战争时期英国的国王。
5. call the members all to naught：把所有的成员骂得一钱不值。naught：无；不存在。
6. an unkind cut：无情的一击。
7. a single assemblage of stars and stripes：许多星与条的奇异集合，即星条旗，美国的国旗。
8. Babylonish jargon：巴比伦的行话，即令人茫然不解的胡言乱语。
9. Tory：托利分子，为英国保守党人的前身，他们对当时刚刚成立的美国颇为仇视。
10. a precise counterpart of himself：与他一模一样的人。类似的意思出现在下一段的 got into my shoes (穿着我的鞋子；与我长得一模一样)。

11. contain：相当于 control。
12. Hedrick Hudson：亨德里克·哈得逊(？—1611)，著名的英国航海家，1609 年发现哈得逊河。同一段的 Half-moon 指的是哈得逊乘坐去冒险的船名“半月号”。
13. old walks and habits：往日的行径和习惯。
14. petticoat government：妇人的专政。petticoat 指妇女穿的衬裙，这里借指妇女。
15. an expression of resignation of his fate, or joy at his deliverance：任凭命运摆布的表达，或者是对自己得到解脱感到喜悦的表达。

五、延伸阅读与批评

《睡谷的传说》是华盛顿·欧文另一部有名的短篇小说。小说在描写美国初期哈得逊河东岸优美而迷人的自然风光以及当地居民淳朴民风的同时，重点叙说流传当地的种种故事。其中，既有令人毛骨悚然的“无头骑士”传说，也有令人忍俊不禁的爱情故事：贫穷而有智慧的教书匠克莱恩和性情暴躁而傲慢的纨绔子弟布鲁姆·布隆特(又称布鲁姆·骨头)如何同时向美女卡特琳娜求爱等。小说的字里行间富有幽默和讽刺的味道。

欧文主要采用两种方式制造幽默讽刺效果：典故和对比。前者提到美国神学家考顿·马特尔(Cotton Mather)和荷马史诗《伊利亚特》中的阿克琉斯等。后者的最典型例子是，克莱恩接到卡特琳娜父亲举办联欢会的邀请函时，让学生立即放学。你能分别指出：这些典故在哪些方面与故事人物描写和当时场景有相似和不同之处？你是否能够指出小说中的其他典故并对之做简要分析？克莱恩在那个特定的时刻对待学生的态度与以前相比明显不同，这个不同点是什么？

Chapter 3 The American Scholar

by Ralph W. Emerson

(*An Excerpt*)

一、作者简介

拉尔夫·瓦尔多·爱默生(1803—1882)，美国19世纪杰出的哲学家、诗人、散文家。他的作品分为三类。早期的作品有散文和演讲：《自然》(1836)、《美国学者》(1837)、《神学院毕业班演说》(1838)；散文集：《散文：第一集》(1841)、《散文：第二集》(1844)，代表性作品有"论自立""论超灵""论诗人""论经验"；此外，他出版了《诗集》(1846)、长篇散文《代表人物》(1850)等。晚期的散文有"女人"(1855)和"梭罗"(1862)等。

爱默生出生于新英格兰一个显赫的牧师家庭，早年就读于哈佛大学，接受唯一神教教义。毕业后当了六年多的牧师，后来因为不满该教的一些刻板教义而辞职。1832至1833年他遍游欧洲，结识了英国浪漫主义诗人柯勒律治、华兹华斯以及集史学家和哲学家于一身的卡莱尔，受他们的影响颇深。回国后爱默生开始著书立说，到处发表演讲。

爱默生强调个人主义思想的自由；号召美国文人挣脱欧洲传统的束缚，创造属于自己民族的文学；主张文学创作与社会现实相结合；关注人和自然的关系、自然与人的和谐统一；相信一切事情都与上帝有关，因此皆有神性和灵性；人可以通过自己的直觉与超灵交流，达到与自然的结合与统一；反对拜金主义思想，赞美人的无限潜能，提倡修炼心灵和精神，做一个真正完整的人。此外，他反对奴隶制，支持林肯的废奴思想。他的作品语言流畅，文字优美；善于引经据典，不乏格言警句。

爱默生是美国超验主义思想的领军人物。超验主义受到唯一神教、德国唯心主义和神秘论、英国浪漫主义文学家以及印度和中国等古典哲学思想的影响，其理论思想在当时的美国宗教、哲学、文学、社会等领域引发一场革命，对美国产生了深刻而深远的影响。在文化和文学界，他的超验主义思想为美国文学复兴提供了直接的思想和理论依据。梭罗、霍桑、麦尔维尔、惠特曼、迪金森等无不受到他思想的滋养而成为美国文学巨匠。

二、文本选读

The American Scholar

Mr. President, and Gentlemen,

I greet you on the re-commencement of our literary year. Our anniversary is one of hope, and, perhaps, not enough of labor. We do not meet for[1] games of strength or skill, for the recitation of histories, tragedies and odes, like the ancient Greeks; for parliaments of love and poesy, like the Troubadours; nor for the advancement of science, like our contemporaries in the British and European capitals. Thus far, our holiday has been simply a friendly sign of the survival of the love of letters amongst a people too busy to give to letters any more. As such, it is precious as the sign of an indestructible instinct. Perhaps the time is already come, when it ought to be, and will be something else; when the sluggard intellect of this continent will look from under its iron lids, and fill the postponed expectation of the world with something better than the exertions of mechanical skill. Our day of dependence, our long apprenticeship to the learning of other lands, draws to a close. The millions that around us are rushing into life, cannot always be fed on the sere remains of foreign harvests. Events, actions arise, that must be sung, that will sing themselves. Who can doubt that poetry will revive and lead in a new age, as the star in the constellation Harp which now flames in our zenith, astronomers announce, shall one day be the pole-star for a thousand years?

In light of this hope, I accept the topic[2] which not only usage but the nature of our association seem to prescribe to this day, —the AMERICAN SCHOLAR. Year by year, we come up hither to read one more chapter of his biography. Let us inquire what new lights, new events and more days and events have thrown on his character, his duties and his hopes.

It is one of those fables which out of an unknown antiquity convey an unlooked-for wisdom, that the gods, in the beginning, divided Man into men, that he might be more helpful to himself; just as the hand was divided into fingers, the better to answer its end.

The old fable covers a doctrine ever new and sublime; that there is One Man[3], —present to all particular men only partially, or through one faculty; and that you must take the whole society to find the whole man. Man is not a farmer, or a professor, or an engineer, but he is all. Man is priest, and scholar, and statesman, and producer, and soldier. In the divided or social state, these functions are parcelled out to individuals, each of whom aims to do his stint of the joint work, whilst each other performs his. The fable implies that the individual, to possess himself, must sometimes return from his own labor to embrace all the other laborers. But unfortunately, this original unit, this fountain of power, has been so distributed to multitudes, has been so minutely subdivided and peddled out, that it is spilled into drops, and cannot be gathered. The state of society is one in which the members have suffered amputation from the trunk, and strut about so many walking monsters, —a good finger, a neck, a stomach, an elbow, but never a man.

Man is thus metamorphosed into a thing, into many things. The planter, who is Man sent out into the field to gather food, is seldom cheered by any idea of the true dignity of his ministry. He sees his bushel and his cart, and nothing beyond, and sinks into the farmer, instead of Man on the farm. The tradesman scarcely ever gives an ideal worth to his work, but is ridden by the routine of his craft, and the soul is subject to dollars. The priest becomes a form; the attorney, a statute-book; the mechanic, a machine; the sailor, a rope of a ship.

In this distribution of functions, the scholar is the delegated intellect. In the right state, he is, Man Thinking. In the degenerate state, when the victim of society, he tends to become a mere thinker, or, still worse, the parrot of other men's thinking.

In this view of him, as Man Thinking, the whole theory of his office is contained. Him Nature solicits, with all her placid, all her monitory pictures. Him the past instructs. Him the future invites. Is not, indeed, every man a student, and do not all things exist for the student's behalf? And, finally, is not the true scholar the only true master? But, as the old oracle said, "All things have two handles. Beware of the wrong one." In life, too often, the scholar errs with mankind and forfeits his privilege. Let us see him in his school, and consider him in reference to the main influences he receives.

I. The first in time and the first in importance of the influences upon the mind is that of Nature. Every day, the sun; and after sunset, night and her stars. Ever the winds blow; ever the grass grows. Every day, men and women, conversing, beholding and beholden. The scholar must needs stand wistful and admiring before this great spectacle. He must settle its value in his mind. What is nature to him? There is never a beginning, there is never an end to the inexplicable continuity of this web of God, but always circular power returning into itself. Therein it resembles his own spirit, whose beginning, whose ending he never can find, —so entire, so boundless. Far, too, as her splendors shine, system on system shooting like rays, upward, downward, without centre, without circumference, —in the mass and in the particle nature hastens to render account of herself to the mind. Classification begins. To the young mind, every thing is individual, stands by itself. By and by, it finds how to join two things, and see in them one nature; then three, then three thousand; and so, tyrannized over by its own unifying instinct, it goes on tying things together, diminishing anomalies, discovering roots running underground, whereby contrary and remote things cohere, and flower out from one stem. It presently learns, that, since the dawn of history, there has been a constant accumulation and classifying of facts. But what is classification but the perceiving that these objects are not chaotic, and are not foreign, but have a law which is also a law of the human mind[4]? The astronomer discovers that geometry, a pure abstraction of the human mind, is the measure of planetary motion. The chemist finds proportions and intelligible method throughout matter; and science is nothing but the finding of analogy, identity, in the most remote parts. The ambitious soul sits down before each refractory fact one after another, reduces all strange constitutions, all new powers, to their class and their law, and goes on forever to animate the last fibre of organization, the outskirts of nature, by insight.

Thus to him, to this school-boy under the bending dome of day, is suggested, that he and it proceed from one root; one is leaf and one is flower; relation, sympathy, stirring in every vein. And what is that Root? Is not that the soul of his soul? —A thought too bold—a dream too wild. Yet when this spiritual light shall have revealed the law of more earthly natures, —when he has learned to worship the soul, and to see that the natural philosophy that now is, is only the first gropings of its gigantic hand, he shall look forward to an ever expanding knowledge as to a becoming creator. He shall see that nature is the opposite of the soul, answering to it part for part. One is seal, and one is print. Its beauty is the beauty of his own mind. Its laws are the laws of his own mind. Nature then becomes to him the measure of his attainments. So much of nature as he is ignorant of, so much of his own mind does he not yet possess. And, in fine, the ancient precept, "Know thyself," and the modern precept, "Study nature," become at last one maxim.

...

I read with joy some of the auspicious signs of the coming days, as they glimmer already through poetry and art, through philosophy and science, through church and state.

One of these signs is the fact that the same movement which effected the elevation[5] of what was called the lowest class in the state, assumed in literature a very marked and as benign an aspect. Instead of the sublime and beautiful, the near, the low, the common, was explored and poetized. That which had been negligently trodden under foot by those who were harnessing and provisioning themselves for long journeys into far countries[6], is suddenly found to be richer than all foreign parts. The literature of the poor, the feelings of the child, the philosophy of the street, the meaning of household life, are the topics of the time[7]. It is a great stride. It is a sign—is it not? of new vigor when the extremities are made active, when currents of warm life run into the hands and the feet. I ask not for the great, the remote, the romantic; what is doing in Italy or Arabia; what is Greek art, or Provencal minstrelsy; I embrace the common, I explore and sit at the feet of the familiar, the low. Give me insight into to-day, and you may have the antique and future worlds. What would we really know the meaning of? The meal in the firkin; the milk in the pan; the ballad in the street; the news of the boat; the glance of the eye; the form and the gait of the body; —show me the ultimate reason of these matters; —show me the sublime presence of the highest spiritual cause lurking, as always it does lurk, in these suburbs and extremities of nature; let me see every trifle bristling with the polarity that ranges it instantly on an eternal law; and the shop, the plough, and the leger, referred to the like cause by which light undulates and poets sing; —and the world lies no longer a dull miscellany and lumber-room, but has form and order; there is no trifle, there is no puzzle, but one design[8] unites and animates the farthest pinnacle and the lowest trench.

This idea has inspired the genius of Goldsmith, Burns, Cowper, and, in a newer time, of Goethe, Wordsworth, and Carlyle. This idea they have differently followed and with various success. In contrast with their writing, the style of Pope, of Johnson, of Gibbon, looks cold and pedantic. This writing is blood-warm. Man is surprised to find that things near are not less beautiful and wondrous than things remote. The near explains the far. The drop is a small ocean. A man is related to all nature. This perception of the worth of the vulgar is fruitful in discoveries. Goethe, in this very thing the most modern of the moderns, has shown us, as none ever did, the genius of the ancients.

There is one man of genius who has done much for this philosophy of life, whose literary value has never yet been rightly estimated; —I mean Emanuel Swedenborg. The most imaginative of men, yet writing with the precision of a mathematician, he endeavored to engraft a purely philosophical Ethics on the popular Christianity of his time. Such an attempt, of course, must have difficulty, which no genius could surmount. But he saw and showed the connection between nature and the affections of the soul. He pierced the emblematic or spiritual character of the visible, audible, tangible world. Especially did his shade-loving muse hover over and interpret the lower parts of nature; he showed the mysterious bond that allies moral evil to the foul material forms, and has given in epical parables a theory of insanity, of beasts, of unclean and fearful things.

Another sign of our times, also marked by an analogous political movement, is the new importance given to the single person. Every thing that tends to insulate the individual, —to surround him with barriers of natural respect, so that each man shall feel the world is his, and man shall treat with man as a sovereign state with a sovereign state; —tends to true union as well as greatness[9]. "I learned," said the melancholy Pestalozzi, "that no man in God's wide earth is either willing or able to help any other man." Help must come from the bosom alone. The scholar is that man who must take up into himself all the ability of the time, all the contributions of the past, all the hopes of the future. He must be an university of knowledges. If there be one lesson more than another; which should pierce his ear, it is, The world is nothing, the man is all; in yourself is the law of all nature, and you know not yet how a globule of sap ascends; in yourself slumbers the whole of Reason; it is for you to know all, it is for you to dare all. Mr. President and Gentlemen, this confidence in the unsearched might of man belongs, by all motives, by all prophecy, by all preparation, to the American Scholar. We have listened too long to the courtly muses of Europe. The spirit of the American freeman is already suspected to be timid, imitative, tame. Public and private avarice make the air we breathe thick and fat. The scholar is decent, indolent, complaisant. See already the tragic consequence. The mind of this country, taught to aim at low objects, eats upon itself. There is no work for any but the decorous and the complaisant. Young men of the fairest promise[10], who begin life upon our shores, inflated by the mountain winds, shined upon by all the stars of God, find the earth below not in unison with these, —but are hindered from action by the disgust which the principles on which business is managed inspire, and turn drudges, or die of disgust, —some of them suicides. What is the remedy? They did not yet see, and thousands of young men as hopeful now crowding to the barriers for the career, do not yet see, that, if the single man plant himself indomitably on his instincts, and there abide, the huge world will come round to him. Patience—patience; —with the shades of all the good and great for company; and for solace the perspective of your own infinite life; and for work the study and the communication of principles, the making those instincts prevalent, the conversion of the world[11]. Is it not the chief disgrace in the world, not to be an unit; —not to be reckoned one character; —not to yield that peculiar fruit which each man was created to bear, but to be reckoned in the gross, in the hundred, or the thousand, of the party, the section, to which we belong; and our opinion predicted geographically, as the north, or the south[12]? Not so, brothers and friends—please God, ours shall not be so. We will walk on our own feet; we will work with our own hands; we will speak our own minds. The study of letters shall be no longer a name for pity, for doubt, and for sensual indulgence. The dread of man and the love of man shall be a wall of defence and a wreath of joy around all[13]. A nation of men will for the first time exist, because each believes himself inspired by the Divine Soul which also inspires all men.

三、修辞解析

《美国学者》是爱默生于1837年8月31日在哈佛大学优等生联谊会上的讲演词。该文被称为"美国思想的独立宣言"。

《美国学者》的主要内容：要想实现美国文化的独立，就必须摆脱他人的影响和控制；宇宙是一个统一的整体，个体的物体有多样性，但它们之间相互关联，互为补充，交织于包含一切的"一"之中；每个人都有两种生活状态，正确的状态是——他拥有自我，是一个大写的"人"，与整个人类相连；为了实现这个更高的思想状态，现代的美国学者不能只做思想家抑或学舌的鹦鹉，必须摒弃古老的思想；"美国学者"像"思考的人"一样有义务看清整个世界，不能受传统或历史的影响，必须用新鲜的眼光扩大理解世界的视野，关注眼前和周围的普通事务。"美国学者"必须调查和理解自然，包括他自己的思想；必须研究过去的思想，如文学、艺术、制度，为创造新思想奠定基础；必须采取行动与世界交流，不当评价过去的隐士式思想家。

爱默生在该文中采用了明喻、暗喻、提喻、拟人、对比、警句式的表达、典故和引用等多种修辞手法，做到说理形象生动，论证视野开阔而有说服力，令人折服和印象深刻。其中，尤为突出的是较多地引用欧洲历史、哲学、文学中的著名人物。如果不了解这些人物及其背后的历史故事，就不能很好地理解原文。

引经据典包含以下主要内容：提到某个人物，让人想到该人物身上某些突出的特征或品质；引用某人的经典话语，它往往富有哲理，放之四海而皆准；提及某个故事，读者透过它能够发现和总结一个道理；提到某个地点，读者由此联想与它相关的人和事，并从中得到启示；突出具有特殊意义的某个行为或动作等。

本文仅以列举历史名人为例。例如，爱默生在提倡文学应关注现实生活时提到英国的华兹华斯和卡莱尔、德国的歌德，在批评文学脱离现实时同样提及英国作家蒲柏、约翰逊、吉本。他还特别欣赏瑞士的哲学家、科学家和神学家伊曼纽尔·斯威登伯格，因为他能看到自然和心灵情感之间的关系，并将二者联系起来。在此仅以英国的华兹华斯和德国的歌德为例加以分析说明。

威廉·华兹华斯(1770—1850)，英国著名的浪漫主义作家，"湖畔派"诗人的最杰出代表。他的主要作品有抒情诗《抒情歌谣集》(1798年与另一位诗人柯勒律治合著，两年后再版时华兹华斯增加了一个长序，阐述自己的浪漫主义文学主张)、《丁登寺旁》，长诗《序曲》，自传体叙事诗《革命与独立》，代表性的诗作有"露西""孤独的刈麦女"和"我像一片云独自漫游"等。华兹华斯反对古典主义的刻板和典雅风格，主张使用普通、平凡、生动、真实的语言创作诗歌，诗歌必须关注现实生活中的普通事物；诗歌必须具有强烈的情感；他认为诗人是人性最坚强的保卫者、支持者、维护者，他所到之处都播下人的情谊和爱；反对资本主义的城市文明和金钱关系，歌颂大自然，宣扬人与自然的和谐统一。《抒情歌谣集》(特别是他的长序)被称为英国浪漫主义诗歌的宣言。

为什么爱默生十分推崇华兹华斯？因为他们之间有若干相似之处：首先，他们都是新生力量的代表，都在各自的领域引起一场革命运动；反对冷漠的古典思想，钟情现实的普遍性和真实性，强调人与自然的统一关系，开创各自领域的新文化(文学)之风。华兹华斯笔下的“诗人”与爱默生心中的“美国学者”十分相似。其次，华兹华斯是英国浪漫主义文学的象征与代表人物，是英国的民族诗人和英国人民的骄傲。既然英国能够产生如此优秀的世界级文人，为什么美国就不能呢？这是爱默生对美国作家的呼唤，而且他相信：美国式的“华兹华斯”一定会出现。果然，在他的感召下，美国产生了一批享誉世界文坛的作家，他们也成为美国文学的代表，是美国民族的作家，也是美国人民的骄傲。

同理，爱默生为什么提到歌德？约翰·歌德(1749—1832)，18世纪中期至19世纪初期欧洲最重要的剧作家、诗人、思想家。代表性的作品有剧本《铁手骑士葛兹·冯·伯理欣根》、中篇小说《少年维特之烦恼》、未完成的诗剧《普罗米修斯》、诗剧《浮士德》等。

歌德的突出贡献在于：敢于反抗旧秩序，勇敢追求新时代，渴求真理和自由；探索人生的意义和社会理想；关心身边普通的人和物等。他的作品中充满了醍醐灌顶的警句名言。例如：“对真理的热爱就像现在：知道怎样去发现和珍惜每一件事物的好处”“关键在于要有一颗爱真理的心灵，随时随地地碰见真理，就把它吸收进来”“艺术家对于自然有着双重关系，他既是自然的主宰，也是自然的奴隶，他是自然的奴隶，因为他必须用人世间的材料进行工作，才能被世人理解；同时他又是自然的主宰，因为他使这种人世间的材料服从他的较高意旨，并且为这较高的意旨服务”。通过比照，读者发现歌德与爱默生的思想主张在某些方面有异曲同工之妙。他们同样是各自国家和民族的思想和文化符号。

四、难点注释

1. We do not meet for：我们(在此)相聚不是为了。
2. topic：(“论美国学者”)演讲题目。
3. One Man：一个大写的人。类似的意思是下文的Man Thinking(思考的人)。
4. But what is classification…human mind?：如果不是认识到物体之间的相互关联、互不陌生，认识到物体之间如同人的心智存在一个规律，谈何分类呢？but 的意思是“除非”“如果不是”。
5. effected the elevation：提高。
6. Harnessing and provisioning themselves for long journey into far countries：准备粮秣整装远行。far countries 指代欧洲国家，暗指一些美国人因自己国家的历史短暂和缺乏文化积淀，而舍近求远，学习外国的文化。
7. The literature of the poor…topics of the time：该句进一步将美国文化的匮乏和欧洲的悠久历史进行对比。句中的 the poor，the child，the street 和 household life 皆指美国文化的贫穷、年轻和俗气。
8. show me the ultimate reason…the sublime presence of the highest spiritual cause… the like

cause … one design：几个分句中诸如事物的“根源”“最高精神存在”“一种意图”等都体现了作者的“超灵”思想。

9. tends to true union as well as greatness：倾向于团结个体，同时使之变得伟大。
10. fairest promise：远大前程。
11. with the shades… for company… the conversion of the world：你有各种善良和伟大的人为朋友，有自己的无限生命的远景为慰藉，有研究和传播原则，普及那些本能，感化世界为责任。理解时注意 for 引导的几个并列成分。
12. Is it not… or the south?：句中的 not to 和 but to 是 it 的真正主语，强调个体人的独立性和特殊性，而不是按数量或地域划分，忽视他的人格个性。
13. a wall of defence and a wreath of joy around all：环绕一切的防御工事和快乐花环。

五、延伸阅读与批评

《瓦尔登湖》或《林中生活》发表于 1854 年，是另一位超验主义的代表人物亨利·戴维·梭罗的散文集。它是梭罗践行超验主义主张的集中表露。有位批评家曾说《瓦尔登湖》有五种读法：简单生活的权威指南，对大自然的真情描述，向金钱社会的讨伐檄文，传世久远的文学名著，一本神圣的书。

作为一部文学作品，《瓦尔登湖》采用了多种修辞手法。以其中的一篇散文“我生活的地方；我为何生活”为例，梭罗引用许多名人逸事和典故来证明自己的观点，例如，他提到他同时代的爱默生的诗句、古代希腊作品中的人物、古代罗马神话中的神、古代印度的作品、古代中国哲人的故事等。梭罗主张生活要简朴、简朴、再简朴。他在表达不要被物质利益蒙蔽自己的心灵，而应注重修炼自我德行和提升精神境界时，引用了蘧伯玉(约公元前 585—约前 484)派使者访问孔子的故事：“蘧伯玉使人于孔子。孔子与之坐而问焉，曰：夫子何为。对曰：夫子欲寡其过而未能也。使者出，子曰：使乎，使乎。”根据《论语·宪问》第 26 节的介绍，蘧伯玉是中国古代春秋时期卫国有名的大夫，他虽然公务缠身，但不忘自我参醒。他与孔子交情甚深，深得孔子的喜欢，于是便留下这段佳话。这段古文是什么意思？孔子最后的反应如何？该故事在哪些方面与梭罗的观点相同？你能否借助工具书，查阅该篇散文中的其他引用信息，并分析它们与此文本的关系？

Chapter 4 I Hear America Singing

by Walt Whitman

一、作者简介

沃尔特·惠特曼(1819—1892)，美国19世纪杰出的浪漫主义和超验主义诗人。从1855年自费出版到1891年的临终版，他的诗集《草叶集》一共出了9版。美国的爱默生和梭罗、英国诗人兼批评家威廉·罗塞蒂为诗集的出版并最终得到世界的认同起了关键作用。1865年，惠特曼还发表了《林肯总统纪念组诗》(起初收入《桴鼓集及其他》诗集里)，后来《桴鼓集及其他》被收入第四版《草叶集》(1867)。《自我之歌》(1855)、《我听见美国在歌唱》(1860)、《当紫丁香最近在庭园里开放的时候》(1865)、《啊，船长，我的船长!》(1865)等是诗集中的名篇。此外，惠特曼还著有散文《民主远景》(1870，1871)。

惠特曼是一位自学成才的作家。他因家庭贫寒于11岁辍学，先后当过法律事务所的勤杂员、医疗所的勤杂工、印刷所的学徒、排字工人、乡村小学教员等。但他勤奋好学，博览群书，欧美的文学、历史、政治等各类书籍无不涉猎。同时，他十分关注现实社会。丰富的人生经历和阅读经历成为他创作的宝贵财富。

惠特曼是美国的民主和自由诗人。他生于美国资本主义上升时期，一个新型理想的美国正在美洲大地矗立。同时，爱默生的“文化宣言”正响遍整个美国。惠特曼正是这个社会和时代的发言人。他歌颂美国的一切：从物质到精神，从美国总统到奴隶和妓女，从自我到他人/她人，从生到死，从精神文化到科技文化，从整个人类到自然万物，从无生命的物质到那男女之间的性爱，从喜乐到哀怒。自由、平等、民主、人与自然的和谐、科技的进步等是他诗作的主要主题。他开创一代诗风——自由体无韵诗：抛弃传统格律，采用日常口语化的语言，使用平行或重叠诗行，辅以倒装、重复、头韵、叠韵等，形成抑扬顿挫的自然节奏，产生气势磅礴和情感深化的艺术效果。

惠特曼被称为“美国现代诗歌之父”。

二、文本选读

I Hear America Singing

I hear America singing, the varied carols I hear[1],
Those of mechanics, each one singing his as it should be blithe and strong[2],
The carpenter singing his as he measures his plank or beam,
The mason singing his as he makes ready for work, or leaves off work,
The boatman singing what belongs to him in his boat, the deck-hand[3] singing on the steamboat

deck,

The shoemaker singing as he sits on his bench, the hatter singing as he stands,
The wood-cutter's song, the ploughboy's on his way in the morning, or at noon intermission or at
sundown,
The delicious singing of the mother, or of the young wife at work, or of the girl sewing or
washing,
Each singing what belongs to him or her and to none else,
The day what belongs to the day[4]—at night the party of young fellows, robust, friendly,
Singing with open mouths their strong melodious songs.

三、修辞解析

《我听见美国在歌唱》是一首歌颂民主与和平的短诗，也是运用自由体无韵律的诗歌典范。诗作的第一行是一个"主题句"——"我听见美国在歌唱，我听到各种各样的歌声。"其余诗行则是"各种各样的歌声"的具体内容：机械师、木匠、石匠、船夫、水手、鞋匠、制帽匠、庄稼汉、母亲、年轻妻子、女孩。他们来自各行各业，不论年龄老少，都在边工作边歌唱；他们精神饱满，情绪高涨，相互友好。他们共同描绘了一幅积极向上、乐观进取的美丽图画。

诗作的突出修辞特色是运用排比和重复句式。从第三行到第八行，每行都以定冠词加名词开始，形成一个整体的对应关系。它们不仅词性相同，而且几乎都是表示职业的名词。这样安排有如下几重艺术效果。第一，从内容上讲，它们表达了诗歌的主题：民主、平等、自由。在诗人看来，这些从业者之间没有高低贵贱之分，都是平等和自由的，都在快乐地工作和快乐地歌唱。第二，从形式上讲，它们相互呼应，起到形式的对称和强调作用，产生一股令人振奋的气势和力量：或抑扬顿挫，或平行演进，或渐进增强。它们既增加了诗歌的乐感和美感，又强化了诗歌主题，达到形式与内容的高度统一。第三，这些排比或重复诗行之间的分行全部使用逗号，只有结尾一个句号。如此安排让读者感觉到这首诗是一个整体，而各个分句(诗行)之间既相互独立又彼此关联，成为整体不可或缺的一部分。这种形式上部分与整体的关系正好对应内容上的局部与整体的关系。那就是，美国人是独立、有创造性的个体，他们集合起来又构成了美国人民的整体。平等、民主、自由、向上既是个体的思想核心，也是整个美国的精神价值。

最后，这些各行各业的人们恰似美国大地上的一片片"草叶"，平凡而伟大，默默无闻又充满生机，看似渺小却潜力无限。他们之所以能够茁壮成长，得益于美国为他们提供了肥沃的土壤和丰富的营养——民主精神。它既是该诗的主题，也是《草叶集》的中心思想。

四、难点注释

1. the varied carols I hear：我听见各种各样的歌。
2. each one singing his as it should be blithe and strong：每个人唱着他那理应快乐和雄壮的

歌。

3. deck-hand：舱面水手；普通水手。
4. The day what belongs to the day：白天唱着属于白天的歌。

五、延伸阅读与批评

《啊，船长，我的船长!》是惠特曼纪念林肯遇难的四首诗中的一首。它用第一人称的对话方式抒发了“我”对林肯去世的深切悼念。林肯是美国著名的民主战士，在美国南北战争时期率领北方联邦军队打败了南方军队，废除了奴隶制。林肯得到美国广大人民的拥护和爱戴。然而美国内战结束不久，林肯遭到奴隶主指使的刺客刺杀而亡。消息传出，诗人惠特曼无比震惊，写下这首不朽的哀歌。

诗作将林肯比做船长，他驾驶美国之船历尽艰难险阻，冲过激流险滩，战胜惊涛骇浪，正在驶向岸边，接受美国人民的欢呼、掌声和鲜花。然而，如今船长倒在血泊中，“浑身冰冷，停止了呼吸”。欢呼声一刹那间变成恸哭声。诗作使用暗喻、类比、重复等修辞手法表达“我”的悲恸之情。诗中的“我”是诗歌作者本人吗？如果是，除此之外是否还指代其他人？诗作有3个诗节。每节的前半部分都由超过10个音节的诗行构成，后半部分诗行的音节几乎是前面的一半，第一节和第三节的最后一行只有5个音节。这种形式安排上的变化与诗歌的主题思想表达之间是什么关系？令人深思。

Chapter 5 Riprap

by Gary Snyder

一、作者介绍

加里·斯奈德(1930—)，美国当代著名诗人，1975 年普利策诗歌奖获得者。1955 年 10 月 7 日参加了由肯尼斯·雷克斯罗斯主持的著名的旧金山“六号画廊诗歌朗诵会”，与艾伦·金斯堡、杰克·克鲁亚克、菲利普·惠伦等一道被人称为“垮掉的一代”。不过与其他垮掉派诗人放荡不羁、沉沦颓废的态度不同，斯奈德以大自然为题材，沉静内敛，修身养性，淡泊避世，远离城市的喧嚣和西方价值体系，别具一格，成为了“垮掉派”作家中极富魅力的“冷派”代表。2003 年，他当选为美国诗人学院院士，先后出版了十六本诗文集，代表性作品有《砌石与寒山诗》(*Riprap and Cold Mountain Poems*)（1965）、《山水无尽头》(*Mountains and Rivers Without End*)（1965）、《龟岛》(*Turtle Island*)(1974)等。

斯奈德出生在旧金山，家庭因大萧条一贫如洗，后搬去华盛顿州西雅图市北部的一个农场。在那里，他与大自然密切接触，逐渐对印第安人的民间传说和神话产生兴趣。1947 年在俄勒冈州的里德学院学习人类学，毕业后从事不少与林业相关的工作，如伐木工和森林防火员。后来于印第安纳大学学习语言学、加州大学伯克利分校学习中国文学，其间翻译了寒山诗，这对他触动很大。1956 至 1968 年间，他远渡重洋，客居日本十余年，学佛参禅，潜心研习禅宗，1969 年与日本妻子回到美国定居在加利福尼亚州北部山区，过着十分简朴的日子。1984 年，他与金斯堡一同来到中国访问。1985 年获聘加州大学戴维斯分校终身教授，并广泛游历、参加诗会和呼吁保护环境。

斯奈德将多种文学传统，特别是来自中国的道家学说、日本的禅宗以及北美印第安文化等融入其诗歌写作中以歌颂自然。他的诗歌作品风格清新易辨：通俗的口语语言，强烈的视觉效果，大量关于自然景色和日常生活的细致观察和描写，对于人类存在的探索闪烁着文化和生态诗学的智慧。不少评论家将其作品和处事与梭罗相提并论，认为他是一个生态诗人。他对于他同时代的诗人也产生了巨大影响，杰克·克鲁亚克在他的作品《达摩浪人》中，以斯奈德为原型，塑造了嘉斐·莱德这一形象。斯奈德翻译了中国唐代诗人寒山的作品，将其介绍到英语世界，是继美国现代诗人庞德等人的中国传统诗词热的延续；同时，斯奈德采用了自由体的诗歌创作手法描写自然和生灵等，并且寄情于景，因此不少批评家认为他承袭了诗人惠特曼的美国诗歌传统，是美国当代最重要的诗人之一。

二、文本选读

Riprap

Lay down[1] these words
Before you mind like rocks.
placed solid, by hands
In choice of place, set
Before the body of the mind
in space and time:
Solidity of bark[2], leaf or wall
riprap of things:
Cobble of milky way[3],
straying planets,
These poems, people,
lost ponies[4] with
Dragging saddles—
and rocky sure-foot trails[5].
The worlds like an endless
four-dimensional
Game of Go[6].
ants and pebbles
In the thin loam, each rock a word
A creek-washed stone
Granite: ingrained[7]
with torment of fire and weight
Crystal and sediment[8] linked hot
all change, in thoughts,
As well as things.

三、修辞解析

斯奈德曾解释“砌石”指的就是“大山里，给狭窄、光滑的岩石铺上的鹅卵石以供马儿通行”。《砌石》一诗发表不久后，斯奈德这样总结自己的诗歌创作：“我最近才意识到我的诗的节奏与我做的工作和我的生活节奏相应……西艾拉·内华达山脉的地理环境，把花岗岩石块铺成坚实路面的修路工作，使我写出了《砌石》。‘你在干什么？’我问老罗伊·马奇班克斯。‘在砌石’，他说。他选石头的本领简直炉火纯青，把琢磨过的石子嵌得天衣无缝。走着、爬着、安放着石子。我也试图用坚实、简单的短词写诗，把复杂性深藏于表面质地之下。我的诗行部分受到我在读的中国五言七言诗的影响，这些中国诗猛烈地撞击我的心灵。”诗人将写诗比作“砌石”，既强调“石头”即写作过程中选词、修辞的重要性，更强调“铺路”即作品的统一与和谐。诗人崇尚自然，因而采用自然式的手法作诗，以表明他的诗作恰如自然界万物生机勃勃，一切浑然天成。

斯奈德《砌石》一诗运用了明喻的修辞手法。第二行的“like”，用具体的事物去提示抽象的事物，让读者能够领会到其作品的深意。他把诗歌写作比作大山里的日常劳作——砌石。他长年在山中做林业工人，双手接触自然，身体和思想在劳作中与自然直接对话。在这首诗里，他将文学创作、普通劳动和山林里秀丽的风光结合在一起，提倡回归原始的、本源的质朴生活，以自己的方式摆脱浮躁紊乱的现代文明，重新寻找工业文明扼杀的人与自然和谐共处的美好理想。第十五行同样出现了“like”，将各个世界比作永不停歇的围棋的四个纬度，将东方的围棋文化与他的诗歌创作联系在一起，一是为获得某种新意，二是借助东方文化中的某种启示，以揭示天地万物生死消涨的规律。

其次，该诗使用了暗喻的修辞手法。在第九、第十行里，他把铺路用的石头比作了银河里散落的行星，从第十九到第二十三行里，他又将石头分别视为语词、被溪水冲刷的石头、被火和沉重长久考验的花岗岩，热物炙烤下的水晶和沉积物，虚实结合，意象优美，给人一种隽永的感觉。第二十二行中的“火”，暗指焚毁特洛伊城的大火和佛教仪式的静寂和焚香，突出了作品东西方文化的双重元素。

诗中还运用了类比、排比以及通感，如第十行中的“迷失的”等修辞手法，从形式和内容上既增强了作品的气势，又丰富了作品的深度和广度，最终使这首诗成为斯奈德最有代表性的作品之一。

四、难点注释

1. lay down：此处喻指像铺路一样将文字排列成诗的形式。
2. bark：树皮。
3. milky way：银河。
4. ponies：小马驹。
5. trails：小路，尤指人迹罕至的小径。
6. Game of Go：指围棋。
7. ingrained：根深蒂固的，长年累月的。
8. sediment：沉积物。

五、延伸阅读与批评

斯奈德把手工劳作、美国西部山林风光与来自东方的文化(包括诗歌和围棋等)融入诗歌写作，以一个普通劳动者的身份在内华达山里过着简朴的生活。在作品中，他摒弃了一切来自现代文明的生活方式和物质，面向农场、山林、岩石、溪水，用简单的劳作与大自然交流，感叹世间万物的变迁、人性的迷失，探索人应该如何自处以获得身心的解放。在他看来，这种质朴的特质正是当代西方社会所缺乏的，因此，他转向“无为而治”“朴素自由”的中国道家文化，思考解决西方社会矛盾的出口，重新审视人与自然的关系，吸取道家文化中的“无为而治”等诗学思想，最终平衡人性与自然性，达到天人合一的境界。

他的另一首短诗是《松树的树冠》："蓝色的夜/ 霜雾，天空中/ 明月朗照。/松树的树冠/弯成霜一般蓝，淡淡地/没入天空，霜，星光。/靴子的吱嘎声。/兔的足迹，鹿的足迹，/我们知道什么。"(赵毅衡译)这首诗以"白描"式的手法将北美山林里的月夜景观进行诗化再现，将松树树冠的形状比作"弯成霜一般蓝"，诗人原本描写印第安人的狩猎场景，却在这些寻常的景物中借修辞手法显现出"道"的法则：一切浑然天成，无我忘我，天人合一。中国文化对他究竟有多深远的影响才能让他得出如此结论？他引用、借用中国文化的目的究竟何在？他从砌石这项工作中参透和领悟的真谛与类比做人作诗又有何关系？诗作的各种修辞手法在传情达意上起到什么作用？这些问题都值得深入探讨。

(周丹撰写，甘文平审校)

参 考 文 献

1. Cleanth Brooks, Robert Penn Warren. *Understanding Fiction*. Beijing: Foreign Language Teaching and Research Press and Pearson Education, 2004.
2. 吴定柏，编注．美国文学欣赏．上海：上海外语教育出版社，2004.
3. 李宜燮，常耀信，主编．美国文学选读(上、下册)．天津：南开大学出版社，2001.
4. 刘海平，王守仁，主编．新编美国文学史(四卷本)．上海：上海外语教育出版社，2000.
5. 杨仁敬．20世纪美国文学史．青岛：青岛出版社，2000.
6. 杨仁敬，杨凌雁．美国文学简史．上海：上海外语教育出版社，2008.
7. 林六辰，编著，姚乃强，审订．英美小说要素解析．上海：上海外语教育出版社，2009.
8. 童明．美国文学史(英文版)．南京：译林出版社，2002.
9. 虞建华．杰克·伦敦研究．上海：上海外语教育出版社，2009.
10. 杨金才，虞建华．英美诗歌：作品与评论．上海：上海外语教育出版社，2008.
11. 周顶之．英美文学作品赏析．长沙：湖南师范大学出版社，2002.

后　记

撰写《美国文学教程：欣赏与评析》的想法源自我对美国文学认识的历史变迁。

大学二年级时，一位年轻美籍教师讲解了霍桑的《年轻的古德曼·布朗》，但我仍然对它一窍不通。惭愧之余，我开始怀疑自己是否有文学细胞。不过我对中国文学很感兴趣。考研时我因为不喜欢语言学而选择了文学方向，也并非完全出于对美国文学的喜爱。读研期间我读了几本原版小说，但也不甚了解，只是在外籍教师的讲解下才找到一点感觉。学习期间我偶尔练笔写散文和散文诗。幸运的是我的几首中文散文诗发表在校报上，这给了我极大的鼓励。从此，我自认为自己具备了一点研习文学的悟性。毕业工作10年，我一直讲授大学英语，很少接触文学，但文学创作和阅读文学的念头时常闯入我的脑海。

2000年是我学术生命的转机之年。我成功地考上美国小说史方向的博士生，并正式将文学作为自己的研究方向和未来的教学职业。三年时间内，在杨仁敬教授的精心指导下，我用勤奋和苦读换来博士学位证书。博士毕业后我如愿地为本科生和硕士研究生主讲美国文学课程。春秋更迭，我坚持学习，用心备课。在历经读博时导师帮我修改论文、翻译文学作品、撰写和发表多篇文学批评论文、指导本科生和研究生撰写文学方向的毕业论文、他们的毕业论文获得答辩优秀、我的博士论文出版、成功地申请校级和省级以及国家级文学研究项目立项等磨炼之后，我逐步积累了文学教学与研究的点滴心得和方法。我多次参加全国美国文学研究会年会和学术专题研讨会，每次总是悉心聆听他人的发言。与此同时，与会者也慢慢地听到了我的声音。这些经历和机遇催生了我自撰美国文学教材的愿望。

该教程涵盖题目、环境、人物、主题、修辞五个部分。每个部分集中从一个方面分析美国文学中的经典作品，重点细说每个方面对解读和批评文学作品所起的作用，突出作品意义的具体性和特殊性。这五个方面是我们解读和批评文学的五个基本视角。每章包括作家简介、文本选读、题目(环境、人物、主题、修辞)解析、难点注释、延伸阅读与批评五个部分。“作家简介”强调作家的独特创作个性，包括主题思想和写作手法的特征，并突出文学与现实的关系。“文本选读”提供作家的原始文本。“题目(环境、人物、主题、修辞)解析”用直观的方式展示作品的内涵，让读者一目了然。“难点注释”尽量为正确理解文本提供有用的信息。“延伸阅读与批评”指的是用相同或相似的方法解读作者的其他作品，或者与作者同时代的其他作家的作品，做到举一反三。

教程强调内容的真实性、讲解的直观性、方法的实用性和文字的可读性，力求为学生自学和教师讲授美国文学提供借鉴和帮助。无论是平时教学抑或学术研究，我始终告诉学生：我的观点只是“……之一”，绝非“唯一”。如果自己的观点能够启发学生从文学中读出“……含义之二或更多”，我则深感欣慰。

此外，本书还参考了一些评论文章和一些英文名著的中译本，在此恕不一一列举。本人对上述著作的作者和译者表示衷心的感谢。

我还要感谢我的同事、长期教授美国文学的王燕萍副教授在百忙之中抽空通读了教材，并提出宝贵的意见。我的几个研究生也帮我通读全文，查找错误。他们从学生的角度与我交流对该书的接受情况，给我有益的启示。我感谢她们为此付出的辛勤劳动。

最后，我要真诚感谢我的妻子王海燕博士，她在我的教材撰写期间承担了大量的家务。她的辛苦付出保证我及时完稿。而且，她在我最后交稿之前帮忙通读全文。

由于时间仓促，加之本人水平有限，教材中的错误和偏颇之处在所难免。诚望各位同仁不吝指正。

甘文平

于武汉理工大学友谊小区